CIMA
STUDY TEXT

Stage 1 Paper 1

Financial Accounting
Fundamentals

First edition 1994
Fourth edition June 1997

ISBN 0 7517 3076 9 (Previous edition 0 7517 3060 2)

British Library Cataloguing-in-Publication Data
A catalogue record for this book
is available from the British Library

Published by

BPP Publishing Limited
Aldine House, Aldine Place
London W12 8AW

Printed and bound by Progressive Printing (U.K.) Limited, Leigh-on-Sea, Essex.

We are grateful to the Chartered Institute of Management Accountants for permission to reproduce past examination questions. The suggested solutions have been prepared by BPP Publishing Limited.

Introduction

PREFACE

Professional exams are not easy. They demand your time and commitment over a period which can feel never-ending. You want to qualify and get on with your career - but you don't want to put your life on hold. You don't want to spend a moment longer studying than you have to ...

At BPP we believe strongly that the secret of success is effective study material which is focused and relevant to the exam *you* will be sitting. It needs to see you through the entire study process - from knowledge acquisition (the Study Text, your core study and reference book), through recap and practice (the Practice and Revision Kit, with exam-standard questions and plenty of revision features) to *final* exam revision (when Passcards are invaluable) - and success!

That's why we have designed and written this Study Text on *Financial Accounting Fundamentals* to set you firmly on the first step - the acquisition of knowledge, skills and application techniques.

- We include the actual syllabus, so you know what you're up against, and we cover it comprehensively. We continually consult with the examiner to make sure we - and you - are right on track.
- We encourage you to study thoroughly and methodically, giving you plenty of opportunity to check that the topics are sinking in, whilst at the same time we help you to 'dip in' if you wish (see the *How to use this Study Text* section).
- We focus your mind on the examination, with recently-examined topics highlighted.
- All topics are up-to-date as at 1 June 1997 - the cut-off date for the November 1997 and May 1998 exams.

Financial Accounting Fundamentals June 1997

Now in its fourth edition, this Study Text has been enhanced in the following ways:

- The new CIMA Syllabus Guidance Notes 1997-98 have been taken into account as the text has been updated
- Material on accounting and information technology has been revised and enhanced
- The new format for cash flow statements (simplified) has been taken into consideration
- Full account has been taken of the new CIMA *Official Terminology*

Market leaders for 20 years in targeted study material for CIMA exams, at BPP we have the experience and the commitment to produce for our customers effective study material which is smart, focused and student-friendly. The rest is up to you. Good luck!

BPP Publishing
June 1997

For details of the other BPP titles relevant to your studies for this examination and for a full list of books in the BPP CIMA range, including our innovative CIMA PASSCARDS, please turn to the end of the text. If you send us your comments on this Study Text, you will automatically be entered in our FREE PRIZE DRAW.

HOW TO USE THIS STUDY TEXT

This Study Text has been designed to help students and lecturers to get to grips as effectively as possible with the content and scope of Paper 1 *Financial Accounting Fundamentals*.

- The framework of this Study Text is structured so that you should find it to be the most coherent way of covering the syllabus. However we have also aimed to help those who choose to take a different path by indicating (in the Introduction section beginning each chapter) the areas which naturally precede the current chapter and those chapters in which topics introduced can be further explored.

- Syllabus coverage in the text is indicated on page (viii) to (x) by chapter references set against each syllabus topic. Syllabus topics are also identified within each chapter of the text. It is thus easy to trace your path through the syllabus.

- As a further guide - and a convenient means of monitoring your progress - we have included a study checklist on page (xvii) on which to chart your completion of chapters and their related illustrative questions.

Each chapter of the Study Text is divided into sections.

- An introduction places the subject of the chapter in its context in the syllabus and the examination.
- The text gives clear, concise topic-by-topic coverage.
- Examples and exercises reinforce learning, confirm understanding and stimulate thought.
- A 'roundup' at the end of the chapter pulls together the key points.
- A test your knowledge quiz helps you to check that you have absorbed the material in the chapter.

Some features of the Study Text are worth looking at in more detail.

Exercises

Exercises are provided throughout the text to enable you to check your progress as you work through the text. These come in a large variety of forms: some test your ability to do a calculation just described, others see whether you have taken in the full significance of a piece of information. Some are meant to be discussed with colleagues, friends or fellow students.

A suggested solution is usually given, but often in an abbreviated form to help you avoid the temptation of merely reading the exercise rather than actively engaging your brain. We think it is preferable on the whole to give the solution immediately after the exercise rather than making you hunt for it at the end of the chapter, losing your place and your concentration. Cover up the solution with a piece of paper if you find the temptation to cheat too great!

Examples can also often be used as exercises, if not the first time you read a passage, then certainly afterwards when you come to revise.

Chapter roundup and Test your knowledge quiz

At the end of each chapter you will find two boxes. The first is the Chapter roundup which summarises key points and arguments and sets out what you should know or be able to do having studied the chapter. The second box is a quiz that serves a number of purposes.

- It is an essential part of the chapter roundup and can be glanced over quickly to remind yourself of key issues covered by the chapter.

- It is a quiz pure and simple. Try doing it first thing in the morning to revise what you read the night before.

- It is a revision tool. Shortly before your examination sit down with pen and paper and try to answer all the questions fully. Many of the questions are typical of the four- or five-mark-earning opportunities that feature so regularly in examination questions.

Illustrative questions and class questions

Each chapter also has at least one illustrative question, in the bank at the end of the Study Text. Initially you might attempt such questions with reference to the chapter you have just covered. Later in your studies, it would be helpful to attempt some without support from the text. Only when you have attempted each question as fully as possible should you refer to the suggested solution to check and correct your performance.

Following the suggested solutions, there are several class questions, without solutions. These are intended to be used by lecturers. The solutions are given in a separate lecturers' pack, available only to bona fide lecturers.

A number of the illustrative questions and class questions are in the style of full exam questions. These questions are provided with mark and time allocations.

Glossary and index

Finally, we have included a glossary to define key terms and a comprehensive index to help you locate key topics.

A note on pronouns

On occasions in this Study Text, 'he' is used for 'he or she', 'him' for 'him or her' and so forth. Whilst we try to avoid this practice it is sometimes necessary for reasons of style. No prejudice or stereotyping according to sex is intended or assumed.

SYLLABUS

The syllabus contains a weighting for each syllabus area, and a ranking of the level of ability required in each topic. The Institute has published the following explanatory notes on these points.

Study weightings

A percentage weighting is shown against each topic in the syllabus; this is intended as a guide to the amount of study time each topic requires.

All topics in a syllabus must be studied, as a question may examine more than one topic, or carry a higher proportion of marks than the percentage study time suggested.

The weightings do not specify the number of marks which will be allocated to topics in the examination.

Abilities required in the examination

Each examination paper contains a number of topics. Each topic has been given a number to indicate the level of ability required of the candidate.

The numbers range from 1 to 4 and represent the following ability levels:

Appreciation (1)
To understand a knowledge area at an early stage of learning, or outside the core of management accounting, at a level which enables the accountant to communicate and work with other members of the management team.

Knowledge (2)
To have detailed knowledge of such matters as laws, standards, facts and techniques so as to advise at a level appropriate to a management accounting specialist.

Skill (3)
To apply theoretical knowledge, concepts and techniques to the solutions of problems where it is clear what technique has to be used and the information needed is clearly indicated.

Application (4)
To apply knowledge and skills where candidates have to determine from a number of techniques which is the most appropriate and select the information required from a fairly wide range of data, some of which might not be relevant; to exercise professional judgement and to communicate and work with members of the management team and other recipients of financial reports.'

Overview

This syllabus gives students with no previous accounting knowledge an introduction to the basics of financial accounting systems. It deals with the reasons for having a financial accounting and bookkeeping system; the processes involved in the operation of such a system; an elementary awareness of controls and audit; and some interpretation of accounting statements.

Aims

To test the candidate's ability to:

- explain the operation of financial accounting systems (manual and computerised) and prepare simple financial statements for incorporated and unincorporated businesses

- relate basic accounting concepts to financial accounting

- interpret simple financial statements and draw conclusions

- read the accounts of a company (without subsidiaries or associates), understand their main components and the reasons for external audit

Content and ability required

	Ability required	Covered in chapter
1(a) Conceptual framework *(study weighting 10%)*		
The users of accounts and the objectives of financial statements; the differing functions of financial accounts and management accounts; the accounting system	2	1
Statutory accounting principles (Companies Acts); fundamental concepts of accounting (SSAP 2); materiality; assets, liabilities, income, expenditure; capital and revenue; profit and cash	2	2
Different methods of asset valuation and their implications for the balance sheet and profitability	2	2
Historical cost accounting convention	2	2
Alternative methods of accounting	1	2
1(b) Accounting systems *(study weighting 40%)*		
Purpose of accounting records	2	1,3
Preparation of accounts for cash and bank; bank reconciliations; imprest system for petty cash	3	5,6,13
Accounting for sales and purchases including personal accounts and control accounts	3	5,6,14
Accounting treatment of Value Added Tax (VAT)	3	15
Components of gross pay and deductions from pay; accounting for payroll, including Pay-As-You-Earn (PAYE) and National Insurance (NI)	3	16
Fixed asset register	3	11
Financial accounting codes and their uses	2	6,18
Nominal ledger accounting, journal entries; trial balance	3	6
Interpretation of outputs from computerised financial accounts	2	18
Stewardship	2	23
The purpose of external and internal audit, and the meaning of true and fair	1	23
Financial controls; audit checks on financial controls; audit trails	1	23
Errors or fraud	1	23

		Ability required	Covered in chapter
1(c)	**Preparation of accounts** *(study weighting 40%)*		
	Simple profit and loss accounts and balance sheets from trial balance; income and expenditure accounts	3	17,19
	Accruals and prepayments; bad debts and provision for doubtful debts	3	8,9
	Methods of depreciation (straight line, declining balance and revaluation methods) and the basic rules of the relevant standard for depreciation)	3	11,12
	Accounting for stocks (excluding long-term contract work in progress); methods of stock valuation (FIFO, average cost)	3	10
	Manufacturing accounts; trading accounts; accounting for appropriations of profit; cash flow statements	3	22
	Completion of accounting records from incomplete data	3	20
1(d)	**Interpretation of accounts** *(study weighting 10%)*		
	Calculation and interpretation of:		
	return on capital employed; gross profit and net profit percentages; cost to sales ratios; asset turnover; debtors turnover, creditors' time to pay; current and quick ratios; financial gearing.	2	24
	Items in company accounting formats (company legislation)	1	24

CIMA SYLLABUS GUIDANCE NOTES 1997-98

The following Guidance Notes will be published by the CIMA in the August 1997 CIMA Student *as an aid to students and lecturers.*

'The following guidelines have been drafted by the chief examiner for each of the subjects. They are intended to inform candidates and lecturers about the scope of the syllabus, the emphasis which should be placed on various topics and the approach which the examination papers will adopt.

These guidance notes are applicable immediately, insofar as they provide a general guidance on each subject. Where any major changes are indicated, these will not be applicable until the May 1998 examination (and will be highlighted, where relevant, in the notes).

The role of the chartered management accountant includes the preparation of information and its provision to other members of the management team. This paper is intended to lay the foundation upon which more detailed and specialised knowledge of accounting techniques may be built.

The examination paper will be divided into three sections, up to 80 per cent of which could be compulsory.

Section A will contain between ten and fifteen multiple-choice sub-questions, taken from across the syllabus.

Section B will contain two compulsory questions. The first of these will require the preparation of final accounts from a trial balance or from incomplete data. It may involve a sole trader, a company, or a not-for-profit organisation, and may include any combination of the 'final accounts' with necessary adjustments and supporting records. Although the question will be substantially numerical, there may be discursive elements included from any area of the syllabus. The other question may be from one or more syllabus areas.

Section C will contain two questions from which candidates will be required to select one to answer. These questions may include material from one or more syllabus areas and candidates must be prepared to view accounting as a whole.

Conceptual framework   *Syllabus reference 1(a)*

Candidates must appreciate the importance of the regulatory framework and its effect on the principles and practices used in the preparation of accounts. Questions in this area will be mainly discursive and may be part of a larger question that examines the candidate's knowledge of other syllabus areas, thereby increasing the practical emphasis of the question.

In the examination, candidates may be required to:

- describe the main user groups of accounting information and their information needs;

- demonstrate an appreciation of the effects of changing price levels on accounting statements and on capital maintenance, and a basic knowledge of the techniques which have been used by accountants in the past to try to solve this problem;

- explain the nature, classification and write off against profits of intangible fixed assets such as purchased goodwill and research and development costs.

The following items are *not* examinable:

- knowledge of specific Statements of Standard Accounting Practice (SSAPs) and other regulatory statements, except for a knowledge of the fundamental accounting concepts (SSAP 2) and of the basic rules of depreciation (SSAP 12);

- the calculation of adjustments for changing price levels.

Accounting Systems   *Syllabus reference 1(b)*

Candidates must be capable of maintaining accounting records and systems efficiently and accurately.

Since those areas of this syllabus which are concerned with recording transactions are ranked at ability level 3, candidates must be able to demonstrate skill in identifying and accurately recording transactions. Questions will *not* be set which require the writing up of numerous ledger accounts, but the underlying double entry principles are important and may be tested using journal entries, control accounts or through other means which restrict the number of ledger accounts required.

In the examination, candidates may be required to:

- demonstrate the ledger entries required to record the purchase, depreciation and disposal of fixed assets, and the issue of shares at par or at a premium;

- explain and demonstrate how control can be assisted by the use of control accounts and totals, reconciliations, segregation of duties and proper authorisation procedures;

- explain the purpose of external and internal audit, and the importance of audit checks and trails, and the prevention of errors or fraud.

The following items are *not* examinable:

- the technical aspect of how computers work, but candidates may benefit from having practical experience in using computer packages and, in particular, using the controls and interpreting outputs from such accounting systems;

- specific knowledge of audit procedures or auditing standards and guidelines.

Preparation of accounts   *Syllabus reference 1(c)*

Candidates must be able to demonstrate skill in the preparation of accounts for various types of organisation, including sole traders, limited companies and not-for-profit organisations.

Many of the questions set on this section will also require knowledge and skills from other areas, particularly those involving adjustments to accounts and the preparation of accounts from incomplete records.

In the examination, candidates may be required to:

- distinguish between items of expense and appropriations of profit in the accounts of limited companies;

- demonstrate an understanding of the different natures and accounting treatment of provisions and reserves;

- deal correctly with the provision for corporation tax for the year;

- prepare cash flow statements using any reasonable format which displays the information required by the question.

The following items are *not* examinable:

- the preparation of accounts in a format suitable for publication;

- the calculation of the provision for corporation tax;

- partnership accounts;

- the content of FRS 1 *Cash flow statements*;

- the LIFO method of stock valuation.

Interpretation of accounts   *Syllabus reference 1(d)*

Candidates must be able to look at a set of company accounts and gain a general understanding of the picture it portrays. They must be able to calculate various ratios as stated in the syllabus, interpret them, compare them with other ratios, and suggest possible reasons for the results obtained.

In the examination candidates may be required to:

- calculate the return on capital employed using the formula:

  Net profit before tax and interest/average capital employed

  where average capital employed includes long-term finance, but does not include short-term finance such as bank overdrafts. As additional guidance, where questions do not include any long-term finance, then any mention of interest payable can be assumed to relate to short-term finance. Where questions include both short-term and long-term finance, the Examiner will clarify the content of any figure for interest payable;

- calculate asset turnover in a variety of ways, including the rate of stock turnover;

- calculate cost to sales ratios involving the major cost headings of the profit and loss account, eg cost of goods sold, materials costs, labour costs, administration costs, etc compared to sales;

- demonstrate an appreciation of the types of headings which appear in company accounts, and the general contents of each heading.

The following items are *not* examinable:

- investors ratios, eg earnings per share, dividend cover etc.

THE EXAMINATION PAPER

Assessment methods and format of the paper

Section A (30 marks): one compulsory question composed of 15 multiple-choice subquestions (special answer sheet provided)

Section B (50 marks): two compulsory questions

Section C (20 marks): one question from two

Time allowed: 3 hours

Analysis of past papers

The analysis below shows the topics which have been examined in the three sittings of the *Financial Accounting Fundamentals* paper and the CIMA Specimen paper.

May 1997

Section A
1   Multiple choice questions - 15 questions worth 2 marks each

Section B (two compulsory questions)
2   Final accounts of sole trader
3   Imprest system; day books; sales ledger control account

Section C (one out of two questions)
4   Capital and revenue; true and fair; adjustments to profit
5   Appropriation accounts; ratios

November 1996

Section A
1   Multiple choice questions - 15 questions worth 2 marks each

Section B (two compulsory questions)
2   Incomplete records; benefits of double entry bookkeeping
3   Ledger accounts; accounting concepts

Section C (one out of two questions)
4   Cash flow statement; liquidity ratios
5   Financial and management accounts; audit; bank reconciliation

May 1996

Section A
1   Multiple choice questions - 15 questions worth 2 marks each

Section B (two compulsory questions)
2   Manufacturing account with VAT
3   Journal entries to correct errors; suspense account

Section C (one out of two questions)
4   Profitability and liquidity ratios; reserves
5   Internal controls; stock valuation

November 1995

Section A
1   Multiple choice questions - 15 questions worth 2 marks each

Section B (two compulsory questions)
2   Preparation of final accounts; cash versus profit
3   Control account reconciliation

Section C (one out of two questions)
4   Gearing ratio; research and development
5   Accounting records; coding system; accounting concepts

May 1995

Section A
1   Multiple choice questions - 15 questions worth 2 marks each

Section B (two compulsory questions)
2   Preparation of final accounts, calculation of ratios and discussion
3   Ledger accounting; stewardship

Section C (one out of two questions)
4   Difference between nominal ledger and fixed assets register
5   Cash flow statement. Accounting information

Specimen paper

Section A
1   Multiple choice questions - 15 questions worth 2 marks each

Section B (two compulsory questions)
2   Preparation of manufacturing, trading and profit and loss account and balance sheet
3   Preparation of VAT and bank accounts; purpose of trial balance

Section C (one out of two questions)
4   Calculation of ratios; effect of different kinds of accounting treatment on ratios
5   Accounting controls

THE MEANING OF EXAMINERS' INSTRUCTIONS

The examinations department of the CIMA has asked the Institute's examiners to be precise when drafting questions. In particular, examiners have been asked to use precise instruction words. It will probably help you to know what instruction words may be used, and what they mean. With the Institute's permission, their list of recommended requirement words, and their meaning, is shown below.

Recommended requirement words are:

Advise/recommend	Present information, opinions or recommendations to someone to enable that recipient to take action
Amplify	Expand or enlarge upon the meaning of (a statement or quotation)
Analyse	Determine and explain the constituent parts of
Appraise/assess/evaluate	Judge the importance or value of
Assess	See 'appraise'
Clarify	Explain more clearly the meaning of
Comment (critically)	Explain
Compare (with)	Explain similarities and differences between
Contrast	Place in opposition to bring out difference(s)
Criticise	Present the faults in a theory or policy or opinion
Demonstrate	Show by reasoning the truth of
Describe	Present the details and characteristics of
Discuss	Explain the opposing arguments
Distinguish	Specify the differences between
Evaluate	See 'appraise'
Explain/interpret	Set out in detail the meaning of
Illustrate	Use an example - chart, diagram, graph or figure as appropriate - to explain something
Interpret	See 'explain'
Justify	State adequate grounds for
List (and explain)	Itemise (and detail meaning of)
Prove	Show by testing the accuracy of
Recommend	See 'advise'
Reconcile	Make compatible apparently conflicting statements or theories
Relate	Show connections between separate matters
State	Express
Summarise	State briefly the essential points (dispensing with examples and details)
Tabulate	Set out facts or figures in a table

Requirement words which will be avoided

Examiners have been asked to avoid instructions which are imprecise or which may not specifically elicit an answer. The following words will not be used.

Consider	As candidates could do this without writing a word
Define	In the sense of stating exactly what a thing is, as CIMA wishes to avoid requiring evidence of rote learning
Examine	As this is what the examiner is doing, not the examinee
Enumerate	'List' is preferred
Identify	
Justify	When the requirement is not 'to state adequate grounds for' but 'to state the advantage of'
List	On its own, without an additional requirement such as 'list and explain'
Outline	As its meaning is imprecise. The addition of the word 'briefly' to any of the suggested action words is more satisfactory
Review	
Specify/Trace	

STUDY CHECKLIST

This page is designed to help you chart your progress through the Study Text, including the illustrative questions at the back of it. You can tick off each topic as you study and try questions on it. Insert the dates you complete the chapters and questions in the relevant boxes. You will thus ensure that you are on track to complete your study before the exam.

	Text chapters	Illustrative questions	
	Date completed	Question number	Date completed

PART A: CONCEPTUAL FRAMEWORK

1 The nature and objectives of accounting
2 Preparing accounts: concepts, conventions and regulations

	Question	
	1	
	2 & 3	

PART B: ACCOUNTING SYSTEMS AND ACCOUNTS PREPARATION

3 Assets, liabilities and the accounting equation
4 An introduction to final accounts
5 Sources, records and the books of prime entry
6 Ledger accounting and double entry
7 From trial balance to financial statements
8 The cost of goods sold, accruals and prepayments
9 Discounts, bad debts and provisions
10 Accounting for stocks
11 Fixed assets - depreciation, revaluation and disposal
12 Intangible fixed assets
13 Bank reconciliations
14 Control accounts
15 Accounting for value added tax
16 Accounting for wages and salaries
17 Correction of errors. Preparation of final accounts
18 Computer applications in accounting

	Question	
	4	
	5	
	6	
	7 & 8	
	9-11	

	Question	
	12 & 13	
	14 & 15	
	16	

	Question	
	17 & 18	
	19	
	20 & 21	
	22 & 23	
	24 & 25	
	26	

	Question	
	27 - 30	
	31	

PART C: FINAL ACCOUNTS AND AUDIT

19 The accounts of unincorporated organisations
20 Incomplete records
21 Limited companies
22 Manufacturing accounts and cash flow statements
23 Internal and external audit

	Question	
	32 & 33	
	34 - 36	
	37	

	Question	
	38 & 39	
	40	

PART D: INTERPRETATION OF ACCOUNTS

24 Interpreting company accounts

	Question	
	41 & 42	

Part A
Conceptual framework

Chapter 1

THE NATURE AND OBJECTIVES OF ACCOUNTING

This chapter covers the following topics.

		Syllabus reference	*Ability required*
1	What is accounting?	1(a)	Knowledge
2	Why keep accounts?	1(a)	Knowledge
3	Users of accounting information	1(a)	Knowledge
4	Management accounting and financial accounting	1(a)	Knowledge
5	The scope of accounting information	1(a)	Knowledge
6	The main financial statements	1(a)	Knowledge

Introduction

The syllabus for the *Financial Accounting Fundamentals* paper starts off with a section entitled 'conceptual framework'. This is because, before you launch into the mechanics of preparing financial statements, it is important that you understand *why* accounting information is necessary and the assumptions on which it is based.

The Syllabus Guidance Notes for this paper state that 'the role of the management accountant includes the preparation of information and its provision to other members of the management team'. You need to consider the nature of such information, its purposes and uses. These are the topics covered in Sections 1 to 3 of this chapter. You may know more about accounting than you realise. Have a go at the first exercise which will encourage you to think about these issues.

As you have chosen to train for the CIMA qualification it is likely that you are already aware that there is a difference between a management accountant and a financial accountant. This topic is covered in Section 4.

Accounting is not an exact science, nor is the information it provides free from drawbacks. It is as well to be aware from the beginning of your studies that there are limitations on the scope and use of accounting information, and this point is explored briefly in Section 5.

Lastly, the chapter introduces you to the main financial statements - the profit and loss account and the balance sheet.

1 WHAT IS ACCOUNTING?

1.1 To set you thinking, attempt the following exercise to assess what you already know about accounting.

Exercise 1

(a) You will often meet with the terms 'an accounting statement' or 'a set of accounts'. Do you know what is meant by these terms?

(b) Who do you think has the task of preparing accounting statements? In an organisation of a reasonable size, would it be one person? One department? Several different departments?

(c)   Who are the users of accounting information?

(d)   What is the purpose of accounting?

Solution

(a)   An accounting statement is any collection of related accounting information. It might be, for example, a profit and loss account or a balance sheet. A set of accounts is a number of accounting statements presented together with the intention of showing an overall view of an organisation's income, expenditure, assets and liabilities.

(b)   Most organisations of reasonable size will have at least one dedicated accounts department, staffed by people with detailed knowledge of accounting systems and theory, perhaps gained while acquiring a professional qualification in accountancy. In large organisations there may be several departments, or groups, responsible for preparing accounting information of many different kinds to meet the needs of accounts users.

(c)   The users of accounts, as explained in the text of this chapter, include a variety of people and organisations, both internal and external. The extent of their information needs of course varies widely.

(d)   There are many purposes of accounting. You may have thought of: control over the use of resources; knowledge of what the business owes and owns; calculation of profits and losses; cash budgeting; effective financial planning.

1.2   A few definitions will get us started.

Accounting could be defined as the process of collecting, recording, summarising and communicating financial information.

Accounts are the records in which this information is recorded. Keeping the most basic records is described as *bookkeeping*. The profession responsible for the summarising and communicating of financial information is the *accountancy* profession.

2   WHY KEEP ACCOUNTS?   *11/95*

2.1   Accounts have been kept for thousands of years because they help to keep track of money, by showing where it came from and how it has been spent.

2.2   The production of accounting information can itself play an important role in the efficient running of a business. For example, a business needs to pay bills in respect of the goods and services it purchases. It must, therefore, keep a record of such bills so that the correct amounts can be paid at the correct times. Similarly a business needs to keep track of cash and cheques received from customers. Such records form one part of a basic accounting system. Additionally, keeping records of a business's assets (eg its motor vehicles or computers) makes it easier to keep them secure.

2.3   Another reason for keeping accounts arises from the complexity of most modern businesses. Centuries ago, a business enterprise might consist of a single venture with a limited life. For example, a merchant might charter a ship to purchase goods from abroad for sale in his own country. In such cases it was easy to ascertain the merchant's profit: it was simply the amount of cash he had left at the end of the venture. Similarly, a small shop needs to generate enough money to pay for all its proprietor's personal expenses and occasional large purchases (eg replacement till or van). The proprietor can quite easily check that this aim is being met by counting the cash in the till.

2.4   However, modern businesses are often much more complicated. They seldom have a single owner (in fact, some very large enterprises, such as British Telecom, may be owned by millions of shareholders). Frequently the owners are not involved in the day-to-day running of the business but appoint managers to act on their behalf. In addition, there are too many activities and assets for the managers to keep track of simply from personal knowledge and an occasional glance at the bank statement. It is therefore desirable that businesses should produce accounts which will indicate how successfully the managers are performing.

2.5   In 1975 a committee established by the UK accountancy bodies published a discussion paper called *The Corporate Report*. (A corporate report is a report, including accounts, prepared by a business enterprise.) One of the questions which the committee attempted to answer was why businesses produce accounts. They concluded that the fundamental objective of a corporate report is:

> '. . . to communicate economic measurements of, and information about, the resources and performance of the reporting entity useful to those having reasonable rights to such information.'

2.6   In other words, a business should produce information about its activities because there are various groups of people who want or need to know that information. This sounds rather vague: to make it clearer, we should look more closely at the classes of people who might need information about a business. We need also to think about what information in particular is of interest to the members of each class. Because large businesses are usually of interest to a greater variety of people than small businesses we will consider the case of a large public company whose shares can be bought and sold on the Stock Exchange.

3   USERS OF ACCOUNTING INFORMATION   MISFIT PEG   5/95

3.1   The people who might be interested in financial information about a large public company may be classified as follows.

(a) *Managers of the company*. These are people appointed by the company's owners to supervise the day-to-day activities of the company. They need information about the company's current financial situation and what it is expected to be in the future. This enables them to manage the business efficiently and to take effective control and planning decisions.

(b) *Shareholders of the company*, ie the company's owners. They will want to assess how effectively management is performing its stewardship function. They will want to know how profitably management is running the company's operations and how much profit they can afford to withdraw from the business for their own use.

(c) *Trade contacts*, including suppliers who provide goods to the company on credit and customers who purchase the goods or services provided by the company. Suppliers will want to know about the company's ability to pay its debts; customers need to know that the company is a secure source of supply and is in no danger of having to close down.

(d) *Providers of finance to the company*. These might include a bank which permits the company to operate an overdraft, or provides longer-term finance by granting a loan. The bank will want to ensure that the company is able to keep up with interest payments, and eventually to repay the amounts advanced.

(e) *The Inland Revenue*, who will want to know about business profits in order to assess the tax payable by the company.

(f) *Employees* of the company. They should have a right to information about the company's financial situation, because their future careers and the level of their wages and salaries depend on it.

(g) *Financial analysts and advisers* need information for their clients or audience. For example, stockbrokers will need information to advise investors in stocks and shares; credit agencies will want information to advise potential suppliers of goods to the company; and journalists need information for their reading public.

(h) *Government and their agencies*. Governments and their agencies are interested in the allocation of resources and therefore in the activities of enterprises. They also require information in order to provide a basis for national statistics.

(i) *The public*. Enterprises affect members of the public in a variety of ways. For example, enterprises may make a substantial contribution to a local economy by providing employment and using local suppliers. Another important factor is the effect of an enterprise on the environment, for example as regards pollution.

Exercise 2

It is easy to see how 'internal' people get hold of accounting information. A manager, for example, can just go along to the accounts department and ask the staff there to prepare whatever accounting statements he needs. But external users of accounts cannot do this. How, in practice, can a business contact or a financial analyst access accounting information about a company?

Solution

The answer is that limited companies (though not other forms of business such as partnerships) are required to make certain accounting information public. They do so by sending copies of the required information to the Registrar of Companies at Companies House. The information filed at Companies House is available, at a fee, to any member of the public who asks for it. Other sources include financial comment in the press and company brochures.

---

4   MANAGEMENT ACCOUNTING AND FINANCIAL ACCOUNTING

4.1   To a greater or lesser extent, accountants aim to satisfy the information needs of all the different groups mentioned above. Managers of a business need the most information, to help them take their planning and control decisions; and they obviously have 'special' access to information about the business, because they are in a position to organise the provision of whatever internally produced statements they require. When managers want a large amount of information about the costs and profitability of individual products, or different parts of their business, they can arrange to obtain it through a system of *cost and management accounting*. The preparation of accounting reports for external use is called *financial accounting*. Bookkeeping and costing are the bases of financial and management accounting respectively.

4.2   Management accounting systems produce detailed information often split between different departments within an organisation (sales, production, finance etc). Although much of the information necessarily deals with past events and decisions, management accountants are also responsible for preparing budgets, helping to set price levels and other decisions about the future activities of a business.

4.3   Financial accountants, however, are usually solely concerned with summarising historical data, often from the same basic records as management accountants, but in a different way. This difference arises partly because external users have different interests from management and have neither the time nor the need for very detailed information, but also because financial statements are prepared under constraints which do not apply to management accounts produced for internal use. This Study Text serves as an introduction to financial accounting.

4.4   These constraints apply particularly to the accounts of limited companies. The owners of a limited company (the shareholders or members of the company) enjoy limited liability, which means that as individuals they are not personally liable to pay the company's debts. If the company's own assets are not sufficient to do so, the company may have to cease trading, but the shareholders are not obliged to make up any shortfall from their own private assets.

4.5   Clearly this system is open to abuse, and one of the safeguards is that limited companies are fenced about with a number of accounting regulations that do not apply to other forms of organisation. For example, they are required by law to prepare financial accounts annually, the minimum content of such accounts being laid down by detailed legal regulations.

4.6   In addition, their annual accounts must, except in the case of some small companies, be audited (ie checked) by an independent person with defined qualifications. The auditor must make a report on the accounts, and will highlight any material areas where they do not comply either with the legal regulations or with other regulations laid down by the accounting profession.

4.7 Different types of financial statements are produced for each external user group. Use the following exercise to develop your understanding of the statements received by the user groups.

Exercise 3

Mark the following statements as true or false.

(a) Shareholders receive annual accounts as prepared in accordance with legal and professional requirements.   T

always

(b) The accounts of limited companies are sometimes filed with the Registrar of Companies.   F

(c) Employees always receive the company's accounts and an employee report.   *NO*   F

(d) The Inland Revenue will receive the published accounts and as much supplementary detail as the Inspector of Taxes needs to assess the corporation tax payable on profits.   T

(e) Banks frequently require more information than is supplied in the published accounts when considering applications for loans and overdraft facilities.   T

Solution

True

(a) Yes, and, in addition, companies listed on the Stock Exchange have to comply with the regulations in the Stock Exchange's Listing Rules (Yellow Book).

(d)

(e) Yes, banks may require cash flow and profit forecasts and budgets prepared to show management's estimates of future activity in the business.

False

(b) The accounts of limited companies MUST be filed with the Registrar of Companies and be available for public inspection. In addition, the company itself will often distribute these accounts on request to potential shareholders, the bank and financial analysts. These accounts are all that is usually available to suppliers and customers.

(c) Employees will not necessarily receive company accounts (unless they are shareholders for example), but many companies do distribute the accounts to employees as a matter of policy. Some companies produce employee reports which summarise and expand on matters which are covered in the annual accounts and are of particular interest to them.

Exercise 4

We have already mentioned that a company's auditors must possess a suitable qualification. In practice this means that auditors will be a members of one or other of the professional accountancy bodies in the United Kingdom and Ireland. Do you know the names of these bodies? They are often mentioned in the financial press.

Solution

The auditors of a company will usually be either chartered accountants (members of the Institute of Chartered Accountants in England and Wales (ICAEW), the Institute of Chartered Accountants in Ireland (ICAI), or the Institute of Chartered Accountants of Scotland (ICAS), or certified accountants (members of the Association of Chartered Certified Accountants, the ACCA). The auditors of some public sector organisations, such as local authorities, are members of the Chartered Institute of Public Finance and Accountancy (CIPFA). Qualified management accountants are usually members of the Chartered Institute of Management Accountants (CIMA), the body whose qualification you are working towards. However, CIMA members are not authorised to conduct audits. The six organisations are jointly responsible for developing detailed accounting regulations known as Financial Reporting Standards (previously Statements of Standard Accounting Practice).

5   THE SCOPE OF ACCOUNTING INFORMATION

5.1   Accounting statements are presented in monetary terms. It follows that they will only include items to which a monetary value can be attributed. For example, in the balance sheet of a business monetary values can be attributed to such assets as machinery (eg the original cost of the machinery, or the amount it would cost to replace it); whereas the flair of a good manager, or the loyalty and commitment of a dedicated workforce, cannot be evaluated in monetary terms and therefore do not appear in the accounts.

5.2   Similarly, there are important factors in the successful running of a business which are non-financial by nature. A manager in a manufacturing business will need a detailed knowledge of his machinery's capabilities, the skills of his production staff and the characteristics of his raw materials. All of these things are important in planning production, but none of them would appear in a set of accounts.

5.3   Subject to these limitations, the range of accounting information which can be prepared is very wide. Accounting statements may cover:

(a)   the profit earned by a business, or by each of its departments or divisions, in a period;

(b)   the assets and liabilities of a business at a particular date;

(c)   the cost of producing and/or selling a particular product or range of products;

(d)   the cost of running a particular department or division;

(e)   the quantity of a product which must be sold in order for it to pay its way (break even);

(f)   the amount of cash coming into and leaving a business over a defined period;

(g)   the expected overdraft requirement of a business at defined intervals in the future.

5.4   The list is far from exhaustive. To ensure you understand the difference between financial and management accountancy, mark each of the above as financial or management statements.

(a)   You could have classified this as both financial and management information. Generally the profit earned by the whole business, included in a historical statement (for example for the past 12 months), will be financial accounting. Forecast information, or information relating to parts of the business, for example departments or divisions is management accounting.

(b)   This usually falls within the scope of financial accounting, although it may be used as an input to management accounting, for example as a basis for a forecast.

(c)   Management accounting.

(d)   Management accounting.

(e)   Management accounting.

(f)   Cash flow accounting is financial information when it is a historical statement and usually management accounting when it is a forecast or budget.

(g)   Management accounting.

Exercise 5

Try to think of two or three other areas that an accounting statement might cover.

Solution

There are many possibilities. Two that you may have heard of in connection with limited companies' financial accounts are a cash flow statement and a five-year summary of key accounting statistics. Other management accounting examples you might suggest are a forecast of sales revenue (perhaps analysed by product, or by geographical area), or an aged debtors analysis (showing the sums of money owed to the business by its customers and the length of time they have been outstanding).

6   THE MAIN FINANCIAL STATEMENTS

6.1   We end this chapter by looking briefly at the two principal financial statements drawn up by accountants: the balance sheet and the profit and loss account.

6.2   The *balance sheet* is simply a list of all the assets owned by a business and all the liabilities owed by a business as at a particular date. It is a snapshot of the financial position of the business at a particular moment. Assets are the business's resources so, for example, a business may buy buildings to operate from, plant and machinery, stock to sell and cars for its employees. These are all resources which it uses in its operations Additionally, it may have bank balances, cash and amounts of money owed to it. These provide the funds it needs to carry out its operations, and are also assets. On the other hand, it may owe money to the bank or to suppliers. These are liabilities.

6.3   A *profit and loss account* is a record of income generated and expenditure incurred over a given period. The period chosen will depend on the purpose for which the statement is produced. The profit and loss account which forms part of the published annual accounts of a limited company will be made up for the period of a year, commencing from the date of the previous year's accounts. On the other hand, management might want to keep a closer eye on a company's profitability by making up quarterly or monthly profit and loss accounts. The profit and loss account shows whether the business has had more income than expenditure (a profit) or vice versa (a loss). Organisations which are not run for profit (charities etc) produce a similar statement called an income and expenditure account which shows the surplus of income over expenditure (or a deficit where expenditure exceeds income).

Accruals concept

6.4   It is very important to grasp the principle, which is applied in nearly all businesses' accounts, that accounts are not prepared on a cash basis but on an accruals (or earnings) basis. That is, a sale or purchase is dealt with in the year in which it is made, even if cash changes hands in a later year. This is important because most businesses, even if they do not sell on credit, make purchases on credit. If cash accounting is used, then accounts do not present a true picture of the business's activities in any given period. Accountants call this convention an application of the accruals concept. This is discussed in more detail in Chapter 2, but in the meantime is explained briefly by means of the example below.

Example: accruals concept

6.5   Emma has a business printing and selling T-shirts. In May 1997 she makes the following purchases and sales.

Invoice date	Numbers bought/sold	Amount	Date paid
Purchases		£	
7.5.97	20	100	1.6.95
Sales			
8.5.97	4	40	1.6.95
12.5.97	6	60	1.6.95
23.5.97	10	100	1.7.95

What is Emma's profit for May?

Solution

6.6 | | £ |
|---|---|
| *Cash basis* | |
| Sales | 0 |
| Purchases | 0 |
| Profit/loss | 0 |
| | |
| *Accruals basis* | |
| Sales (£40 + £60 + £100) | 200 |
| Purchases | 100 |
| Profit | 100 |

6.7 Obviously, the accruals basis gives a truer picture than the cash basis. Emma has no cash to show for her efforts until June but her customers are legally bound to pay her and she is legally bound to pay for her purchases.

6.8 Her balance sheet as at 31 May 1997 would therefore show her assets and liabilities as follows.

	£
Assets	
Debtors (£40 + £60 + £100)	200
Liabilities	
Creditors	100
Net assets	100
Proprietor's capital	100

6.9 *Capital* is a special form of liability, representing the amount owed by the business to its proprietor(s). In Emma's case it represents the profit earned in May, which she, as sole proprietor of the business, is entitled to in full. Usually, however, capital will also include the proprietor's initial capital, introduced as cash and perhaps equipment or other assets.

6.10 For example, if Emma had begun her business on 30 April 1997 by opening a business bank account and paying in £100, her balance sheet immediately after this transaction would look like this.

	£
Assets	
Bank	100
Proprietor's capital	100

On 31 May 1997 the balance sheet would look like this.

	£
Assets	
Debtors	200
Bank	100
	300
Liabilities	
Creditors	100
Net assets	200
Proprietor's capital	
Brought forward	100
Profit for the period	100
Carried forward	200

6.11 This simple example shows that both the balance sheet and the profit and loss account are summaries of a great many transactions. In later chapters we will look in detail at the ways in which these transactions are recorded and financial statements prepared.

Exercise 6

By looking at the example of Emma, you may be able to see that there is a simple arithmetical relationship linking capital at the beginning of a period, capital at the end of the period, and profit earned during the period. Can you formulate the relationship?

Solution

The relationship is: opening capital + profit = closing capital. In more complicated examples it would be necessary to make adjustments for new capital introduced during the period, and for any capital withdrawn during the period.

6.12   Accountancy textbooks often write 19X6 or 19X7 and so on for dates instead of 1997 etc. You will find both conventions in this Study Text, but in the CIMA exams set so far only 'real dates' (1997 etc) have been used.

Chapter roundup

- You should now have an understanding of accounting and its main uses.

- Accounting is the process of collecting, recording, summarising and communicating financial information.

- Accounting information is essential to the efficient running of a business. It helps managers to control the use of resources, keep track of the assets and liabilities of the business and plan effectively for the future.

- Accounting information is required by a wide range of interested parties both within and outside of the organisation.

- The scope of accounting information is very wide, but it does not embrace every aspect of an organisation's affairs. Even within its own province, the scope of accounting is limited by its restriction to items which have a monetary value.

- The two most important financial statements prepared by accountants are the profit and loss account and the balance sheet. Both are prepared on an accruals basis, not a cash basis.

- In Chapter 2 we will develop your understanding of accountancy by considering the concepts, conventions and regulations used in preparing accounts.

Test your knowledge

1   How has the increasing complexity of modern business contributed to the development of accounting? (see para 2.3)

2   List five categories of people who might want accounting information about a business. How do their information needs differ? (3.1)

3   Explain the distinction between financial accounting and management accounting. (4.1-4.3)

4   What safeguards are in place to prevent the abuse of limited liability? (4.5)

5   What limitations are there on the scope of accounting information? (5.1, 5.2)

6   Explain briefly:

(a) what a balance sheet is; (6.2) and
(b) what a profit and loss account is. (6.3)

7   In what sense is the capital of a business a liability of the business? (6.9)

Now try illustrative question 1 at the end of the Study Text

Chapter 2

PREPARING ACCOUNTS: CONCEPTS, CONVENTIONS AND REGULATIONS

This chapter covers the following topics.

		Syllabus reference	Ability required
1	Accounting concepts	1(a)	Knowledge
2	Costs and values	1(a)	Appreciation
3	The regulatory framework of accounts	1(a)	Knowledge

Introduction

Accounting practice has developed gradually over a period of centuries. Many of its procedures are operated automatically by people who have never questioned whether alternative methods exist which have equal validity. However, the procedures in common use imply the acceptance of certain concepts which are by no means self-evident; nor are they the only possible concepts which could be used to build up an accounting framework.

Our next step is to look at some of the more important concepts which are taken for granted in preparing accounts. A statement of standard accounting practice (SSAP 2 *Disclosure of accounting policies*) describes four concepts as *fundamental accounting concepts*: they are going concern, prudence, accruals and consistency. These four are also identified as fundamental by companies legislation (the Companies Act 1985), which adds a fifth to the list (the separate valuation principle). But there is no universally agreed list of fundamental concepts, and others besides these have been described as fundamental by various authors.

In this chapter we shall single out the following concepts for discussion.

(a) The entity concept
(b) The money measurement concept
(c) The going concern concept
(d) The prudence concept
(e) The accruals or matching concept
(f) The consistency concept
(g) The separate valuation principle
(h) The materiality concept

In the last chapter we saw that one of the limitations of accounting information is that such information is always, by definition, in monetary terms, thus ignoring factors which are not readily quantifiable, but which may nevertheless be important to the success of a business. In Section 2 of this chapter we take the point further and argue that, even when you accept that monetary value is paramount, determining that monetary value is by no means a straightforward uncontroversial task.

In Section 3, we take a look at the regulatory framework within which accounts, particularly those of limited companies, are prepared. Do not feel you have to memorise all the details at this stage, the purpose of the section is to impress upon you the *importance* of this framework, which is to be studied in much more detail in the later stages of your qualification.

1   ACCOUNTING CONCEPTS   11/95, 5/96

The entity concept

1.1   This will be discussed more fully in the next chapter. Briefly, the concept is that accountants regard a business as a separate entity, distinct from its owners or managers. The concept applies whether the business is a limited company (and so recognised in law as a separate entity) or a sole proprietorship or partnership (in which case the business is not separately recognised by the law). So, in the example of Emma in the previous chapter, the money she transferred to her business bank account becomes, in accounting terms, a *business* asset (but legally remains a *personal* asset).

1.2   Acceptance of this concept has important practical consequences. Particularly in the case of a small business run by a single individual, the owner's personal affairs and business affairs may appear to be inextricably linked; for example, Emma may conduct her business from home. But in preparing the business accounts it is essential to distinguish her private transactions and keep them separate.

1.3   Suppose that Emma withdraws a number of T-shirts from her stock to give to friends, how would this be reflected in her accounts?

1.4   The correct accounting treatment is to regard her as having purchased the goods from the business, which is a completely separate entity; the subsequent gift to her friends is then a private transaction and is not recorded anywhere in the books of the business. Emma should pay for the T-shirts by taking money from her own purse and putting it into the till, or she should regard the withdrawal as a repayment of capital. Otherwise, the business accounts will give a misleading picture.

The money measurement concept

1.5   In Chapter 1, we stated that accounts deal only with items to which a monetary value can be attributed. This is the money measurement concept. We distinguished between an asset such as a machine (which might be valued at its original purchase cost, its replacement cost etc) and an asset such as the flair of a manager or the dedication of the workforce.

1.6   Although these latter assets are very hard to quantify in monetary terms, they can be of enormous significance to the success of a business. Recognising their importance, accountants in recent years have tried to suggest ways of 'bringing them on to the balance sheet' by attributing values to them. These methods of 'human resource accounting' are beyond the scope of this book, but you should be aware at least of the problems they attempt to address.

Exercise 1

Perhaps it is too glib to say that monetary values can never be attributed to the skill of the workforce. There is at least one high-profile industry where such valuations are commonplace. Can you think of it? And do you know what the accounting consequences are in that industry?

Solution

The industry referred to is of course the world of sport, particularly football, where transfer fees appear to provide an objective valuation of a player's worth. Many football clubs are run as substantial businesses, some of them with shares quoted on the Stock Exchange. As such, their accounting practices are widely publicised and discussed. In almost all cases, however, they make no attempt to include the value of players on their balance sheet, presumably because such values fluctuate wildly with the form and fitness of the players concerned. Almost invariably transfer fees are therefore shown simply as a cost in the profit and loss account.

The going concern concept

1.7   The going concern concept implies that the business will continue in operational existence for the foreseeable future, and that there is no intention to put the company into liquidation or to make drastic cutbacks to the scale of operations.

1.8   The main significance of the going concern concept is that the assets of the business should not be valued at their 'break-up' value, which is the amount that they would sell for if they were sold off piecemeal and the business were thus broken up.

1.9   Suppose, for example, that Emma acquires a T-shirt-printing machine at a cost of £60,000. The asset has an estimated life of six years, and it is normal to write off the cost of the asset to the profit and loss account over this time. In this case a depreciation cost of £10,000 per annum will be charged. (This topic will be covered in more detail in later chapters.)

1.10   Using the going concern concept, it would be presumed that the business will continue its operations and so the asset will live out its full six years in use. A depreciation charge of £10,000 will be made each year, and the value of the asset in the balance sheet will be its cost less the accumulated amount of depreciation charged to date. After one year, the net book value of the asset would therefore be £(60,000 – 10,000) = £50,000, after two years it would be £40,000, after three years £30,000 etc, until it has been written down to a value of 0 after 6 years.

1.11   Now suppose that this asset has no other operational use outside the business, and in a forced sale it would only sell for scrap. After one year of operation, its scrap value might be, say, £8,000. What would the net book value be after one year?

1.12   The net book value of the asset, applying the going concern concept, would be £50,000 after one year, but its immediate sell-off value only £8,000. It might be argued that the asset is over-valued at £50,000 and that it should be written down to its break-up value (ie in the balance sheet it should be shown at £8,000 and the balance of its cost should be treated as an expense). However, provided that the going concern concept is valid, so that the asset will continue to be used and will not be sold, it is appropriate accounting practice to value the asset at its net book value.

Exercise 2

Now try this example yourself.

A retailer commences business on 1 January and buys a stock of 20 washing machines, each costing £100. During the year he sells 17 machines at £150 each. How should the remaining machines be valued at 31 December if:

(a)   he is forced to close down his business at the end of the year and the remaining machines will realise only £60 each in a forced sale; or

(b)   he intends to continue his business into the next year?

Solution

(a)   If the business is to be closed down, the remaining three machines must be valued at the amount they will realise in a forced sale, ie 3 × £60 = £180.

(b)   If the business is regarded as a going concern, the stock unsold at 31 December will be carried forward into the following year, when the cost of the three machines will be matched against the eventual sale proceeds in computing that year's profits. The three machines will therefore appear in the balance sheet at 31 December at cost, 3 × £100 = £300.

The prudence concept

1.13 This is the concept which states that where alternative procedures, or alternative valuations, are possible, the one selected should be the one which gives the most cautious presentation of the business's financial position or results. For example, you may have wondered why the three washing machines in Exercise 2 were stated in the balance sheet at their cost (£100 each) rather than their selling price (£150 each). This is simply an aspect of the prudence concept: to value the machines at £150 would be to anticipate making a profit before the profit had been realised. (After all, what if you only sold them for £130?)

1.14 The other aspect of the prudence concept is that where a loss is foreseen, it should be anticipated and taken into account immediately. If a business purchases stock for £1,200 but because of a sudden slump in the market only £900 is likely to be realised when the stock is sold the prudence concept dictates that the stock should be valued at £900. It is not enough to wait until the stock is sold, and then recognise the £300 loss; it must be recognised as soon as it is foreseen.

1.15 A profit can be considered to be a realised profit when it is in the form of:

(a) cash; or

(b) another asset which has a reasonably certain cash value. This includes amounts owing from debtors, provided that there is a reasonable certainty that the debtors will eventually pay up what they owe.

1.16 SSAP 2 describes the prudence concept as follows.

> 'Revenue and profits are not anticipated, but are recognised by inclusion in the profit and loss account only when realised in the form either of cash or of other assets the ultimate cash realisation of which can be assessed with reasonable certainty; provision is made for all known ... expenses and losses whether the amount of these is known with certainty or is a best estimate in the light of the information available.'

1.17 An exercise may help you to understand how the prudence concept is applied in practice.

Exercise 3

(a) A company begins trading on 1 January 1995 and sells goods worth £100,000 during the year to 31 December. At 31 December there are debts of £15,000 owed to the business by customers. Of these, the company is now doubtful whether £6,000 will ever be paid. What is the effect of this on the company's balance sheet and profit and loss account?

(b) Samson Feeble trades as a carpenter. He has undertaken to make a range of kitchen furniture for a customer at an agreed price of £1,000. At the end of Samson's accounting year the job is unfinished (being two thirds complete) and the following data has been assembled.

	£
Costs incurred in making the furniture to date	800
Further estimated cost to completion of the job	400
Total cost	1,200

The incomplete job represents *work in progress* at the end of the year which is an asset, like stock. Its cost to date is £800, but by the time the job is completed Samson will have made a loss of £200. What is the effect of this on Samson's balance sheet and profit and loss account?

Solution

(a) The company should make a *provision for doubtful debts* of £6,000. Sales for 1995 will be shown in the profit and loss account at their full value of £100,000, but the provision for doubtful debts would be a cost of £6,000. Because there is some uncertainty that the sales will be realised in the form of cash, the prudence concept dictates that the £6,000 should not be included in the profit for the year. Debtors in the balance sheet will be shown at a valuation of £9,000.

(b)   The full £200 loss should be charged against profits of the current year. The value of work in progress at the year end should be its *net realisable value*, which is lower than its cost. The net realisable value can be calculated in either of two ways.

	(i) £		(ii) £
Eventual sales value	1,000	Work in progress at cost	800
Less further costs to completion		Less loss foreseen	200
in order to make the sale	400		
Net realisable value	600		600

1.18   It is important to understand the relationship - sometimes a conflict - between the accruals concept and the prudence concept.

(a)   How should we value an asset? If you refer back to our discussion of the going concern concept, you will see that assets are commonly valued at amounts in excess of their realisable value. Is this prudent?

(b)   When should we recognise a sale as having been made? According to the accruals concept Emma shows sales revenue in her profit and loss account in the period when she sells goods to a customer. But is this prudent, given that the customer has purchased on credit and has not yet paid Emma the cash?

1.19   The first problem is covered in our earlier discussion. For the second case, the generally accepted rules are as follows.

1.20   Sales revenue should only be 'realised' and so 'recognised' in the trading, profit and loss account when:

(a)   the sale transaction is for a specific quantity of goods at a known price, so that the sales value of the transaction is known for certain;

(b)   the sale transaction has been completed, or else it is certain that it will be completed (eg in the case of long-term contract work, when the job is well under way but not yet completed by the end of an accounting period);

(c)   the *critical event* in the sale transaction has occurred. The critical event is the event after which either:

(i)   it becomes virtually certain that cash will eventually be received from the customer; or

(ii)   cash is actually received.

1.21   Usually, revenue is 'recognised' either:

(a)   when a cash sale is made; or

(b)   when the customer promises to pay on or before a specified future date, and the debt is legally enforceable.

1.22   The prudence concept is applied here in the sense that revenue should not be anticipated, and included in the trading, profit and loss account, before it is reasonably certain to 'happen'.

Exercise 4

Given that prudence is the main consideration, consider under what circumstances, if any, revenue might be recognised at the following stages of a sale.

(a)   Goods have been acquired by the business which it confidently expects to resell very quickly.

(b)   A customer places a firm order for goods.

(c)   Goods are delivered to the customer.

(d)   The customer is invoiced for goods.

(e)   The customer pays for the goods.

(f)   The customer's cheque in payment for the goods has been cleared by the bank.

Solution

(a)   A sale must never be recognised before the goods have even been ordered. There is no certainty about the value of the sale, nor when it will take place, even if it is virtually certain that goods will be sold.

(b)   A sale must never be recognised when the customer places an order. Even though the order will be for a specific quantity of goods at a specific price, it is not yet certain that the sale transaction will go through. The customer may cancel the order, or the supplier might be unable to deliver the goods as ordered.

(c)   A sale will be recognised when delivery of the goods is made only when:

(i)   the sale is for cash, and so the cash is received at the same time; or

(ii)   the sale is on credit and the customer accepts delivery (eg by signing a delivery note).

(d)   The critical event for a credit sale is usually the dispatch of an invoice to the customer. There is then a legally enforceable debt, payable on specified terms, for a completed sale transaction.

(e)   The critical event for a cash sale is when delivery takes place and when cash is received; both take place at the same time.

It would be too cautious or 'prudent' to await cash payment for a credit sale transaction before recognising the sale, unless the customer is a high credit risk and there is a serious doubt about his ability or intention to pay.

(f)   It would again be over-cautious to wait for clearance of the customer's cheques before recognising sales revenue. Such a precaution would only be justified in cases where there is a very high risk of the bank refusing to honour the cheque.

The accruals concept or matching concept

1.23   This concept states that, in computing profit, revenue earned must be matched against the expenditure incurred in earning it. This is illustrated in the example of Emma; profit of £100 was computed by matching the revenue (£200) earned from the sale of 20 T-shirts against the cost (£100) of acquiring them.

1.24   If, however, Emma had only sold 18 T-shirts, it would have been incorrect to charge her profit and loss account with the cost of 20 T-shirts, as she still has two T-shirts in stock. If she intends to sell them in June she is likely to make a profit on the sale. Therefore, only the purchase cost of 18 T-shirts (£90) should be matched with her sales revenue, leaving her with a profit of £90.

1.25   Her balance sheet would therefore look like this.

	£
Assets	
Stock (at cost, ie 2 × £5)	10
Debtors (18 × £10)	180
	190
Liabilities	
Creditors	100
Net assets	90
Proprietor's capital (profit for the period)	90

1.26   In this example, the concepts of going concern and matching are linked. Because the business is assumed to be a going concern it is possible to carry forward the cost of the unsold T-shirts as a charge against profits of the next period.

1.27   If Emma decided to give up selling T-shirts, how would the two T-shirts in the balance sheet be valued?

1.28   If Emma decided to give up selling T-shirts, then the going concern concept would no longer apply and the value of the two T-shirts in the balance sheet would be a break-up valuation rather than cost. Similarly, if the two unsold T-shirts were now unlikely to be sold at more than their cost of £5 each (say, because of damage or a fall in demand) then they should be recorded on the balance sheet at their net realisable value (ie the likely eventual sales price less any expenses to be incurred to make them saleable, eg paint) rather than cost. This shows the application of the prudence concept.

The accruals concept defined

1.29   The 'accruals' or 'matching' concept is described in SSAP 2 as follows.

> 'Revenues and costs are accrued (that is, recognised as they are earned or incurred, not as money is received or paid), matched with one another so far as their relationship can be established or justifiably assumed, and dealt with in the profit and loss account of the period to which they relate ... Revenue and profits dealt with in the profit and loss account of the period are matched with associated costs and expenses by including in the same account the costs incurred in earning them (so far as these are material and identifiable)'.

1.30   Company legislation gives legal recognition to the accruals concept, stating that: 'all income and charges relating to the financial year to which the accounts relate shall be taken into account, without regard to the date of receipt or payment.' This has the effect, as we have seen, of requiring businesses to take account of sales and purchases when made, rather than when paid for, and also to carry unsold stock forward in the balance sheet rather than to deduct its cost from profit for the period.

The consistency concept

1.31   Accounting is not an exact science. There are many areas in which judgement must be exercised in attributing money values to items appearing in accounts. Over the years certain procedures and principles have come to be recognised as good accounting practice, but within these limits there are often various acceptable methods of accounting for similar items.

1.32   The consistency concept states that in preparing accounts consistency should be observed in two respects.

(a)   Similar items within a single set of accounts should be given similar accounting treatment.

(b)   The same treatment should be applied from one period to another in accounting for similar items. This enables valid comparisons to be made from one period to the next.

The separate valuation principle

1.33   Company law recognises the same four fundamental accounting concepts as SSAP 2, although it describes them not as concepts but as *accounting principles*. The Act also mentions a fifth principle, which may be called the separate valuation principle. Although it is not described by SSAP 2 as a fundamental accounting concept it has long been recognised as good accounting practice.

1.34   The separate valuation principle states that, in determining the amount to be attributed to an asset or liability in the balance sheet, each component item of the asset or liability must be valued separately. These separate valuations must then be aggregated to arrive at the balance sheet figure. For example, if a company's stock comprises 50 separate items, a valuation must (in theory) be arrived at for each item separately; the 50 figures must then be aggregated and the total is the stock figure which should appear in the balance sheet.

Exercise 5

The following true/false exercise will allow you to ensure that you have understood the concepts and conventions covered so far in this chapter.

Mark the following statements as true or false.

(a)   The entity concept is that accountants regard a business as a separate legal entity, distinct from its owners or managers.

(b)   Accounts deal only with items to which a monetary value can be attributed.

(c)   Where the prudence and accruals concepts conflict, preparers of accounts may follow either.

(d)   The accruals, prudence, going concern and consistency concepts are contained in SSAP 2.

Solution

True

(b)

(d)   Yes. Company law also recognises them as principles and adds a fifth, the separate valuation principle.

False

(a)   No. Although it is certainly true that the entity concept is that accountants regard a business as a separate entity, it is not always a legal difference. For example, legally a sole trader is not separate from his business.

(c)   Where the prudence and accruals concepts conflict, prudence overrides accruals.

The materiality concept

1.35   As we stated above in discussing the consistency concept, accounts preparation is not an exact science. Apart from the possibility of downright error, there will be many areas where two different accountants would come up with different figures for the same item. The materiality concept is relevant in this context.

1.36   An error which is too trivial to affect anyone's understanding of the accounts is referred to as *immaterial*. In preparing accounts it is important to assess what is material and what is not, so that time and money are not wasted in the pursuit of excessive detail.

1.37   Determining whether or not an item is material is a very subjective exercise. There is no absolute measure of materiality. It is common to apply a convenient rule of thumb (for example to define material items as those with a value greater than 5% of the net profit disclosed by the accounts). But some items disclosed in accounts are regarded as particularly sensitive and even a very small misstatement of such an item would be regarded as a material error. An example in the accounts of a limited company might be the amount of remuneration paid to directors of the company.

1.38   The assessment of an item as material or immaterial may affect its treatment in the accounts. For example, the profit and loss account of a business will show the expenses incurred by the business grouped under suitable captions (heating and lighting expenses, rent and rates expenses etc); but in the case of very small expenses it may be appropriate to lump them together under a caption such as 'sundry expenses', because a more detailed breakdown would be inappropriate for such immaterial amounts.

1.39 In assessing whether or not an item is material, it is not only the amount of the item which needs to be considered. The context is also important.

(a) If a balance sheet shows fixed assets of £2 million and stocks of £30,000 an error of £20,000 in the fixed asset valuation might not be regarded as material, whereas an error of £20,000 in the stock valuation would be. In other words, the total of which the erroneous item forms a part must be considered.

(b) If a business has a bank loan of £50,000 and a £55,000 balance on bank deposit account, it might well be regarded as a material misstatement if these two amounts were displayed on the balance sheet as 'cash at bank £5,000'. In other words, incorrect presentation may amount to material misstatement even if there is no monetary error.

Exercise 6

(a) You depreciate your office equipment by 20% each year because it has a useful life, on average, of five years. This year your profitability is down and you think you can squeeze an extra year's life out of your equipment. Is it acceptable not to charge any depreciation this year?

(b) You have recently paid £4.95 for a waste paper bin which should have a useful life of about five years. Should you treat it as a fixed asset?

Solution

(a) No, because of the consistency concept. Once the depreciation policy has been established, it should not be changed without good cause.

(b) No, because of the materiality concept. The cost of the bin is very small. Rather than cluttering up the balance sheet for five years, treat the £4.95 as an expense in this year's profit and loss account.

---

2 COSTS AND VALUES

2.1 Accounting concepts are a part of the theoretical framework on which accounting practice is based. Before we proceed to the chapters which discuss accounting practice in detail, it is worth looking at one further general point, the problem of attributing monetary values to the items which appear in accounts.

2.2 A basic principle of accounting (some writers include it in the list of fundamental accounting concepts) is that resources are normally stated in accounts at historical cost, ie at the amount which the business paid to acquire them. An important advantage of this procedure is that the objectivity of accounts is maximised: there is usually objective, documentary evidence to prove the amount paid to purchase an asset or pay an expense.

2.3 In general, accountants prefer to deal with costs, rather than with 'values'. This is because valuations tend to be subjective and to vary according to what the valuation is for. For example, suppose that a company acquires a machine to manufacture its products. The machine has an expected useful life of four years. At the end of two years the company is preparing a balance sheet and has to decide what monetary amount to attribute to the asset.

2.4 Numerous possibilities might be considered:

(a) the original cost (historical cost) of the machine;

(b) half of the historical cost, on the ground that half of its useful life has expired;

(c) the amount the machine might fetch on the secondhand market;

(d)   the amount it would cost to replace the machine with an identical machine;

(e)   the amount it would cost to replace the machine with a more modern machine incorporating the technological advances of the previous two years;

(f)   the machine's economic value, ie the amount of the profits it is expected to generate for the company during its remaining life.

2.5   All of these valuations have something to commend them, but the great advantage of the first two is that they are based on a figure (the machine's historical cost) which is objectively verifiable. (Some authors regard objectivity as an accounting concept in its own right.) The subjective judgement involved in the other valuations, particularly (f), is so great as to lessen the reliability of any accounts in which they are used. As we will see in later chapters, method (b), or a variation of it, is the one which would normally be used.

2.6   The method chosen has important consequences for the measurement of profit, as the following example will show.

Example: costs and values

2.7   Brian sets up in business on 1 January 1996 selling accountancy textbooks. He buys 100 books for £5 each and by 31 December 1996 he manages to sell his entire stock, all for cash, at a price of £8 each. On 1 January 1997 he replaces his stock by purchasing another 100 books; by this time the cost of the books has risen to £6 each. Calculate the profit earned by Brian in 1996.

Solution

2.8   In conventional historical cost accounting, Brian's profit would be computed as follows.

	£
Sale of 100 books (@ £8 each)	800
Cost of 100 books (@ £5 each)	500
Profit for the year	300

2.9   The purchase of the books is stated at their historical cost. Although this is accepted accounting practice, and is the method we will be using almost invariably throughout this book, it involves an anomaly which can be seen if we look at how well off the business is.

2.10 On 1 January 1996 the assets of the business consist of the 100 books which Brian has purchased as stock. On 1 January 1997 the business has an identical stock of 100 books, and also has cash of £200 (ie £800 received from customers, less the £600 cost of replacing stock). So despite making a profit of £300, measured in the conventional way, the business appears to be only £200 better off.

2.11 This anomaly could be removed if an alternative accounting convention were used. Suppose that profit was measured as the difference between the selling price of goods and the cost of replacing the goods sold. Brian's profit would then be computed as follows.

	£
Sale of 100 books	800
Cost of replacing 100 books sold @ £6 each	600
Profit for the year	200

2.12 Now the profit for the year is exactly matched by the increase in the company's assets over the year.

Capital maintenance

2.13 The example above leads us on to the important concept of capital maintenance. The capital of a business (also called its net worth) represents the excess of its assets over its liabilities, and, as we saw in the example of Emma in Chapter 1, represents the proprietor's interest in the business. One way of measuring profit would be to measure how well off a business is at the beginning of a period, and compare it with how well off it is at the end of the period; the difference (after allowing for withdrawals of capital and injections of new capital) would be the profit or loss for the period. On this basis, measurement of profit depends on the methods we use to value the assets and liabilities of the business at the beginning and end of the period.

2.14 It is worth looking again at the example of Brian. Using historical cost as our basis of valuation, the value of his business at 1 January 1996 and 1 January 1997 is as follows.

	1996	1997
	£	£
Stocks (at historical cost)	500	600
Cash	0	200
	500	800

2.15 The value of the business has risen by £300 over the year and this is the amount of profit we calculated on the historical cost basis. We can say that the original capital of the business, £500, has been maintained and an addition to capital of £300 has been created.

2.16 Instead of using historical costs, it is theoretically possible to measure capital in physical terms. Brian's physical capital was originally 100 books; on 1 January 1997, it consists of an identical 100 books plus £200 cash. We can say that Brian's original physical capital has been maintained and an addition to capital of £200 has been created. This is equivalent to the profit we computed on a replacement cost basis.

2.17 A system of accounting based principally on replacement costs, and measuring profit as the increase in physical capital, was used in the UK for some years. It is called *current cost accounting*. The main accounting system has always been, and will continue to be, historical cost accounting but current cost accounting was developed as a possible solution to certain problems which arise in periods of rising prices. Theoretical and practical objections to the current cost accounting system led to its withdrawal in the UK.

Accounting in periods of rising prices

2.18 In periods of *inflation*, businessmen and accountants face a number of problems.

2.19 For businessmen the major difficulty is in decision making. Successful decisions depend on correct estimates of future events and this is complicated when future costs and prices are affected by inflation. The difficulty is more acute when the effects of the decision extend over a long period of time, but even short-term decisions such as price increases are affected.

2.20 Another difficulty is that businessmen rely on accounts to show the profit earned by a business, and this is at least partly so that an assessment can be made of how much profit can safely be withdrawn from the business by its owners. But when prices are rising, at least some of the profit shown by historical cost accounts must be ploughed back into the business just to maintain its previous capacity.

2.21 The job of the accountant is also complicated by inflation. The accounts he or she prepares must be expressed in terms of a monetary unit (eg the £ in the UK). In times of rising prices the value of the unit is not constant and comparisons between the accounts of the current year with those of previous years may be misleading.

2.22   The accountant must cope with difficulties in measuring asset values and profit. Asset values can become out of date, particularly in the case of fixed assets; for example, a freehold factory purchased 20 years ago will be shown in the accounts at its original cost, even though its value is likely to have increased greatly over the period of ownership. Profit figures are likely to be distorted by increases in the cost of goods purchased during the accounting period. This is because the cost of goods sold is computed in the profit and loss account on the basis of their historical cost. But a continuing business will want to replace stocks sold and will have to do so at ever higher prices. This means that some of the 'profit' shown by the accounts is not profit at all, but must be spent just in restoring the assets of the business to their previous level.

2.23   Attempts to get round the problems of inflation have a long history in the UK and abroad. One step which has long been common in practice is to prepare *modified* historical cost accounts. This usually means that up-to-date valuations are included in the historical cost balance sheet for some or all of a company's fixed assets, without any other adjustments being made. No attempt is made to tackle the difficulties of profit measurement.

2.24   More active measures have been taken to find alternatives to the historical cost convention. The two alternative systems which have found favour, at different times, in the UK are *current cost accounting* (CCA) and *current purchasing power accounting* (CPP). CCA has already been briefly described. CPP tackles the problems of inflation by attempting to express accounting values in terms of a stable monetary unit.

2.25   For the foreseeable future, historical cost accounting is likely to be the most important system in the UK, despite its inability to reflect the effects of inflation.

Exercise 7

To try and get your mind around the concept of capital maintenance, try to work out the answer to this question. In a period when prices are rising, the profit shown under the historical cost convention will differ from that shown under the current cost convention. In the case of a retail trading company, which of the two profit figures will be higher?

Solution

The profit shown under the historical cost convention will be higher. This is because the value of the resources consumed by the business is measured by their cost at the time they were purchased. Under the current cost convention, the value of these resources is measured by their cost at the (later) time when they were replaced. Given that prices are rising, this cost will be higher and so reported profits will be less.

---

3   THE REGULATORY FRAMEWORK OF ACCOUNTS

3.1   We have already seen that there is a wide range of accounting concepts in use, not all of them by any means self-evident and for the most part accorded different levels of importance and priority by accounting theorists. There are also different conventions under which accounts can be prepared. It may seem as though almost anything goes. What rules are there to guide us on how accounts should be prepared?

3.2   One important point to grasp is that the answer to this question is very different for a limited company compared with almost any other organisation. As we have already noted, the activities of limited companies, including the way they prepare their accounts, are closely regulated. For an unincorporated business, any form of accounting information is adequate if it gives the owner(s) of the business a basis for planning and control, and satisfies the requirements of external users such as the Inland Revenue.

3.3   As far as limited companies are concerned, the regulations on accounts come from four main sources.

(a) Company law enacted by the UK Parliament

(b) Statements of standard accounting practice and financial reporting standards issued by the professional accountancy bodies in the UK and Ireland

(c) International accounting standards

(d) The requirements of the Stock Exchange. These of course only apply to 'listed' companies, being those large companies whose shares are bought and sold on the Stock Exchange.

Company law

3.4 Limited companies are required by law to prepare accounts annually for distribution to their shareholders. A copy of these accounts must be lodged with the Registrar of Companies and is available for inspection by any member of the public. For this reason a company's statutory annual accounts are often referred to as its published accounts.

3.5 In 1985, all existing companies legislation was brought together in a number of consolidating Acts, of which by far the most important is the Companies Act 1985 (CA 1985). This was substantially amended on the enactment of the Companies Act 1989 (CA 1989) The 1989 Act repealed parts of the 1985 Act and inserted new sections. This book reflects the 1985 Act *as amended by the 1989 Act*; unless otherwise stated, all statutory references are to the amended Companies Act 1985. Occasionally, where there is no parallel provision, a section number is followed by 'CA 1989' to indicate a section of the new Act itself.

3.6 There are many differences between accounting systems found in the various European Union (EU) member states. For example, in the UK a 'true and fair view' is sought, whereas in West Germany a more 'legal and correct view' is observed. Taxation and accounting principles differ and consolidation practices vary.

3.7 Since the United Kingdom became a member of the EU it has been obliged to comply with legal requirements decided on by the EU. It does this by enacting UK laws to implement EU directives. For example, the CA 1989 was enacted in part to implement the provisions of the seventh and eighth EU directives, which deal with consolidated accounts and auditors.

3.8 As far as the preparation of accounts is concerned, the overriding requirement of companies legislation is that accounts should show a 'true and fair view'. This is a slippery phrase which is nowhere defined in the Companies Acts. What it certainly does *not* mean is that company accounts are to be exact to the penny in every respect. For one thing, as we shall see later, many of the figures appearing in a set of accounts are arrived at least partly by the exercise of judgement. For another, the amount of time and effort that such a requirement would cost would be out of all proportion to the advantages derived from it: see the discussion earlier in this chapter of the materiality concept.

3.9 The legislation also requires that the accounts of a limited company (except certain small companies) must be *audited*. An audit, for this purpose, may be defined as an 'independent examination of, and expression of opinion on, the financial statements of an enterprise'. This means in practice that a limited company must engage a firm of chartered or certified accountants to conduct an examination of its accounting records and its financial statements in order to form an opinion as to whether the accounts present a 'true and fair view'. At the conclusion of their audit work, the auditors issue a report (addressed to the owners of the company, ie its *members* or *shareholders*) which is published as part of the accounts. Audit is discussed in more detail in Chapter 23 of this Study Text.

Non-statutory regulation

3.10   Apart from company law, the main regulations affecting accounts in the UK derive from pronouncements issued by the professional accounting bodies (though later we will look briefly at *international* accounting regulations and the regulations of the Stock Exchange).

Six accountancy bodies in the UK are represented on the Consultative Committee of Accountancy Bodies (CCAB). They are as follows.

(a)   The Chartered Institute of Management Accountants (CIMA)
(b)   The Institute of Chartered Accountants in England and Wales (ICAEW)
(c)   The Institute of Chartered Accountants of Scotland (ICAS)
(d)   The Institute of Chartered Accountants in Ireland (ICAI)
(e)   The Association of Chartered Certified Accountants (ACCA)
(f)   The Chartered Institute of Public Finance and Accountancy (CIPFA)

3.11   Through a number of operating arms the CCAB is a major influence on the way in which accounts are prepared. Our main interest at this stage will be in the accounting standards published to lay down prescribed accounting treatments in areas where a variety of approaches might be taken. Clearly the value of accounts would be reduced if users were not able to count on a measure of comparability between them; the aim of accounting standards is to ensure that such comparability exists.

The Accounting Standards Committee (ASC) and the Accounting Standards Board (ASB)

3.12   The ASC was set up in January 1970 with the aim of publishing accounting standards in order to crack down on manipulation of published accounts. This was the beginning of a long line of attempts to protect investors in the wake of accounting scandals.

Exercise 8

You will be aware from your reading that such attempts have not yet been entirely successful. For fun, list a few of the more recent accounting scandals you can think of.

Solution

The list is almost endless, but among the most recent you will certainly have thought of Polly Peck, BCCI, the Maxwell empire and Barings Bank.

3.13   The procedure of the ASC was to publish an *exposure draft* (ED), outlining its proposed accounting treatment for the area under consideration. Comments were invited from interested parties, and in the light of such comments a final document was issued in the form of a *Statement of Standard Accounting Practice* (SSAP) Under the Companies Act 1989, large companies are required to state that their accounts have been prepared in accordance with applicable accounting standards. The ASC issued 25 SSAPs before it was replaced by a successor body on 1 August 1990.

3.14   In response to criticisms of the ASC's ineffectiveness, CCAB appointed a committee under the chairmanship of Sir Ron Dearing to review and make recommendations on the process by which accounting standards are issued. The Committee reported in 1988 and as a result of its recommendations a new standard-setting process was introduced. Under the new system, there are four bodies you need to know about.

(a)   The Financial Reporting Council (FRC)
(b)   The Accounting Standards Board (ASB)
(c)   The Financial Reporting Review Panel (FRRP)
(d)   The Urgent Issues Task Force (UITF)

3.15   The *Financial Reporting Council*. The FRC draws its membership from a wide spectrum of accounts preparers and users. Its chairman is appointed by the Government.

3.16   The *Accounting Standards Board*. The FRC operates through two arms: the FRRP (see below) and the ASB. The ASB is, in effect, the successor body to the ASC and is responsible for the issue of accounting standards. Accounting standards issued by the ASB will be called *Financial Reporting Standard* (FRSs), of which three have so far been published. Prior to publication, the ASB circulates its proposals in the form of a financial reporting exposure draft (inevitably referred to as a FRED) and invites comments. To avoid chaos, the ASB has 'adopted' those SSAPs still extant, and they therefore remain in force.

3.17   The *Financial Reporting Review Panel*. The FRRP is the second operating arm of the FRC. Its task is to examine accounts published by companies if it appears that Companies Act requirements have been breached - in particular, the requirement that accounts should show a true and fair view. The panel has legal backing: if a public company departs from an accounting standard, the panel may apply to the courts, which may in turn instruct the company to prepare revised accounts.

3.18   The *Urgent Issues Task Force*. The UITF is an offshoot of the ASB. Its role is to assist the ASB in areas where an accounting standard or Companies Act provision already exists, but where unsatisfactory or conflicting interpretations have developed. As its name suggests, the UITF is designed to act quickly (more quickly than the full standard-setting process is capable of) when an authoritative ruling is urgently needed.

International accounting standards

3.19   The International Accounting Standards Committee (IASC) was set up in June 1973 in an attempt to co-ordinate the development of international accounting standards. It includes representatives from many countries throughout the world, including the USA and the UK.

3.20   International standards are not intended to override local regulations. In the UK, however, the ASC expressed their support for international standards by incorporating them within the UK standards. Not every IAS has so far been incorporated in this way. The ASB has also stated support for international standards.

The Stock Exchange regulations

3.21   The Stock Exchange is a market for stocks and shares, and a company whose securities are traded in this market is known as a 'quoted' or 'listed' company.

3.22   When a share is granted a quotation on The Stock Exchange, it appears on the 'Official List' which is published in London for each business day. The Official List shows the 'official quotation' or price for the share for that particular day; it is drawn up by the Quotations Department of The Stock Exchange, which derives its prices from those actually ruling in this market.

3.23   In order to receive a quotation for its securities, a company must conform with Stock Exchange Listing Rules issued by the Council of The Stock Exchange. The company commits itself to certain procedures and standards, including matters concerning the disclosure of accounting information, which are more extensive than the disclosure requirements of the Companies Acts.

3.24   To ensure you understand which regulations apply to which type of business, fill in the table below with a 'yes' where compliance is required and 'no' where it is not.

Type Of Business	Companies Act	FRSs/SSAPs	IASs	Stock Exchange Listing Rules
Public Listed Company				
Private Limited Company				
Sole Tradership				

3.25 Your table should look like this.

Type Of Business	Companies Act	FRSs/SSAPs	IASs	Stock Exchange Listing Rules
Public Listed Company	YES	YES	NO	YES
Private Limited Company	YES	YES	NO	NO
Sole Tradership	NO	NO	NO	NO

Exercise 9

One of the Stock Exchange's accounting requirements is that listed companies give financial information regularly. How long do you think a listed company can go without providing some sort of accounts?

Solution

Six months. Listed companies are required to publish interim accounts covering the first half of each year as well as accounts covering the whole year. It is common to see statements of six-monthly profit (or loss) figures published by leading companies in the pages of the quality newspapers.

Chapter roundup

- Having completed this chapter you should understand the following points.

- A large number of accounting concepts are at work in the preparation of a set of accounts. To some extent the selection of concepts is an arbitrary exercise, but in fact a large measure of consensus exists among practising accountants.

- Different accounting conventions can lead to different reported results. Of the various possible conventions that could be adopted, the historical cost convention is the only one enjoying wide currency at present. However, you should also be aware of the current cost and current purchasing power conventions.

- Order in this apparent chaos is provided by a comprehensive regulatory framework, based on UK company legislation, accounting standards (both UK and international) and Stock Exchange requirements.

Test your knowledge

1   List the four accounting concepts identified as fundamental by SSAP 2. (see introduction)

2   Briefly re-cap what is meant by: the entity concept; the money measurement concept; the going concern concept; the prudence concept; (see para 1.2) the accruals concept and the consistency concept? (1.1 - 1.32)

3   At what stage is it normal to recognise the revenue arising from a credit sale? (1.20)

4   The separate valuation principle is a provision of SSAP 2. True or false? (1.33)

5   List six possible values that might be attributed in the accounts to a piece of machinery. (2.4)

6   What is the concept of capital maintenance that underlies:

    (a)   the historical cost convention? (2.17)
    (b)   the current cost convention? (2.25)

7   What is meant by modified historical cost accounts? (2.23)

8   What is the main statute governing the content of limited company accounts in the UK? (3.5)

9   Name the four bodies now responsible for the issue and enforcement of accounting regulations in the UK. (3.14)

Now try illustrative questions 2 and 3 at the end of the Study Text

Part B
Accounting systems and accounts preparation

Chapter 3

ASSETS, LIABILITIES AND THE ACCOUNTING EQUATION

This chapter covers the following topics.

		Syllabus reference	Ability required
1	The nature of a business: assets and liabilities	1(b)	Skill
2	The accounting equation	1(b)	Skill
3	The business equation	1(b)	Skill

Introduction

Part A of this Study Text gave you a broad overview of the nature and purpose of accounting. Part B should provide you with a understanding of the mechanics of preparing financial accounts.

Up until now, we have used the terms 'business', 'assets' and 'liabilities' without looking too closely at their meaning. This has been possible because the terms are common in everyday speech. From now on we will be examining accounting practice in more detail and it is important to have a thorough understanding of how these terms are used in an accounting context.

Sections 2 and 3 of the chapter introduce two concepts which it is important for you to grasp: the *accounting equation* and the *business equation*. You may already realise that a balance sheet has to balance. You are about to learn why!

Do not rush this chapter. Without an understanding of these essential points you will find it impossible to master more complex aspects later in your studies.

---

1 THE NATURE OF A BUSINESS: ASSETS AND LIABILITIES

1.1 Try this exercise to set you thinking.

Exercise 1

You may already be familiar with the more technical uses of certain terms. Can you distinguish, for example, between the terms 'an enterprise', 'a business', 'a company' and 'a firm'?

Solution

An 'enterprise' is the most general term, referring to just about any organisation in which people join together to achieve a common end. In the context of accounting it can refer to a multinational conglomerate, a small club, a local authority and so on *ad infinitum*.

A 'business' is also a very general term, but it does not extend as widely as the term 'enterprise': for example, it would not include a charity or a local authority. But any organisation existing to trade and make a profit could be called a business.

A 'company' is an enterprise constituted in a particular legal form, usually involving limited liability for its members. Companies need not be businesses; for example, many charities are constituted as companies.

A 'firm' is a much vaguer term. It is sometimes used loosely in the sense of a business or a company. Some writers, more usefully, try to restrict its meaning to that of an unincorporated business (ie a business not constituted as a company, for example a partnership).

What is a business?

1.2 There are a number of different ways of looking at a business. Some ideas are listed below.

(a) A business is a commercial or industrial concern which exists to deal in the manufacture, re-sale or supply of goods and services.

(b) A business is an organisation which uses economic resources to create goods or services which customers will buy.

(c) A business is an organisation providing jobs for people to work in.

(d) A business invests money in resources (eg it buys buildings, machinery etc, it pays employees) in order to make even more money for its owners.

1.3 This last definition introduces the important idea of profit which was briefly discussed in the last chapter. Business enterprises vary in character, size and complexity. They range from very small businesses (the local shopkeeper or plumber) to very large ones (ICI). But the objective of earning profit is common to all of them.

1.4 Profit is the excess of income over expenditure. When expenditure exceeds income, the business is running at a loss. One of the jobs of an accountant is to measure income, expenditure and profit. It is not such a straightforward problem as it may seem and in later chapters we will look at some of the theoretical and practical difficulties involved.

There are some organisations which do not have a profit motive.

(a) Charities exist to provide help to the needy. However, a charity must keep its expenditure within the level of its income or it could not continue in operation.

(b) Public sector organisations exist to serve the community rather than to make profits. Such organisations include government departments and services (eg the fire service, police force, national health service etc). But even though their purpose is not primarily to make a profit, they can only spend the money allowed to them by the government. Like charities, they must be cost-conscious.

(c) Certain clubs and associations exist to provide services to their members. Profit is not their primary objective, but to maintain and improve the services they offer they must ensure that their income is at least as great as their expenditure.

Assets and liabilities

1.5 An *asset* is something valuable which a business owns or has the use of. Examples of assets are factories, office buildings, warehouses, delivery vans, lorries, plant and machinery, computer equipment, office furniture, cash and also goods held in store awaiting sale to customers, and raw materials and components held in store by a manufacturing business for use in production.

1.6 Some assets are held and used in operations for a long time. An office building might be occupied by administrative staff for years; similarly, a machine might have a productive life of many years before it wears out. Other assets are held for only a short time. The owner of a newsagent's shop, for example, will have to sell his newspapers on the same day that he gets them, and weekly newspapers and monthly magazines also have a short shelf life. The more quickly a business can sell the goods it has in store, the more profit it is likely to make.

1.7 A *liability* is something which is owed to somebody else. 'Liabilities' is the accounting term for the debts of a business. Here are some examples of liabilities.

(a) *A bank loan or bank overdraft.* The liability is the amount which must eventually be repaid to the bank.

(b) *Amounts owed to suppliers* for goods purchased but not yet paid for. For example, a boat builder might buy some timber on credit from a timber merchant, which means that the boat builder does not have to pay for the timber until some time after it has been delivered. Until the boat builder pays what he owes, the timber merchant will be his creditor for the amount owed.

(c) *Taxation owed to the government.* A business pays tax on its profits but there is a gap in time between when a company declares its profits and becomes liable to pay tax and the time when the tax bill must eventually be paid.

Exercise 2

Attempt to classify the following items as long-term assets ('fixed assets'), short-term assets ('current assets') or liabilities.

(a)   A personal computer used in the accounts department of a retail store

(b)   A personal computer on sale in an office equipment shop

(c)   Wages due to be paid to staff at the end of the week

(d)   A van for sale in a motor dealer's showroom

(e)   A delivery van used in a grocer's business

(f)   An amount owing to a leasing company for the acquisition of a van

Solution

(a)   Fixed asset
(b)   Current asset
(c)   Liability
(d)   Current asset
(e)   Fixed asset
(f)   Liability

Note that the same item can be categorised differently in different businesses.

The business as a separate entity

1.8   So far we have spoken of assets and liabilities 'of a business'. In the previous chapter, it was pointed out that in accounting terms, a business is always a separate entity; but there are two aspects to this question: the strict legal position and the convention adopted by accountants.

1.9   Many businesses are carried on in the form of *limited companies*. The owners of a limited company are its shareholders, who may be few in number (as with a small, family-owned company) or very numerous (eg in the case of a large public company whose shares are quoted on the Stock Exchange).

1.10   The law recognises a company as a legal entity, quite separate from its owners. A company may, in its own name, acquire assets, incur debts, and enter into contracts. If a company's assets become insufficient to meet its liabilities, the company as a separate entity might become 'bankrupt', but the owners of the company could not usually be required to pay the debts from their own private resources: the debts are not debts of the shareholders, but of the company. This is *limited liability*: the liability of shareholders to the company is *limited* to the amount the company asks for their shares on issue.

1.11   The case is different, in law, when a business is carried on not by a company, but by an individual (a sole trader) or by a group of individuals (a partnership). Suppose that Fiona Middleton sets herself up in business as a hairdresser trading under the business name 'Fiona's Salon'. The law recognises no distinction between Fiona Middleton, the individual, and the business known as 'Fiona's Salon'. Any debts of the business which cannot be met from business assets must be met from Fiona's private resources.

Exercise 3

Fill in the missing words to make sure you understand the entity concept and how the law differs from accounting practice.

The entity concept regards a business as a _____ entity, distinct from its____ . The concept applies to ____ businesses. However, the law only recognises a ____ as a legal entity separate from its _____. The liability of shareholders to the company is ____ to the amount the company asks them to pay for their shares.

Solution

The missing words are:

separate; owners; all; company; owners; limited.

1.12 The crucial point which must be understood at the outset is that the convention adopted in preparing accounts (the *entity concept*) is *always* to treat a business as a separate entity from its owner(s). This applies whether or not the business is recognised in law as a separate entity, so it applies whether the business is carried on by a company or by a sole trader.

1.13 This is an idea which at first sight seems illogical and unrealistic; students often have difficulty in understanding it. Nevertheless, it is an idea which you must try to appreciate. It is the basis of a fundamental rule of accounting, which is that the assets and liabilities of a business must always be equal. A simple example may clarify the idea of a business as a separate entity from its owners.

2   THE ACCOUNTING EQUATION

2.1 We will begin our discussion of the preparation of financial accounts by illustrating how to account for a business's transactions from the time that trading first begins. We will use an example to illustrate the 'accounting equation', ie the rule that the assets of a business will at all times equal its liabilities.

Example: the accounting equation

2.2 On 1 July 19X6, Courtney Spice decided to open up a stall in the market, to sell herbs and spices. She had saved up some money in her savings account, and had £2,500 to put into her business.

2.3 When the business is set up, an 'accountant's picture' can be drawn of what it owns and what it owes.

The business begins by owning the cash that Courtney has put into it, £2,500. But does it owe anything? The answer is yes.

The business is a separate entity in accounting terms. It has obtained its assets, in this example cash, from its owner, Courtney Spice. It therefore owes this amount of money to its owner. If Courtney changed her mind and decided not to go into business after all, the business would be dissolved by the 'repayment' of the cash by the business to Courtney.

2.4 The money put into a business by its owners is *capital*. In accounting, capital is an investment of money (funds) with the intention of earning a return. A business proprietor invests capital with the intention of earning profit. As long as that money is invested, accountants will treat the capital as money owed to the proprietor by the business.

2.5   When Courtney Spice sets up her business:

Capital invested	=	£2,500
Cash	=	£2,500

Capital invested is a form of liability, because it is an amount owed by the business to its owner(s). Adapting this to the idea that liabilities and assets are always equal amounts, we can state the accounting equation as follows.

Assets	=	*Capital*	+	*Liabilities*

For Courtney Spice, as at 1 July 19X6:

£2,500 (cash)	=	£2,500	+	£0

Example continued

2.6   Courtney Spice uses some of the money invested to purchase a market stall from Noel Jarvis, who is retiring from his fruit and vegetables business. The cost of the stall is £1,800.

She also purchases some herbs and spices from a trader in the Albert Square wholesale market, at a cost of £650.

This leaves £50 in cash, after paying for the stall and goods for resale, out of the original £2,500. Courtney kept £30 in the bank and drew out £20 in small change. She was now ready for her first day of market trading on 3 July 19X6.

2.7   The assets and liabilities of the business have now altered, and at 3 July, before trading begins, the state of her business is as follows.

Assets	£	=	*Capital*	+	*Liabilities*
Stall	1,800	=	£2,500	+	£0
Herbs and spices	650				
Cash at bank	30				
Cash in hand	20				
	2,500				

The stall and the herbs and spices are physical items, but they must be given a money value. As explained in the last chapter, this money value will usually be their historical cost.

Profit introduced into the accounting equation

2.8   Let us now suppose that on 3 July Courtney has a very successful day. She is able to sell all of her herbs and spices, for £900. All of her sales are for cash.

Since Courtney has sold goods costing £650 to earn revenue of £900, we can say that she has earned a profit of £250 on the day's trading.

Profits belong to the owners of a business. In this case, the £250 belongs to Courtney Spice. However, so long as the business retains the profits, and does not pay anything out to its owners, the retained profits are accounted for as an addition to the proprietor's capital.

Assets		=	*Capital*		+	*Liabilities*
	£			£		
Stall	1,800		Original investment	2,500		
Herbs and spices	0					
Cash in hand and at bank						
(30+20+900)	950		Retained profit	250		
	2,750			2,750	+	£0

2.9   We can re-arrange the accounting equation to help us to calculate the capital balance.

Assets – liabilities	=	Capital, which is the same as
Net assets	=	Capital

2.10 At the beginning and then at the end of 3 July 19X6 Courtney Spice's financial position was as follows.

		Net Assets	Capital
(a)	At the beginning of the day:	£(2,500 – 0) = £2,500 =	£2,500
(b)	At the end of the day:	£(2,750 – 0) = £2,750 =	£2,750

There has been an increase of £250 in net assets, which is the amount of profits earned during the day.

Drawings

2.11 Drawings are amounts of money taken out of a business by its owner.

Since Courtney Spice has made a profit of £250 from her first day's work, she might well feel fully justified in drawing some of the profits out of the business. After all, business owners, like everyone else, need income for living expenses. We will suppose that Courtney decides to pay herself £180, in 'wages'.

2.12 The payment of £180 is probably regarded by Courtney as a fair reward for her day's work, and she might think of the sum as being in the nature of wages. However, the £180 is not an expense to be deducted before the figure of net profit is arrived at. In other words, it would be incorrect to calculate the net profit earned by the business as follows.

	£
Profit on sale of flowers etc	250
Less 'wages' paid to Courtney	180
Net profit earned by business (incorrect)	70

2.13 This is because any amounts paid by a business to its proprietor are treated by accountants as withdrawals of profit (the usual term is appropriations of profit), and not as expenses incurred by the business. In the case of Courtney's business, the true position is that the net profit earned is the £250 surplus on sale of flowers.

	£
Net profit earned by business	250
Less profit withdrawn by Courtney	180
Net profit retained in the business	70

2.14 Profits are capital as long as they are retained in the business. Once they are appropriated, they are no longer capital. When they are paid out, the business suffers a reduction in capital.

2.15 The drawings are taken in cash, and so the business loses £180 of its cash assets. After the drawings have been made, the accounting equation would be restated.

(a)

Assets		=	Capital		+	Liabilities
	£			£		
Stall	1,800		Original investment	2,500		
Herbs and spices	0		Retained profit	70		
Cash (950-180)	770					
	2,570			2,570	+	£0

(b) Alternatively

	Net assets		Capital
	£(2,570 – 0) =		£2,570

The increase in net assets since trading operations began is now only £(2,570 – 2,500) = £70, which is the amount of the retained profits.

3 THE BUSINESS EQUATION

3.1   The business equation gives a definition of profits earned. The preceding example has attempted to show that the amount of profit earned can be related to the increase in the net assets of the business, and the drawings of profits by the proprietor.

3.2   The business equation is:

$$P = I + D - C_i$$

where

P represents profit

I represents the increase in net assets, after drawings have been taken out by the proprietor

D represents drawings

C_i represents the amount of extra capital introduced into the business during the period. This is a negative figure in the equation, because when a business is given new capital, perhaps in the form of extra money paid in by the proprietor himself, there will be an increase in the net assets of the business without any profits being earned. This means, say, that if a proprietor puts an extra £5,000 into his business the profit from the transaction, according to the business equation would be P = £5,000 + 0 – £5,000 = £0.

3.3   In our example of Courtney Spice's business on 3 July 19X6, after drawings have been taken:

Profit = £ 70 + £180 – £0
        = £250

Example continued

3.4   The next market day is on 10 July, and Courtney gets ready by purchasing more herbs and spices for cash, at a cost of £740. She was not feeling well, however, because of a heavy cold, and so she decided to accept the offer of help for the day from her cousin Bianca. Bianca would be paid a wage of £40 at the end of the day.

Trading on 10 July was again very brisk, and Courtney and Bianca sold all their goods for £1,100 cash. Courtney paid Bianca her wage of £40 and drew out £200 for herself.

Required

(a)   State the accounting equation before trading began on 10 July.

(b)   State the accounting equation at the end of 10 July, after paying Bianca:

   (i)   but before drawings are taken out;
   (ii)   after drawings have been made.

(c)   State the business equation to compute profits earned on 10 July.

You are reminded that the accounting equation for the business at the end of transactions for 3 July is given in Paragraph 2.15(a).

Solution

3.5   (a)   After the purchase of the goods for £740.

Assets		=	Capital	+	Liabilities
	£				
Stall	1,800				
Goods	740				
Cash (770 – 740)	30				
	2,570	=	£ 2,570	+	£0

(b) (i)   On 10 July, all the goods are sold for £1,100 cash, and Bianca is paid £40. The profit for the day is £320.

	£	£
Sales		1,100
Less cost of goods sold	740	
Bianca's wage	40	
		780
Profit		320

Assets		=	*Capital*		+	*Liabilities*
	£			£		
Stall	1,800		At beginning of 10 July	2,570		
Goods	0		Profits earned on 10 July	320		
Cash						
(30+ 1,100 – 40)	1,090					
	2,890			2,890		£0
					+	

(ii)   After Courtney has taken drawings of £200 in cash, retained profits will be only £(320 - 200) = £120.

Assets		=	*Capital*		+	*Liabilities*
	£			£		
Stall	1,800		At beginning of 10 July	2,570		
Goods	0		Retained profits for 10 July	120		
Cash						
(1,090 – 200)	890					
	2,690			2,690	+	£0

(c)   The increase in net assets on 10 July, after drawings have been taken, is as follows.

	£
Net assets at end of 10 July	2,690
Net assets at beginning of 10 July	2,570
Increase in net assets	120

The business equation is:

$$P = I + D - C_i$$
$$= £120 + £200 - £0$$
$$= £320$$

This confirms the calculation of profit made in b(i).

Tutorial note. It is very important you should understand the principles described so far. Do not read on until you are confident that you understand the solution to this example.

Creditors and debtors

3.6   A *creditor* is a person to whom a business owes money.

A trade creditor is a person to whom a business owes money for debts incurred in the course of trading operations, and in an examination question, this term might refer to debts still outstanding which arise from the purchase from suppliers of materials, components or goods for resale.

3.7   A business does not always pay immediately for goods or services it buys. It is a common business practice to make purchases on credit, with a promise to pay within 30 days, or two months or three months of the date of the bill or 'invoice' for the goods. For example, if A buys goods costing £2,000 on credit from B, B might send A an invoice for £2,000, dated say 1 March, with credit terms that payment must be made within 30 days. If A then delays payment until 31 March, B will be a creditor of A between 1 and 31 March, for £2,000.

3.8   A creditor is a liability of a business.

3.9   Just as a business might buy goods on credit, so too might it sell goods to customers on credit. A customer who buys goods without paying cash for them straight away is a *debtor*. For example, suppose that C sells goods on credit to D for £6,000 on terms that the debt must be settled within two months of the invoice date 1 October. If D does not pay the £6,000 until 30 November, D will be a debtor of C for £6,000 from 1 October until 30 November.

3.10   A debtor is an asset of a business. When the debt is finally paid, the debtor 'disappears' as an asset, to be replaced by 'cash at bank and in hand'.

Example continued

3.11   The example of Courtney Spice's market stall will be continued further, by looking at the consequences of the following transactions in the week to 17 July 19X6. (See Paragraph 3.5 (b)(ii) for the situation as at the end of 10 July.)

   (a) Courtney Spice realises that she is going to need more money in the business and so she makes the following arrangements.

      (i)   She invests immediately a further £250 of her own capital.

      (ii) She persuades her Uncle Felix to lend her £500 immediately. Uncle Felix tells her that she can repay the loan whenever she likes, but in the meantime, she must pay him interest of £5 per week each week at the end of the market day. They agree that it will probably be quite a long time before the loan is eventually repaid.

   (b) She is very pleased with the progress of her business, and decides that she can afford to buy a second hand van to pick up herbs and spices from her supplier and bring them to her stall in the market. She finds a car dealer, Laurie Loader, who agrees to sell her a van on credit for £700. Courtney agrees to pay for the van after 30 days' trial use.

   (c) During the week before the next market day (which is on 17 July), Courtney's Uncle Grant telephones her to ask whether she would be interested in selling him some spice racks and herb chopping boards as presents for his friends. Courtney tells him that she will look for a supplier. After some investigations, she buys what Uncle Grant has asked for, paying £300 in cash to the supplier. Uncle Grant accepts delivery of the goods and agrees to pay £350 to Courtney for them, but he asks if she can wait until the end of the month for payment. Courtney agrees.

   (d) The next market day approaches, and Courtney buys herbs and spices costing £800. Of these purchases £750 are paid in cash, with the remaining £50 on seven days' credit. Courtney decides to use Bianca's services again as an assistant on market day, at an agreed wage of £40.

   (e) For the third market day running, on 17 July, Courtney succeeds in selling all her goods earning revenue of £1,250 (all in cash). She decides to take out drawings of £240 for her week's work. She also pays Bianca £40 in cash. She decides to make the interest payment to her Uncle Felix the next time she sees him.

   (f) We shall ignore any van expenses for the week, for the sake of relative simplicity.

   Required

   (a) State the accounting equation:

      (i)   after Courtney and Uncle Felix have put more money into the business and after the purchase of the van;

      (ii)   after the sale of goods to Uncle Grant;

      (iii) after the purchase of goods for the weekly market;

      (iv)   at the end of the day's trading on 17 July, and after drawings have been appropriated out of profit.

   (b) State the business equation showing profit earned during the week ended 17 July.

Solution

3.12 There are a number of different transactions to account for here. This solution deals with them one at a time in chronological order. (In practice, it would be possible to do one set of calculations which combines the results of all the transactions, but we shall defer such 'shortcut' methods until later.)

(a) (i) *The addition of Courtney's extra capital and Uncle Felix's loan*

An investment analyst might define the loan of Uncle Felix as a capital investment on the grounds that it will probably be for the long term. Uncle Felix is not the owner of the business, however, even though he has made an investment of a loan in it. He would only become an owner if Courtney offered him a partnership in the business, and she has not done so. To the business, Uncle Felix is a long-term creditor, and it is more appropriate to define his investment as a liability of the business and not as business capital.

The accounting equation after £(250 + 500) = £750 cash is put into the business will be:

Assets		=	Capital		+	Liabilities	
	£			£			£
Stall	1,800		As at end of 10 July	2,690		Loan	500
Goods	0		Additional capital put in	250			
Cash (890+750)	1,640						
	3,440	=		2,940	+		500

The purchase of the van (cost £700) is on credit.

Assets		=	Capital		+	Liabilities	
	£			£			£
Stall	1,800		As at end of 10 July	2,690		Loan	500
Van	700		Additional capital	250		Creditor	700
Cash	1,640						
	4,140	=		2,940	+		1,200

(ii) *The sale of goods to Uncle Grant on credit (£350) which cost the business £300 (cash paid)*

Assets		=	Capital		+	Liabilities		
	£			£				£
Stall	1,800		As at end of 10 July	2,690		Loan	500	
Van	700		Additional capital	250		Creditor	700	
Debtors	350		Profit on sale to					
Cash(1,640 − 300)	1,340		Uncle Grant	50				
	4,190	=		2,990	+		1,200	

(iii) *After the purchase of goods for the weekly market (£750 paid in cash and £50 of purchases on credit)*

Assets		=	Capital		+	Liabilities	
	£			£			£
Stall	1,800		As at end of 10 July	2,690		Loan	500
Van	700					Creditor for car	700
Goods	800		Additional capital	250		Creditor for goods	50
Debtors	350		Profit on sale to				
Cash(1,340 − 750)	590		Uncle Grant	50			
	4,240	=		2,990	+		1,250

(iv) *After market trading on 17 July*

Sales of goods costing £800 earned revenues of £1,250. Bianca's wages were £40 (paid), Uncle Felix's interest charge is £5 (not paid yet) and drawings out of profits were £240 (paid). The profit for 17 July may be calculated as follows, taking the full £5 of interest as a cost on that day.

	£	£
Sales		1,250
Cost of goods sold	800	
Wages	40	
Interest	5	
		845
Profit earned on 17 July		405
Profit on sale of goods to Uncle Grant		50
Profit for the week		455
Drawings appropriated out of profits		240
Retained profit		215

Assets		=	Capital		+	Liabilities	
	£			£			£
Stall	1,800		As at end of 10 July	2,690		Loan	500
Van	700		Additional capital	250		Creditor for van	700
Stocks	0					Creditor for goods	50
Debtors	350						
Cash (590+ 1,250 – 40 – 240)	1,560		Profits retained	215		Creditor for interest payment	5
	4,410			3,155			1,255

(b) The increase in the net assets of the business during the week was as follows.

	£
Net assets as at the end of 17 July £(4,410 – 1,255)	3,155
Net assets as at the end of 10 July (Paragraph 3.5(b)(ii))	2,690
Increase in net assets	465

The business equation for the week ended 17 July is as follows.

(Remember that extra capital of £250 was invested by the proprietor.)

$$P = I + D - Ci$$
$$= £465 + £240 - £250$$
$$= £455$$

This confirms the calculation of profit above in (a)(iv).

Exercise 4

Calculate the profit for the year ended 31 December 19X1 from the following information.

	1 January 19X1		31 December 19X1	
	£	£	£	£
Assets				
Property	20,000		20,000	
Machinery	6,000		9,000	
Debtors	4,000		8,000	
Cash	1,000		1,500	
		31,000		38,500
Liabilities				
Overdraft	6,000		9,000	
Creditors	5,000		3,000	
		(11,000)		(12,000)
Net assets		20,000		26,500
Drawings during the year				£4,500
Additional capital introduced by the proprietor during the year				£5,000

Solution

The increase in net assets during the year was £(26,500 - 20,000) = £6,500.

$$P = I + D - C_i$$
$$= £6,500 + £4,500 - £5,000$$
$$= £6,000$$

Chapter roundup

- A *business* owns assets and owes liabilities. It is important to keep business assets and liabilities separate from the personal assets and liabilities of the proprietor(s).

- *Assets* are items belonging to a business and based on the running of the business. They may be fixed (such as machinery or office premises), or current (such as stock, debtors and cash).

- *Liabilities* are sums of money owed by a business to outsiders such as a bank or a trade creditor.

- The assets of a business are always equal to its liabilities (including capital).

- The accounting equation and the business equation are useful introductory concepts in accounting for the following reasons.

  o The accounting equation emphasises the equality between assets and liabilities (including capital as a liability).

  o The business equation emphasises the inter-relationship between profits, net assets, appropriations of profit (drawings) and new capital investment.

- You should now be aware, for example, that when business transactions are accounted for, it should be possible to do two things as follows.

  o Restate the assets and liabilities of the business after the transactions have taken place.
  o State the profit or loss, if any, arising as a result of the transactions.

- In practice, the accounting equation and business equation are rarely used to state assets and liabilities and profit.

  o The assets and liabilities of a business at any moment in time are shown in a balance sheet. This is very similar to the accounting equation.

  o The profit (or loss) earned by a business during a given period of time is shown in a trading, profit and loss account.

  These will be described in the following chapter.

Test your knowledge

1   What is meant by profit? (see para 1.4)

2   List as may organisations as you can which do not have profit as their main objective. (1.4)

3   Briefly explain the legal distinction between a sole trader and a limited company (1.9 - 1.11)

4   In what sense can a proprietor's capital be regarded as a liability of the business. (2.4)

5   What is the accounting equation? (2.5)

6   What are drawings? (2.11)

7   What is the business equation? (3.2)

8   Distinguish between a debtor and a creditor. (3.6, 3.10)

Now try illustrative question 4 at the end of the Study Text

Chapter 4

AN INTRODUCTION TO FINAL ACCOUNTS

This chapter covers the following topics.

		Syllabus reference	Ability required
1	The balance sheet	1(b)	Skill
2	The trading, profit and loss account	1(b)	Skill
3	Capital and revenue expenditure	1(b)	Skill

Introduction

In Chapter 3 you were introduced to the idea of the accounting equation. If you understand this, you should now have little difficulty in getting to grips with the balance sheet. You should already have some idea of what is meant by the profit and loss account. In this chapter you will see this in more detail.

A *balance sheet* is a statement of the liabilities, capital and assets of a business at a given moment in time. It is like a 'snapshot' photograph, since it captures on paper a still image, frozen at a single moment in time, of something which is dynamic and continually changing. Typically, a balance sheet is prepared to show the liabilities, capital and assets as at the end of the accounting period to which the financial accounts relate.

As you should readily appreciate, a balance sheet is therefore very similar to the accounting equation. In fact, there are only two differences between a balance sheet and an accounting equation are as follows.

(a) The manner or format in which the liabilities and assets are presented
(b) The extra detail which is usually contained in a balance sheet

The details shown in a balance sheet will not be described in full in this chapter. Instead, we will make a start in this chapter, and add more detail in later chapters as we go on to look at other ideas and methods in accounting.

The *profit and loss account* has been mentioned several times. It is a statement which matches the revenue earned in a period with the costs incurred in earning it. It is usual to distinguish between a gross profit (sales revenue less the cost of goods sold) and a net profit (being the gross profit less the expenses of selling, distribution, administration etc).

There is a fair amount to learn before you will be able to prepare these statements yourself, although you will be surprised how quickly you will be in that enviable position. It is important to introduce the financial statements now so you can see what you are aiming at. Keep them in your mind as you tackle the 'nuts and bolts' of ledger accounting in the next few chapters.

Common sense may tell you that, if you spend money on something which you could use in the business over the next twenty years, it would be misleading to charge all the expenses in the first year. This is the principle behind the important distinction between *capital and revenue expenditure* which is explored in Section 3 of the chapter.

1 THE BALANCE SHEET

1.1 A balance sheet is divided into two halves, with either:

(a) capital and liabilities in one half and assets in the other; or

(b) capital in one half and net assets in the other.

1.2 In other words, a balance sheet might be presented in either of the following ways.

(a) Either

NAME OF BUSINESS
BALANCE SHEET AS AT (DATE)

	£
Assets (item by item)	X
	X
	X̄
	£
Capital	X
Liabilities (item by item)	X
	X̄

(b) Or

NAME OF BUSINESS
BALANCE SHEET AS AT (DATE)

	£
Assets	X
Less liabilities	X
Net assets	X̄
Capital	X

Method (a) puts capital and liabilities in the same half of the balance sheet, whereas method (b) shows capital on its own, and nets off liabilities against assets in the other half. This Study Text generally uses method (b).

1.3 In either form of presentation, the total value in one half of the balance sheet will equal the total value in the other half. You should readily understand this from the accounting equation.

1.4 Since each half of the balance sheet has an equal value, one half balances the other. However, the equal value of the two halves is not the origin of the term balance sheet. A balance sheet is so called because it is a statement of the outstanding balances on the ledger accounts for the capital, liabilities and assets of the business, at a given moment in time. Ledger accounts are described in a later chapter.

1.5 Capital, liabilities and assets are usually shown in some detail in a balance sheet. The following paragraphs describe the sort of detail we might expect to find.

Capital (sole trader)

1.6 The proprietor's capital might well be analysed into its component parts.

	£	£
Capital as at the beginning of the accounting period (ie capital 'brought forward')		X
Add additional capital introduced during the period		X
		X̄
Add profit earned during the period	X	
Less drawings	(X)	
Retained profit for the period		X
Capital as at the end of the accounting period (ie capital 'carried forward')		X̄

1.7 'Brought forward' means 'brought forward from the previous period', and 'carried forward' means 'carried forward to the next period'. The carried forward amount at the end of one period is also the brought forward amount of the next period.

Liabilities

1.8   The various liabilities should be itemised separately. In addition, a distinction is made between current liabilities and long-term liabilities.

Current liabilities

1.9   These are debts of the business that must be paid within a fairly short period of time. By convention, a 'fairly short period of time' has come to be accepted as one year. In the accounts of limited companies, the Companies Act 1985 requires use of the term 'creditors: amounts falling due within one year' rather than 'current liabilities' although they mean the same thing.

Examples of current liabilities are:

(a)   loans repayable within one year;

(b)   a bank overdraft (see Paragraph 1.10);

(c)   trade creditors;

(d)   bills of exchange which are payable by the business;

(e)   taxation payable;

(f)   'accrued charges'. These are expenses already built up by the business, for which no invoice has yet been received, or for which the date of payment by standing order has not yet arrived. An example of accrued charges would be the cost of gas or electricity bills. If a business ends its accounting year on 31 December, but does not expect its next quarterly gas bill until the end of January, there will be two months of accrued gas charges, ie charges for which no invoice has been received and no debt is yet 'officially' payable, to record in the balance sheet as a liability. Accruals will be described more fully in a later chapter.

1.10   It is often argued that a bank overdraft is not a current liability, because a business is usually able to negotiate an overdraft facility for a long period of time. If an overdraft thus becomes a more permanent source of borrowing, it is really a long-term liability. However, you should normally expect to account for an overdraft as a current liability, since banks reserve the right to demand repayment at short notice.

Long-term liabilities ('deferred liabilities')

1.11   A long-term liability is a debt which is not payable within the 'short term' and so any liability which is not current must be long-term. (A deferred liability is a debt due to someone else which has been put off till sometime in the future. In other words, a deferred liability is a long-term liability.) Just as 'short-term' by convention means one year or less, 'long-term' means more than one year. In the accounts of limited companies, the Companies Act 1985 requires use of the term: 'Creditors: amounts falling due after more than one year'.

1.12   Examples of long-term liabilities are as follows.

(a)   Loans which are not repayable for more than one year, such as a bank loan, or a loan from an individual to a business.

(b)   A mortgage loan, which is a loan specifically secured against a freehold property. (If the business fails to repay the loan, the lender then has 'first claim' on the property, and is entitled to repayment from the proceeds from the enforced sale of the property.)

(c)   Debentures or debenture loans. These are common with limited companies. Debentures are securities issued by a company at a fixed rate of interest. They are repayable on agreed terms by a specified date in the future. Holders of debentures are therefore lenders of money to a company. Their interests, including security for the loan, are protected by the terms of a trust deed.

Assets

1.13   Assets in the balance sheet are divided into two groups.

(a)   Fixed assets:

(i)   tangible fixed assets;
(ii)   intangible fixed assets;
(iii)   investments (long term)

(b)   Current assets

Fixed assets

1.14   A fixed asset is an asset acquired for continuing use within the business, with a view to earning income or making profits from its use, either directly or indirectly. A fixed asset is not acquired for sale to a customer.

(a)   In a manufacturing industry, a production machine would be a fixed asset, because it makes goods which are then sold.

(b)   In a service industry, equipment used by employees giving service to customers would be classed as fixed assets (eg the equipment used in a garage, and furniture in a hotel).

(c)   Less obviously, factory premises, office furniture, computer equipment, company cars, delivery vans or pallets in a warehouse are all fixed assets.

1.15   To be classed as a fixed asset in the balance sheet of a business, an item must satisfy two further conditions.

(a)   Clearly, it must be used by the business. For example, the proprietor's own house would not normally appear on the business balance sheet.

(b)   The asset must have a 'life' in use of more than one year (strictly, more than one 'accounting period' which might be more or less than one year).

1.16   A *tangible* fixed asset is a physical asset, ie one that can be touched. It has a real, 'solid' existence. All of the examples of fixed assets mentioned above are tangible.

An *intangible* fixed asset is an asset which does not have a physical existence. It cannot be 'touched'. The idea of intangible assets might well puzzle you at the moment, and a description of them will be deferred until a later chapter.

An *investment* might also be a fixed asset. Investments are commonly found in the published accounts of large limited companies. A large company A might invest in another company B by purchasing some of the shares or debentures of B. These investments would earn income for A in the form of interest or dividends paid out by B. If the investments are purchased by A with a view to holding on to them for more than one year, they would be classified as fixed assets of A.

In this chapter, we shall restrict our attention to tangible fixed assets.

Fixed assets and depreciation

1.17   Fixed assets might be held and used by a business for a number of years, but they wear out or lose their usefulness in the course of time. Every tangible fixed asset has a limited life. The only exception is land held freehold or on a very long leasehold.

1.18   The accounts of a business try to recognise that the cost of a fixed asset is gradually consumed as the asset wears out. This is done by gradually writing off the asset's cost in the profit and loss account over several accounting periods. For example, in the case of a machine costing £1,000 and expected to wear out after ten years, it might be appropriate to reduce the balance sheet value by £100 each year. This process is known as depreciation.

1.19 If a balance sheet were drawn up four years, say, after the asset was purchased, the amount of depreciation which would have accumulated would be 4 × £100 = £400. The machine would then appear in the balance sheet as follows.

	£
Machine at original cost	1,000
Less accumulated depreciation	400
Net book value*	600

* ie the value of the asset in the books of account, net of depreciation. After ten years the asset would be fully depreciated and would appear in the balance sheet with a net book value of zero.

Current assets

1.20 Current assets are either:

(a) items owned by the business with the intention of turning them into cash within one year; or

(b) cash, including money in the bank, owned by the business.

These assets are 'current' in the sense that they are continually flowing through the business.

1.21 The definition in (a) above needs explaining further. Let us suppose that a trader, David Wickes, runs a business selling motor cars, and purchases a showroom which he stocks with cars for sale. We will also suppose that he obtains the cars from a manufacturer, and pays for them in cash on delivery.

(a) If he sells a car in a cash sale, the goods are immediately converted into cash. The cash might then be used to buy more cars for re-sale.

(b) If he sells a car in a credit sale, the car will be given to the customer, who then becomes a debtor of the business. Eventually, the debtor will pay what he owes, and David Wickes will receive cash. Once again, the cash might then be used to buy more cars for sale.

1.22 Current assets can be identified in this example as follows.

(a) The cars (goods) held in stock for re-sale are current assets, because David Wickes intends to sell them within one year, in the normal course of trade.

(b) Any debtors are current assets, if they are expected to pay what they owe within one year.

(c) Cash is a current asset.

1.23 The transactions described above could be shown as a cash cycle.

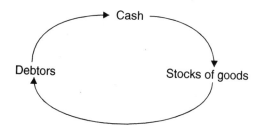

1.24 Cash is used to buy goods which are sold. Sales on credit create debtors, but eventually cash is earned from the sales. Some, perhaps most, of the cash will then be used to replenish stocks.

1.25 The main items of current assets are therefore:

(a) stocks;
(b) debtors;
(c) cash.

1.26 It is important to realise that cars are current assets of David Wickes because he is in the business of buying and selling them, ie he is a car trader. If he also has a car which he keeps and uses for business purposes, this car would be a fixed asset. The distinction between a fixed asset and a current asset is not what the asset is physically, but for what purpose it is obtained and used by the business.

1.27 There are some other categories of current assets.

(a) *Short-term investments*. These are stocks and shares of other businesses, currently owned, but with the intention of selling them in the near future. For example, if a business has a lot of spare cash for a short time, its managers might decide to 'have a flutter' on the stock exchange, and buy shares in, say, Marks and Spencer, ICI or GEC. The shares will later be sold when the business needs the cash again. If share prices rise in the meantime, the business will make a profit from its short-term investment.

(b) *Prepayments*. These are amounts of money already paid by the business for benefits which have not yet been enjoyed but will be enjoyed within the next accounting period. Suppose, for example, that a business pays an annual insurance premium of £240 to insure its premises against fire and theft, and that the premium is payable annually in advance on 1 December. Now, if the business has an accounting year end of 31 December it will pay £240 on 1 December, but only enjoy one month's insurance cover by the end of the year. The remaining 11 months' cover (£220 cost, at £20 per month) will be enjoyed in the next year. The prepayment of £220 would therefore be shown in the balance sheet of the business, at 31 December, as a current asset.

A prepayment might be thought of as a form of debtor. In the example above, at 31 December the insurance company still owes the business 11 months' worth of insurance cover.

Trade debtors and other debtors

1.28 Although it is convenient to think of debtors as customers who buy goods on credit, it is more accurate to say that a debtor is anyone who owes the business money. Continuing the example of an insurance policy, if a business makes an insurance claim for fire damage, the insurance company would be a debtor for the money payable on the claim.

1.29 A distinction can be made between two groups of debtors.

(a) Trade debtors, ie customers who still owe money for goods or services bought on credit in the course of the trading activities of the business.

(b) Other debtors, ie anyone else owing money to the business.

Example: balance sheet preparation

1.30 We shall now look at how the various types of assets and liabilities are shown in the balance sheet of a business. You might like to attempt to prepare a balance sheet yourself before reading the solution which follows.

Exercise 1

You are required to prepare a balance sheet for the Ted Hills Hardware Store as at 31 December 19X6, given the information below.

	£
Capital as at 1 January 19X6	47,600
Profit for the year to 31 December 19X6	8,000
Freehold premises, net book value at 31 December 19X6	50,000
Motor vehicles, net book value at 31 December 19X6	9,000
Fixtures and fittings, net book value at 31 December 19X6	8,000
Long-term loan (mortgage)	25,000
Bank overdraft*	2,000
Goods held in stock for resale	16,000
Debtors	500
Cash in hand*	100
Creditors	1,200
Taxation payable	3,500
Drawings	4,000
Accrued costs of rent	600
Prepayment of insurance	300

* A shop might have cash in its cash registers, but an overdraft at the bank.

Solution

TED HILLS BALANCE SHEET
AS AT 31 DECEMBER 19X6

	£	£
Fixed assets at net book value		
Freehold premises		50,000
Fixtures and fittings		8,000
Motor vehicles		9,000
		67,000
Current assets		
Stocks	16,000	
Debtors	500	
Prepayment	300	
Cash	100	
	16,900	
Current liabilities		
Bank overdraft	2,000	
Creditors	1,200	
Taxation payable	3,500	
Accrued costs	600	
	7,300	
Net current assets		9,600
		76,600
Long-term liabilities		
Loan		(25,000)
		51,600
Capital		
Capital as at 1 January 19X6		47,600
Profit for the year		8,000
		55,600
Less drawings		(4,000)
		51,600

The order of items in the balance sheet

1.31 By convention, a balance sheet lists liabilities and assets in a particular order. This order is not compulsory, nor will you find that it is used all the time; however, you should try to get into the habit of using the conventional order of items yourself.

1.32 The format most commonly used is the vertical balance sheet format, which lists:

(a)   net assets above and capital below; or

(b)   fixed assets and net current assets above, with capital and long-term liabilities below; or

(c)   assets above and liabilities (including capital) below; or

(d)   capital and liabilities above, with assets below.

As you will appreciate, there is no hard and fast rule about the order of items in a vertical balance sheet, except that the Companies Act 1985 requires (a) to be used for the published accounts of most limited companies. This format is therefore one in particular you should try to familiarise yourself with and use as a matter of habit.

Order of items within categories

1.33   Note the following points.

(a)   *Fixed assets* are listed in a descending order of 'length of useful life'. Property has a longer life than fixtures and fittings, which in turn perhaps have a longer life than motor vehicles. This is why the fixed assets are listed in the order shown above.

(b)   *Current assets* are listed in descending order of the length of time it might be before the asset will be converted into cash. Broadly speaking, stocks will convert into debtors, and debtors will convert into cash, and so stock, debtors and cash will be listed in that order. Prepayments, because they are similar to debtors, should be listed after debtors and before cash.

Working capital, or net current assets

1.34   The 'working' capital of a business is the difference between its current assets and current liabilities, ie working capital is the amount of net current assets. In the balance sheet above, the Ted Hills Hardware Store has net current assets of £(16,900 – 7,300) = £9,600. This is a figure which is shown separately when a balance sheet is prepared in a vertical format.

1.35   The balance sheet of the Ted Hills Hardware Store could be arranged in either of the following ways, using formats (a) and (b) above.

Method (a)			*Method (b)*		
TED HILLS BALANCE SHEET			TED HILLS BALANCE SHEET		
AS AT 31 DECEMBER 19X6			AS AT 31 DECEMBER 19X6		
	£	£		£	£
Fixed assets at net book value			*Fixed assets at net book value*		
Freehold premises		50,000	Freehold premises		50,000
Fixtures and fittings		8,000	Fixtures and fittings		8,000
Motor vehicles		9,000	Motor vehicles		9,000
		67,000			67,000
Current assets			*Current assets*		
Stocks	16,000		Stocks	16,000	
Debtors	500		Debtors	500	
Prepayment	300		Prepayment	300	
Cash	100		Cash	100	
	16,900			16,900	
Less *current liabilities*			Less *current liabilities*		
Bank overdraft	2,000		Bank overdraft	2,000	
Creditors	1,200		Creditors	1,200	
Taxation payable	3,500		Taxation payable	3,500	
Accrued costs	600		Accrued costs	600	
	7,300			7,300	
Net current assets		9,600			9,600
		76,600			76,600
Less *long-term liabilities*					
Loan		25,000			
		51,600			
Capital			*Capital*		
Capital as at 1 January 19X6		47,600	Capital as at 1 January 19X6		47,600
Profit for the year		8,000	Profit for the year		8,000
		55,600			55,600
Less drawings		4,000	Less drawings		4,000
		51,600			51,600
			Long-term liabilities		
			Loan		25,000
					76,600

It should be stressed that method (a) is now the format of balance sheet we would recommend that you try to use unless examination questions specify otherwise.

2   THE TRADING, PROFIT AND LOSS ACCOUNT

2.1   The profit and loss account has already been mentioned several times as a statement in which revenues and expenditure are compared to arrive at a figure of profit or loss. Many businesses try to distinguish between a gross profit earned on trading, and a net profit. They prepare a statement called a trading, profit and loss account: in the first part of the statement (the trading account) revenue from selling goods is compared with direct costs of acquiring or producing the goods sold to arrive at a gross profit figure; from this, deductions are made in the second half of the statement (the profit and loss account) in respect of indirect costs (overheads).

2.2   The trading, profit and loss account is a statement showing in detail how the profit (or loss) of a period has been made. The owners and managers of a business obviously want to know how much profit or loss has been made, but there is only a limited information value in the profit figure alone. In order to exercise financial control effectively, managers need to know how much income has been earned, what various items of costs have been, and whether the performance of sales or the control of costs appears to be satisfactory. This is the basic reason for preparing the trading, profit and loss account.

2.3   The two parts of the statement may be examined in more detail.

(a)   *The trading account.* This shows the gross profit for the accounting period. Gross profit is the difference between:

(i)   the value of sales (excluding value added tax); and

(ii)   the purchase cost or production cost of the goods sold.

In the retail business, the cost of the goods sold is their purchase cost from the suppliers. In a manufacturing business, the production cost of goods sold is the cost of raw materials in the finished goods, plus the cost of the labour required to make the goods, and often plus an amount of production 'overhead' costs.

(b)   *The profit and loss account.* This shows the net profit of the business. The net profit is:

(i)   the gross profit;

(ii)   plus any other income from sources other than the sale of goods;

(iii)   minus other expenses of the business which are not included in the cost of goods sold.

Detail in the profit and loss account

2.4   Income from other sources will include the following.

(a)   Dividends or interest received from investments.

(b)   Profits on the sale of fixed assets.

(c)   Bad debts written off in a previous accounting period which were unexpectedly paid in the current period (see Paragraph 2.5(a)(vii) below).

2.5   Other business expenses that will appear in the profit and loss account are as follows.

(a)   *Selling and distribution expenses.* These are expenses associated with the process of selling and delivering goods to customers. They include the following items.

(i)   The salaries of a sales director and sales management.

(ii)   The salaries and commissions of salesmen.

(iii)   The travelling and entertainment expenses of salesmen.

(iv)   Marketing costs (eg advertising and sales promotion expenses).

(v)   The costs of running and maintaining delivery vans.

(vi)   Discounts allowed to customers for early payment of their debt. For example, a business might sell goods to a customer for £100 and offer a discount of 5% for payment in cash. If the customer takes the discount, the accounts of the business would not record the sales value at £95; they would instead record sales at the full £100, with a cost for discounts allowed of £5. Discounts are described more fully in a later chapter.

(vii)   Bad debts written off. Sometimes debtors fail to pay what they owe, and a business might have to decide at some stage of chasing after payment that there is now no prospect of ever being paid. The debt has to be written off as 'bad'. The amount of the debt written off is charged as an expense in the profit and loss account. Bad debts will be described more fully in a later chapter.

(b)   *Administration expenses.* These are the expenses of providing management and administration for the business. They include:

(i)   the salaries of directors, management and office staff;

(ii)   rent and rates;

(iii)   insurance;

(iv)   telephone and postage;

(v)   printing and stationery;

(vi)   heating and lighting.

(c)   *Finance expenses.* These include, for example:

(i)   interest on a loan;

(ii)   bank overdraft interest.

As far as possible, you should try to group items of expenses (selling and distribution, administration and finance) but this is not something that you should worry about unnecessarily at this stage.

Example: trading, profit and loss account

2.6   On 1 June 19X5, Jock Heiss commenced trading as an ice cream salesman, selling ice creams from a van which he drove around the streets of his town.

(a)   He rented the van at a cost of £1,000 for three months. Running expenses for the van averaged £300 per month.

(b)   He hired a part time helper at a cost of £100 per month.

(c)   He borrowed £2,000 from his bank, and the interest cost of the loan was £25 per month.

(d)   His main business was to sell ice cream to customers in the street, but he also did some special catering arrangements for business customers, supplying ice creams for office parties. Sales to these customers were usually on credit.

(e)   For the three months to 31 August 19X5, his total sales were:

(i)   cash sales £8,900;
(ii)   credit sales £1,100.

(f)   He purchased his ice cream from a local manufacturer, Floors Ltd. The cost of purchases in the three months to 31 August 19X5 was £6,200, and at 31 August he had sold every item of stock. He still owed £700 to Floors Ltd for unpaid purchases on credit.

(g)   One of his credit sale customers has gone bankrupt, owing Jock £250. Jock has decided to write off the debt in full, with no prospect of getting any of the money owed.

(h)   He used his own home for his office work. Telephone and postage expenses for the three months to 31 August were £150.

(i)   During the period he paid himself £300 per month.

Required

Prepare a trading, profit and loss account for the three months 1 June to 31 August 19X5.

Solution

2.7   A trading, profit and loss account can be presented in either a horizontal format or a vertical format.

(a)   *Horizontal format*

JOCK HEISS
TRADING, PROFIT AND LOSS ACCOUNT
FOR THE THREE MONTHS ENDED 31 AUGUST 19X5

	£		£
Cost of sales	6,200	Sales	10,000
Gross profit carried down	3,800		
	10,000		10,000
Wages	300	Gross profit brought down	3,800
Van rental	1,000		
Van expenses	900		
Bad debt written off	250		
Telephone and postage	150		
Interest charges	75		
Net profit transferred to the balance sheet	1,125		
	3,800		3,800

Notes

(i)   In a horizontal trading account, the cost of sales is shown on the left hand side and sales are shown on the right. The difference between the two amounts is the gross profit (or loss).

(ii)   The gross profit so calculated is carried down into the profit and loss account, where it is shown on the right hand side. The various expenses are itemised on the left, and the difference between the gross profit and total expenses is the net profit. A net profit appears on the left, whereas a net loss would be shown on the right.

(iii) The net profit is the profit for the period, and it is transferred to the balance sheet of the business as part of the proprietor's capital.

(iv)   Drawings are appropriations of profit and not expenses. They must not be included in the profit and loss account. In this example, the payments that Jock Heiss makes to himself (£900) are drawings.

(v)   The cost of sales is £6,200, even though £700 of the costs have not yet been paid for, and Floors Ltd is still a creditor for £700 in the balance sheet.

The horizontal format is uncommon in practice and in this Study Text the vertical format will be used.

(b)   *Vertical format*

A vertical trading, profit and loss account shows the same information, but with a different layout of figures.

JOCK HEISS
TRADING, PROFIT AND LOSS ACCOUNT
FOR THE THREE MONTHS ENDED 31 AUGUST 19X5

	£	£
Sales		10,000
Less cost of sales		6,200
Gross profit		3,800
Wages	300	
Van rental	1,000	
Van expenses	900	
Bad debt written off	250	
Telephone and postage	150	
Interest charges	75	
		2,675
Net profit (transferred to the balance sheet)		1,125

3   CAPITAL AND REVENUE EXPENDITURE

3.1   Capital expenditure is expenditure which results in the acquisition of fixed assets, or an improvement in their earning capacity.

(a)   Capital expenditure is not charged as an expense in the profit and loss account, although a depreciation charge will usually be made to write off the capital expenditure gradually over time. Depreciation charges are expenses in the profit and loss account.

(b)   Capital expenditure on fixed assets results in the appearance of a fixed asset in the balance sheet of the business.

3.2   Revenue expenditure is expenditure which is incurred for either of the following reasons.

(a)   For the purpose of the trade of the business. This includes expenditure classified as selling and distribution expenses, administration expenses and finance charges.

(b)   To maintain the existing earning capacity of fixed assets.

3.3   Revenue expenditure is charged to the profit and loss account of a period, provided that it relates to the trading activity and sales of that particular period. For example, if a business buys ten widgets for £200 (£20 each) and sells eight of them during an accounting period, it will have two widgets left in stock at the end of the period. The full £200 is revenue expenditure but only £160 is a cost of goods sold during the period. The remaining £40 (cost of two units) will be included in the balance sheet in the stock of goods held - ie as a current asset valued at £40.

3.4 Suppose that a business purchases a building for £30,000. It then adds an extension to the building at a cost of £10,000. The building needs to have a few broken windows mended, its floors polished and some missing roof tiles replaced. These cleaning and maintenance jobs cost £900.

In this example, the original purchase (£30,000) and the cost of the extension (£10,000) are capital expenditures, because they are incurred to acquire and then improve a fixed asset. The other costs of £900 are revenue expenditure, because these merely maintain the building and thus the 'earning capacity' of the building.

Capital income and revenue income

3.5 Capital income is the proceeds from the sale of non-trading assets (ie proceeds from the sale of fixed assets, including fixed asset investments). The profits (or losses) from the sale of fixed assets are included in the profit and loss account of a business, for the accounting period in which the sale takes place.

3.6 Revenue income is income derived from the following sources.

(a) The sale of trading assets
(b) Interest and dividends received from investments held by the business

Capital transactions

3.7 The categorisation of capital and revenue items given above does not mention raising additional capital from the owner(s) of the business, or raising and repaying loans. These are transactions which either:

(a) add to the cash assets of the business, thereby creating a corresponding liability (capital or loan); or

(b) when a loan is repaid, reduce the liabilities (loan) and the assets (cash) of the business.

None of these transactions would be reported through the profit and loss account.

Why is the distinction between capital and revenue items important?

3.8 Revenue expenditure results from the purchase of goods and services that will either:

(a) be used fully in the accounting period in which they are purchased, and so be a cost or expense in the trading, profit and loss account; or

(b) result in a current asset as at the end of the accounting period because the goods or services have not yet been consumed or made use of. The current asset would be shown in the balance sheet and is not yet a cost or expense in the trading, profit and loss account.

3.9 Capital expenditure results in the purchase or improvement of fixed assets, which are assets that will provide benefits to the business in more than one accounting period, and which are not acquired with a view to being resold in the normal course of trade. The cost of purchased fixed assets is not charged in full to the trading, profit and loss account of the period in which the purchase occurs. Instead, the fixed asset is gradually depreciated over a number of accounting periods.

3.10   Since revenue items and capital items are accounted for in different ways, the correct and consistent calculation of profit for any accounting period depends on the correct and consistent classification of items as revenue or capital.

Exercise 2

State whether each of the following items should be classified as 'capital' or 'revenue' expenditure or income for the purpose of preparing the trading, profit and loss account and the balance sheet of the business.

(a)   The purchase of leasehold premises.

(b)   The annual depreciation of leasehold premises.

(c)   Solicitors' fees in connection with the purchase of leasehold premises.

(d)   The costs of adding extra storage capacity to a mainframe computer used by the business.

(e)   Computer repairs and maintenance costs.

(f)   Profit on the sale of an office building.

(g)   Revenue from sales by credit card.

(h)   The cost of new machinery.

(i)   Customs duty charged on the machinery when imported into the country.

(j)   The 'carriage' costs of transporting the new machinery from the supplier's factory to the premises of the business purchasing the machinery.

(k)   The cost of installing the new machinery in the premises of the business.

(l)   The wages of the machine operators

Solution

(a)   Capital expenditure.

(b)   Depreciation of a fixed asset is a revenue expenditure.

(c)   The legal fees associated with the purchase of a property may be added to the purchase price and classified as capital expenditure. The cost of the leasehold premises in the balance sheet of the business will then include the legal fees.

(d)   Capital expenditure (enhancing an existing fixed asset).

(e)   Revenue expenditure.

(f)   Capital income (net of the costs of sale).

(g)   Revenue income.

(h)   Capital expenditure.

(i)   If customs duties are borne by the purchaser of the fixed asset, they may be added to the cost of the machinery and classified as capital expenditure.

(j)   Similarly, if carriage costs are paid for by the purchaser of the fixed asset, they may be included in the cost of the fixed asset and classified as capital expenditure.

(k)   Installation costs of a fixed asset are also added to the fixed asset's cost and classified as capital expenditure.

(l)   Revenue expenditure.

Chapter roundup

- The purpose of this chapter has been to introduce in broad outline the characteristics of the balance sheet and the trading, profit and loss account. In the next chapters, we shall go on to consider in detail some of the techniques and principles applied to prepare the trading, profit and loss account.

- A balance sheet is a statement of the financial position of a business at a given moment in time.

- A trading, profit and loss account is a financial statement showing in detail how the profit or loss of a period has been made.

- A distinction is made in the balance sheet between long-term liabilities and current liabilities, and between fixed assets and current assets.

- 'Current' means 'within one year'. Current assets are expected to be converted into cash within one year. Current liabilities are debts which are payable within one year.

- Fixed assets are those acquired for long-term use within the business. They are normally valued at cost less depreciation.

- Capital expenditure is expenditure which results in the acquisition of fixed assets or an improvement in their earning capacity.

- Revenue expenditure is incurred:

  o for the purpose of the trade of the business; or

  o to maintain the existing earning capacity of fixed assets.

Test your knowledge

1 What are the component parts of the item 'proprietor's capital' in a balance sheet? (see para 1.6

2 Give two examples of long-term liabilities. (1.12)

3 What are the main items of current assets in a balance sheet? (1.25)

4 What is the 'working capital' of a business? (1.34)

5 What is the difference between gross profit and net profit? (2.3)

6 Identify a source of income other than the sale of goods. (2.4)

7 What items might be included in selling and distribution expenses? (2.5)

8 What is the distinction between capital expenditure and revenue expenditure. (3.1, 3.2)

Now try illustrative question 5 at the end of the Study Text

Chapter 5

SOURCES, RECORDS AND THE BOOKS OF PRIME ENTRY

This chapter covers the following topics.

		Syllabus reference	*Ability required*
1	The role of source documents	1(b)	Knowledge
2	The need for books of prime entry	1(b)	Knowledge
3	Sales and purchase day books	1(b)	Skill
4	Cash books	1(b)	Skill

Introduction

From your studies of the first four chapters you should have grasped some important points about the nature and purpose of accounting. You should have realised that most organisations exist to provide products and services in the ultimate hope of making a surplus or profit for their owners, which they do by receiving payment in money for goods and services provided. The role of the accounting system is to record these monetary effects and create information about them.

You should also, by now, understand the basic principles underlying the balance sheet and profit and loss account and have an idea of what they look like.

We now turn our attention to the process by which a business transaction works its way through to the financial statements.

It is usual to record a business transaction on a *document*. Such documents include invoices, orders, credit notes and goods received notes, all of which will be discussed in Section 1 of this chapter. In terms of the accounting system these are known as *source documents*. The information on them is processed by the system by, for example, aggregating (adding together) or classifying.

Records of source documents are kept in 'books of prime entry', which, as the name suggests, are the first stage at which a business transaction enters into the accounting system. The various types of books of prime entry are discussed in Sections 2 to 4.

In the next chapter we consider what happens to transactions after the books of prime entry stage.

1 THE ROLE OF SOURCE DOCUMENTS

1.1 Whenever a business transaction takes place, involving sales or purchases, receiving or paying money, or owing or being owed money, it is usual for the transaction to be recorded on a document. These documents are the source of all the information recorded by a business.

1.2 Documents used to record the business transactions in the 'books of account' of the business include the following.

(a) *Sales order*. A customer writes out an order or signs an order for goods or services he wishes to buy.

(b) *Purchase order*. A business makes an order from another business for the purchase of goods or services, such as material supplies.

(c) *Invoices* and *credit notes*. These are discussed further below.

1.3   An *invoice* relates to a sales order or a purchase order.

(a)   When a business sells goods or services on credit to a customer, it sends out an invoice. The details on the invoice should match up with the details on the sales order. The invoice is a request for the customer to pay what he owes.

(b)   When a business buys goods or services on credit it receives an invoice from the supplier. The details on the invoice should match up with the details on the purchase order.

1.4   The invoice is primarily a demand for payment, but it is used for other purposes as well, as we shall see. Because it has several uses, an invoice is often produced on multi-part stationery, or photocopied, or carbon-copied. The top copy will go to the customer and other copies will be used by various people within the business.

What does an invoice show?

1.5   Most invoices are numbered, so that the business can keep track of all the invoices it sends out. Information usually shown on an invoice includes the following.

(a)   Name and address of the seller and the purchaser.

(b)   Date of the sale.

(c)   Description of what is being sold.

(d)   Quantity and unit price of what has been sold (eg 20 pairs of shoes at £25 a pair).

(e)   Details of trade discount, if any (eg 10% reduction in cost if buying over 100 pairs of shoes). We shall look at discounts in a later chapter.

(f)   Total amount of the invoice including (in the UK) any details of VAT.

(g)   Sometimes, the date by which payment is due, and other terms of sale.

The credit note

1.6   Suppose that Student Supplies sent out its invoice for 450 rulers, but the typist accidentally typed in a total of £162.10, instead of £62.10. The county council has been *overcharged* by £100. What is Student Supplies to do?

1.7   Alternatively, suppose that when the primary school received the rulers, it found that they had all been broken in the post and that it was going to send them back. Although the county council has received an invoice for £62.10, it has no intention of paying it, because the rulers were useless. Again, what is Student Supplies to do?

1.8   The answer is that the supplier (in this case, Student Supplies) sends out a *credit note*. A credit note is sometimes printed in red to distinguish it from an invoice. Otherwise, it will be made out in much the same way as an invoice, but with less detail and 'Credit Note Number' instead of 'Invoice Number'.

1.9   Other documents sometimes used in connection with sales and purchases are:

(a)   debit notes;
(b)   goods received notes.

1.10   A *debit note* might be issued instead of raising an invoice to *adjust* an invoice already issued. This is also commonly achieved by issuing a revised invoice after raising a credit or debit note purely for internal purposes (ie to keep the records straight).

1.11   More commonly, a debit note is issued to a supplier as a means of formally requesting a credit note.

1.12   *Goods received notes* (GRNs) are filled in to record a receipt of goods, most commonly in a warehouse. They may be used in addition to suppliers' advice notes. Often the accounts department will require to see the relevant GRN before paying a supplier's invoice. Even where GRNs are not routinely used, the details of a consignment from a supplier which arrives without an advice note must always be recorded.

2   THE NEED FOR BOOKS OF PRIME ENTRY

2.1   We have seen that in the course of business, source documents are created. The details on these source documents need to be summarised, as otherwise the business might forget to ask for some money, or forget to pay some, or even accidentally pay something twice. In other words, it needs to keep records of source documents - of transactions - so that it can keep tabs on what is going on.

2.2   Such records are made in *books of prime entry*. The main books of prime entry which we need to look at are as follows.

(a)   Sales day book
(b)   Purchase day book
(c)   Sales returns day book
(d)   Purchases returns day book
(e)   Journal (described in the next chapter)
(f)   Cash book
(g)   Petty cash book

2.3   It is worth bearing in mind that, for convenience, this chapter describes books of prime entry as if they are actual books. Nowadays, books of prime entry are often not books at all, but rather files hidden in the memory of a computer. However, the principles remain the same whether they are manual or computerised.

3   SALES AND PURCHASE DAY BOOKS

The sales day book

3.1   The *sales day book* is used to keep a list of all invoices sent out to customers each day. An extract from a sales day book might look like this.

SALES DAY BOOK

Date 19X0	Invoice	Customer	Sales ledger folio	Total amount invoiced £
Jan 10	247	Jones & Co	SL14	105.00
	248	Smith Ltd	SL 8	86.40
	249	Alex & Co	SL 6	31.80
	250	Enor College	SL 9	1,264.60
				1,487.80

3.2   The column called 'sales ledger folio' is a reference to the sales ledger. It means, for example, that the sale to Jones & Co for £105 is also recorded on page 14 of the sales ledger.

3.3   Most businesses 'analyse' their sales. For example, suppose that the business sells boots and shoes, and that the sale to Smith was entirely boots, the sale to Alex was entirely shoes, and the other two sales were a mixture of both.

3.4   Then the sales day book might look like this.

SALES DAY BOOK

Date	Invoice	Customer	Sales ledger folio	Total amount invoiced	Boot sales	Shoe sales
19X0				£	£	£
Jan 10	247	Jones & Co	SL 14	105.00	60.00	45.00
	248	Smith Ltd	SL 8	86.40	86.40	
	249	Alex & Co	SL 6	31.80		31.80
	250	Enor College	SL 9	1,264.60	800.30	464.30
				1,487.80	946.70	541.10

3.5   This sort of analysis gives the managers of the business useful information which helps them to decide how best to run the business.

The purchase day book

3.6   A business also keeps a record in the purchase day book of all the invoices it receives.

3.7   An extract from a purchase day book might look like this.

PURCHASE DAY BOOK

Date	Supplier	Purchase ledger folio	Total amount invoiced	Purchases	Electricity etc
19X8			£	£	£
Mar 15	Cook & Co	PL 31	315.00	315.00	
	W Butler	PL 46	29.40	29.40	
	EEB	PL 42	116.80		116.80
	Show Fair Ltd	PL 12	100.00	100.00	
			561.20	444.40	116.80

3.8   You should note the following points.

(a)   The 'purchase ledger folio' is a reference to the purchase ledger just as the sales ledger folio was to the sales ledger. Again, we will see the purpose of this in the next chapter.

(b)   There is no 'invoice number' column, because the purchase day book records other people's invoices, which have all sorts of different numbers.

(c)   Like the sales day book, the purchase day book analyses the invoices which have been sent in. In this example, three of the invoices related to goods which the business intends to re-sell (called simply 'purchases') and the fourth invoice was an electricity bill.

The sales returns day book

3.9   When customers return goods for some reason, the returns are recorded in the sales return day book. An extract from the sales returns day book might look like this:

SALES RETURNS DAY BOOK

Date	Customer and goods	Sales ledger folio	Amount
19X8			£
30 April	Owen Plenty		
	3 pairs 'Texas' boots	SL 82	135.00

3.10   Not all sales returns day books analyse what goods were returned, but it makes sense to keep as complete a record as possible.

The purchase returns day book

3.11 There are no prizes for guessing that the purchase returns day book is kept to record goods which the business sends back to its suppliers. The business might expect a cash refund from the supplier. In the meantime, however, it might issue a debit note to the supplier, indicating the amount by which the business expects its total debt to the supplier to be reduced.

3.12 An extract from the purchase returns day book might look like this:

PURCHASE RETURNS DAY BOOK

Date 19X8	Supplier and goods	Purchase ledger folio	Amount £
29 April	Boxes Ltd 300 cardboard boxes	PL 123	46.60

4   CASH BOOKS

The cash book

4.1 The cash book is also a day book, which is used to keep a cumulative record of money received and money paid out by the business. The cash book deals with money paid into and out of the business *bank* account. This could be money received on the business premises in notes, coins and cheques. There are also receipts and payments made by bank transfer, standing order, direct debit and, in the case of bank interest and charges, directly by the bank.

4.2 Some cash, in notes and coins, is usually kept on the business premises in order to make occasional payments for odd items of expense. This cash is usually accounted for separately in a *petty cash book* (which we will look at shortly).

4.3 One part of the cash book is used to record receipts of cash, and another part is used to record payments. The best way to see how the cash book works is to follow through an example.

Example: cash book

4.4 At the beginning of 1 September, Robin Plenty had £900 in the bank.

4.5 During 1 September 19X7, Robin Plenty had the following receipts and payments.

   (a) Cash sale - receipt of £80
   (b) Payment from credit customer Hay £400 less discount allowed £20
   (c) Payment from credit customer Been £720
   (d) Payment from credit customer Seed £150 less discount allowed £10
   (e) Cheque received for cash to provide a short-term loan from Len Dinger £1,800
   (f) Second cash sale - receipts of £150
   (g) Cash received for sale of machine £200
   (h) Payment to supplier Kew £120
   (i) Payment to supplier Hare £310
   (j) Payment of telephone bill £400
   (k) Payment of gas bill £280
   (l) £100 in cash withdrawn from bank for petty cash
   (m) Payment of £1,500 to Hess for new plant and machinery

4.6 If you look through these transactions, you will see that seven of them are receipts and six of them are payments.

4.7 The receipts part of the cash book for 1 September would look like this.

CASH BOOK (RECEIPTS)

Date	Narrative	Folio	Total
19X7			£
1 Sept	Balance b/d*		900
	Cash sale		80
	Debtor: Hay		380
	Debtor: Been		720
	Debtor: Seed		140
	Loan: Len Dinger		1,800
	Cash sale		150
	Sale of fixed asset		200
			4,370
2 Sept	Balance b/d*		1,660

* 'b/d' = brought down (ie brought forward)

4.8 You should note the following points.

(a) There is space on the right hand side of the cash book so that the receipts can be analysed under various headings - for example, 'receipts from debtors', 'cash sales' and 'other receipts'.

(b) The cash received in the day amounted to £3,470. Added to the £900 at the start of the day, this comes to £4,370. But this is not, of course, the amount to be carried forward to the next day, because first we have to subtract all the payments made during 1 September.

4.9 The payments part of the cash book for 1 September would look like this.

CASH BOOK (PAYMENTS)

Date	Narrative	Folio	Total
19X7			£
1 Sept	Creditor: Kew		120
	Creditor: Hare		310
	Telephone		400
	Gas bill		280
	Petty cash		100
	Machinery purchase		1,500
	Balance c/d		1,660
			4,370

4.10 As you can see, this is very similar to the receipts part of the cash book. The only points to note are as follows.

(a) The analysis on the right would be under headings like 'payments to creditors', 'payments into petty cash', 'wages' and 'other payments'.

(b) Payments during 1 September totalled £2,710. We know that the total of receipts was £4,370. That means that there is a balance of £4,370 – £2,710 = £1,660 to be 'carried down' to the start of the next day. As you can see this 'balance carried down' is noted at the end of the payments column, so that the receipts and payments totals show the same figure of £4,370 at the end of 1 September. And if you look to the receipts part of this example, you can see that £1,660 has been brought down ready for the next day.

4.11 With analysis columns completed, the cash book given in the examples above might look as follows.

CASH BOOK (RECEIPTS)

Date	Narrative	Folio	Total £	Debtors £	Cash sales £	Other £
19X7						
1 Sept	Balance b/d		900			
	Cash sale		80		80	
	Debtor - Hay		380	380		
	Debtor - Been		720	720		
	Debtor - Seed		140	140		
	Loan - Len Dinger		1,800			1,800
	Cash sale		150		150	
	Sale of fixed asset		200			200
			4,370	1,240	230	2,000

CASH BOOK (PAYMENTS)

Date	Narrative	Folio	Total £	Creditors £	Petty cash £	Wages £	Other £
19X7							
1 Sept	Creditor - Kew		120	120			
	Creditor - Hare		310	310			
	Telephone		400				400
	Gas bill		280				280
	Petty cash		100		100		
	Machinery purchase		1,500				1,500
	Balance c/d		1,660				
			4,370	430	100	-	2,180

Bank statements

4.12 Weekly or monthly, a business will receive a bank statement. Bank statements should be used to check that the amount shown as a balance in the cash book agrees with the amount on the bank statement, and that no cash has 'gone missing'. This agreement or 'reconciliation' of the cash book with a statement is the subject of a later chapter.

Petty cash book

4.13 Most businesses keep a small amount of cash on the premises to make occasional small payments in cash - eg to pay the milkman, to buy a few postage stamps, to pay the office cleaner, to pay for some bus or taxi fares etc. This is often called the cash float or petty cash account. The cash float can also be the resting place for occasional small receipts, such as cash paid by a visitor to make a phone call, or take some photocopies etc.

4.14 There are usually more payments than receipts, and petty cash must be 'topped up' from time to time with cash from the business bank account.

4.15 Under what is called the *imprest system*, the amount of money in petty cash is kept at an agreed sum or 'float' (say £100). Expense items are recorded on vouchers as they occur, so that at any time:

	£
Cash still held in petty cash	X
Plus voucher payments	X
Must equal the agreed sum or float	X

The total float is made up regularly (to £100, or whatever the agreed sum is) by means of a cash payment from the bank account into petty cash. The amount of the 'top-up' into petty cash will be the total of the voucher payments since the previous top-up.

4.16 The format of a petty cash book is much the same as for the cash book, with analysis columns (chiefly for expenditure items, such as travel, postage, cleaning etc).

4.17   Try the following exercise on books of prime entry.

Exercise

State which books of prime entry the following transactions would be entered into.

(a)   Your business pays A Brown (a supplier) £450.00.
(b)   You send D Smith (a customer) an invoice for £650.
(c)   Your accounts manager asks you for £12 urgently in order to buy some envelopes.
(d)   You receive an invoice from A Brown for £300.
(e)   You pay D Smith £500.
(f)   F Jones (a customer) returns goods to the value of £250.
(g)   You return goods to J Green to the value of £504.
(h)   F Jones pays you £500.

Solution

(a)   Cash book
(b)   Sales day book
(c)   Petty cash book
(d)   Purchases day book
(e)   Cash book
(f)   Sales returns day book
(g)   Purchase returns day book
(h)   Cash book

4.18   Another book of prime entry is the *journal* which is considered in the next chapter.

Chapter roundup

- Business transactions are recorded on source documents. These include the following.

  o   Sales orders
  o   Purchase orders
  o   Invoices
  o   Credit notes

- These transactions are recorded in books of prime entry of which there are seven.

  o   Sales day book
  o   Sales returns day book
  o   Purchase day book
  o   Purchase returns day book
  o   Cash book
  o   Petty cash book
  o   Journal

- Most businesses keep petty cash on the premises which is topped up from the main bank account. Under the imprest system the petty cash is kept at an agreed sum.

- You should be aware of which transactions go in a given book of prime entry.

Test your knowledge

1   Name four pieces of information normally shown on an invoice. (see para 1.5)

2   Name the seven books of prime entry. (2.2)

3   What information is summarised in the sales day book? (3.1 - 3.4)

4   What is the purchase returns day book used for? (3.11)

5   What is the difference between the cash book and the petty cash book? (4.1, 4.2)

6   Describe how the imprest system works. (4.15)

Now try illustrative question 6 at the end of the Study Text

Chapter 6

LEDGER ACCOUNTING AND DOUBLE ENTRY

This chapter covers the following topics.

		Syllabus reference	*Ability required*
1	The nominal ledger	1(b)	Skill
2	Double entry bookkeeping	1(b)	Skill
3	The journal	1(b)	Skill
4	Day book analysis	1(b)	Skill
5	The imprest system	1(b)	Skill
6	The sales and purchase ledgers	1(b)	Skill

Introduction

In earlier chapters we looked at the theory of preparing accounts for the proprietor(s) of a business, by presenting a profit and loss account for a given period of time and a balance sheet as at the end of that period. We have also seen, by means of the accounting equation and the business equation, that it would be possible to prepare a statement of the affairs of a business at any time we like, and that a profit and loss account and a balance sheet could be drawn up on any date, relating to any period of time. A business is continually making transactions, buying and selling etc, and we would not want to prepare a profit and loss account and a balance sheet on completion of every individual transaction. To do so would be a time-consuming and cumbersome administrative task.

It is common sense that a business should keep a record of the transactions that it makes, the assets it acquires and liabilities it incurs, and when the time comes to prepare a profit and loss account and a balance sheet, the relevant information can be taken from those records.

The records of transactions, assets and liabilities should be kept:

(a)   in chronological order, and dated so that transactions can be related to a particular period of time; and

(b)   built up in cumulative totals. For example, a business may build up the total of its sales:

  (i)   day by day (eg total sales on Monday, total sales on Tuesday);
  (ii)   week by week;
  (iii)   month by month;
  (iv)   year by year.

We have already seen the first step in this process, which is to list all the transactions in various books of prime entry. Now we must turn our attention to the method used to summarise these records.

This chapter introduces *double entry bookkeeping*. This is the cornerstone of accounts preparation, and is surprisingly simple.

1   THE NOMINAL LEDGER

1.1   The nominal ledger is an accounting record which summarises the financial affairs of a business. It contains details of assets, liabilities and capital, income and expenditure and so profit and loss. It consists of a large number of different accounts, each account having its own purpose or 'name' and an identity or code. There may be various subdivisions, whether for convenience, ease of handling, confidentiality, security, or to meet the needs of computer software design.

1.2   The nominal ledger is sometimes called the 'general ledger'.

1.3   Examples of accounts in the nominal ledger include the following.

(a)   Plant and machinery at cost (fixed asset)
(b)   Motor vehicles at cost (fixed asset)
(c)   Plant and machinery, provision for depreciation (liability)
(d)   Motor vehicles, provision for depreciation (liability)
(e)   Proprietor's capital (liability)
(f)   Stocks - raw materials (current asset)
(g)   Stocks - finished goods (current asset)
(h)   Total debtors (current asset)
(i)   Total creditors (current liability)
(j)   Wages and salaries (expense item)
(k)   Rent and rates (expense item)
(l)   Advertising expenses (expense item)
(m)   Bank charges (expense item)
(n)   Motor expenses (expense item)
(o)   Telephone expenses (expense item)
(p)   Sales (income)
(q)   Total cash or bank overdraft (current asset or liability)

The format of a ledger account

1.4   If a ledger account were to be kept in an actual book rather than as a computer record, its format might be as follows:

ADVERTISING EXPENSES

Date	Narrative	Folio	£	Date	Narrative	Folio	£
19X6							
15 April	JFK Agency for quarter to 31 March	PL 348	2,500				

Only one entry in the account is shown here, because the example is introduced simply to illustrate the general format of a ledger account.

1.5   There are two sides to the account, and an account heading on top, and so it is convenient to think in terms of 'T' accounts:

(a)   on top of the account is its name;
(b)   there is a left hand side, or debit side; and
(c)   there is a right hand side, or credit side.

NAME OF ACCOUNT

DEBIT SIDE	£	CREDIT SIDE	£

2   DOUBLE ENTRY BOOKKEEPING   5/95

2.1   As we have seen, since the total of liabilities plus capital is always equal to total assets, any transaction which changes the amount of total assets must also change the total liabilities plus capital, and vice versa. Alternatively, a transaction might use up assets of a certain value to obtain other assets of the same value. For example, if a business pays £50 in cash for some goods, its total assets will be unchanged, but as the amount of cash falls by £50, the value of goods in stocks rises by the same amount.

2.2   Ledger accounts, with their debit and credit side, are kept in a way which allows the two-sided nature of business transactions to be recorded. This system of accounting was first expounded in Venice in 1494 AD and it is known as the 'double entry' system of bookkeeping, so called because every transaction is recorded twice in the accounts. This is sometimes referred to as the concept of *duality*.

2.3   Double entry bookkeeping is not entirely standardised, and there are some variations found in practice in the way that business transactions are recorded. In this text, double entry bookkeeping will be explained according to a given set of well practised 'rules'. Variations in these rules that are made in accounting systems of some businesses might be mentioned from time to time; however, if you learn the system as described here, you should be able to adapt your knowledge to any (minor) differences which either might appear in an examination question, or you might come across in your practical experience.

The rules of double entry bookkeeping

2.4   The basic rule which must always be observed is that *every* financial transaction gives rise to two accounting entries, one a debit and the other a credit. The total value of debit entries in the nominal ledger is therefore always equal at any time to the total value of credit entries. Which account receives the credit entry and which receives the debit depends on the nature of the transaction.

   (a)   An increase in an expense (eg a purchase of stationery) or an increase in an asset (eg a purchase of office furniture) is a *debit*.

   (b)   An increase in income (eg a sale) or an increase in a liability (eg buying goods on credit) is a *credit*.

   (c)   A decrease in an asset (eg making a cash payment) is a *credit*.

   (d)   A decrease in a liability (eg paying a creditor) is a *debit*.

2.5   Students coming to the subject for the first time often have difficulty in knowing where to begin. A good starting point is the cash account, ie the nominal ledger account in which receipts and payments of cash are recorded. The rule to remember about the cash account is as follows.

   (a)   A cash *payment* is a *credit* entry in the cash account. Here the asset is decreasing. Cash may be paid out, for example, to pay an expense (such as rates) or to purchase an asset (such as a machine). The matching debit entry is therefore made in the appropriate expense account or asset account.

   (b)   A cash *receipt* is a *debit* entry in the cash account. Here the asset is increasing. Cash might be received, for example, by a retailer who makes a cash sale. The credit entry would then be made in the sales account.

Example: double entry for cash transactions

2.6   In the cash book of a business, the following transactions have been recorded.

   (a)   A cash sale (ie a receipt) of £2
   (b)   Payment of a rent bill totalling £150
   (c)   Buying some goods for cash at £100
   (d)   Buying some shelves for cash at £200

2.7   How would these four transactions be posted to the ledger accounts? For that matter, which ledger accounts should they be posted to? Don't forget that each transaction will be posted twice, in accordance with the rule of double entry.

Solution

2.8   (a)   The two sides of the transaction are:

   (i)   cash is received (debit entry in the cash account);
   (ii)   sales increase by £2 (credit entry in the sales account),

CASH ACCOUNT

	£		£
Sales a/c	2		

SALES ACCOUNT

	£		£
		Cash a/c	2

(Note how the entry in the cash account is cross-referenced to the sales account and vice-versa. This enables a person looking at one of the accounts to trace where the other half of the double entry can be found.)

   (b)   The two sides of the transaction are:

   (i)   cash is paid (credit entry in the cash account);
   (ii)   rent expense increases by £150 (debit entry in the rent account).

CASH ACCOUNT

	£		£
		Rent a/c	150

RENT ACCOUNT

	£		£
Cash a/c	150		

   (c)   The two sides of the transaction are:

   (i)   cash is paid (credit entry in the cash account);
   (ii)   purchases increase by £100 (debit entry in the purchases account).

CASH ACCOUNT

	£		£
		Purchases a/c	100

PURCHASES ACCOUNT

	£		£
Cash a/c	100		

   (d)   The two sides of the transaction are:

   (i)   cash is paid (credit entry in the cash account);

   (ii)   assets - in this case, shelves - increase by £200 (debit entry in shelves account).

CASH ACCOUNT

	£		£
		Shelves a/c	200

SHELVES (ASSET) ACCOUNT

	£		£
Cash a/c	200		

2.9 If all four of these transactions related to the same business, the cash account of that business would end up looking as follows.

CASH ACCOUNT

	£		£
Sales a/c	2	Rent a/c	150
		Purchases a/c	100
		Shelves a/c	200

Credit transactions

2.10 Not all transactions are settled immediately in cash. A business might purchase goods or fixed assets from its suppliers on credit terms, so that the suppliers would be creditors of the business until settlement was made in cash. Equally, the business might grant credit terms to its customers who would then be debtors of the business. Clearly no entries can be made in the cash book when a credit transaction occurs, because initially no cash has been received or paid. Where then can the details of the transactions be entered?

2.11 The solution to this problem is to use debtors and creditors accounts. When a business acquires goods or services on credit, the credit entry is made in an account designated 'creditors' instead of in the cash account. The debit entry is made in the appropriate expense or asset account, exactly as in the case of cash transactions. Similarly, when a sale is made to a credit customer the entries made are a debit to the total debtors account (instead of cash account) and a credit to sales account.

Example: credit transactions

2.12 Recorded in the sales day book and the purchase day book are the following transactions.

(a) The business sells goods on credit to a customer Mr A for £2,000.
(b) The business buys goods on credit from a supplier B Ltd for £100.

2.13 How and where are these transactions posted in the ledger accounts?

Solution

2.14 (a)

DEBTORS ACCOUNT

	£		£
Sales a/c	2,000		

SALES ACCOUNT

	£		£
		Debtors account	2,000

(b)

CREDITORS ACCOUNT

	£		£
		Purchases a/c	100

PURCHASES ACCOUNT

	£		£
Creditors a/c	100		

When cash is paid to creditors or by debtors

2.15 What happens when a credit transaction is eventually settled in cash? Suppose that, in the example above, the business paid £100 to B Ltd one month after the goods were acquired. The two sides of this new transaction are:

(a) cash is paid (credit entry in the cash account);
(b) the amount owing to creditors is reduced (debit entry in the creditors account).

CASH ACCOUNT

	£		£
		Creditors a/c (B Ltd)	100

CREDITORS ACCOUNT

	£		£
Cash a/c	100		

2.16 If we now bring together the two parts of this example, the original purchase of goods on credit and the eventual settlement in cash, we find that the accounts appear as follows.

CASH ACCOUNT

	£		£
		Creditors a/c	100

PURCHASES ACCOUNT

	£		£
Creditors a/c	100		

CREDITORS ACCOUNT

	£		£
Cash a/c	100	Purchases a/c	100

2.17 The two entries in the creditors account cancel each other out, indicating that no money is owing to creditors any more. We are left with a credit entry of £100 in the cash account and a debit entry of £100 in the purchases account. These are exactly the entries which would have been made to record a *cash* purchase of £100 (compare example above). This is what we would expect: after the business has paid off its creditors it is in exactly the position of a business which has made cash purchases of £100, and the accounting records reflect this similarity.

2.18 Similar reasoning applies when a customer settles his debt. In the example above when Mr A pays his debt of £2,000 the two sides of the transaction are:

(a) cash is received (debit entry in the cash account);
(b) the amount owed by debtors is reduced (credit entry in the debtors account).

CASH ACCOUNT

	£		£
Debtors a/c	2,000		

DEBTORS ACCOUNT

	£		£
		Cash a/c	2,000

2.19 The accounts recording this sale to, and payment by, Mr A now appear as follows.

CASH ACCOUNT

	£		£
Debtors A/C	2,000		

SALES ACCOUNT

	£		£
		Debtors a/c	2,000

DEBTORS ACCOUNT

	£		£
Sales a/c	2,000	Cash a/c	2,000

2.20 The two entries in the debtors account cancel each other out; while the entries in the cash account and sales account reflect the same position as if the sale had been made for cash (see above).

2.21 Now try the following exercises.

Exercise 1

See if you can identify the debit and credit entries in the following transactions.

(a) Bought a machine on credit from A, cost £8,000.
(b) Bought goods on credit from B, cost £500.
(c) Sold goods on credit to C, value £1,200.
(d) Paid D (a creditor) £300.
(e) Collected £180 from E, a debtor.
(f) Paid wages £4,000.
(g) Received rent bill of £700 from landlord G.
(h) Paid rent of £700 to landlord G.
(i) Paid insurance premium £90.

Solution

			£	£
(a)	DEBIT	Machine account (fixed asset)	8,000	
	CREDIT	Creditors (A)		8,000
(b)	DEBIT	Purchases account	500	
	CREDIT	Creditors (B)		500
(c)	DEBIT	Debtors (C)	1,200	
	CREDIT	Sales		1,200
(d)	DEBIT	Creditors (D)	300	
	CREDIT	Cash		300
(e)	DEBIT	Cash	180	
	CREDIT	Debtors (E)		180
(f)	DEBIT	Wages account	4,000	
	CREDIT	Cash		4,000
(g)	DEBIT	Rent account	700	
	CREDIT	Creditors (G)		700
(h)	DEBIT	Creditors (G)	700	
	CREDIT	Cash		700
(i)	DEBIT	Insurance costs	90	
	CREDIT	Cash		90

Exercise 2

See now whether you can record the ledger entries for the following transactions. Ron Knuckle set up a business selling keep fit equipment, trading under the name of Buy Your Biceps Shop. He put £7,000 of his own money into a business bank account (transaction A) and in his first period of trading, the following transactions occurred.

Transaction		£
B	Paid rent of shop for the period	3,500
C	Purchased equipment (stocks) on credit	5,000
D	Raised loan from bank	1,000
E	Purchase of shop fittings (for cash)	2,000
F	Sales of equipment: cash	10,000
G	Sales of equipment: on credit	2,500
H	Payments to trade creditors	5,000
I	Payments from debtors	2,500
J	Interest on loan (paid)	100
K	Other expenses (all paid in cash)	1,900
L	Drawings	1,500

All stocks purchased during the period was sold, and so there were no closing stocks of equipment.

Try to do as much of this exercise as you can by yourself before reading the solution.

Solution

Clearly, there should be an account for cash, debtors, creditors, purchases, a shop fittings account, sales, a loan account and a proprietor's capital account. It is also useful to keep a separate *drawings account* until the end of each accounting period. Other accounts should be set up as they seem appropriate and in this exercise, accounts for rent, bank interest and other expenses would seem appropriate.

It has been suggested to you that the cash account is a good place to start, if possible. You should notice that cash transactions include the initial input of capital by Ron Knuckle, subsequent drawings, the payment of rent, the loan from the bank, the interest, some cash sales and cash purchases, and payments to creditors and by debtors. (The transactions are identified below by their reference, to help you to find them.)

CASH

	£		£
Capital - Ron Knuckle (A)	7,000	Rent (B)	3,500
Bank loan (D)	1,000	Shop fittings (E)	2,000
Sales (F)	10,000	Trade creditors (H)	5,000
Debtors (I)	2,500	Bank loan interest (J)	100
		Incidental expenses (K)	1,900
		Drawings (L)	1,500
			14,000
		Balancing figure - the amount of cash left over after payments have been made	
			6,500
	20,500		20,500

CAPITAL (RON KNUCKLE)

	£		£
		Cash (A)	7,000

BANK LOAN

	£		£
		Cash (D)	1,000

PURCHASES

	£		£
Trade creditors (C)	5,000		

TRADE CREDITORS

	£		£
Cash (H)	5,000	Purchases (C)	5,000

RENT

	£		£
Cash (B)	3,500		

FIXED ASSETS

	£		£
Cash (E)	2,000		

SALES

	£		£
		Cash (F)	10,000
		Debtors (G)	2,500
			12,500

DEBTORS

	£		£
Sales (G)	2,500	Cash (I)	2,500

BANK LOAN INTEREST

	£		£
Cash (J)	100		

OTHER EXPENSES

	£		£
Cash (K)	1,900		

DRAWINGS ACCOUNT

	£		£
Cash (L)	1,500		

(a)   If you want to make sure that this solution is complete, you should go through the transactions A to L and tick off each of them twice in the ledger accounts, once as a debit and once as a credit. When you have finished, all transactions in the 'T' account should be ticked, with only totals left over.

(b)   In fact, there is an easier way to check that the solution to this sort of problem does 'balance' properly, which we will meet in the next chapter.

3   THE JOURNAL

3.1   You should remember that one of the books of prime entry from the previous chapter was the journal. The journal keeps a record of unusual movement between accounts. It is used to record any double entries made which do not arise from the other books of prime entry. For example, journal entries are made when errors are discovered and need to be corrected.

3.2   Whatever type of transaction is being recorded, the format of a journal entry is:

Date	Folio	Debit	Credit
		£	£
Account to be debited		X	
Account to be credited			X
(Narrative to explain the transaction)			

(Remember: in due course, the ledger accounts will be written up to include the transactions listed in the journal.)

3.3   A narrative explanation must accompany each journal entry. It is required for audit and control, to indicate the purpose and authority of every transaction which is not first recorded in a book of prime entry.

Examples: journal entries

3.4   Some examples might help to illustrate the format. Note that an examination question might ask you to 'journalise' transactions which would not in practice be recorded in the journal at all. If you are faced with such a problem, you should simply record the debit and credit entries for every transaction you can recognise, giving some supporting narrative to each transaction.

3.5   The following is a summary of the transactions of Hair by Fiona Middleton of which Fiona is the sole proprietor.

1 January	Put in cash of £2,000 as capital
	Purchased brushes and combs for cash £50
	Purchased hair driers from Gilroy Ltd on credit £150
30 January	Paid three months rent to 31 March £300
	Collected and paid in takings £600
31 January	Gave Mrs Sullivan a perm, highlights etc on credit £80

Show the transactions by means of journal entries.

Solution

3.6   JOURNAL

				£	£
1 January	DEBIT	Cash		2,000	
	CREDIT	Fiona Middleton - capital account			2,000
	Initial capital introduced				
1 January	DEBIT	Brushes and combs account		50	
	CREDIT	Cash			50
	The purchase for cash of brushes and combs as fixed assets				
1 January	DEBIT	Hair dryer account		150	
	CREDIT	Sundry creditors account ★			150
	The purchase on credit of hair driers as fixed assets				
30 January	DEBIT	Rent account		300	
	CREDIT	Cash			300
	The payment of rent to 31 March				
30 January	DEBIT	Cash		600	
	CREDIT	Sales (or takings account)			600
	Cash takings				
31 January	DEBIT	Debtors account		80	
	CREDIT	Sales account (or takings account)			80
	The provision of a hair-do on credit				

★ *Note.* Creditors who have supplied fixed assets are included amongst sundry creditors, as distinct from creditors who have supplied raw materials or goods for resale, who are trade creditors. It is quite common to have separate 'total creditors' accounts, one for trade creditors and another for sundry other creditors.

The correction of errors

3.7   The journal is most commonly used to record corrections to errors that have been made in writing up the nominal ledger accounts. Errors corrected by the journal must be capable of correction by means of a double entry in the ledger accounts. (When errors are made which break the rule of double entry, that debits and credits must be equal, the initial step in identifying and correcting the error is to open up a suspense account, to restore equality between total debits and total credits. Errors leading to the creation of a suspense account are corrected initially by making a record in the journal. However, suspense accounts are the subject of a separate chapter in this text.)

3.8   There are several types of error which can occur. They are looked at in some detail in the section of this text on internal control along with the method of using journal entries to correct them.

4   DAY BOOK ANALYSIS   5/97

4.1   In the previous chapter, we used the following example of four transactions entered into the sales day book.

SALES DAY BOOK

Date 19X0	Invoice	Customer	Sales ledger folios	Total amount invoiced £	Boot sales £	Shoe sales £
Jan 10	247	Jones & Co	SL 14	105.00	60.00	45.00
	248	Smith Ltd	SL 8	86.40	86.40	
	249	Alex & Co	SL 6	31.80		31.80
	250	Enor College	SL 9	1,264.60	800.30	464.30
				1,487.80	946.70	541.10

4.2   We have already seen that in theory these transactions are posted to the ledger accounts as follows:

DEBIT	Total debtors account	£1,487.80	
CREDIT	Sales account		£1,487.80

4.3   But a total sales account is not very informative, particularly if the business sells lots of different products. So, using our example, the business might open up a 'sale of shoes' account and a 'sale of boots' account, then at the end of the day, the ledger account postings are:

		£	£
DEBIT	Debtors account	1,487.80	
CREDIT	Sale of shoes account		541.10
	Sale of boots account		946.70

4.4   That is why the analysis of sales is kept. Exactly the same reasoning lies behind the analyses kept in other books of prime entry.

5   THE IMPREST SYSTEM   *5/97*

5.1   In the last chapter, we saw how the petty cash book was used to operate the imprest system for petty cash. It is now time to see how the double entry works in the imprest system.

5.2   Suppose a business starts off a cash float on 1.3.19X7 with £250. This will be a payment from cash at bank to petty cash, ie:

DEBIT	Petty cash	£250	
CREDIT	Cash at bank		£250

5.3   Suppose further that five payments were made out of petty cash during March 19X7. The petty cash book might look as follows.

					Payments	
Receipts £	*Date*	*Narrative*	*Total* £	*Postage* £		*Travel* £
250.00	1.3.X7	Cash				
	2.3.X7	Stamps	12.00	12.00		
	8.3.X7	Stamps	10.00	10.00		
	19.3.X7	Travel	16.00			16.00
	23.3.X7	Travel	5.00			5.00
	28.3.X7	Stamps	11.50	11.50		
250.00			54.50	33.50		21.00

5.4   At the end of each month (or at any other suitable interval) the total credits in the petty cash book are posted to ledger accounts. For March 19X7, £33.50 would be debited to postage account, and £21.00 to travel account. The cash float would need to be topped up by a payment of £54.50 from the main cash book, ie:

		£	£
DEBIT	Petty cash	54.50	
CREDIT	Cash		54.50

5.5   So the rules of double entry have been satisfied, and the petty cash book for the month of March 19X7 will look like this.

Receipts £	Date	Narrative	Total £	Payments Postage £	Travel £
250.00	1.3.X7	Cash			
	2.3.X7	Stamps	12.00	12.00	
	8.3.X7	Stamps	10.00	10.00	
	19.3.X7	Travel	16.00		16.00
	23.3.X7	Travel	5.00		5.00
	28.3.X7	Stamps	11.50	11.50	
	31.3.X7	Balance c/d	195.50		
250.00			250.00	33.50	21.00
195.50	1.4.X7	Balance b/d			
54.50	1.4.X7	Cash			

5.6   As you can see, the cash float is back up to £250 on 1.4.X7, ready for more payments to be made.

6   THE SALES AND PURCHASE LEDGERS

Impersonal accounts and personal accounts

6.1   The accounts in the nominal ledger (ledger accounts) relate to types of income, expense, asset, liability - rent, rates, sales, debtors, creditors etc - rather than to the person to whom the money is paid or from whom it is received. They are therefore called *impersonal* accounts. However, there is also a need for *personal* accounts, most commonly for debtors and creditors, and these are contained in the sales ledger and purchase ledger.

6.2   Personal accounts include details of transactions which have already been summarised in ledger accounts (eg sales invoices are recorded in sales and total debtors, payments to creditors in the cash and creditors accounts). The personal accounts do not therefore form part of the double entry system, as otherwise transactions would be recorded twice over (ie two debits and two credits for each transaction). They are *memorandum* accounts only.

The sales ledger

6.3   The sales day book provides a chronological record of invoices sent out by a business to credit customers. For many businesses, this might involve very large numbers of invoices per day or per week. The same customer might appear in several different places in the sales day book, for purchases he has made on credit at different times. So at any point in time, a customer may owe money on several unpaid invoices.

6.4   In addition to keeping a chronological record of invoices, a business should also keep a record of how much money each individual credit customer owes, and what this total debt consists of. The need for a *personal account* for each customer is a practical one.

(a)   A customer might telephone, and ask how much he currently owes. Staff must be able to tell him.

(b)   It is a common practice to send out statements to credit customers at the end of each month, showing how much they still owe, and itemising new invoices sent out and payments received during the month.

(c)   The managers of the business will want to keep a check on the credit position of an individual customer, and to ensure that no customer is exceeding his credit limit by purchasing more goods.

(d)   Most important is the need to match payments received against debts owed. If a customer makes a payment, the business must be able to set off the payment against the customer's debt and establish how much he still owes on balance.

6.5 Sales ledger accounts are written up as follows.

(a) When entries are made in the sales day book (invoices sent out), they are subsequently also made in the *debit side* of the relevant customer account in the sales ledger; and

(b) Similarly, when entries are made in the cash book (payments received), or in the sales returns day book, they are also made in the *credit side* of the relevant customer account.

6.6 Each customer account is given a reference or code number, and it is that reference which is the 'sales ledger folio' in the *sales day book*. We say that amounts are *posted* from the sales day book to the sales ledger.

6.7 Here is an example of how a sales ledger account is laid out.

ENOR COLLEGE

A/c no: SL 9

	£			£
Balance b/f	250.00			
10.1.X0 Sales - SDB 48				
(invoice no 250)	1,264.60	Balance c/d		1,514.60
	1,514.60			1,514.60
11.1.X0 Balance b/d	1,514.60			

6.8 The debit side of this personal account, then, shows amounts owed by Enor College. When Enor pays some of the money it owes it will be entered into the cash book (receipts) and subsequently 'posted' to the credit side of the personal account. For example, if the college paid £250 on 10.1.19X0, it would appear as follows.

ENOR COLLEGE

A/c no: SL 9

	£			£
Balance b/f	250.00	10.1.X0 Cash		250.00
10.1.X0 Sales - SDB 48				
(invoice no 250)	1,264.60	Balance c/d		1,264.60
	1,514.60			1,514.60
11.1.X0 Balance b/d	1,264.60			

6.9 The opening balance owed by Enor College on 11.1.X0 is now £1,264.60 instead of £1,514.60, because of the £250 receipt which came in on 10.1.X0.

The purchase ledger (bought ledger)

6.10 The purchase ledger, like the sales ledger, consists of a number of personal accounts. These are separate accounts for each individual supplier, and they enable a business to keep a continuous record of how much it owes each supplier at any time.

6.11 After entries are made in the purchase day book, cash book, or purchase returns day book - ie after entries are made in the books of prime entry - they are also made in the relevant supplier account in the purchase ledger. Again we say that the entries in the purchase day book are *posted* to the suppliers' personal accounts in the purchase ledger.

6.12 Here is an example of how a purchase ledger account is laid out.

COOK & CO

A/c no: SL 31

	£			£
Balance c/d	515.00		Balance b/f	200.00
			15 Mar 19X8	
			Invoice received	
			PDB 37	315.00
	515.00			515.00
			16 March 19X8	
			Balance b/d	515.00

6.13   The credit side of this personal account, then, shows amounts owing to Cook & Co. If the business paid Cook & Co some money, it would be entered into the cash book (payments) and subsequently be posted to the debit side of the personal account. For example, if the business paid Cook & Co £100 on 15 March 19X8, it would appear as follows:

COOK & CO

A/c no: SL 31

		£				£
15.3.X8	Cash	100.00		Balance b/f		200.00
			15.3.X8	Invoice received		
	Balance c/d	415.00	PDB 37			315.00
		515.00				515.00
			16.3.X8	Balance b/d		415.00

6.14   The opening balance owed to Cook & Co on 16.3.X8 is now £415.00 instead of £515.00 because of the £100 payment made during 15.3.X8.

6.15   The roles of the sales day book and purchases day book are very similar, with one book dealing with invoices sent out and the other with invoices received. The sales ledger and purchases ledger also serve similar purposes, with one consisting of personal accounts for credit customers and the other consisting of personal accounts for creditors.

Chapter roundup

- Double entry bookkeeping is based on the same idea as the accounting equation. Every accounting transaction alters the make-up of a business's assets and liabilities. But because the equality of assets and liabilities is always preserved, it follows that each transaction must have two equal but opposite effects.

- In a system of double entry bookkeeping every accounting event must be entered in ledger accounts both as a debit and as an equal but opposite credit. The principal accounts are contained in a ledger called the nominal ledger.

- Some accounts in the nominal ledger represent the total of very many smaller balances. For example, the debtors accounts represents all the balances owed by individual customers of the business, while the creditors account represents all amounts owed by the business to its suppliers.

- To keep track of individual customer and supplier balances, it is common to maintain subsidiary ledgers (called the sales ledger and the purchase ledger respectively). Each account in these ledgers represents the balance owed by or to an individual customer or supplier. These subsidiary ledgers are kept purely for reference and are therefore known as *memorandum* records. They do *not* normally form part of the double entry system.

- The rules of double entry bookkeeping are best learnt by considering the cash book. In the cash book a *credit* entry indicates a payment made by the business; the matching debit entry is then made in an account denoting an expense paid, an asset purchased or a liability settled. A *debit* entry in the cash book indicates cash received by the business; the matching credit entry is then made in an account denoting revenue received, a liability created or an asset sold.

Test your knowledge

1   Give six examples of nominal ledger accounts. (see para 1.3)

2   What is the double entry to record a cash sale of £50? (2.8(a))

3   What is the double entry to record a purchase of office chairs for £1,000? (2.8(d))

4   What is the double entry to record a credit sale? (2.14(a))

5   Name one reason for making a journal entry. (3.1)

6   What is the difference between the creditors account in the nominal ledger and the purchase ledger? (6.1)

Now try illustrative questions 7 and 8 at the end of the Study Text

Chapter 7

FROM TRIAL BALANCE TO FINANCIAL STATEMENTS

This chapter covers the following topics.

		Syllabus reference	Ability required
1	The trial balance	1(c)	Skill
2	The trading, profit and loss account	1(c)	Skill
3	The balance sheet	1(c)	Skill
4	Balancing accounts and preparing financial statements	1(c)	Skill

Introduction

In the previous chapter you learned the principles of double entry and how to post to the ledger accounts. The next step in our progress towards the financial statements is the trial balance.

Before transferring the relevant balances at the year end to the profit and loss account and putting closing balances carried forward into the balance sheet, it is usual to test the accuracy of double entry bookkeeping records by preparing a trial balance. This is done by taking all the balances on every account. Because of the self-balancing nature of the system of double entry the total of the debit balances will be exactly equal to the total of the credit balances.

In very straightforward circumstances, where no complications arise and where the records are complete, it is possible to prepare accounts directly from a trial balance. This is covered in Section 4.

Exam questions at all levels in financial accounting sometimes involve preparation of final accounts from trial balance. Last but not least, you may end up having to do it in 'real life'.

1 THE TRIAL BALANCE

1.1 Imagine that an examination question has given you a list of transactions, and has asked you to post them to the relevant ledger accounts. You do it as quickly as possible and find that you have a little time left over at the end of the examination. How do you check that you have posted all the debit and credit entries properly?

There is no foolproof method, but a technique which shows up the more obvious mistakes is to prepare a *trial balance*.

The first step

1.2 Before you draw up a trial balance, you must have a collection of ledger accounts. For the sake of convenience, we will use the accounts of Ron Knuckle, which we drew up in the previous chapter.

CASH

	£		£
Capital - Ron Knuckle (A)	7,000	Rent	3,500
Bank loan	1,000	Shop fittings	2,000
Sales	10,000	Trade creditors	5,000
Debtors	2,500	Bank loan interest	100
		Incidental expenses	1,900
		Drawings	1,500
			14,000
		Balancing figure - the amount of cash left over after payments have been made	6,500
	20,500		20,500

CAPITAL (RON KNUCKLE)

	£		£
		Cash	7,000

BANK LOAN

	£		£
		Cash	1,000

PURCHASES

	£		£
Trade creditors	5,000		

TRADE CREDITORS

	£		£
Cash	5,000	Purchases	5,000

RENT

	£		£
Cash	3,500		

SHOP FITTINGS

	£		£
Cash	2,000		

SALES

	£		£
		Cash	10,000
		Debtors	2,500
			12,500

DEBTORS

	£		£
Sales	2,500	Cash	2,500

BANK LOAN INTEREST

	£		£
Cash	100		

OTHER EXPENSES

	£		£
Cash	1,900		

DRAWINGS ACCOUNT

	£		£
Cash	1,500		

1.3   The next step is to 'balance' each account.

Balancing ledger accounts

1.4   At the end of an accounting period, a balance is struck on each account in turn. This means that all the debits on the account are totalled and so are all the credits. If the total debits exceed the total credits there is said to be a debit balance on the account; if the credits exceed the debits then the account has a credit balance.

1.5   In our simple example, there is very little balancing to do.

(a)   Both the trade creditors account and the debtors account balance off to zero.
(b)   The cash account has a debit balance of £6,500.
(c)   The total on the sales account is £12,500, which is a credit balance.

Otherwise, the accounts have only one entry each, so there is no totalling to do to arrive at the balance on each account.

Collecting the balances

1.6   If the basic principle of double entry has been correctly applied throughout the period it will be found that the credit balances equal the debit balances in total. This can be illustrated by collecting together the balances on Ron Knuckle's accounts.

	Debit £	Credit £
Cash	6,500	
Capital		7,000
Bank loan		1,000
Purchases	5,000	
Trade creditors	-	-
Rent	3,500	
Shop fittings	2,000	
Sales		12,500
Debtors	-	-
Bank loan interest	100	
Other expenses	1,900	
Drawings	1,500	
	20,500	20,500

1.7   This list of balances is called the trial balance. It does not matter in what order the various accounts are listed, because the trial balance is not a document that a company *has* to prepare. It is just a method used to test the accuracy of the double entry bookkeeping methods.

What if the trial balance shows unequal debit and credit balances?

1.8   If the two columns of the trial balance are not equal, there must be an error in recording the transactions in the accounts. A trial balance, however, will not disclose the following types of errors.

(a) The complete omission of a transaction, because neither a debit nor a credit is made.

(b) The posting of a debit or credit to the correct side of the ledger, but to a wrong account.

(c) Compensating errors (eg an error of £100 is exactly cancelled by another £100 error elsewhere).

(d) Errors of principle, eg cash received from debtors being debited to the debtors account and credited to cash instead of the other way round.

Example: trial balance

1.9 As at 30.3.19X7, your business has the following balances on its ledger accounts.

Accounts	Balance
	£
Bank loan	12,000
Cash	11,700
Capital	13,000
Rates	1,880
Trade creditors	11,200
Purchases	12,400
Sales	14,600
Sundry creditors	1,620
Debtors	12,000
Bank loan interest	1,400
Other expenses	11,020
Vehicles	2,020

During the year the business made the following transactions.

(a) Bought materials for £1,000, half for cash and half on credit.
(b) Made £1,040 sales, £800 of which was for credit.
(c) Paid wages to shop assistants of £260 in cash.

You are required to draw up a trial balance showing the balances as at the end of 31.3.X7.

Solution

1.10 First it is necessary to put the original balances into a trial balance - ie decide which are debit and which are credit balances.

Account	Dr	Cr
	£	£
Bank loan		12,000
Cash	11,700	
Capital		13,000
Rates	1,880	
Trade creditors		11,200
Purchases	12,400	
Sales		14,600
Sundry creditors		1,620
Debtors	12,000	
Bank loan interest	1,400	
Other expenses	11,020	
Vehicles	2,020	
	52,420	52,420

1.11   Now we must take account of the effects of the three transactions which took place on 31.3.X7.

			£	£
(a)	DEBIT	Purchases	1,000	
	CREDIT	Cash		500
		Trade creditors		500
(b)	DEBIT	Cash	240	
		Debtors	800	
	CREDIT	Sales		1,040
(c)	DEBIT	Other expenses	260	
	CREDIT	Cash		260

1.12   When these figures are included in the trial balance, it becomes:

Account	Dr	Cr
	£	£
Bank loan		12,000
Cash	11,180	
Capital		13,000
Rates	1,880	
Trade creditors		11,700
Purchases	13,400	
Sales		15,640
Sundry creditors		1,620
Debtors	12,800	
Bank loan interest	1,400	
Other expenses	11,280	
Vehicles	2,020	
	53,960	53,960

2   THE TRADING, PROFIT AND LOSS ACCOUNT

2.1   The first step in the process of preparing the financial statements is to open up another ledger account, called the trading, profit and loss account. In it a business summarises its results for the period by gathering together all the ledger account balances relating to income and expenses. This account is still part of the double entry system, so the basic rule of double entry still applies: every debit must have an equal and opposite credit entry.

2.2   This trading, profit and loss account we have opened up is not the financial statement we are aiming for, even though it has the same name. The difference between the two is not very great, because they contain the same information. However, the financial statement lays it out differently and may be much less detailed.

2.3   So what do we do with this new ledger account? The first step is to look through the ledger accounts and identify which ones relate to income and expenses. In the case of Ron Knuckle, the income and expense accounts consist of purchases, rent, sales, bank loan interest, and other expenses.

2.4   The balances on these accounts are transferred to the new trading, profit and loss account. For example, the balance on the purchases account is £5,000 DR. To balance this to zero, we write in £5,000 CR. But to comply with the rule of double entry, there has to be a debit entry somewhere, so we write £5,000 DR in the trading, profit and loss account. Now the balance on the purchases account has been moved to the trading, profit and loss account.

2.5   If we do the same thing with all the income and expense accounts of Ron Knuckle, the result is as follows.

PURCHASES

Trade creditors	£ 5,000	Trading, P & L a/c	£ 5,000

RENT

\Cash	£ 3,500	Trading, P & L a/c	£ 3,500

SALES

Trading, P & L a/c	£ 12,500 12,500	Cash Debtors	£ 10,000 2,500 12,500

BANK LOAN INTEREST

Cash	£ 100	Trading, P & L a/c	£ 100

OTHER EXPENSES

Cash	£ 1,900	Trading, P & L a/c	£ 1,900

TRADING, PROFIT AND LOSS ACCOUNT

	£		£
Purchases	5,000	Sales	12,500
Rent	3,500		
Bank loan interest	100		
Other expenses	1,900		

(Note that the trading, profit and loss account has not yet been balanced off but we will return to that later.)

2.6 If you look at the items we have gathered together in the trading, profit and loss account, they should strike a chord in your memory. They are the same items that we need to draw up the trading, profit and loss account in the form of a financial statement. With a little rearrangement they could be presented as follows.

RON KNUCKLE: TRADING, PROFIT AND LOSS ACCOUNT

	£	£
Sales		12,500
Cost of sales (= purchases in this case)		(5,000)
Gross profit		7,500
Expenses		
Rent	3,500	
Bank loan interest	100	
Other expenses	1,900	
		(5,500)
Net profit		2,000

3   THE BALANCE SHEET

3.1 Look back at the ledger accounts of Ron Knuckle. Now that we have dealt with those relating to income and expenses, which ones are left? The answer is that we still have to find out what to do with cash, capital, bank loan, trade creditors, shop fittings, debtors and the drawings account.

3.2 Are these the only ledger accounts left? No: don't forget there is still the last one we opened up, called the trading, profit and loss account. The balance on this account represents the profit earned by the business, and if you go through the arithmetic, you will find that it has a credit balance - a profit - of £2,000. (Not surprisingly, this is the figure that is shown in the trading profit and loss account financial statement.)

3.3 These remaining accounts must also be balanced and ruled off, but since they represent assets and liabilities of the business (not income and expenses) their balances are not transferred to the trading profit and loss account. Instead they are *carried down* in the books of the business. This means that they become opening balances for the next accounting period and indicate the value of the assets and liabilities at the end of one period and the beginning of the next.

3.4 The conventional method of ruling off a ledger account at the end of an accounting period is illustrated by the bank loan account in Ron Knuckle's books.

BANK LOAN ACCOUNT

	£		£
Balance carried down (c/d)	1,000	Cash (D)	1,000
		Balance brought down (b/d)	1,000

3.5 Ron Knuckle therefore begins the new accounting period with a credit balance of £1,000 on this account. A credit balance brought down denotes a liability. An asset would be represented by a debit balance brought down.

3.6 One further point is worth noting before we move on to complete this example. You will remember that a proprietor's capital comprises any cash introduced by him, plus any profits made by the business, less any drawings made by him. At the stage we have now reached these three elements are contained in different ledger accounts: cash introduced of £7,000 appears in the capital account; drawings of £1,500 appear in the drawings account; and the profit made by the business is represented by the £2,000 credit balance on the trading profit and loss account. It is convenient to gather together all these amounts into one capital account, in the same way as we earlier gathered together income and expense accounts into one trading and profit and loss account.

3.7 If we go ahead and gather the three amounts together, the results are as follows.

DRAWINGS

	£		£
Cash	1,500	Capital a/c	1,500

TRADING, PROFIT AND LOSS ACCOUNT

	£		£
Purchases	5,000	Sales	12,500
Rent	3,500		
Bank loan interest	100		
Other expenses	1,900		
Capital a/c	2,000		
	12,500		12,500

CAPITAL

	£		£
Drawings	1,500	Cash	7,000
Balance c/d	7,500	Trading, P & L a/c	2,000
	9,000		9,000
		Balance b/d	7,500

3.8   A re-arrangement of these balances will complete Ron Knuckle's simple balance sheet:

RON KNUCKLE
BALANCE SHEET AT END OF FIRST TRADING PERIOD

	£
Fixed assets	
Shop fittings	2,000
Current assets	
Cash	6,500
Total assets	8,500
Liabilities	
Bank loan	(1,000)
Net assets	7,500
Proprietor's capital	7,500

3.9   When a balance sheet is drawn up for an accounting period which is not the first one, then it ought to show the capital at the start of the accounting period and the capital at the end of the accounting period. This will be illustrated in the next example.

3.10   In an examination question, you might not be given the ledger accounts - you might have to draw them up in the first place. That is the case with the following exercise - see if you can do it by yourself before looking at the solution.

4   BALANCING ACCOUNTS AND PREPARING FINANCIAL STATEMENTS

4.1   The exercise which follows is by far the most important in this text so far. It uses all the accounting steps from entering up ledger accounts to preparing the financial statements, and is set out in a style which you might well find in an examination. It is very important that you try the question by yourself: if you do not, you will be missing out a vital part of this text.

Exercise

A business is established with capital of £2,000, and this amount is paid into a business bank account by the proprietor. During the first year's trading, the following transactions occurred:

	£
Purchases of goods for resale, on credit	4,300
Payments to trade creditors	3,600
Sales, all on credit	5,800
Payments from debtors	3,200
Fixed assets purchased for cash	1,500
Other expenses, all paid in cash	900

The bank has provided an overdraft facility of up to £3,000.

Prepare the ledger accounts, a trading, profit and loss account for the year and a balance sheet as at the end of the year.

Solution

The first thing to do is to open ledger accounts so that the transactions can be entered up. The relevant accounts which we need for this example are: cash; capital; trade creditors; purchases; fixed assets; sales and debtors; other expenses.

The next step is to work out the double entry bookkeeping for each transaction. Normally you would write them straight into the accounts, but to make this example easier to follow, they are first listed below.

(a) Establishing business (£2,000)   DR Cash;   CR Capital
(b) Purchases (£4,300)   DR Purchases;   CR Creditors
(c) Payments to creditors (£3,600)   DR Creditors;   CR Cash
(d) Sales (£5,800)   DR Debtors;   CR Sales
(e) Payments by debtors (£3,200)   DR Cash;   CR Debtors
(f) Fixed assets (£1,500)   DR Fixed assets; CR Cash
(g) Other (cash) expenses (£900)   DR Other expenses; CR Cash

So far, the ledger accounts will look like this.

CASH

	£		£
Capital	2,000	Creditors	3,600
		Fixed assets	1,500
Debtors	3,200	Other expenses	900

CAPITAL

	£		£
		Cash	2,000

CREDITORS

	£		£
Cash	3,600	Purchases	4,300

PURCHASES

	£		£
Creditors	4,300		

FIXED ASSETS

	£		£
Cash	1,500		

SALES

	£		£
		Debtors	5,800

DEBTORS

	£		£
Sales	5,800	Cash	3,200

OTHER EXPENSES

	£		£
Cash	900		

The next thing to do is to balance all these accounts. It is at this stage that you could, if you wanted to, draw up a trial balance to make sure the double entries are accurate. There is not very much point in this simple example, but if you did draw up a trial balance, it would look like this.

	Dr £	Cr £
Cash		800
Capital		2,000
Creditors		700
Purchases	4,300	
Fixed assets	1,500	
Sales		5,800
Debtors	2,600	
Other expenses	900	
	9,300	9,300

After balancing the accounts, the trading, profit and loss account should be opened. Into it should be transferred all the balances relating to income and expenses (ie purchases, other expenses, and sales). At this point, the ledger accounts will be:

CASH

	£		£
Capital	2,000	Trade creditors	3,600
Debtors	3,200	Fixed assets	1,500
Balance c/d	800	Other expenses	900
	6,000		6,000
		Balance b/d	800*

* A credit balance b/d means that this cash item is a liability, not an asset. This indicates a bank overdraft of £800, with cash income of £5,200 falling short of payments of £6,000 by this amount.

CAPITAL

	£		£
Balance c/d	2,600	Cash	2,000
		P & L a/c	600
	2,600		2,600

TRADE CREDITORS

	£		£
Cash	3,600	Stores (purchases)	4,300
Balance c/d	700		
	4,300		4,300
		Balance b/d	700

PURCHASES ACCOUNT

	£		£
Trade creditors	4,300	Trading a/c	4,300

FIXED ASSETS

	£		£
Cash	1,500	Balance c/d	1,500
Balance b/d	1,500		

SALES

	£		£
Trading a/c	5,800		5,800

DEBTORS

	£		£
Sales	5,800	Cash	3,200
		Balance c/d	2,600
	5,800		5,800
Balance b/d	2,600		

OTHER EXPENSES

	£		£
Cash	900	P & L a/c	900

TRADING, PROFIT AND LOSS ACCOUNT

	£		£
Purchases account	4,300	Sales	5,800
Gross profit c/d	1,500		
	5,800		5,800
Other expenses	900	Gross profit b/d	1,500
Net profit (transferred to capital account)	600		
	1,500		1,500

So the trading, profit and loss account financial statement will be:

TRADING, PROFIT AND LOSS ACCOUNT
FOR THE ACCOUNTING PERIOD

	£
Sales	5,800
Cost of sales (purchases)	(4,300)
Gross profit	1,500
Expenses	900
Net profit	600

Listing and then rearranging the balances on the ledger accounts gives the balance sheet as:

BALANCE SHEET AS AT THE END OF THE PERIOD

	£	£
Fixed assets		1,500
Current assets		
Debtors	2,600	
Current liabilities		
Bank overdraft	800	
Trade creditors	700	
	1,500	
Net current assets		1,100
		2,600
Capital		
At start of period		2,000
Net profit for period		600
At end of period		2,600

4.2   In an examination you need not spell out your answer in quite such detail. The detail is given here to help you to work through the example properly, and you may wish to do things this way yourself until you get more practised in accounting techniques and are confident enough to take short cuts.

Chapter roundup

- At suitable intervals, the entries in each ledger accounts are totalled and a balance is struck. Balances are usually collected in a trial balance which is then used as a basis for preparing a profit and loss account and a balance sheet.

- A trial balance can be used to test the accuracy of the double entry accounting records. It works by listing the balances on ledger accounts, some of which will be debits and some credits, to see if they balance off to zero.

- A profit and loss ledger account is opened up to gather all items relating to income and expenses. When rearranged, the items make up the profit and loss account financial statement.

- The balances on all remaining ledger accounts (including the profit and loss account) can be listed and rearranged to form the balance sheet.

Test your knowledge

1   What is the purpose of a trial balance? (see para 1.1)

2   Give four circumstances in which a trial balance might balance although some of the balances are wrong. (1.8)

3   What is the difference between the ledger account and the financial statement both called the trading, profit and loss account? (2.1, 2.2)

4   What is the difference between balancing off an expense account and balancing off a liability account? (3.3)

Now try illustrative questions 9 to 11 at the end of the Study Text

Chapter 8

THE COST OF GOODS SOLD, ACCRUALS AND PREPAYMENTS

This chapter covers the following topics.

		Syllabus reference	*Ability required*
1	The accounting treatment of stocks and carriage costs	1(b)	Skill
2	Accruals and prepayments	1(b)	Skill

Introduction

When we looked at the trading, profit and loss account near the start of this text, we defined profit as the value of sales less the cost of sales and expenses. This definition might seem simple enough; however, it is not always immediately clear how much the cost of sales or expenses are. A variety of difficulties can arise in measuring them: some of these problems can be dealt with fairly easily, whereas others are less obvious to solve. The purpose of this chapter is to describe some of these problems and their solutions.

In this chapter, we shall consider unsold goods in stock at the beginning and end of an accounting period, carriage costs, writing off or writing down stock values, and the accounting treatment of accruals and prepayments. Their common feature is that they are applications of the accruals concept or matching concept described in Chapter 2.

---

1   THE ACCOUNTING TREATMENT OF STOCKS AND CARRIAGE COSTS

Unsold goods in stock at the end of an accounting period

1.1   Goods might be unsold at the end of an accounting period and so still be held in stock at the end of the period. The purchase cost of these goods should not be included therefore in the cost of sales of the period.

Example: closing stock

1.2   Suppose that Perry P Louis, trading as the Umbrella Shop, ends his financial year on 30 September each year. On 1 October 19X4 he had no goods in stock. During the year to 30 September 19X5, he purchased 30,000 umbrellas costing £60,000 from umbrella wholesalers and suppliers. He resold the umbrellas for £5 each, and sales for the year amounted to £100,000 (20,000 umbrellas). At 30 September there were 10,000 unsold umbrellas left in stock, valued at £2 each.

What was Perry P Louis's gross profit for the year?

Solution

1.3   Perry P Louis purchased 30,000 umbrellas, but only sold 20,000. Purchase costs of £60,000 and sales of £100,000 do not represent the same quantity of goods.

The gross profit for the year should be calculated by 'matching' the sales value of the 20,000 umbrellas sold with the cost of those 20,000 umbrellas. The cost of sales in this example is therefore the cost of purchases minus the cost of goods in stock at the year end.

	£	£
Sales (20,000 units)		100,000
Purchases (30,000 units)	60,000	
Less closing stock (10,000 units @ £2)	20,000	
Cost of sales (20,000 units)		40,000
Gross profit		60,000

Example continued

1.4   We shall continue the example of the Umbrella Shop into its next accounting year, 1 October 19X5 to 30 September 19X6. Suppose that during the course of this year, Perry P Louis purchased 40,000 umbrellas at a total cost of £95,000. During the year he sold 45,000 umbrellas for £230,000. At 30 September 19X6 he had 5,000 umbrellas left in stock, which had cost £12,000.

What was his gross profit for the year?

Solution

1.5   In this accounting year, he purchased 40,000 umbrellas to add to the 10,000 he already had in stock at the start of the year. He sold 45,000, leaving 5,000 umbrellas in stock at the year end. Once again, gross profit should be calculated by matching the value of 45,000 units of sales with the cost of those 45,000 units.

The cost of sales is the value of the 10,000 umbrellas in stock at the beginning of the year, plus the cost of the 40,000 umbrellas purchased, less the value of the 5,000 umbrellas in stock at the year end.

	£	£
Sales (45,000 units)		230,000
Opening stock (10,000 units) *	20,000	
Add purchases (40,000 units)	95,000	
	115,000	
Less closing stock (5,000 units)	12,000	
Cost of sales (45,000 units)		103,000
Gross profit		127,000

*Taken from the closing stock value of the previous accounting year, see paragraph 1.3.

The cost of goods sold

1.6   The cost of goods sold is found by applying the following formula.

	£
Opening stock value	X
Add cost of purchases (or, in the case of a manufacturing company, the cost of production)	X
	X
Less closing stock value	(X)
Equals cost of goods sold	X

In other words, to match 'sales' and the 'cost of goods sold', it is necessary to adjust the cost of goods manufactured or purchased to allow for increases or reduction in stock levels during the period.

1.7   You might agree that the 'formula' above is based on a logical idea. You should learn it, because it is fundamental among the principles of accounting.

Test your knowledge of the formula with the following example.

Example: cost of goods sold and variations in stock levels

1.8 On 1 January 19X6, the Grand Union Food Stores had goods in stock valued at £6,000. During 19X6 its proprietor, who ran the shop, purchased supplies costing £50,000. Sales turnover for the year to 31 December 19X6 amounted to £80,000. The cost of goods in stock at 31 December 19X6 was £12,500.

Calculate the gross profit for the year.

Solution

1.9 GRAND UNION FOOD STORES
TRADING ACCOUNT FOR THE YEAR ENDED 31 DECEMBER 19X6

	£	£
Sales		80,000
Opening stocks	6,000	
Add purchases	50,000	
	56,000	
Less closing stocks	12,500	
Cost of goods sold		43,500
Gross profit		36,500

The cost of carriage inwards and outwards

1.10 'Carriage' refers to the cost of transporting purchased goods from the supplier to the premises of the business which has bought them. Someone has to pay for these delivery costs: sometimes the supplier pays, and sometimes the purchaser pays. When the purchaser pays, the cost to the purchaser is carriage inwards. When the supplier pays, the cost to the supplier is known as carriage outwards.

1.11 The cost of carriage inwards is usually added to the cost of purchases, and is therefore included in the trading account.

The cost of carriage outwards is a selling and distribution expense in the profit and loss account.

Example: carriage inwards and carriage outwards

1.12 Gwyn Tring, trading as Clickety Clocks, imports and resells cuckoo clocks and grandfather clocks. He must pay for the costs of delivering the clocks from his supplier in Switzerland to his shop in Wales.

He resells the clocks to other traders throughout the country, paying the costs of carriage for the consignments from his business premises to his customers.

On 1 July 19X5, he had clocks in stock valued at £17,000. During the year to 30 June 19X6 he purchased more clocks at a cost of £75,000. Carriage inwards amounted to £2,000. Sales for the year were £162,100. Other expenses of the business amounted to £56,000 excluding carriage outwards which cost £2,500. Gwyn Tring took drawings of £20,000 from the business during the course of the year. The value of the goods in stock at the year end was £15,400.

Required

Prepare the trading, profit and loss account of Clickety Clocks for the year ended 30 June 19X6.

Solution

1.13   CLICKETY CLOCKS
       TRADING, PROFIT AND LOSS ACCOUNT FOR THE YEAR ENDED 30 JUNE 19X6

	£	£
Sales		162,100
Opening stock	17,000	
Purchases	75,000	
Carriage inwards	2,000	
	94,000	
Less closing stock	15,400	
Cost of goods sold		78,600
Gross profit		83,500
Carriage outwards	2,500	
Other expenses	56,000	
		58,500
Net profit (transferred to balance sheet)		25,000

Goods written off or written down

1.14   A trader might be unable to sell all the goods that he purchases, because a number of things might happen to the goods before they can be sold. For example:

   (a)   goods might be lost or stolen;

   (b)   goods might be damaged, and so become worthless. Such damaged goods might be thrown away;

   (c)   goods might become obsolete or out of fashion. These might have to be thrown away, or possibly sold off at a very low price in a clearance sale.

1.15   When goods are lost, stolen or thrown away as worthless, the business will make a loss on those goods because their 'sales value' will be nil.

       Similarly, when goods lose value because they have become obsolete or out of fashion, the business will make a loss if their clearance sales value is less than their cost. For example, if goods which originally cost £500 are now obsolete and could only be sold for £150, the business would suffer a loss of £350.

1.16   If, at the end of an accounting period, a business still has goods in stock which are either worthless or worth less than their original cost, the value of the stocks should be written down to:

   (a)   nothing, if they are worthless; or
   (b)   their net realisable value, if this is less than their original cost.

       This means that the loss will be reported as soon as the loss is foreseen, even if the goods have not yet been thrown away or sold off at a cheap price. This is an application of another concept - the prudence concept - which we will look at in a later chapter.

1.17   The costs of stock written off or written down should not usually cause any problems in calculating the gross profit of a business, because the cost of goods sold will include the cost of stocks written off or written down, as the following example shows.

Example: stocks written off and written down

1.18   Lucas Wagg, trading as Fairlock Fashions, ends his financial year on 31 March. At 1 April 19X5 he had goods in stock valued at £8,800. During the year to 31 March 19X6, he purchased goods costing £48,000. Fashion goods which cost £2,100 were still held in stock at 31 March 19X6, and Lucas Wagg believes that these could only now be sold at a sale price of £400. The goods still held in stock at 31 March 19X6 (including the fashion goods) had an original purchase cost of £7,600. Sales for the year were £81,400.

Required

Calculate the gross profit of Fairlock Fashions for the year ended 31 March 19X6.

Solution

1.19 Initial calculation of closing stock values:

STOCK COUNT

	At cost £	Realisable value £	Amount written down £
Fashion goods	2,100	400	1,700
Other goods (balancing figure)	5,500	5,500	
	7,600	5,900	1,700

FAIRLOCK FASHIONS
TRADING ACCOUNT FOR THE YEAR ENDED 31 MARCH 19X6

	£	£
Sales		81,400
Value of opening stock	8,800	
Purchases	48,000	
	56,800	
Less closing stock	5,900	
Cost of goods sold		50,900
Gross profit		30,500

2 ACCRUALS AND PREPAYMENTS

11/96

Introduction

2.1 It has already been stated that the gross profit for a period should be calculated by matching sales and the cost of goods sold. In the same way, the net profit for a period should be calculated by charging the expenses which relate to that period. For example, in preparing the profit and loss account of a business for a period of, say, six months, it would be appropriate to charge six months' expenses for rent and rates, insurance costs and telephone costs etc.

2.2 Expenses might not be paid for during the period to which they relate. For example, if a business rents a shop for £20,000 per annum, it might pay the full annual rent on, say, 1 April each year. Now if we were to calculate the profit of the business for the first six months of the year 19X7, the correct charge for rent in the profit and loss account would be £10,000 even though the rent payment would be £20,000 in that period. Similarly, the rent charge in a profit and loss account for the business in the second six months of the year would be £10,000, even though no rent payment would be made in that six month period.

2.3 Accruals or accrued expenses are expenses which are charged against the profit for a particular period, even though they have not yet been paid for. Prepayments are payments which have been made in one accounting period, but should not be charged against profit until a later period, because they relate to that later period.

2.4 Accruals and prepayments might seem difficult at first, but the following examples might help to clarify the principle involved, that expenses should be matched against the period to which they relate.

Example: accruals

2.5 Horace Goodrunning, trading as Goodrunning Motor Spares, ends his financial year on 28 February each year. His telephone was installed on 1 April 19X6 and he receives his telephone account quarterly at the end of each quarter. He pays it promptly as soon as it is received. On the basis of the following data, you are required to calculate the telephone expense to be charged to the profit and loss account for the year ended 28 February 19X7.

Goodrunning Motor Spares - telephone expense for the three months ended:

	£
30.6.19X6	23.50
30.9.19X6	27.20
31.12.19X6	33.40
31.3.19X7	36.00

Solution

2.6 The telephone expenses for the year ended 28 February 19X7 are:

	£
1 March - 31 March 19X6 (no telephone)	0.00
1 April - 30 June 19X6	23.50
1 July - 30 September 19X6	27.20
1 October - 31 December 19X6	33.40
1 January - 28 February 19X7 (two months)	24.00
	108.10

The charge for the period 1 January - 28 February 19X7 is two-thirds of the quarterly charge received on 31 March. As at 28 February 19X7, no telephone bill has been received for the quarter, because it is not due for another month. However, it would be inappropriate to ignore the telephone expenses for January and February, and so an accrued charge of £24 should be made, being two-thirds of the quarter's bill of £36.

The accrued charge will also appear in the balance sheet of the business as at 28 February 19X7, as a current liability.

Exercise 1

Ratsnuffer is a business dealing in pest control. Its owner, Roy Dent, employs a team of eight who were paid £12,000 per annum each in the year to 31 December 19X5. At the start of 19X6 he raised salaries by 10% to £13,200 per annum each.

On 1 July 19X6, he hired a trainee at a salary of £8,400 per annum.

He pays his work force on the first working day of every month, one month in arrears, so that his employees receive their salary for January on the first working day in February, etc.

Required

(a) Calculate the cost of salaries which would be charged in the profit and loss account of Ratsnuffer for the year ended 31 December 19X6.

(b) Calculate the amount actually paid in salaries during the year (ie the amount of cash received by the work force).

(c) State the amount of accrued charges for salaries which would appear in the balance sheet of Ratsnuffer as at 31 December 19X6.

Solution

(a) Salaries cost in the profit and loss account

	£
Cost of 8 employees for a full year at £13,200 each	105,600
Cost of trainee for a half year	4,200
	109,800

(b) *Salaries actually paid in 19X6*

	£
December 19X5 salaries paid in January (8 employees × £1,000 per month)	8,000
Salaries of 8 employees for January - November 19X6 paid in February - December (8 employees × £1,100 per month × 11 months)	96,800
Salaries of trainee (for July - November paid in August - December 19X6: 5 months × £700 per month)	3,500
Salaries actually paid	108,300

(c)   *Accrued salaries costs as at 31 December 19X6*
      (ie costs charged in the P & L account, but not yet paid)

	£
8 employees x 1 month x £1,100 per month	8,800
1 trainee x 1 month x £700 per month	700
	9,500

(d)   *Summary*

	£
Accrued wages costs as at 31 December 19X5	8,000
Add salaries cost for 19X6 (P & L account)	109,800
	117,800
Less salaries paid	108,300
Equals accrued wages costs as at 31 December 19X6	9,500

Example: prepayments

2.7   The Square Wheels Garage pays fire insurance annually in advance on 1 June each year. The firm's financial year end is 28 February. From the following record of insurance payments you are required to calculate the charge to profit and loss for the financial year to 28 February 19X8.

	Insurance paid
	£
1.6.19X6	600
1.6.19X7	700

2.8   Insurance cost for:

	£
(a) the 3 months, 1 March - 31 May 19X7 (3/12 × £600)	150
(b) the 9 months, 1 June 19X7 - 28 February 19X8 (9/12 × £700)	525
Insurance cost for the year, charged to the P & L account	675

At 28 February 19X8 there is a prepayment for fire insurance, covering the period 1 March - 31 May 19X8. This insurance premium was paid on 1 June 19X7, but only nine months worth of the full annual cost is chargeable to the accounting period ended 28 February 19X8. The prepayment of (3/12 × £700) £175 as at 28 February 19X8 will appear as a current asset in the balance sheet of the Square Wheels Garage as at that date.

In the same way, there was a prepayment of (3/12 × £600) £150 in the balance sheet one year earlier as at 28 February 19X7.

Summary	£
Prepaid insurance premiums as at 28 February 19X7	150
Add insurance premiums paid 1 June 19X7	700
	850
Less insurance costs charged to the P & L account for the year ended 28 February 19X8	675
Equals prepaid insurance premiums as at 28 February 19X8	175

Exercise 2

The Batley Print Shop rents a photocopying machine from a supplier for which it makes a quarterly payment as follows:

(a)   three months rental in advance;
(b)   a further charge of 2 pence per copy made during the quarter just ended.

The rental agreement began on 1 August 19X4 and the first six quarterly bills were as follows.

Bills dated and received	Rental	Costs of copies taken	Total
	£	£	£
1 August 19X4	2,100	0	2,100
1 November 19X4	2,100	1,500	3,600
1 February 19X5	2,100	1,400	3,500
1 May 19X5	2,100	1,800	3,900
1 August 19X5	2,700	1,650	4,350
1 November 19X5	2,700	1,950	4,650

The bills are paid promptly, as soon as they are received.

(a) Calculate the charge for photocopying expenses for the year to 31 August 19X4 and the amount of prepayments and/or accrued charges as at that date.

(b) Calculate the charge for photocopying expenses for the following year to 31 August 19X5, and the amount of prepayments and/or accrued charges as at that date.

Solution

(a) *Year to 31 August 19X4*   £

One months' rental (1/3 × £2,100) *   700
Accrued copying charges (1/3 × £1,500) **   500
Photocopying expense (P & L account)   1,200

*   From the quarterly bill dated 1 August 19X4
**   From the quarterly bill dated 1 November 19X4

There is a prepayment for 2 months' rental (£1,400) as at 31 August 19X4.

(b) *Year to 31 August 19X5*

	£	£
Rental from 1 September 19X4 - 31 July 19X5 (11 months at £2,100 per quarter or £700 per month)		7,700
Rental from 1 August - 31 August 19X5 (1/3 × £2,700)		900
Rental charge for the year		8,600
Copying charges		
1 September - 31 October 19X4 (2/3 × £1,500)	1,000	
1 November 19X4 - 31 January 19X5	1,400	
1 February - 30 April 19X5	1,800	
1 May - 31 July 19X5	1,650	
Accrued charges for August 19X5 (1/3 × £1,950)	650	
		6,500
Total photocopying expenses (P & L account)		15,100

There is a prepayment for 2 months' rental (£1,800) as at 31 August 19X5.

Summary of year 1 September 19X4 - 31 August 19X5

	Rental charges	Copying costs
	£	£
Prepayments as at 31.8.19X4	1,400	
Accrued charges as at 31.8.19X4		(500)
Bills received during the year		
1 November 19X4	2,100	1,500
1 February 19X5	2,100	1,400
1 May 19X5	2,100	1,800
1 August 19X5	2,700	1,650
Prepayment as at 31.8.19X5	(1,800)	
Accrued charges as at 31.8.19X5		650
Charge to the P & L account for the year	8,600	6,500
Balance sheet items as at 31 August 19X5		
Prepaid rental (current asset)	1,800	
Accrued copying charges (current liability)		650

Further example: accruals

2.9   Suppose that Willie Woggle opens a shop on 1 May 19X6 to sell hiking and camping equipment. The rent of the shop is £12,000 per annum, payable quarterly in arrears (with the first payment on 31 July 19X6). Willie decides that his accounting period should end on 31 December each year.

2.10 The rent account as at 31 December 19X6 will record only two rental payments (on 31 July and 31 October) and there will be two months' accrued rental expenses for November and December 19X6, (£2,000) since the next rental payment is not due until 31 January 19X7.

The charge to the P & L account for the period to 31 December 19X6 will be for 8 months' rent (May-December inclusive) and so it follows that the total rental cost should be £8,000.

2.11 So far, the rent account appears as follows.

RENT ACCOUNT

		£			£
19X6			*19X6*		
31 July	Cash	3,000			
31 Oct	Cash	3,000	31 Dec	P & L account	8,000

2.12 To complete the picture, the accruals of £2,000 have to be put in, not only to balance the account, but also to have an opening balance of £2,000 ready for next year. So the accrued rent of £2,000 is debited to the rent account as a balance to be carried down, and credited to the rent account as a balance brought down.

RENT ACCOUNT

		£			£
19X6			*19X6*		
31 July	Cash *	3,000			
31 Oct	Cash *	3,000			
31 Dec	Balance c/d (accruals)	2,000	31 Dec	P & L account	8,000
		8,000			8,000
			19X7		
			1 Jan	Balance b/d	2,000

* The corresponding credit entry would be cash if rent is paid without the need for an invoice - eg with payment by standing order or direct debit at the bank. If there is always an invoice where rent becomes payable, the double entry would be:

DEBIT	Rent account	£2,000	
CREDIT	Creditors		£2,000

Then when the rent is paid, the ledger entries would be:

DEBIT	Creditors	£2,000	
CREDIT	Cash		£2,000

2.13 The rent account for the *next* year to 31 December 19X7, assuming no increase in rent in that year, would be as follows.

RENT ACCOUNT

		£			£
19X7			*19X7*		
31 Jan	Cash	3,000	1 Jan	Balance b/d	2,000
30 Apr	Cash	3,000			
31 Jul	Cash	3,000			
31 Oct	Cash	3,000			
31 Dec	Balance c/d (accruals)	2,000	31 Dec	P & L account	12,000
		14,000			14,000
			19X8		
			1 Jan	Balance b/d	2,000

2.14 Here, you will see that for a full year, a full twelve months' rental charges are taken as an expense to the P & L account.

Further example: prepayments

2.15 Prepayments are expenses which have been paid (or for which an invoice demanding payment has been received) but which relate to a future accounting period, and so should be an expense in the P & L account of that future period.

2.16 Suppose that Terry Trunk commences business as a landscape gardener on 1 September 19X5. He immediately decides to join his local trade association, the Confederation of Luton Gardeners, for which the annual membership subscription is £180, payable annually in advance. He paid this amount on 1 September. Terry decides that his account period should end on 30 June each year.

In the first period to 30 June 19X6 (10 months), a full year's membership will have been paid, but only ten twelfths of the subscription should be charged to the period (ie 10/12 × £180 = £150). There is a prepayment of two months of membership subscription - ie 2/12 × £180 = £30.

2.17 It is therefore necessary to recognise the prepayment in the ledger account for subscriptions. This is done in much the same way as accounting for accruals, by using the balance carried down/brought down technique.

CREDIT	Subscriptions account with prepayment as a balance c/d	£30
DEBIT	Subscriptions account with the same balance b/d £30	

The remaining expenses in the subscriptions account should then be taken to the P & L account. The balance on the account will appear as a current asset (prepaid subscriptions) in the balance sheet as at 30 June 19X6.

SUBSCRIPTIONS ACCOUNT

		£			£
19X5			*19X6*		
1 Sept	Cash	180	30 Jun	P & L account	150
			30 Jun	Balance c/d (prepayment)	30
		180			180
19X6					
1 Jul	Balance b/d	30			

2.18 The subscription account for the next year, assuming no increase in the annual charge and that Terry Trunk remains a member of the association, will be:

SUBSCRIPTIONS ACCOUNT

		£			£
19X6			*19X7*		
1 Jul	Balance b/d	30	30 Jun	P & L account	180
1 Sep	Cash	180	30 Jun	Balance c/d (prepayment)	30
		210			210
19X67					
1 Jul	Balance b/d	30			

2.19 Again, we see here for a full accounting year, the charge to the P & L account is for a full year's subscriptions.

Chapter roundup

- This chapter has illustrated how the amount of profit is calculated when:
    - there are opening or closing stocks of goods in hand;
    - there is carriage inwards and/or carriage outwards;
    - stocks are written off or written down in value;
    - there are accrued charges;
    - there are prepayments of expenses.

- The cost of goods sold is calculated by adding the value of opening stock in hand to the cost of purchases and subtracting the value of closing stock.

- Accrued expenses are expenses which relate to an accounting period but have not yet been paid for. They are a charge against the profit for the period and they are shown in the balance sheet as at the end of the period as a current liability.

- Prepayments are expenses which have already been paid but relate to a future accounting period. They are not charged against the profit of the current period, and they are shown in the balance sheet a at the end of the period as a current asset.

- Accruals and prepayments are aspects of the accruals concept which is one of the fundamental concepts in accounting (and which we have looked at earlier).

Test your knowledge

1 How is the cost of goods sold calculated? (see para 1.6)

2 Distinguish between carriage inwards and carriage outwards. (1.10)

3 How is carriage inwards treated in the trading, profit and loss account? (1.11)

4 Give three reasons why goods purchased might have to be written off. (1.14)

5 If a business has paid rates of £1,000 for the year to 31 March 19X9, what is the prepayment in the accounts for the year to 31 December 19X9? (2.2)

6 Define an accrual. (2.3)

Now try illustrative questions 12 and 13 at the end of the Study Text

Chapter 9

DISCOUNTS, BAD DEBTS AND PROVISIONS

This chapter covers the following topics.

		Syllabus reference	*Ability required*
1	Discounts	1(b)	Skill
2	Accounting for bad and doubtful debts	1(b)	Skill

Introduction

As a general rule, for the purpose of accounting (as distinct from the legal aspects of the law of contract), sales and purchases are treated as follows.

(a) A sale takes place at one of two points in time (this is called *revenue recognition*).

    (i) *Cash sales.* If the sale is for cash, it occurs when the goods or services are given in exchange for an immediate payment, in notes and coins, or by cheque or credit card.

    (ii) *Credit sales.* If the sale is on credit, it occurs when the business making the sale sends out an invoice for the goods or services supplied.

(b) The purchase of goods or services by a business also takes place at one of two points in time.

    (i) *Purchases for cash.* If the goods are paid for promptly (ie in cash) the purchase occurs when the goods and cash exchange hands.

    (ii) *Purchases on credit.* If the goods are bought on credit, the purchase normally occurs when the business receives the goods, accompanied by an invoice from the supplier.

The accounting problems discussed in this chapter are concerned with sales or purchases on credit. With credit transactions, the point in time when a sale or purchase is recognised in the accounts of the business is not the same as the point in time when cash is eventually received or paid for the sale or purchase. There is a gap in time between the sale or purchase and the eventual cash settlement, and it is possible that something might happen during that time which results in the amount of cash eventually paid (if any) being different from the original value of the sale or purchase on the invoice.

We shall consider three such 'happenings':

(a) discounts allowed by the supplier for goods purchased by the business;

(b) discounts allowed to customers for goods sold by the business;

(c) bad debts, which arise when the business decides that a credit customer will never pay the money he owes.

1 DISCOUNTS

Types of discount

1.1 A discount is a reduction in the price of goods below the amount at which those goods would normally be sold to other customers of the supplier. A distinction must be made between:

    (a) trade discount; and

(b) cash discount, or settlement discount.

1.2 *Trade discount* is a reduction in the cost of goods owing to the nature of the trading transaction. It usually results from buying goods in bulk. For example:

(a) a customer might be quoted a price of £1 per unit for a particular item, but a lower price of, say, 95 pence per unit if the item is bought in quantities of, say, 100 units or more at a time;

(b) an important customer or a regular customer might be offered a discount on all the goods he buys, regardless of the size of each individual order, because the total volume of his purchases over time is so large.

1.3 *Cash discount* is a reduction in the amount payable to the supplier, in return for immediate payment in cash, rather than purchase on credit. For example, a supplier might charge £1,000 for goods, but offer a discount of, say, 5% if the goods are paid for immediately in cash.

1.4 *Settlement discount* is similar to cash discount. It is a discount on the price of the goods purchased for credit customers who pay their debts promptly. For example, a supplier might charge £1,000 to a credit customer for goods purchased, but offer a discount of, say, 5% for payment within so many days of the invoice date.

Accounting for trade discount

1.5 Trade discount is a reduction in the amount of money demanded from a customer.

(a) If trade discount is received by a business for goods purchased from a supplier, the amount of money demanded from the business by the supplier will be net of discount (ie it will be the normal sales value less the discount).

(b) Similarly, if a trade discount is given by a business for goods sold to a customer, the amount of money demanded by the business will be after deduction of the discount.

1.6 Trade discount should therefore be accounted for as follows.

(a) Trade discount received should be deducted from the gross cost of purchases. In other words, the cost of purchases in the trading account will be stated at gross cost minus discount (ie it will be stated at the invoiced amount).

(b) Trade discount allowed should be deducted from the gross sales price, so that sales for the period will be reported in the trading account at their invoice value.

Cash discounts and settlement discounts received

1.7 When a business is given the opportunity to take advantage of a cash discount or a settlement discount for prompt payment, the decision as to whether or not to take the discount is a matter of financing policy, not of trading policy.

1.8 Suppose that A buys goods from B, on the understanding that A will be allowed a period of credit before having to pay for the goods. The terms of the transaction might be as follows.

(a) Date of sale: 1 July 19X6

(b) Credit period allowed: 30 days

(c) Invoice price of the goods: £2,000 (the invoice will be issued at this price when the goods are delivered)

(d) Cash discount offered: 4% discount for prompt payment

1.9   A has the choice between:

(a)   holding on to his money for 30 days and then paying the full £2,000;
(b)   paying £2,000 less 4% - ie £1,920 now.

This is a financing decision about whether it is worthwhile for A to save £80 by paying its debts sooner, or whether it can employ its cash more usefully for 30 days, and pay the debt at the latest acceptable moment.

1.10   If A decides to take the cash discount, he will pay £1,920, instead of the invoiced amount £2,000. The cash discount received (£80) will be accounted for in the books of A as follows.

(a)   In the trading account, the cost of purchases will be at the invoiced price (or 'full trade' price) of £2,000. When the invoice for £2,000 is received by A, it will be recorded in his books of account at that price, and the subsequent financing decision about accepting the cash discount is ignored.

(b)   In the profit and loss account, the cash discount received is shown as though it were income received. There is no expense in the P & L account from which the cash discount can be deducted, and so there is no alternative other than to show the discount received as income.

1.11   In our example, we would have:

	£
Cost of purchase from B by A (trading account)	2,000
Discount received (income in the P & L account)	(80)
Net cost	1,920

Settlement discounts received are accounted for in exactly the same way as cash discounts received.

Cash discounts and settlement discounts allowed

1.12   The same principle is applied in accounting for cash discounts or settlement discounts allowed to customers. Goods are sold at a trade price, and the offer of a discount on that price is a matter of financing policy for the business and not a matter of trading policy.

1.13   Suppose that X sells goods to Y at a price of £5,000. Y is allowed 60 days' credit before payment, but is also offered a settlement discount of 2% for payment within 10 days of the invoice date.

X will issue an invoice to Y for £5,000 when the goods are sold. X has no idea whether or not Y will take advantage of the discount. In trading terms, and in terms of the amount charged in the invoice to Y, Y is a debtor for £5,000.

1.14   If Y subsequently decides to take the discount, he will pay £5,000 less 2% - ie £4,900 - ten days later. The discount allowed (£100) will be accounted for by X as follows:

(a)   in the trading account, sales will be valued at their full invoice price, £5,000;
(b)   in the profit and loss account, the discount allowed will be shown as an expense.

1.15   In our example, we would have:

	£
Sales (trading account)	5,000
Discounts allowed (P & L account)	(100)
Net sales	4,900

Cash discounts allowed are accounted for in exactly the same way as settlement discounts allowed.

Exercise 1

You are required to prepare the trading, profit and loss account of Seesaw Timber Merchants for the year ended 31 March 19X6, given the following information.

	£
Goods in stock, 1 April 19X5	18,000
Purchases at gross cost	120,000
Trade discounts received	4,000
Cash and settlement discounts received	1,500
Goods in stock, 31 March 19X6	25,000
Cash sales	34,000
Credit sales at invoice price	150,000
Cash and settlement discounts allowed	8,000
Selling expenses	32,000
Administrative expenses	40,000
Drawings by proprietor, Tim Burr	22,000

Solution

SEESAW TIMBER MERCHANTS
TRADING, PROFIT AND LOSS ACCOUNT
FOR THE YEAR ENDED 31 MARCH 19X6

	£	£
Sales (note 1)		184,000
Opening stocks	18,000	
Purchases (note 2)	116,000	
	134,000	
Less closing stocks	25,000	
Cost of goods sold		109,000
Gross profit		75,000
Discounts received		1,500
		76,500
Expenses		
Selling expenses	32,000	
Administrative expenses	40,000	
Discounts allowed	8,000	
		80,000
Net loss transferred to balance sheet		(3,500)

Notes

1   £(34,000 + 150,000)
2   £(120,000 − 4,000)
3   Drawings are not an expense, but an appropriation of profit.

2   ACCOUNTING FOR BAD AND DOUBTFUL DEBTS   *11/96*

2.1   Customers who buy goods on credit might fail to pay for them, perhaps out of dishonesty or perhaps because they have gone bankrupt and cannot pay. Customers in another country might be prevented from paying by the unexpected introduction of foreign exchange control restrictions by their country's government during the credit period.

For one reason or another, a business might decide to give up expecting payment and to write the debt off as a 'lost cause'.

Writing off bad debts

2.2   When a business decides that a particular debt is unlikely ever to be repaid, the amount of the debt should be 'written off' as an expense in the profit and loss account.

2.3   For example, if Alfred's Mini-Cab Service sends an invoice for £300 to a customer who subsequently does a 'moonlight flit' from his office premises, never to be seen or heard of again, the debt of £300 must be written off. It might seem sensible to record the business transaction as:

Sales £(300 – 300) = £0.

2.4   However, bad debts written off are accounted for as follows.

(a)   Sales are shown at their invoice value in the trading account. The sale has been made, and gross profit should be earned. The subsequent failure to collect the debt is a separate matter, which is reported in the P & L account.

(b)   Bad debts written off are shown as an expense in the profit and loss account.

2.5   In our example of Alfred's Mini-Cab Service:

	£
Sale (in the trading account)	300
Bad debt written off (expense in the P & L account)	300
Net profit on this transaction	0

2.6   Obviously, when a debt is written off, the value of the debtor as a current asset falls to zero. If the debt is expected to be uncollectable, its 'net realisable value' is nil, and so it has a zero balance sheet value.

Bad debts written off and subsequently paid

2.7   A bad debt which has been written off might occasionally be unexpectedly paid. The only accounting problem to consider is when a debt written off as bad in one accounting period is subsequently paid in a later accounting period. The amount paid should be recorded as additional income in the profit and loss account of the period in which the payment is received.

2.8   For example, a trading, profit and loss account for the Blacksmith's Forge for the year to 31 December 19X5 could be prepared as shown below from the following information.

	£
Stocks of goods in hand, 1 January 19X5	6,000
Purchases of goods	122,000
Stocks of goods in hand, 31 December 19X5	8,000
Cash sales	100,000
Credit sales	70,000
Discounts allowed	1,200
Discounts received	5,000
Bad debts written off	9,000
Debts paid in 19X5 which were previously written off as bad in 19X4	2,000
Other expenses	31,800

BLACKSMITH'S FORGE
TRADING, PROFIT AND LOSS ACCOUNT FOR THE YEAR ENDED 31.12.19X5

	£	£
Sales		170,000
Opening stock	6,000	
Purchases	122,000	
	128,000	
Less closing stock	8,000	
Cost of goods sold		120,000
Gross profit		50,000
Add: discounts received		5,000
debts paid, previously written off as bad		2,000
		57,000
Expenses		
Discounts allowed	1,200	
Bad debts written off	9,000	
Other expenses	31,800	
		42,000
Net profit		15,000

A provision for doubtful debts

2.9   When bad debts are written off, specific debts owed to the business are identified as unlikely ever to be collected.

However, because of the risks involved in selling goods on credit, and it might be accepted that a certain percentage of outstanding debts at any time are unlikely to be collected. But although it might be estimated that, say, 5% of debts will turn out bad, the business will not know until later which specific debts are bad.

2.10   Suppose that a business commences operations on 1 July 19X4, and in the twelve months to 30 June 19X5 makes sales of £300,000 (all on credit) and writes off bad debts amounting to £6,000. Cash received from customers during the year is £244,000, so that at 30 June 19X5, the business has outstanding debtors of £50,000.

	£
Credit sales during the year	300,000
Add debtors at 1 July 19X4	0
Total debts owed to the business	300,000
Less cash received from credit customers	244,000
	56,000
Less bad debts written off	6,000
Debtors outstanding at 30 June 19X5	50,000

Now, some of these outstanding debts might turn out to be bad. The business does not know on 30 June 19X5 which specific debts in the total £50,000 owed will be bad, but it might guess (from experience perhaps) that 5% of debts will eventually be found to be bad.

2.11   When a business expects bad debts amongst its current debtors, but does not yet know which specific debts will be bad, it can make a provision for doubtful debts.

2.12   A 'provision' is a 'providing for' and so a provision for doubtful debts provides for future bad debts, as a prudent precaution by the business. The business will be more likely to avoid claiming profits which subsequently fail to materialise because some debts turn out to be bad.

(a)   When a provision is first made, the amount of this initial provision is charged as an expense in the profit and loss account of the business, for the period in which the provision is created.

(b)   When a provision already exists, but is subsequently increased in size, the amount of the *increase* in provision is charged as an expense in the profit and loss account, for the period in which the increased provision is made.

(c)   When a provision already exists, but is subsequently reduced in size, the amount of the *decrease* in provision is recorded as an item of 'income' in the profit and loss account, for the period in which the reduction in provision is made.

2.13   The balance sheet, as well as the profit and loss account of a business, must be adjusted to show a provision for doubtful debts. *The value of debtors in the balance sheet must be shown after deducting the provision for doubtful debts.* This is because the net realisable value of all the debtors of the business is estimated to be less than their 'sales value'. After all, this is the reason for making the provision in the first place. The net realisable value of debtors is the total value of debtors minus the provision for doubtful debts. Such a provision is an example of the *prudence concept*, discussed in detail in Chapter 2.

2.14   In the example above (in paragraph 2.10) the newly created provision for doubtful debts at 30 June 19X5 will be 5% of £50,000 = £2,500. This means that although total debtors are £50,000, eventual payment of only £47,500 is expected.

(a)   In the P & L account, the newly created provision of £2,500 will be shown as an expense.

(b)   In the balance sheet, debtors will be shown as:

	£
Total debtors at 30 June 19X5	50,000
Less provision for doubtful debts	2,500
	47,500

Example: provision for doubtful debts

2.15   Corin Flakes owns and runs the Aerobic Health Foods Shop in Dundee. He commenced trading on 1 January 19X1, selling health foods to customers, most of whom make use of a credit facility that Corin offers. (Customers are allowed to purchase up to £200 of goods on credit but must repay a certain proportion of their outstanding debt every month.)

This credit system gives rise to a large number of bad debts, and Corin Flake's results for his first three years of operations are as follows.

Year to 31 December 19X1
Gross profit	£27,000
Bad debts written off	£8,000
Debts owed by customers as at 31 December 19X1	£40,000
Provision for doubtful debts	2½% of outstanding debtors
Other expenses	£20,000

Year to 31 December 19X2
Gross profit	£45,000
Bad debts written off	£10,000
Debts owed by customers as at 31 December 19X2	£50,000
Provision for doubtful debts	2½% of outstanding debtors
Other expenses	£28,750

Year to 31 December 19X3
Gross profit	£60,000
Bad debts written off	£11,000
Debts owed by customers as at 31 December 19X3	£30,000
Provision for doubtful debts	3% of outstanding debtors
Other expenses	£32,850

Required

For each of these three years, prepare the profit and loss account of the business, and state the value of debtors appearing in the balance sheet as at 31 December.

Solution

2.16 AEROBIC HEALTH FOOD SHOP
PROFIT AND LOSS ACCOUNTS FOR THE YEARS ENDED 31 DECEMBER

	19X1		*19X2*		*19X3*	
	£	£	£	£	£	£
Gross profit		27,000		45,000		60,000
Standard income reduction in provision for						
doubtful debts*						350
						60,350
Expenses:						
Bad debts written off	8,000		10,000		11,000	
Increase in provision for doubtful						
debts*	1,000		250		-	
Other expenses	20,000		28,750		32,850	
		29,000		39,000		43,850
Net(loss)/profit		(2,000)		6,000		16,500

*At 1 January 19X1 when Corin began trading the provision for doubtful debts was nil. At 31 December 19X1 the provision required was $2^1/_2$% of £40,000 = £1,000. The increase in the provision is therefore £1,000. At 31 December 19X2 the provision required was 2½% of £50,000 = £1,250. The 19X1 provision must therefore be increased by £250. At 31 December 19X3 the provision required is 3% × £30,000 = £900. The 19X2 provision is therefore reduced by £350.

VALUE OF DEBTORS IN THE BALANCE SHEET

	As at *31.12.19X1*	*As at* *31.12.19X2*	*As at* *31.12.19X3*
	£	£	£
Total value of debtors	40,000	50,000	30,000
Less provision for doubtful debts	1,000	1,250	900
Balance sheet value	39,000	48,750	29,100

Other provisions

2.17 A provision for doubtful debts is not the only type of provision you will come across in accounting. Companies legislation defines a provision as 'any amount written off or retained by way of providing for depreciation, renewals or diminution in value of assets or retained by way of providing for any known liability of which the amount cannot be determined with substantial accuracy'.

2.18 For most businesses, by far the largest provision in their accounts is the provision for depreciation which is described in a later chapter.

You should now try to use what you have learned to attempt a solution to the following exercise, which involves preparing a trading, profit and loss account and balance sheet.

Exercise 2

The financial affairs of Newbegin Tools prior to the commencement of trading were as follows.

NEWBEGIN TOOLS
BALANCE SHEET AS AT 1 AUGUST 19X5

	£	£
Fixed assets		
Motor vehicle	2,000	
Shop fittings	3,000	
		5,000
Current assets		
Stocks	12,000	
Cash	1,000	
	13,000	
Current liabilities		
Bank overdraft	2,000	
Trade creditors	4,000	
	6,000	
Net current assets		7,000
		12,000
Financed by		
Capital		12,000

At the end of six months the business had made the following transactions.

(a)   Goods were purchased on credit at a gross amount of £10,000.

(b)   Trade discount received was 2% on this gross amount and there was a settlement discount received of 5% on settling debts to suppliers of £8,000. These were the only payments to suppliers in the period.

(c)   Closing stocks of goods were valued at £5,450.

(d)   Cash sales and credit sales together totalled £27,250.

(e)   Outstanding debtors balances at 31 January 19X6 amounted to £3,250 of which £250 were to be written off. A further provision for doubtful debts is to be made amounting to 2% of the remaining outstanding debtors

(f)   Cash payments were made in respect of the following expenses.

		£
(i)	Stationery, postage and wrapping	500
(ii)	Telephone charges	200
(iii)	Electricity	600
(iv)	Cleaning and refreshments	150

(g)   Cash drawings by the proprietor, Alf Newbegin, amounted to £6,000.

(h)   The outstanding overdraft balance as at 1 August 19X5 was paid off. Interest charges and bank charges on the overdraft amounted to £40.

Alf Newbegin knew the balance of cash on hand at 31 January 19X6 but he wanted to know if the business had made a profit for the six months that it had been trading, and so he asked his friend, Harry Oldhand, if he could tell him.

Prepare the trading, profit and loss account of Newbegin Tools for the six months to 31 January 19X6 and a balance sheet as at that date.

Solution

The trading, profit and loss account should be fairly straightforward.

TRADING AND PROFIT AND LOSS ACCOUNT
FOR THE SIX MONTHS ENDED 31 JANUARY 19X6

	£	£
Sales		27,250
Opening stocks	12,000	
Purchases (note (a))	9,800	
	21,800	
Less closing stocks	5,450	
Cost of goods sold		16,350
Gross profit		10,900
Discounts received (note (b))		400
		11,300
Electricity (note (c))	600	
Stationery, postage and wrapping	500	
Bad debts written off	250	
Provision for doubtful debts (note (d))	60	
Telephone charges	200	
Cleaning and refreshments	150	
Interest and bank charges	40	
		1,800
Net profit		9,500

Notes

(a)   Purchases at cost £10,000 less 2% trade discount.

(b)   5% of £8,000 = £400

(c)   Expenses are grouped into sales and distribution expenses (here assumed to be electricity, stationery and postage, bad debts and provision for doubtful debts) administration expenses (here assumed to be telephone charges and cleaning) and finance charges.

(d)   2% of £3,000 = £60.

The preparation of a balance sheet is not so easy, because we must calculate the value of creditors and cash in hand.

(a)   *Creditors as at 31 January 19X6*

The amount owing to creditors is the sum of the amount owing at the beginning of the period, plus the cost of purchases during the period (net of all discounts), less the payments already made for purchases. If you think carefully about this, you might see that this calculation is logical. What is still owed is the total amount of costs incurred less payments already made.

	£
Creditors as at 1 August 19X5	4,000
Add purchases during the period, net of trade discount	9,800
	13,800
Less settlement discounts received	(400)
	13,400
Less payments to creditors during the period*	(7,600)
	5,800

   * £8,000 less cash discount of £400.

(b)   *Cash at bank and in hand at 31 January 19X6*

This too requires a fairly lengthy calculation. You need to identify cash payments received and cash payments made.

			£
(i)	*Cash received from sales*		
	Total sales in the period		27,250
	Add debtors as at 1 August 19X5		0
			27,250
	Less unpaid debts as at 31 January 19X6		3,250
	Cash received		24,000

		£
(ii)	*Cash paid*	
	Trade creditors (see (a))	7,600
	Stationery, postage and wrapping	500
	Telephone charges	200
	Electricity	600
	Cleaning and refreshments	150
	Bank charges and interest	40
	Bank overdraft repaid	2,000
	Drawings by proprietor	6,000
		17,090

Note. It is easy to forget some of these payments, especially drawings.

		£
(iii)	Cash in hand at 1 August 19X5	1,000
	Cash received in the period	24,000
		25,000
	Cash paid in the period	(17,090)
	Cash at bank and in hand as at 31 January 19X6	7,910

(c) When bad debts are written off, the value of outstanding debtors must be reduced by the amount written off. This is because the debtors are no longer expected to pay, and it would be misleading and absurd to show them in the balance sheet as current assets of the business for which cash payment is expected within one year. Debtors in the balance sheet will be valued at £3,000 less the provision for doubtful debts of £60 - ie at £2,940.

(d) Fixed assets should be depreciated. However, in this exercise depreciation has been ignored.

NEWBEGIN TOOLS
BALANCE SHEET AS AT 31 JANUARY 19X6

	£	£
Fixed assets		
Motor vehicles	2,000	
Shop fittings	3,000	
		5,000
Current assets		
Stocks	5,450	
Debtors	2,940	
Cash	7,910	
		16,300
		21,300
Current liabilities		
Trade creditors		(5,800)
		15,500
Capital		
Capital at 1 August 19X5		12,000
Net profit for the period		9,500
		21,500
Less drawings		6,000
Capital at 31 January 19X6		15,500

The bank overdraft has now been repaid and is therefore not shown.

Bad debts written off: ledger accounting entries

2.19   For bad debts written off, there is a bad debts account. The double-entry bookkeeping is fairly straightforward, but there are two separate transactions to record.

    (a)   When it is decided that a particular debt will not be paid, the customer is no longer called an outstanding debtor, and becomes a bad debt. We therefore:

        DEBIT   Bad debts account (expense)
        CREDIT   Debtors account

    (b)   At the end of the accounting period, the balance on the bad debts account is transferred to the P & L ledger account (like all other expense accounts):

        DEBIT   P & L account
        CREDIT   Bad debts account.

Example: bad debts written off

2.20   At 1 October 19X5 a business had total outstanding debts of £8,600. During the year to 30 September 19X6:

    (a)   credit sales amounted to £44,000;

    (b)   payments from various debtors amounted to £49,000;

    (c)   two debts, for £180 and £420, were declared bad and the customers are no longer purchasing goods from the company. These are to be written off.

Required

Prepare the debtors account and the bad debts account for the year.

Solution

2.21

DEBTORS

	£		£
Opening balance b/f	8,600	Cash	49,000
Sales	44,000	Bad debts	180
		Bad debts	420
		Closing balance c/d	3,000
	52,600		52,600
Opening balance b/d	3,000		

BAD DEBTS

	£		£
Debtors	180	P & L a/c: bad debts written off	600
Debtors	420		
	600		600

2.22   In the sales ledger, personal accounts of the customers whose debts are bad will be taken off the ledger. The business should then take steps to ensure that it does not sell goods on credit to those customers again.

Provision for doubtful debts: ledger accounting entries

2.23   A provision for doubtful debts is rather different. A business might know from past experience that, say 2% of debtors' balances are unlikely to be collected. It would then be considered prudent to make a general provision of 2%. It may be that no particular customers are regarded as suspect and so it is not possible to write off any individual customer balances as bad debts. The procedure is then to leave the total debtors balances completely untouched, but to open up a provision account by the following entries:

    DEBIT   Doubtful debts account (expense)
    CREDIT   Provision for doubtful debts

When preparing a balance sheet, the credit balance on the provision account is deducted from the total debit balances in the debtors ledger.

2.24   *In subsequent years*, adjustments may be needed to the amount of the provision. The procedure to be followed then is as follows.

(a)   Calculate the new provision required.

(b)   Compare it with the existing balance on the provision account (ie the balance b/f from the previous accounting period).

(c)   Calculate increase or decrease required.

　　(i)   If a higher provision is required now:

　　　　CREDIT   Provision for doubtful debts
　　　　DEBIT   P & L account

　　with the amount of the increase.

　　(ii)   If a lower provision is needed now than before:

　　　　DEBIT   Provision for doubtful debts
　　　　CREDIT   P & L account

　　with the amount of the decrease.

Example: accounting entries for provision for doubtful debts

2.25   Alex Gullible has total debtors' balances outstanding at 31 December 19X2 of £28,000. He believes that about 1% of these balances will not be collected and wishes to make an appropriate provision. Before now, he has not made any provision for doubtful debts at all.

On 31 December 19X3 his debtors balances amount to £40,000. His experience during the year has convinced him that a provision of 5% should be made.

What accounting entries should Alex make on 31 December 19X2 and 31 December 19X3, and what figures for debtors will appear in his balance sheets as at those dates?

Solution

2.26   *At 31 December 19X2*

Provision required   = 1% × £28,000
　　　　　　　　　　　　= £280

Alex will make the following entries.

DEBIT	P & L account (doubtful debts)	£280	
CREDIT	Provision for doubtful debts		£280

In the balance sheet debtors will appear as follows under current assets.

	£
Sales ledger balances	28,000
Less provision for doubtful debts	280
	27,720

At 31 December 19X3

Following the procedure described above, Alex will calculate as follows.

	£
Provision required now (5% × £40,000)	2,000
Existing provision	(280)
∴ Additional provision required	1,720

He will make the following entries.

DEBIT	P & L account (doubtful debts)	£1,720	
CREDIT	Provision for doubtful debts		£1,720

The provision account will by now appear as follows.

PROVISION FOR DOUBTFUL DEBTS

19X2		£	*19X2*		£
31 Dec	Balance c/d	280	31 Dec	P & L account	280
19X3			*19X3*		
31 Dec	Balance c/d	2,000	1 Jan	Balance b/d	280
			31 Dec	P & L account	1,720
		2,000			2,000
			19X4		
			1 Jan	Balance b/d	2,000

For the balance sheet debtors will be valued as follows.

	£
Sales ledger balances	40,000
Less provision for doubtful debts	2,000
	38,000

2.27 In practice, it is unnecessary to show the total debtors balances and the provision as separate items in the balance sheet. A balance sheet would normally show only the net figure (£27,720 in 19X2, £38,000 in 19X3). However, it might be good practice at this stage in your studies to show the provision in the balance sheet, so that the examiner/marker can check that you have got your accounting procedures correct.

2.28 Now try the following exercise on provision for doubtful debts for yourself.

Exercise 3

Horace Goodrunning fears that his business will suffer an increase in defaulting debtors in the future and so he decides to make a provision for doubtful debts of 2% of outstanding debtors at the balance sheet date from 28 February 19X6. On 28 February 19X8, Horace decides that the provision has been over-estimated and he reduces it to 1% of outstanding debtors. Outstanding debtors balances at the various balance sheet dates are as follows.

	£
28.2.19X6	15,200
28.2.19X7	17,100
28.2.19X8	21,400

You are required to show extracts from the following accounts for each of the three years above.

(a) Debtors
(b) Provision for doubtful debts
(c) Profit and loss

Show how debtors would appear in the balance sheet at the end of each year.

Solution

The entries for the three years are denoted by (a), (b) and (c) in each account.

DEBTORS (EXTRACT)

			£	£
(a)	28.2.19X6	Balance	15,200	
(b)	28.2.19X7	Balance	17,100	
(c)	28.2.19X8	Balance	21,400	

PROVISION FOR DOUBTFUL DEBTS

			£				£
(a)	28.2.19X6	Balance c/d		28.2.19X6	Profit and loss		304
		(2% of 15,200)	304				
			304				304
(b)	28.2.19X7	Balance c/d		1.3.19X6	Balance b/d		304
		(2% of 17,100)	342	28.2.19X7	Profit and loss (note (i))		38
			342				342
(c)	28.2.19X8	Profit and loss (note (ii))	128	1.3.19X7	Balance b/d		342
	28.2.19X8	Balance c/d					
		(1% of 21,400)	214				
			342				342
				1.3.19X8	Balance b/d		214

PROFIT AND LOSS (EXTRACT)

		£
28.2.19X6	Provision for doubtful debts	304
28.2.19X7	Provision for doubtful debts	38
28.2.19X8	Provision for doubtful debts	128

Notes

(i)   The increase in the provision is £(342 - 304) = £38
(ii)   The decrease in the provision is £(342 - 214) = £128
(iii) We calculate the net debtors figure for inclusion in the balance sheet as follows.

	19X6	19X7	19X8
	£	£	£
Current assets			
Debtors	15,200	17,100	21,400
Less provision for doubtful debts	304	342	214
	14,896	16,758	21,186

Chapter roundup

- In this chapter, the following terms were defined.

  o *Trade discount* is a reduction in the catalogue price of an article, given by a wholesaler or manufacturer to a retailer. It is often given in return for bulk purchase orders.

  o *Cash discount* is a reduction in the amount payable for the purchase of goods or services in return for payment in cash rather than taking credit.

  o *Settlement discount* is a reduction in the amount payable for the purchase of goods or services in return for prompt payment within an agreed credit period.

  o *Bad debts* are specific debts owed to a business which it decides are never going to be paid.

  o *Doubtful debts* are debts which might become bad in the future but are not yet bad.

  o A *provision* is an amount written off to provide for depreciation or the fall in value of an asset, or to provide for any known liability of uncertain value. The amount is written off by:

    - charging the amount of the extra provision as an expense in the P & L account, and also

    - reducing the value of the asset in the balance sheet by the amount of the provision.

- We looked at the accounting treatment of each of these items.

  o *Trade discounts received* are deducted from the cost of purchases. *Cash and settlement discounts received* are included as 'other income' of the period in the profit and loss account. Similarly, cash and settlement discounts allowed are shown as expenses in the profit and loss account.

  o *Bad debts written off* are an expense in the profit and loss account.

- An *increase* in the provision for doubtful debts is an expense in the profit and loss account whereas a decrease in the provision for doubtful debts is shown as 'other income' in the P & L account.

- *Debtors* are valued in the balance sheet after deducting any provision for doubtful debts.

Test your knowledge

1 When is a cash sale recorded? (see introduction)

2 When is a purchase on credit recorded? (introduction)

3 Define a trade discount. (1.2)

4 How does cash discount differ from settlement discount? (1.4)

5 Explain how cash discount allowed is accounted for. (1.12)

6 If a doubtful debts provision is increased, what is the effect on the P & L account? (2.12)

7 What is the double entry to record a bad debt written off? (2.19)

Now try illustrative questions 14 and 15 at the end of the Study Text

Chapter 10

ACCOUNTING FOR STOCKS

This chapter covers the following topics.

		Syllabus reference	Ability required
1	Accounting for opening and closing stocks	1(c)	Skill
2	Stocktaking	1(c)	Skill
3	Valuing stocks	1(c)	Skill

Introduction

Stock is one of the most important assets in a company's balance sheet. As we have seen it also affects the profit and loss account.

In an earlier chapter, we saw that in order to calculate gross profit it is necessary to work out the cost of goods sold, and in order to calculate the cost of goods sold it is necessary to have values for the opening stock (ie stock in hand at the beginning of the accounting period) and closing stock (ie stock in hand at the end of the accounting period).

You should remember, in fact, that the trading part of a profit and loss account includes:

	£
Opening stock	X
Plus purchases	X
Less closing stock	(X)
Equals cost of goods sold	X

However, just writing down this formula hides three basic problems.

(a) How do you manage to get a precise count of stock in hand at any one time?
(b) Even once it has been counted, how do you value the stock?
(c) Assuming the stock is given a value, how does the double entry bookkeeping for stock work?

The purpose of this chapter is to answer all three of these questions. In order to make the presentation a little easier to follow, it is convenient to tackle the last question first.

---

1   ACCOUNTING FOR OPENING AND CLOSING STOCKS

Ledger accounting for stocks

1.1   It has already been shown that purchases are introduced to the trading account by means of the double entry:

DEBIT	Trading account	£X
CREDIT	Purchases account	£X

1.2   But what about opening and closing stocks? How are their values accounted for in the double entry bookkeeping system? The answer is that a stock account must be kept. This stock account is only ever used at the end of an accounting period, when the business counts up and values the stock in hand, in a stocktake.

(a)   When a stocktake is made, the business will have a value for its closing stock, and the double entry is:

DEBIT	Stock account (closing stock value)	£X
CREDIT	Trading account	£X

However, rather than show the closing stock as a 'plus' value in the trading account (eg by adding it to sales) it is usual to show it as a 'minus' figure in arriving at cost of sales. This is illustrated in the formula in the introduction. The debit balance on stock account represents an asset, which will be shown as part of current assets in the balance sheet.

(b) Closing stock at the end of one period becomes opening stock at the start of the next period. The stock account remains unchanged until the end of the next period, when the value of opening stock is taken to the trading account; ie

DEBIT	Trading account	£X
CREDIT	Stock account (value of opening stock)	£X

1.3 Partly as an example of how this ledger accounting for stocks works, and partly as revision on ledger accounting in general, try the following exercise. It is an example from an earlier part of this text which has had a closing stocks figure included.

Exercise

A business is established with capital of £2,000 and this amount is paid into a business bank account by the proprietor. During the first year's trading, the following transactions occurred:

	£
Purchases of goods for resale, on credit	4,300
Payments to trade creditors	3,600
Sales, all on credit	4,000
Payments from debtors	3,200
Fixed assets purchased for cash	1,500
Other expenses, all paid in cash	900

The bank has provided an overdraft facility of up to £3,000.

All 'other expenses' relate to the current year.

Closing stocks of goods are valued at £1,800. (Because this is the first year of the business, there are no opening stocks.)

Ignore depreciation and drawings.

Required

Prepare the ledger accounts, a trading, profit and loss account for the year and a balance sheet as at the end of the year.

Solution

CASH

	£		£
Capital	2,000	Trade creditors	3,600
Debtors	3,200	Fixed assets	1,500
Balance c/d	800	Other expenses	900
	6,000		6,000
		Balance b/d	800

CAPITAL

	£		£
Balance c/d	2,600	Cash	2,000
		P & L a/c	600
	2,600		2,600
		Balance b/d	2,600

TRADE CREDITORS

	£		£
Cash	3,600	Purchases	4,300
Balance c/d	700		
	4,300		4,300
		Balance b/d	700

PURCHASES ACCOUNT

	£		£
Trade creditors	4,300	Trading a/c	4,300

FIXED ASSETS

	£		£
Cash	1,500	Balance c/d	1,500
Balance b/d	1,500		

SALES

	£		£
Trading a/c	4,000	Debtors	4,000

DEBTORS

	£		£
Sales	4,000	Cash	3,200
		Balance c/d	800
	4,000		4,000
Balance b/d	800		

OTHER EXPENSES

	£		£
Cash	900	P & L a/c	900

TRADING, PROFIT AND LOSS ACCOUNT

	£		£
Purchases account	4,300	Sales	4,000
Gross profit c/d	1,500	Closing stock (stock account)	1,800
	5,800		5,800
Other expenses	900	Gross profit b/d	1,500
Net profit (transferred to			
capital account)	600		
	1,500		1,500

Alternatively, closing stock could be shown as a minus value on the debit side of the trading account, instead of a credit entry, giving purchases £4,300 less closing stock £1,800 equals cost of goods sold £2,500.

STOCK ACCOUNT

	£		£
Trading account (closing stock)	1,800	B/S	1,800

BALANCE SHEET AS AT THE END OF THE PERIOD

	£	£
Fixed assets		1,500
Current assets		
Goods in stock	1,800	
Debtors	800	
	2,600	
Current liabilities		
Bank overdraft	800	
Trade creditors	700	
	1,500	
Net assets		1,100
		2,600
Capital		
At start of period		2,000
Profit for period		600
		2,600

Make sure you can see what has happened here. The balance on the stock account was £1,800, which appears in the balance sheet as a current asset. As it happens, the £1,800 closing stock was the only entry in the stock account - there was no figure for opening stock.

If there had been, it would have been eliminated by transferring it as a debit balance to the trading account, ie:

DEBIT   Trading account (with value of opening stock)
CREDIT   Stock account (with value of opening stock)

The debit in the trading account would then have increased the cost of sales, ie opening stock is added to purchases in calculating cost of sales. Again, this is illustrated in the formula: opening stock + purchases – closing stock = cost of sales.

1.4   So if we can establish the value of stocks on hand, the above paragraphs and exercise show us how to account for that value. That takes care of one of the problems noted in the introduction of this chapter. But now another of those problems becomes apparent - how do we establish the value of stocks on hand? The first step must be to establish how much stock is held.

2   STOCKTAKING

2.1   Business trading is a continuous activity, but accounting statements must be drawn up at a particular date. In preparing a balance sheet it is necessary to 'freeze' the activity of a business so as to determine its assets and liabilities at a given moment. This includes establishing the quantities of stocks on hand, which can create problems.

2.2   A business buys stocks continually during its trading operations and either sells the goods onwards to customers or incorporates them as raw materials in manufactured products. This constant movement of stocks makes it difficult to establish what exactly is held at any precise moment.

2.3   In simple cases, when a business holds easily counted and relatively small amounts of stock, quantities of stocks on hand at the balance sheet date can be determined by physically counting them in a stocktake.

2.4   The continuous nature of trading activity may cause a problem in that stock movements will not necessarily cease during the time that the physical stocktake is in progress. Two possible solutions are:

(a)   to close down the business while the count takes place; or
(b)   to keep detailed records of stock movements during the course of the stocktake.

2.5   Closing down the business for a short period for a stocktake (eg over a weekend or at Christmas) is considerably easier than trying to keep detailed records of stock movements during a stocktake. So most businesses prefer that method unless they happen to keep detailed records of stock movements anyway (for example, because they wish to keep strict control on stock movements).

2.6   In more complicated cases, where a business holds considerable quantities of varied stock, an alternative approach to establishing stock quantities is to maintain continuous stock records. This means that a card is kept for every item of stock, showing receipts and issues from the stores, and a running total. A few stock items are counted each day to make sure their record cards are correct - this is called a 'continuous' stocktake because it is spread out over the year rather than completed in one stocktake at a designated time.

2.7   One obstacle is overcome once a business has established how much stock is on hand. But another of the problems noted in the introduction immediately raises its head. What value should the business place on those stocks?

3   VALUING STOCKS   *11/95, 5/96*

The basic rule

3.1   There are several methods which, in theory, might be used for the valuation of stock items.

(a)   Stocks might be valued at their expected selling price.

(b)   Stocks might be valued at their expected selling price, less any costs still to be incurred in getting them ready for sale and then selling them. This amount is referred to as the *net realisable value (NRV)* of the stocks.

(c)   Stocks might be valued at their historical cost (ie the cost at which they were originally bought).

(d)   Stocks might be valued at the amount it would cost to replace them. This amount is referred to as the current replacement cost of stocks.

3.2   Current replacement costs are not used in the type of accounts dealt with in this syllabus.

3.3   The use of selling prices in stock valuation is ruled out because this would create a profit for the business before the stock has been sold.

3.4   A simple example might help to explain this. Suppose that a trader buys two items of stock, each costing £100. He can sell them for £140 each, but in the accounting period we shall consider, he has only sold one of them. The other is closing stock in hand.

3.5   Since only one item has been sold, you might think it is common sense that profit ought to be £40. But if closing stock is valued at selling price, profit would be £80 - ie profit would be taken on the closing stock as well.

	£	£
Sales		140
Opening stock	-	
Purchases (2 × 100)	200	
	200	
Less closing stock (at selling price)	140	
Cost of sale		60
Profit		80

This would contradict the accounting concept of prudence - because a profit is being claimed before the item has actually been sold.

3.6   The same objection *usually* applies to the use of NRV in stock valuation. Say that the item purchased for £100 requires £5 of further expenditure in getting it ready for sale and then selling it (eg £5 of processing costs and distribution costs). If its expected selling price is £140, its NRV is £(140 – 5) = £135. To value it at £135 in the balance sheet would still be to anticipate a £35 profit.

3.7   We are left with historical cost as the normal basis of stock valuation. The only time when historical cost is not used is in the exceptional cases where the prudence concept requires a lower value to be used.

3.8   Staying with the example in Paragraph 3.6, suppose that the market in this kind of product suddenly slumps and the item's expected selling price is only £90. The item's NRV is then £(90 – 5) = £85 and the business has in effect made a loss of £15 (£100 – £85). The prudence concept requires that losses should be recognised as soon as they are foreseen. This can be achieved by valuing the stock item in the balance sheet at its NRV of £85.

3.9   The argument developed above suggests that the rule to follow is that stocks should be valued at cost, or if lower, net realisable value. The accounting treatment of stock is governed by an accounting standard, SSAP 9 *Stocks and long-term contracts*. SSAP 9 states that *stock should be valued at the lower of cost and net realisable value*. This is an important rule and one which you should learn by heart.

Applying the basic valuation rule

3.10   If a business has many stock items on hand the comparison of cost and NRV should theoretically be carried out for each item separately. It is not sufficient to compare the total cost of all stock items with their total NRV. An example will show why.

3.11   Suppose a company has four items of stock on hand at the end of its accounting period. Their cost and NRVs are as follows.

Stock item	Cost	NRV	Lower of cost/NRV
	£	£	£
1	27	32	27
2	14	8	8
3	43	55	43
4	29	40	29
	113	135	107

3.12   It would be incorrect to compare total costs (£113) with total NRV (£135) and to state stocks at £113 in the balance sheet. The company can foresee a loss of £6 on item 2 and this should be recognised. If the four items are taken together in total the loss on item 2 is masked by the anticipated profits on the other items. By performing the cost/NRV comparison for each item separately the prudent valuation of £107 can be derived. This is the value which should appear in the balance sheet.

3.13   However, for a company with large amounts of stock this procedure may be impracticable. In this case it is acceptable to group similar items into categories and perform the comparison of cost and NRV category by category, rather than item by item.

3.14   So have we now solved the problem of how a business should value its stocks? It seems that all the business has to do is to choose the lower of cost and net realisable value. This is true as far as it goes, but there is one further problem, perhaps not so easy to foresee: for a given item of stock, what was the cost?

Determining the purchase cost

3.15 Stock may be raw materials or components bought from suppliers, finished goods which have been made by the business but not yet sold, or work in the process of production, but only part-completed (this type of stock is called work in progress or WIP). It will simplify matters, however, if we think about the historical cost of purchased raw materials and components, which ought to be their purchase price.

3.16 A business may be continually purchasing consignments of a particular component. As each consignment is received from suppliers they are stored in the appropriate bin or on the appropriate shelf or pallet, where they will be mingled with previous consignments. When the storekeeper issues components to production he will simply pull out from the bin the nearest components to hand, which may have arrived in the latest consignment or in an earlier consignment or in several different consignments. Our concern is to devise a pricing technique, a rule of thumb which we can use to attribute a cost to each of the components issued from stores.

3.17 There are several techniques which are used in practice.

(a) *FIFO (first in, first out)*. Using this technique, we assume that components are used in the order in which they are received from suppliers. The components issued are deemed to have formed part of the oldest consignment still unused and are costed accordingly.

(b) *Average cost*. As purchase prices change with each new consignment, the average price of components in the bin is constantly changed. Each component in the bin at any moment is assumed to have been purchased at the average price of all components in the bin at that moment.

(c) *LIFO (last in, first out)*. This involves the opposite assumption, that components issued to production originally formed part of the most recent delivery, while older consignments lie in the bin undisturbed.

(d) *Standard cost*. A pre-determined standard cost is applied to all stock items. If this standard price differs from prices actually paid during the period it will be necessary to write off the difference as a 'variance' in the profit and loss account.

(e) *Replacement cost*. The arbitrary assumption is made that the cost at which a stock unit was purchased is the amount it would cost to replace it. This is often (but not necessarily) the unit cost of stocks purchased in the next consignment *following* the issue of the component to production. For this reason, a method which produces similar results to replacement costs is called NIFO (next in, first out).

Only the first two methods, FIFO and average cost are examinable in your syllabus.

3.18 Any or all of these methods might provide a suitable basis for valuing stocks. But it is worth mentioning here that if you are preparing *financial* accounts you would normally expect to use FIFO or average costs for the balance sheet valuation of stock. SSAP 9 specifically discourages the use of LIFO and replacement costs. (CA 85 allows any method the directors think appropriate, so long as, under the historical cost accounting rules, stock is stated at production cost or purchase price.) You should note furthermore that terms such as LIFO and FIFO refer to *pricing techniques* only. The actual components can be used in any order.

3.19 To illustrate the two pricing methods, the following transactions will be used in each case.

TRANSACTIONS DURING MAY 19X3

	Quantity Units	Unit cost £	Total cost £	Market value per unit on date of transactions £
Opening balance 1 May	100	2.00	200	
Receipts 3 May	400	2.10	840	2.11
Issues 4 May	200			2.11
Receipts 9 May	300	2.12	636	2.15
Issues 11 May	400			2.20
Receipts 18 May	100	2.40	240	2.35
Issues 20 May	100			2.35
Closing balance 31 May	200			2.38
			1,916	

Receipts mean goods are received into store and issues represent the issue of goods from store.

The problem is to put a valuation on:

(a)   the issues of materials;
(b)   the closing stock.

How would issues and closing stock be valued using:

(a)   FIFO;
(b)   average cost?

FIFO (first in, first out)

3.20   FIFO assumes that materials are issued out of stock in the order in which they were delivered into stock, ie issues are priced at the cost of the earliest delivery remaining in stock.

The cost of issues and closing stock value in the example, using FIFO would be as follows (note that o/s stands for opening stock).

Date of issue	Quantity Units	Value issued	Cost of issues £	£
4 May	200	100 o/s at £2	200	
		100 at £2.10	210	
				410
11 May	400	300 at £2.10	630	
		100 at £2.12	212	
				842
20 May	100	100 at £2.12		212
				1,464
Closing stock value	200	100 at £2.12	212	
		100 at £2.40	240	
				452
				1,916

Note that the cost of materials issued plus the value of closing stock equals the cost of purchases plus the value of opening stock (£1,916).

Average cost

3.21   There are various ways in which costs may be used in pricing stock issues. The most common (cumulative weighted average pricing) is illustrated below.

3.22   The cumulative weighted average pricing method calculates a weighted average price for all units in stock. Issues are priced at this average cost, and the balance of stock remaining would have the same unit valuation.

A new weighted average price is calculated whenever a new delivery of materials into store is received. This is the key feature of cumulative weighted average pricing.

3.23   In our example, issue costs and closing stock values would be:

Date	Received Units	Issued Units	Balance Units	Total stock value £	Unit cost £	Price of issue £
Opening stock			100	200	2.00	
3 May	400			840	2.10	
			500	1,040	2.08 *	
4 May		200		(416)	2.08 **	416
			300	624	2.08	
9 May	300			636	2.12	
			600	1,260	2.10 *	
11 May		400		(840)	2.10 **	840
			200	420	2.10	
18 May	100			240	2.40	
			300	660	2.20 *	
20 May		100		(220)	2.20 **	220
						1,476
Closing stock value			200	440	2.10	440
						1,916

* A new unit cost of stock is calculated whenever a new receipt of materials occurs.

** Whenever stocks are issued, the unit value of the items issued is the current weighted average cost per unit at the time of the issue.

For this method too, the cost of materials issued plus the value of closing stock equals the cost of purchases plus the value of opening stock (£1,916).

Stock valuations and profit

3.24   In the previous descriptions of FIFO and average costing, the example used raw materials as an illustration. Each method of valuation produced different costs both of closing stocks and also of material issues. Since raw material costs affect the cost of production, and the cost of production works through eventually into the cost of sales, it follows that different methods of stock valuation will provide different profit figures. An example may help to illustrate this point.

Example: stock valuations and profit

3.25   On 1 November 19X2 a company held 300 units of finished goods item No 9639 in stock. These were valued at £12 each. During November 19X2 three batches of finished goods were received into store from the production department as follows.

Date	Units received	Production cost per unit
10 November	400	£12.50
20 November	400	£14
25 November	400	£15

Goods sold out of stock during November were as follows.

Date	Units sold	Sale price per unit
14 November	500	£20
21 November	500	£20
28 November	100	£20

What was the profit from selling stock item 9639 in November 19X2, applying the following principles of stock valuation:

(a)   FIFO;
(b)   cumulative weighted average costing?

Ignore administration, sales and distribution costs.

Solution

3.26 (a) *FIFO*

		Issue cost Total £	*Closing stock* £
Date	*Issue costs*		
14 November	300 units × £12 plus		
	200 units × £12.50	6,100	
21 November	200 units × £12.50 plus		
	300 units × £14	6,700	
28 November	100 units × £14	1,400	
Closing stock	400 units × £15		6,000
		14,200	6,000

(b) *Cumulative weighted average costs*

		Unit cost	*Balance in stock* £	*Total cost of issues* £	*Closing stock* £
1 November	Opening stock 300	12	3,600		
10 November	400	12.50	5,000		
	700	12.286	8,600		
14 November	500	12.286	6,143	6,143	
	200	12.286	2,457		
20 November	400	14	5,600		
	600	13.428	8,057		
21 November	500	13.428	6,714	6,714	
	100	13.428	1,343		
25 November	400	15	6,000		
	500	14.686	7,343		
28 November	100	14.686	1,469	1,469	
30 November	400	14.686	5,874	14,326	5,874

	FIFO £	*Weighted average* £
Profit:		
Opening stock	3,600	3,600
Cost of production	16,600	16,600
	20,200	20,200
Closing stock	6,000	5,874
Cost of sales	14,200	14,326
Sales (1,100 × £20)	22,000	22,000
Profit	7,800	7,674

3.27 Different stock valuations have produced different cost of sales figures, and therefore different profits. In our example opening stock values are the same, therefore the difference in the amount of profit under each method is the same as the difference in the valuations of closing stock.

3.28 The profit differences are only temporary. In our example, the opening stock in December 19X2 will be £6,000 or £5,874, depending on the stock valuation used. Different opening stock values will affect the cost of sales and profits in December, so that in the long run inequalities in costs of sales each month will even themselves out.

Chapter roundup

- The quantity of stocks held at the year end is established by means of a physical count of stock in an annual stocktaking exercise, or by a 'continuous' stocktake.

- The value of these stocks is then calculated, taking the lower of cost and net realisable value for each separate item or group of stock items.

- In order to value the stocks, some rule of thumb must be adopted. The possibilities include FIFO, LIFO, average costs and standard costs. But remember that in *financial* accounts FIFO or average cost should normally be used. These are the two methods which you need to know for the purposes of your examination.

- NRV is the selling price less all costs to completion and less selling costs.

- Cost comprises purchase costs and costs of conversion.

- The value of closing stocks is accounted for in the nominal ledger by debiting a stock account and crediting the trading account at the end of an accounting period. The stock will therefore always have a debit balance at the end of a period, and this balance will be shown in the balance sheet as a current asset for stocks.

- Opening stocks brought forward in the stock account are transferred to the trading account, and so at the end of the accounting year, the balance on the stock account ceases to be the opening stock value b/f, and becomes instead the closing stock value c/f.

Test your knowledge

1   When is a stock account used? (see para 1.2)

2   How is closing stock incorporated in financial statements? (1.2)

3   What is 'continuous' stocktaking? (2.6)

4   Define net realisable value. (3.1)

5   Why is stock not valued at expected selling price? (3.3 - 3.5)

6   Give five methods of pricing a stock item at historical cost. (3.17)

Now try illustrative question 16 at the end of the Study Text

Chapter 11

FIXED ASSETS - DEPRECIATION, REVALUATION AND DISPOSAL

This chapter covers the following topics.

		Syllabus reference	Ability required
1	Depreciation	1(c)	Skill
2	Revaluation of fixed assets	1(c)	Skill
3	Accounting for depreciation provisions; fixed asset disposals	1(c)	Skill
4	SSAP 12 *Accounting for depreciation*	1(c)	Skill
5	The fixed assets register	1(c)	Skill

Introduction

You should by now be familiar with the distinction between fixed and current assets, a fixed asset being one bought for ongoing use in the business. If you are unsure of this look back to Chapter 3 to refresh your memory.

Fixed assets might be held and used by a business for a number of years, but they wear out or lose their usefulness in the course of time. Every tangible fixed asset has a limited life. The only exception is land held freehold or very long leasehold.

The accounts of a business try to recognise that the cost of a fixed asset is gradually consumed as the asset wears out. This is done by gradually writing off the asset's cost in the profit and loss account over several accounting periods. For example, in the case of a machine costing £1,000 and expected to wear out after ten years, it might be appropriate to reduce the balance sheet value by £100 each year. This process is known as depreciation and is the subject of Section 1 of this chapter.

Occasionally, particularly in the case of land or buildings, the market value of a fixed asset will rise with time. The asset may then be *revalued*. The accounting treatment of revaluations and the effect on depreciation are considered in Section 2. Section 3 deals with disposals of fixed assets. A profit may arise on the sale of a fixed asset if too much depreciation has been charged.

Depreciation is the subject of an *accounting standard* (SSAP 12), which you will need to know for your exam. The standard is fairly straightforward and is discussed in Section 4. Section 5 deals with a more practical issue: the fixed assets register. You are sure to encounter this in real life - nearly all organisations have one.

1   DEPRECIATION   5/95

1.1   A fixed asset is acquired for use within a business with a view to earning profits. Its life extends over more than one accounting period, and so it earns profits over more than one period.

1.2   With the exception of land held on freehold or very long leasehold, every fixed asset eventually wears out over time. Machines, cars and other vehicles, fixtures and fittings, and even buildings do not last for ever. When a business acquires a fixed asset, it will have some idea about how long its useful life will be, and it might decide either:

(a) to keep on using the fixed asset until it becomes completely worn out, useless, and worthless; or

(b) to sell off the fixed asset at the end of its useful life, either by selling it as a second-hand item or as scrap.

1.3 Since a fixed asset has a cost and a limited useful life, and its value eventually declines, it follows that a charge should be made in the trading, profit and loss account to reflect the use that is made of the asset by the business. This charge is called depreciation.

Definition of depreciation

1.4 Suppose that a business buys a machine for £40,000. Its expected life is four years, and at the end of that time it is expected to be worthless.

1.5 Since the fixed asset is used to make profits for four years, it would be reasonable to charge the cost of the asset over those four years (perhaps by charging £10,000 per annum) so that at the end of the four years the total cost of £40,000 would have been charged against profits.

1.6 Indeed, one way of defining depreciation is to describe it as a means of spreading the cost of a fixed asset over its useful life, and so matching the cost against the full period during which it earns profits for the business. Depreciation charges are an example of the application of the accruals concept to calculate profits.

1.7 A better definition of depreciation is given by SSAP 12 *Accounting for depreciation.*

'Depreciation is the measure of the wearing out, consumption or other reduction in the useful economic life of a fixed asset, whether arising from use, effluxion of time or obsolescence through technological or market changes. Depreciation should be allocated so as to charge a fair proportion of cost or valuation of the asset to each accounting period expected to benefit from its use.'

1.8 This definition makes two important points.

(a) Depreciation is a measure of the wearing out or depletion of a fixed asset through use, time or obsolescence.

(b) Depreciation charges should be spread fairly over a fixed asset's life, and so allocated to the accounting periods which are expected to benefit (ie make profits) from the asset's use.

The total charge for depreciation: the depreciable amount

1.9 The total amount to be charged over the life of a fixed asset ('the depreciable amount') is usually its cost less any expected 'residual' sales value or disposal value at the end of the asset's life.

(a) A fixed asset costing £20,000 which has an expected life of five years and an expected residual value of nil should be depreciated by £20,000 in total over the five year period.

(b) A fixed asset costing £20,000 which has an expected life of five years and an expected residual value of £3,000 should be depreciated by £17,000 in total over the five year period.

Depreciation in the accounts of a business

1.10 When a fixed asset is depreciated, two things must be accounted for.

(a) The charge for depreciation is a cost or expense of the accounting period. For the time being, we shall charge depreciation as an expense in the profit and loss account.

(b) At the same time, the fixed asset is wearing out and diminishing in value, and so the value of the fixed asset in the balance sheet must be reduced by the amount of depreciation charged. The balance sheet value of the fixed asset will be its 'net book value' which is the value net of depreciation in the books of account of the business.

1.11 The amount of depreciation deducted from the cost of a fixed asset to arrive at its net book value will build up (or 'accumulate') over time, as more depreciation is charged in each successive accounting period. This accumulated depreciation is a 'provision' because it provides for the fall in value of the fixed asset. The term 'provision for depreciation' refers to the 'accumulated depreciation' of a fixed asset.

1.12 For example, if a fixed asset costing £40,000 has an expected life of four years and an estimated residual value of nil, it might be depreciated by £10,000 per annum.

	Depreciation charge for the year (P & L a/c) (A) £	Accumulated depreciation at end of year (B) £	Cost of the asset (C) £	Net book value at end of year (C-B) £
At beginning of its life	-	-	40,000	40,000
Year 1	10,000	10,000	40,000	30,000
Year 2	10,000	20,000	40,000	20,000
Year 3	10,000	30,000	40,000	10,000
Year 4	10,000	40,000	40,000	0
	40,000			

At the end of year 4, the full £40,000 of depreciation charge has been made in the profit and loss accounts of the four years. The net book value of the fixed asset is now nil. In theory (although perhaps not in practice) the business will no longer use the fixed asset, which would now need replacing.

Methods of depreciation

1.13 There are several different methods of depreciation. Of these, the ones you need to know about are:

(a) the straight-line method;
(b) the reducing balance method; and
(c) the machine hour method (sometimes called the units of output method).

The straight line method

1.14 This is the most commonly used method of all. The total depreciable amount is charged in equal instalments to each accounting period over the expected useful life of the asset. (In this way, the net book value of the fixed asset declines at a steady rate, or in a 'straight line' over time.)

1.15 The annual depreciation charge is calculated as:

$$\frac{\text{Cost of asset minus residual value}}{\text{Expected useful life of the asset}}$$

Example: straight line depreciation

1.16 (a) A fixed asset costing £20,000 with an estimated life of 10 years and no residual value would be depreciated at the rate of:

$$\frac{£20,000}{10 \text{ years}} = £2,000 \text{ per annum}$$

(b) A fixed asset costing £60,000 has an estimated life of 5 years and a residual value of £7,000. The annual depreciation charge using the straight line method would be:

$$\frac{£(60,000 - 7,000)}{5 \text{ years}} = £10,600 \text{ per annum}$$

The net book value of the fixed asset would be:

	After 1 year £	After 2 years £	After 3 years £	After 4 years £	After 5 years £
Cost of the asset	60,000	60,000	60,000	60,000	60,000
Accumulated depreciation	10,600	21,200	31,800	42,400	53,000
Net book value	49,400	38,800	28,200	17,600	7,000 ★

★ ie its estimated residual value.

1.17 Since the depreciation charge per annum is the same amount every year with the straight line method, it is often convenient to state that depreciation is charged at the rate of x per cent per annum on the cost of the asset. In the example in Paragraph 1.16(a) above, the depreciation charge per annum is 10% of cost (ie 10% of £20,000 = £2,000).

Examination questions often describe straight line depreciation in this way.

1.18 The straight line method of depreciation is a fair allocation of the total depreciable amount between the different accounting periods, provided that it is reasonable to assume that the business enjoys equal benefits from the use of the asset in every period throughout its life.

Assets acquired in the middle of an accounting period

1.19 A business can purchase new fixed assets at any time during the course of an accounting period, and so it might seem fair to charge an amount for depreciation in the period when the purchase occurs which reflects the limited amount of use the business has had from the asset in that period.

Example: assets acquired in the middle of an accounting period

1.20 Suppose that a business which has an accounting year which runs from 1 January to 31 December purchases a new fixed asset on 1 April 19X1, at a cost of £24,000. The expected life of the asset is 4 years, and its residual value is nil. What should be the depreciation charge for 19X1?

Solution

1.21 The annual depreciation charge will be $\dfrac{24,000}{4 \text{ years}} = £6,000$ per annum

However, since the asset was acquired on 1 April 19X1, the business has only benefited from the use of the asset for 9 months instead of a full 12 months. It would therefore seem fair to charge depreciation in 19X1 of only:

$$\frac{9}{12} \times £6,000 = £4,500$$

1.22 If an examination question gives you the purchase date of a fixed asset, which is in the middle of an accounting period, you should generally assume that depreciation should be calculated in this way, as a 'part-year' amount. However:

(a) you will only be given such a problem when the straight line method of depreciation is used; and

(b) in practice, many businesses ignore the niceties of part-year depreciation, and charge a full year's depreciation on fixed assets in the year of their purchase, regardless of the point in time during the year at which they were acquired.

The reducing balance method

1.23 The reducing balance method of depreciation calculates the annual depreciation charge as a fixed percentage of the net book value of the asset, as at the end of the previous accounting period.

1.24 For example, suppose that a business purchases a fixed asset at a cost of £10,000. Its expected useful life is 3 years and its estimated residual value is £2,160. The business wishes to use the reducing balance method to depreciate the asset, and calculates that the rate of depreciation should be 40% of the reducing (net book) value of the asset. (The method of deciding that 40% is a suitable annual percentage is a problem of mathematics, not financial accounting, and is not described here.)

The total depreciable amount is £(10,000 – 2,160) = £7,840.

The depreciation charge per annum and the net book value of the asset as at the end of each year will be as follows:

	£	Accumulated depreciation £	
Asset at cost	10,000		
Depreciation in year 1 (40%)	4,000	4,000	
Net book value at end of year 1	6,000		
Depreciation in year 2			
(40% of reducing balance)	2,400	6,400	(4,000 + 2,400)
Net book value at end of year 2	3,600		
Depreciation in year 3 (40%)	1,440	7,840	(6,400 + 1,440)
Net book value at end of year 3	2,160		

1.25 You should note that with the reducing balance method, the annual charge for depreciation is higher in the earlier years of the asset's life, and lower in the later years. In the example above, the annual charges for years 1, 2 and 3 are £4,000, £2,400 and £1,440 respectively.

1.26 The reducing balance method might therefore be used when it is considered fair to allocate a greater proportion of the total depreciable amount to the earlier years and a lower proportion to later years, on the assumption that the benefits obtained by the business from using the asset decline over time.

The machine hour method of depreciation

1.27 As the name of this method implies, it is a method of depreciation which might be considered suitable for plant and machinery, where it is assumed that the fixed asset wears out through use rather than over time. Instead of calculating a depreciation charge relating to a period of time, depreciation is calculated according to the number of hours of use made of the machine by the business during the course of the period.

1.28 The life of the asset is estimated in hours (or miles or other conventional units) and each unit is given a money value for depreciation purposes. The rate of depreciation is calculated as:

$$\frac{\text{Cost of asset minus estimated residual value}}{\text{Expected useful life of the asset in hours of used time}}$$

Example: the machine hour method

1.29 A business purchases a machine at a cost of £45,000. Its estimated useful life is 8,000 hours of running time, and its estimated residual value is £5,000.

The rate of depreciation by the machine hour method will be:

$$\frac{£(45,000 - 5,000)}{8,000 \text{ hours}} = £5 \text{ per machine hour}$$

1.30 Suppose that the actual use of the machine each year is:

	Hours
Year 1	3,000
Year 2	1,500
Year 3	2,500
Year 4	1,000
	8,000

We can calculate the annual depreciation charge and net book value of the machine as at the end of each year as follows.

Year	Depreciation charge in the P & L account of the year £	Accumulated depreciation as at end of the year £	Fixed asset at cost £	Net book value as at end of the year £
Start of life			45,000	45,000
Year 1 (3,000 × £5)	15,000	15,000	45,000	30,000
Year 2 (1,500 × £5)	7,500	22,500	45,000	22,500
Year 3 (2,500 × £5)	12,500	35,000	45,000	10,000
Year 4 (1,000 × £5)	5,000	40,000	45,000	5,000
	40,000			

1.31 This method is sometimes modified so as to base each year's depreciation on the number of units produced by the machine in that year, rather than on the number of hours in which the machine is active. In this case the depreciation method is referred to as the units of output method.

Applying a depreciation method consistently

1.32 It is up to the business concerned to decide which method of depreciation to apply to its fixed assets. Once that decision has been made, however, it should not be changed - the chosen method of depreciation should be applied consistently from year to year. This is an instance of the consistency concept, which we will look at later in the chapter on accounting concepts.

1.33 Similarly, it is up to the business to decide what a sensible life span for a fixed asset should be. Again, once that life span has been chosen, it should not be changed unless something unexpected happens to the fixed asset.

1.34 It is permissible for a business to depreciate different categories of fixed assets in different ways. For example, if a business owns three cars, then each car would normally be depreciated in the same way (eg by the straight line method) but another category of fixed asset, say, photocopiers, might be depreciated using a different method (eg by the machine hour method).

Exercise 1

A lorry bought for a business cost £17,000. It is expected to last for five years and then be sold for scrap for £2,000. Usage over the five years is expected to be:

Year 1	200 days
Year 2	100 days
Year 3	100 days
Year 4	150 days
Year 5	40 days

Required

Work out the depreciation to be charged each year under:

(a)   the straight line method;
(b)   the reducing balance method (using a rate of 35%); and
(c)   the machine hour method.

Solution

(a)   Under the straight line method, depreciation for each of the five years is:

$$\text{Annual depreciation} = \frac{£17,000 - 2,000}{5} = £3,000$$

(b)   Under the reducing balance method, depreciation for each of the five years is:

Year	Depreciation	
1	35% × £17,000	= £5,950
2	35% × (£17,000 – £5,950) = 35% × £11,050	= £3,868
3	35% × (£11,050 – £3,868) = 35% × £7,182	= £2,514
4	35% × (£7,182 – £2,514) = 35% × £4,668	= £1,634
5	Balance to bring book value down to £2,000 = £4,668 – £1,634 – £2,000	= £1,034

(c)   Under the machine hour method, depreciation for each of the five years is calculated as follows.

Total usage (days) = 200 + 100 + 100 + 150 + 40 = 590 days

$$\text{Depreciation per day} = \frac{£17,000 - 2,000}{590} = £25.42$$

Year	Usage (days)	Depreciation (£) (days × £25.42)
1	200	5,084.00
2	100	2,542.00
3	100	2,542.00
4	150	3,813.00
5	40	1,016.80
		14,997.80

(The answer does not come to exactly £15,000 because of the rounding carried out at the 'depreciation per day' stage of the calculation.)

A fall in the value of a fixed asset

1.35   When the 'market' value of a fixed asset falls so that it is worth less than the amount of its net book value, and the fall in value is expected to be permanent, the asset should be written down to its new low market value. The charge in the profit and loss account for the diminution in the value of the asset during the accounting period should then be:

	£
Net book value at the beginning of the period	X
Less: new reduced value	(X)
Equals: the charge for the diminution in the asset's value in the period.	X

Example: fall in asset value

1.36   A business purchased a leasehold property on 1 January 19X1 at a cost of £100,000. The lease has a 20 year life. After 5 years' use, on 1 January 19X6, the business decides that since property prices have fallen sharply, the leasehold is now worth only £60,000, and that the value of the asset should be reduced in the accounts of the business.

The leasehold was being depreciated at the rate of 5% per annum on cost.

1.37   Before the asset is reduced in value, the annual depreciation charge is:

$$\frac{£100,000}{20 \text{ years}} = £5,000 \text{ per annum} (= 5\% \text{ of } £100,000)$$

After 5 years, the accumulated depreciation would be £25,000, and the net book value of the leasehold £75,000, which is £15,000 more than the new asset value. This £15,000 should be written off as a charge for depreciation or fall in the asset's value in year 5, so that the total charge in year 5 is:

	£
Net book value of the leasehold after 4 years (£100,000 − 20,000)	80,000
Revised asset value at end of year 5	60,000
Charge against profit in year 5	20,000

An alternative method of calculation is:

	£
'Normal' depreciation charge per annum	5,000
Further fall in value, from net book value at end of year 5 to revised value	15,000
Charge against profit in year 5	20,000

1.38   The leasehold has a further 15 years to run, and its value is now £60,000. From year 6 to year 20, the annual charge for depreciation will be:

$$\frac{£60,000}{15 \text{ years}} = £4,000 \text{ per annum}$$

Change in expected life of an asset

1.39   The depreciation charge on a fixed asset depends not only on the cost (or value) of the asset and its estimated residual value, but also on its estimated useful life.

1.40   Suppose that a business purchased a fixed asset costing £12,000 with an estimated life of four years and no residual value. If it used the straight line method of depreciation, it would make an annual provision of 25% of £12,000 = £3,000.

Now what would happen if the business decided after two years that the useful life of the asset has been underestimated, and it still had five more years in use to come (making its total life seven years)?

For the first two years, the asset would have been depreciated by £3,000 per annum, so that its net book value after two years would be £(12,000 − 6,000) = £6,000. If the remaining life of the asset is now revised to five more years, the remaining amount to be depreciated (here £6,000) should be spread over the remaining life, giving an annual depreciation charge for the final five years of:

$$\frac{\text{Net book value at time of life readjustment, minus residual value}}{\text{New estimate of remaining useful life}}$$

$$= \frac{£6,000}{5 \text{ years}} = £1,200 \text{ per annum}$$

Depreciation is not a cash expense

1.41 Depreciation spreads the cost of a fixed asset (less its estimated residual value) over the asset's life. The cash payment for the fixed asset will be made when, or soon after, the asset is purchased. Annual depreciation of the asset in subsequent years is not a cash expense - rather it allocates costs to those later years for a cash payment that has occurred previously.

1.42 For example, suppose a business purchased some shop fittings for £6,000 on 1 July 19X5 and paid for them in cash on that date.

Subsequently, depreciation may be charged at £600 pa for ten years. So each year £600 is deducted from profits and the net book value of the fittings goes down, but no actual cash is being paid. The cash was all paid on 1 July 19X5. So annual depreciation is not a cash expense, but rather an allocation of the original cost to later years.

2   REVALUATION OF FIXED ASSETS

2.1 Largely because of inflation, it is now quite common for the market value of certain fixed assets to go up, in spite of getting older. The most obvious example of rising market values is land and buildings (both freehold and leasehold).

A business which owns fixed assets which are rising in value is not obliged to revalue those assets in its balance sheet. However, in order to give a more 'true and fair view' of the position of the business, it might be decided that some fixed assets should be revalued upwards; otherwise the total value of the assets of the business might seem unrealistically low. When fixed assets are revalued, depreciation should be charged on the revalued amount.

Example: the revaluation of fixed assets

2.2 When Ira Vann commenced trading as a car hire dealer on 1 January 19X1, he purchased business premises freehold at a cost of £50,000.

For the purpose of accounting for depreciation, he decided that:

(a) the freehold land part of the business premises was worth £20,000. This would not be depreciated;

(b) the building part of the business premises was worth the remaining £30,000. This would be depreciated by the straight-line method to a nil residual value over 30 years.

After five years of trading on 1 January 19X6, Ira decides that his business premise is now worth £150,000, divided into:

	£
Land	75,000
Building	75,000
	150,000

He estimates that the building still has a further 25 years of useful life remaining.

Calculate the annual charge for depreciation in each of the 30 years of its life, and the balance sheet value of the land and building as at the end of each year.

Solution

2.3 *Before the revaluation*, the annual depreciation charge is £1,000 per annum on the building. This charge is made in each of the first five years of the asset's life.

The net book value of the asset will decline by £1,000 per annum, to:

(a) £49,000 as at 31.12.X1;
(b) £48,000 as at 31.12.X2;
(c) £47,000 as at 31.12.X3;

(d)   £46,000 as at 31.12.X4;
(e)   £45,000 as at 31.12.X5.

2.4   *When the revaluation takes place*, the amount of the revaluation is:

	£
New asset value	150,000
Net book value as at end of 19X5	45,000
Amount of revaluation	105,000

The asset will be revalued by £105,000 to £150,000. If you remember the accounting equation, that the total value of assets must be equalled by the total value of capital and liabilities you should recognise that if assets go up in value by £105,000, capital or liabilities must also go up by the same amount. Since the increased value benefits the owners of the business, the amount of the revaluation is added to capital.

2.5   *After the revaluation*, depreciation will be charged on the building at a new rate of:

$$\frac{£75,000}{25 \text{ years}} = £3,000 \text{ per annum}$$

The net book value of the property will then fall by £3,000 per annum over 25 years, from £150,000 as at 1 January 19X6 to only £75,000 at the end of the 25 years - ie the building part of the property value will have been fully depreciated.

2.6   The consequence of a revaluation is therefore a higher annual depreciation charge.

3   ACCOUNTING FOR DEPRECIATION PROVISIONS; FIXED ASSET DISPOSALS

The disposal of fixed assets   5/95

3.1   Fixed assets are not purchased by a business with the intention of reselling them in the normal course of trade. However, they might be sold off at some stage during their life, either when their useful life is over, or before then. A business might decide to sell off a fixed asset long before its useful life has ended.

3.2   Whenever a business sells something, it will make a profit or a loss. When fixed assets are disposed of, there will be a profit or loss on disposal. Because it is a capital item being sold, the profit or loss will be a capital gain or a capital loss. These gains or losses are reported in the profit and loss account of the business (and not as a trading profit in the trading account). They are commonly referred to as 'profit on disposal of fixed assets' or 'loss on disposal'.

3.3   Examination questions on the disposal of fixed assets usually ask for ledger accounts to be prepared, showing the entries in the accounts to record the disposal. But before we look at the ledger accounting for disposing of assets, we had better look at the principles behind calculating the profit (or loss) on disposing of assets.

The principles behind calculating the profit or loss on disposal

3.4   The profit or loss on the disposal of a fixed asset is the difference between:

(a)   the net book value of the asset at the time of its sale; and
(b)   its net sale price, which is the price minus any costs of making the sale.

A profit is made when the sale price exceeds the net book value, and a loss is made when the sale price is less than the net book value.

Example: disposal of a fixed asset

3.5   A business purchased a fixed asset on 1 January 19X1 for £25,000. It had an estimated life of six years and an estimated residual value of £7,000. The asset was eventually sold after three years on 1 January 19X4 to another trader who paid £17,500 for it.

What was the profit or loss on disposal, assuming that the business uses the straight line method for depreciation?

Solution

3.6   Annual depreciation $= \dfrac{£(25,000 - 7,000)}{6 \text{ years}}$

   $= £3,000$ per annum

	£
Cost of asset	25,000
Less accumulated depreciation (three years)	9,000
Net book value at date of disposal	16,000
Sale price	17,500
Profit on disposal	1,500

This profit will be shown in the profit and loss account of the business where it will be an item of other income added to the gross profit brought down from the trading account.

Second example: disposal of a fixed asset

3.7   A business purchased a machine on 1 July 19X1 at a cost of £35,000. The machine had an estimated residual value of £3,000 and a life of eight years. The machine was sold for £18,600 on 31 December 19X4, the last day of the accounting year of the business. To make the sale, the business had to incur dismantling costs and costs of transporting the machine to the buyer's premises. These amounted to £1,200.

The business uses the straight line method of depreciation. What was the profit or loss on disposal of the machine?

Solution

3.8   Annual depreciation $\dfrac{£(35,000 - 3,000)}{8 \text{ years}} = £4,000$ per annum

It is assumed that in 19X1 only one-half year's depreciation was charged, because the asset was purchased six months into the year.

	£	£
Fixed asset at cost		35,000
Depreciation in 19X1 (1 year)	2,000	
19X2, 19X3 and 19X4	12,000	
Accumulated depreciation		14,000
Net book value at date of disposal		21,000
Sale price	18,600	
Costs incurred in making the sale	(1,200)	
Net sale price		17,400
Loss on disposal		(3,600)

This loss will be shown as an expense in the profit and loss account of the business. It is a capital loss, not a trading loss, and it should not therefore be shown in the trading account.

Provision for depreciation

3.9   A provision for depreciation is the amount set aside as a charge for the wearing out of fixed assets. There are two basic aspects of the provision for depreciation to remember.

(a) A depreciation charge (provision) is made in the profit and loss account in each accounting period for every depreciable fixed asset. Nearly all fixed assets are depreciable, the most important exceptions being freehold land and long-term investments.

(b) The total accumulated depreciation on a fixed asset builds up as the asset gets older. Unlike a provision for doubtful debts, therefore, the total provision for depreciation is always getting larger, until the fixed asset is fully depreciated.

3.10 If you understand these points, the similarity in the accounting treatment of the provision for doubtful debts and the provision for depreciation may become apparent to you.

3.11 The ledger accounting entries for the provision for depreciation are as follows.

(a) There is a provision for depreciation account for each separate category of fixed assets, for example, plant and machinery, land and buildings, fixtures and fittings.

(b) The depreciation charge for an accounting period is a charge against profit. It is an extra provision for depreciation and is accounted for as follows:

DEBIT   P & L account (depreciation expense)
CREDIT   Provision for depreciation account

with the depreciation charge for the period.

(c) The balance on the provision for depreciation account is the total accumulated depreciation. This is always a credit balance brought forward in the ledger account for depreciation.

(d) The fixed asset accounts are unaffected by depreciation. Fixed assets are recorded in these accounts at cost (or, if they are revalued, at their revalued amount).

(e) In the balance sheet of the business, the total balance on the provision for depreciation account (ie accumulated depreciation) is set against the value of fixed asset accounts (ie fixed assets at cost or revalued amount) to derive the net book value of the fixed assets.

Example: provision for depreciation

3.12 Brian Box set up his own computer software business on 1 March 19X6. He purchased a computer system on credit from a manufacturer, at a cost of £16,000. The system has an expected life of three years and a residual value of £2,500. Using the straight line method of depreciation, the fixed asset account, provision for depreciation account and P & L account (extract) and balance sheet (extract) would be as follows, for each of the next three years, 28 February 19X7, 19X8 and 19X9.

FIXED ASSET - COMPUTER EQUIPMENT

	Date		£	*Date*		£
(a)	1.3.X6	Creditor	16,000	28.2.X7	Balance c/d	16,000
(b)	1.3.X7	Balance b/d	16,000	28.2.X8	Balance c/d	16,000
(c)	1.3.X8	Balance b/d	16,000	28.2.X9	Balance c/d	16,000
(d)	1.3.X9	Balance b/d	16,000			

In theory, the fixed asset has now lasted out its expected useful life. However, until it is sold off or scrapped, the asset will still appear in the balance sheet at cost (less accumulated depreciation) and it should remain in the ledger account for computer equipment until it is eventually disposed of.

PROVISION FOR DEPRECIATION

	Date		£	Date		£
(a)	28.2.X7	Balance c/d	4,500	28.2.X7	P & L account	4,500
(b)	28.2.X8	Balance c/d	9,000	1.3.X7	Balance b/d	4,500
				28.2.X8	P & L account	4,500
			9,000			9,000
(c)	28.2.X9	Balance c/d	13,500	1.3.X8	Balance b/d	9,000
				28.2.X9	P & L account	4,500
			13,500			13,500
				1 Mar 19X9	Balance b/d	13,500

The annual depreciation charge is $\dfrac{(£16,000 - 2,500)}{3 \text{ years}} = £4,500$ pa

At the end of three years, the asset is fully depreciated down to its residual value. If it continues to be used by Brian Box, it will not be depreciated any further (unless its estimated value is reduced).

P & L ACCOUNT (EXTRACT)

	Date		£
(a)	28 Feb 19X7	Provision for depreciation	4,500
(b)	28 Feb 19X8	Provision for depreciation	4,500
(c)	28 Feb 19X9	Provision for depreciation	4,500

BALANCE SHEET (EXTRACT) AS AT 28 FEBRUARY

	19X7	19X8	19X9
	£	£	£
Computer equipment at cost	16,000	16,000	16,000
Less accumulated depreciation	4,500	9,000	13,500
Net book value	11,500	7,000	2,500

Example: provision for depreciation with assets acquired part-way through the year

3.13 Brian Box prospers in his computer software business, and before long he purchases a car for himself, and later for his chief assistant Bill Ockhead. Relevant data is as follows.

	Date of purchase	Cost	Estimated life	Estimated residual value
Brian Box car	1 June 19X6	£20,000	3 years	£2,000
Bill Ockhead car	1 June 19X7	£8,000	3 years	£2,000

The straight line method of depreciation is to be used.

3.14 Prepare the motor vehicles account and provision for depreciation of motor vehicle account for the years to 28 February 19X7 and 19X8. (You should allow for the part-year's use of a car in computing the annual charge for depreciation.)

Calculate the net book value of the motor vehicles as at 28 February 19X8.

Solution

3.15 (a) (i) Brian Box car Annual depreciation $\dfrac{£(20,000 - 2,000)}{3 \text{ years}} =$ £6,000 pa

	Monthly depreciation £500	
Depreciation	1 June-19X6 - 28 February 19X7 (9 months)	£4,500
	1 March 19X7 - 28 February 19X8	£6,000

(ii) Bill Ockhead car Annual depreciation $\dfrac{£(8,000 - 2,000)}{3 \text{ years}} =$ £2,000 pa

Depreciation	1 June 19X7 - 28 February 19X8 (9 months)	£1,500

(b)

MOTOR VEHICLES

Date		£	Date		£
1 Jun 19X6	Creditors (or cash) (car purchase)	20,000	28 Feb 19X7	Balance c/d	20,000
1 Mar 19X7	Balance b/d	20,000			
1 Jun 19X7	Creditors (or cash) (car purchase)	8,000	28 Feb 19X8	Balance c/d	28,000
		28,000			28,000
1 Mar 19X8	Balance b/d	28,000			

PROVISION FOR DEPRECIATION OF MOTOR VEHICLES

Date		£	Date		£
28 Feb 19X7	Balance c/d	4,500	28 Feb 19X7	P & L account	4,500
			1 Mar 19X7	Balance b/d	4,500
28 Feb 19X8	Balance c/d	12,000	28 Feb 19X8	P & L account (6,000+1,500)	7,500
		12,000			12,000
			1 March 19X8	Balance b/d	12,000

BALANCE SHEET (WORKINGS) AS AT 28 FEBRUARY 19X8

	Brian Box car £	£	Bill Ockhead car £	£	Total £
Asset at cost		20,000		8,000	28,000
Accumulated depreciation:					
Year to:					
28 Feb 19X7	4,500		-		
28 Feb 19X8	6,000		1,500		
		10,500		1,500	12,000
Net book value		9,500		6,500	16,000

The disposal of fixed assets: ledger accounting entries

3.16 We have already seen how the profit or loss on disposal of a fixed asset should be computed. A profit on disposal is an item of 'other income' in the P & L account, and a loss on disposal is an item of expense in the P & L account.

3.17 It is customary in ledger accounting to record the disposal of fixed assets in a *disposal of fixed assets* account.

(a) The profit or loss on disposal is the difference between:

(i)   the sale price of the asset (if any); and
(ii)   the net book value of the asset at the time of sale.

(b) The relevant items which must appear in the disposal of fixed assets account are therefore:

(i)   the value of the asset (at cost, or revalued amount★);

    (ii)   the accumulated depreciation up to the date of sale;

    (iii) the sale price of the asset.

    ★To simplify the explanation of the rules, we will assume now that the fixed assets disposed of are valued at cost.

(c) The ledger accounting entries are as follows.

    (i)   DEBIT   Disposal of fixed asset account
           CREDIT   Fixed asset account
          with the cost of the asset disposed of.

    (ii)   DEBIT   Provision for depreciation account
           CREDIT   Disposal of fixed asset account
          with the accumulated depreciation on the asset as at the date of sale.

    (iii) DEBIT   Debtor account or cash book
           CREDIT   Disposal of fixed asset account
          with the sale price of the asset. The sale is therefore not recorded in a sales account, but in the disposal of fixed asset account itself.

    (iv) The balance on the disposal account is the profit or loss on disposal and the corresponding double entry is recorded in the P & L account itself.

Example: disposal of assets: ledger accounting entries

3.18 A business has £110,000 worth of machinery at cost. Its policy is to make a provision for depreciation at 20% per annum straight line. The total provision now stands at £70,000. The business now sells for £19,000 a machine which it purchased exactly two years ago for £30,000.

Show the relevant ledger entries.

Solution

3.19

PLANT AND MACHINERY ACCOUNT

	£		£
Balance b/d	110,000	Plant disposals account	30,000
		Balance c/d	80,000
	110,000		110,000
Balance b/d	80,000		

PLANT AND MACHINERY DEPRECIATION PROVISION

	£		£
Plant disposals (20% of £30,000 for 2 years)	12,000	Balance b/d	70,000
Balance c/d	58,000		
	70,000		70,000
		Balance b/d	58,000

PLANT DISPOSALS

	£		£
Plant and machinery account	30,000	Depreciation provision	12,000
Profit and loss a/c (profit on sale)	1,000	Cash	19,000
	31,000		31,000

Check:

	£
Asset at cost	30,000
Accumulated depreciation at time of sale	12,000
Net book value at time of sale	18,000
Sale price	19,000
Profit on sale	1,000

Example continued

3.20 Taking the example above assume that, instead of the machine being sold for £19,000, it was exchanged for a new machine costing £60,000, a credit of £19,000 being received upon exchange. In other words £19,000 is the trade-in price of the old machine. Now what are the relevant ledger account entries?

Solution

3.21

PLANT AND MACHINERY ACCOUNT

	£		£
Balance b/d	110,000	Plant disposal	30,000
Cash (60,000 - 19,000)	41,000	Balance c/d	140,000
Plant disposals	19,000		
	170,000		170,000
Balance b/d	140,000		

The new asset is recorded in the fixed asset account at cost £(41,000 + 19,000) = £60,000.

PLANT AND MACHINERY DEPRECIATION PROVISION

	£		£
Plant disposals (20% of £30,000 for 2 years)	12,000	Balance b/d	70,000
Balance c/d	58,000		
	70,000		70,000
		Balance b/d	58,000

PLANT DISPOSALS

	£		£
Plant and machinery	30,000	Depreciation provision	12,000
Profit transferred to P & L	1,000	Plant and machinery	19,000
	31,000		31,000

Exercise 2

A business purchased two widget-making machines on 1 January 19X5 at a cost of £15,000 each. Each had an estimated life of five years and a nil residual value. The straight line method of depreciation is used.

Owing to an unforeseen slump in market demand for widgets, the business decided to reduce its output of widgets, and switch to making other products instead. On 31 March 19X7, one widget-making machine was sold (on credit) to a buyer for £8,000.

Later in the year, however, it was decided to abandon production of widgets altogether, and the second machine was sold on 1 December 19X7 for £2,500 cash.

Prepare the machinery account, provision for depreciation of machinery account and disposal of machinery account for the accounting year to 31 December 19X7.

Solution

MACHINERY ACCOUNT

		£			£
19X7			*19X7*		
1 Jan	Balance b/f	30,000	31 Mar	Disposal of machinery account	15,000
			1 Dec	Disposal of machinery account	15,000
		30,000			30,000

PROVISION FOR DEPRECIATION OF MACHINERY

		£			£
19X7			*19X7*		
31 Mar	Disposal of machinery account*	6,750	1 Jan	Balance b/f	12,000
1 Dec	Disposal of machinery account**	8,750	31 Dec	P & L account***	3,500
		15,500			15,500

*   Depreciation at date of disposal £6,000 + £750
**   Depreciation at date of disposal £6,000 + £2,750
***   Depreciation charge for the year = £750 + £2,750

DISPOSAL OF MACHINERY

19X7		£	*19X7*		£
31 Mar	Machinery account	15,000	31 Mar	Debtor account (sale price)	8,000
			31 Mar	Provision of depreciation	6,750
1 Dec	Machinery	15,000	1 Dec	Cash (sale price)	2,500
			1 Dec	Provision of depreciation	8,750
			31 Dec	P & L account (loss on disposal)	4,000
		30,000			30,000

You should be able to calculate that there was a loss on the first disposal of £250, and on the second disposal of £3,750, giving a total loss of £4,000.

Workings

1   At 1 January 19X7, accumulated depreciation on the machines will be

   2 machines × 2 years × $\dfrac{£15,000}{5}$ per machine pa = £12,000,

   or £6,000 per machine

2   Monthly depreciation is $\dfrac{£3,000}{12}$ = £250 per machine per month

3   The machines are disposed of in 19X7.

   (a)   On 31 March - after 3 months of the year.
      Depreciation for the year on the machine = 3 months × £250 = £750.

   (b)   On 1 December - after 11 months of the year.
      Depreciation for the year on the machine = 11 months × £250 = £2,750

4   SSAP 12 ACCOUNTING FOR DEPRECIATION

4.1   The Companies Act 1985 requires that all fixed assets having a limited economic life should be depreciated. SSAP 12 gives a useful discussion of the purpose of depreciation and supplements the statutory requirements in important respects. (Note that the following paragraphs cover some of the ground you have already covered but with particular relevance to SSAP 12.)

4.2   Depreciation is defined in SSAP 12 as 'the measure of the wearing out, consumption or other reduction in the useful economic life of a fixed asset whether arising from use, effluxion of time or obsolescence through technological or market changes'. This definition covers the amortisation of assets with a pre-determined life, such as a leasehold, and the depletion of wasting assets such as mines.

4.3   The need to depreciate fixed assets arises from the accruals concept. If money is expended in purchasing an asset then the amount expended must at some time be charged against profits. If the asset is one which contributes to an enterprise's revenue over a number of accounting periods it would be inappropriate to charge any single period (eg the period in which the asset was acquired) with the whole of the expenditure. Instead, some method must be found of spreading the cost of the asset over its useful economic life.

4.4 This view of depreciation as a process of allocation of the cost of an asset over several accounting periods is the view adopted by SSAP 12. It is worth mentioning here two common misconceptions about the purpose and effects of depreciation.

(a) It is sometimes thought that the net book value (NBV) of an asset is equal to its net realisable value and that the object of charging depreciation is to reflect the fall in value of an asset over its life. This misconception is the basis of a common, but incorrect, argument which says that freehold properties (say) need not be depreciated in times when property values are rising. It is true that historical cost balance sheets often give a misleading impression when a property's NBV is much below its market value, but in such a case it is open to a business to incorporate a revaluation into its books, or even to prepare its accounts on the current cost convention. This is a separate problem from that of allocating the property's cost over successive accounting periods.

(b) Another misconception is that depreciation is provided so that an asset can be replaced at the end of its useful life. This is not the case.

(i) If there is no intention of replacing the asset, it could then be argued that there is no need to provide for any depreciation at all.

(ii) If prices are rising, the replacement cost of the asset will exceed the amount of depreciation provided.

4.5 SSAP 12 contains no detailed guidance on the calculation of depreciation or the suitability of the various depreciation methods and merely requires that the method chosen should be fair and appropriate.

Factors affecting depreciation

4.6 SSAP 12 states that:

'the assessment of depreciation, and its allocation to accounting periods, involves the consideration of three factors:

(a) the carrying amount of the asset (whether cost or valuation);

(b) the length of the asset's expected useful economic life to the business of the enterprise, having due regard to the incidence of obsolescence; and

(c) the estimated residual value of the asset at the end of its useful economic life in the business of the enterprise.'

4.7 The cost at which fixed assets are to be stated in the accounts is defined by the Companies Act 1985, and is, broadly speaking, purchase price or manufacturing cost less incidental expenses.

4.8 The estimated residual value of an asset is of necessity a matter of judgement. Where it is expected to be a relatively small amount in relation to the asset's cost (and therefore immaterial) it is convenient to assume that the residual value is nil.

4.9 The expected life of an asset is again a matter of judgement. SSAP 12 comments that an asset's useful life may be:

(a) pre-determined, as in leaseholds;
(b) directly governed by extraction or consumption (eg a mine or quarry);
(c) dependent on the extent of use (eg a motor car);
(d) reduced by economic or technological obsolescence.

4.10 If it becomes clear that the original estimate of an asset's useful life was incorrect, it should be revised. Normally, no adjustment should be made in respect of the depreciation charged in previous years; instead the remaining net book value of the asset should be depreciated over the new estimate of its remaining useful life. But if future results could be materially distorted, the adjustment to accumulated depreciation should be recognised in the accounts.

Methods of depreciation

4.11 The cost of an asset less its residual value is known as the depreciable amount of the asset. For example, if plant has a five year expected life and the anticipated capital costs are:

	£
Purchase cost	19,000
Delivery	1,500
Installation by own employees	2,700
	23,200

while the residual value at the end of the fifth year is expected to be £3,200, the depreciable amount would be £20,000. Any repair and maintenance costs incurred during the period are written off as running costs in the year in which they are incurred.

4.12 However, if major improvements are made to an asset, thereby increasing its expected life, the depreciable amount should be adjusted. For example, if at the beginning of year 3, £11,000 was spent on technological improvements to the plant so prolonging its expected life by three years (with a residual value of £1,200 at the end of the eighth year), the depreciable amount would be adjusted.

	£
Original depreciable amount	20,000
Less amount already depreciated (say 2 × £4,000)	8,000
	12,000
Add fall in residual value £(3,200 – 1,200)	2,000
	14,000
Add further capital expenditure	11,000
New depreciable amount	25,000

The new depreciable amount would be written off over the remaining useful life of the asset, ie 6 years.

4.13 There are a number of different methods of calculating the depreciation charge for an accounting period, each giving a different result. The most common are:

(a) the straight line method;
(b) the reducing balance method;
(c) the sum of digits method;
(d) the machine hour method;
(e) revaluation;
(f) the annuity (actuarial) method;
(g) the outside investments involved.

The last three methods are rare in practice.

4.14 The *straight line method* is the simplest and the most commonly used in practice. The *reducing balance* and *sum of digits* methods are accelerated methods which lead to a higher charge in earlier years. Since repair and maintenance costs tend to increase as assets grow older these methods lead to a more even allocation of total fixed asset costs (depreciation plus maintenance).

4.15 The *machine hour method* is suited to assets which depreciate primarily through use rather than through effluxion of time. Such assets might include mines and quarries, which are subject to gradual exhaustion of the minerals etc that they contain, and also delivery lorries, which may be argued to depreciate in accordance with the number of miles travelled.

4.16 Neither the CA 1985 nor SSAP 12 prescribes which method should be used. Management must exercise its judgement and SSAP 12 prescribes that:

> '19. If at any time there is a permanent diminution in the value of an asset and the net book amount is considered not to be recoverable in full (perhaps as a result of obsolescence or a fall in demand for a product) the net book amount should be written down immediately to the estimated recoverable amount, which should then be written off over the remaining useful economic life of the asset. If at any time the reasons for making such a provision cease to apply, the provision should be written back to the extent that it is no longer necessary.'

4.17 SSAP 12 also states that a change from one method of providing depreciation to another is permissible only if the new method will give a fairer presentation of the company's results and financial position. Such a change would not constitute a change of accounting policy and disclosure as a prior year adjustment would therefore not be appropriate. Instead, the asset's net book amount should be written off over its remaining useful economic life. The change of method, the reason for the change, and its quantitative effect, should be disclosed by note.

4.18 Many companies carry fixed assets in their balance sheets at revalued amounts, particularly in the case of freehold buildings. When this is done, the depreciation charge should be calculated on the basis of the revalued amount (not the original cost).

Disclosure requirements of SSAP 12

4.19 In addition to the requirements of CA 1985, SSAP 12 requires disclosure of:

    (a)   the depreciation methods used and the useful lives or the depreciation rates used;

    (b)   the effect of revaluation of assets during the financial period. The CA 1985 requires disclosure of movements on reserves, including the revaluation reserve.

5   THE FIXED ASSETS REGISTER   5/95

5.1 Nearly all but the smallest organisations keep a fixed assets register. This is a listing of all fixed assets owned by the organisation, broken down perhaps by department, location or asset type.

5.2 A fixed assets register is maintained primarily for internal purposes. It does not record rights over or obligations towards third parties but shows an organisation's investment in capital equipment. A fixed asset register is also part of the *internal control system*. Fixed assets registers or ledgers are sometimes called *real accounts*, to distinguish them from *impersonal accounts* such as 'rent' in the nominal ledger and *personal accounts* such as 'A Detta' in the sales ledger. They tend to include very few transactions and for this reason they are separated from those accounts that are more heavily used.

Data kept in a fixed assets register

5.3 Details held about each fixed asset might include the following.

    (a)   The organisation's internal reference number (for physical identification purposes)
    (b)   Manufacturer's serial number (for maintenance purposes)
    (c)   Description of asset
    (d)   Location of asset
    (e)   Department which 'owns' asset
    (f)   Purchase date (for calculation of depreciation)
    (g)   Cost
    (h)   Depreciation method and estimated useful life (for calculation of depreciation)
    (i)   Net book value

5.4 The main events giving rise to entries in a fixed asset register or 'inputs' in the case of a computerised one, would be:

    (a)   purchase of an asset;
    (b)   sale of an asset;

(c) loss or destruction of an asset;
(d) transfer of assets between departments;
(e) revision of estimated useful life of an asset;
(f) scrapping of an asset.

5.5 'Outputs' from a fixed assets register would be made:

(a) to enable reconciliations to be made to the nominal ledger;
(b) to enable depreciation charges to be posted to the nominal ledger; and
(c) for physical verification/audit purposes.

Layout of fixed assets register

5.6 The layout of a fixed assets register and the degree of detail included will depend on the organisation in question. Below is a fairly typical layout from a fixed assets register.

Plant No.	Assets	Depreciation Rate	WDV bf	Adds (Disps)	Profit/ (Loss)	Depreciation	WDV cf

Control

5.7 It is important, both from the point of view of external reporting (ie the audit) and for internal purposes, that there are controls over fixed assets. The fixed assets register has already been mentioned. Four further points should be made in this context.

(a) *Purchase* of fixed assets, which can involve a great deal of capital expenditure, must be authorised and must only be made by a responsible official.

(i) The purchaser should obtain several quotations.

(ii) The person authorising the expenditure should not be the same as the person who is using the asset.

(b) Procedures should exist and be enforced for *disposal* of fixed assets to ensure that the sales proceeds are not misappropriated.

(c) The fixed assets register must reconcile with the nominal ledger.

(d) The fixed assets register must reconcile with the physical presence of capital items.

The first two points are self explanatory. The second two will be examined in more detail.

The fixed assets register and the nominal ledger

5.8 Generally, the fixed assets register is not integrated with the nominal ledger. If you look at our example of a fixed assets register in paragraph 5.6 above, you will see that the entry lists the nominal ledger accounts (cost account, accumulated depreciation account and depreciation expense account) to which the relevant amounts must be posted and also contains other details not required in those nominal ledger accounts. In other words, the fixed assets register is not part of the double entry and is there for memorandum and control purposes.

5.9 The fixed assets register must therefore be reconciled to the nominal ledger to make sure that all additions, disposals and depreciation provisions and charges have been posted. For example, the total of all the 'cost' figures in the fixed assets register for motor vehicles should equal the balance on the 'motor vehicles cost' account in the nominal ledger, and the same goes for accumulated depreciation.

5.10 If an asset is sold off, this should be properly authorised, the asset released, the register completed and the necessary entries made in the journal and ledger accounts. If discrepancies arise between the register and the nominal ledger, these must be investigated. It could be, for example, that there is a delay in sending the appropriate authorisation form where an asset has been disposed of.

The fixed assets register and the fixed assets

5.11 It is possible that the fixed assets register may not reconcile with the fixed assets actually present. This may be for the following reasons.

(a) An asset has been stolen or damaged and this has not been noticed or not recorded.

(b) A fixed asset may have become obsolete or damaged and need to be written down but the appropriate entries have not been made.

(c) New assets have been purchased but not yet recorded in the register because the register has not been kept up to date.

(d) Errors have been made in entering details in the register.

5.12 It is important therefore that the company:

(a) physically inspects all the items in the fixed assets register; and
(b) keeps the fixed assets register up to date.

The nature of the inspection will obviously vary between organisations. A large company might carry out a fixed asset inspection of, for example, 25% of assets by value each year, aiming to cover all categories every five years. A small company might be able to inspect all its fixed assets each day, although this 'inspection' will probably not be formally recorded.

Dealing with discrepancies

5.13 As mentioned in 5.11 above, some assets may require an adjustment in their expected life due to excessive wear and tear. The proper authority to change any estimations as to the life of an asset must have the correct authorisation, and the information should be communicated to the accounts department who will need to make the right adjustments in the journal, the register and the ledger.

5.14 When discrepancies are discovered, the appropriate action must be taken. It may be possible to resolve the discrepancy by updating the fixed assets register and/or nominal ledger to reflect the new position. It may not be possible for the person who discovers the discrepancy to resolve it himself. For example, if a fixed asset has to be revalued downwards due to wear and tear or obsolescence, he may have to refer the matter to his superior who has more experience and judgement in such matters.

5.15 The May 1995 examination involved an adjustment of the nominal ledger where it did not reconcile with the fixed assets register.

Example: Extract from a computerised fixed assets register

5.16 Most fixed assets registers will be computerised. Below is an extract from a fixed asset register showing one item as it might appear when the details are printed out.

FASSET HOLDINGS PLC

Asset Code: 938

Next depreciation: 539.36

A   Description:

1 × Seisha Laser printer YCA40809 office publisher

B   Date of purchase: 25/05/96

C   Cost: 1618.25

D   Accumulated depreciation: 584.35

E   Depreciation %:   33.33%

F   Depreciation type: straight line

G   Date of disposal: NOT SET

H   Sale proceeds: 0.00

I   Accumulated depreciation amount: 55Q O/EQPT DEP CHARGE

J   Depreciation expense account: 34F DEPN O/EQPT

K   Depreciation period: standard

L   Comments: electronic office

M   Residual value: 0.00

N   Cost account: 65C O/E ADDITIONS

Chapter roundup

- This has been a long chapter with a lot to take in, so do not be surprised if it has taken you longer than you expected to work through it. Now that you have finally reached the end, you should understand the following points.

- The cost of a fixed asset, less its estimated residual value, is allocated fairly between accounting periods by means of depreciation. The provision for depreciation is both:
  - o   charged against profit; and
  - o   deducted from the value of the fixed asset in the balance sheet.

- There are several different methods of depreciation, but the straight line method and the reducing balance method are most commonly used in practice. You also need to know how to use the machine hour method of depreciation. Every method described in this chapter allocates the total depreciable amount between accounting periods, although in different ways.

- When a fixed asset is revalued, depreciation is charged on the residual amount.

- When a fixed asset is sold, there is likely to be a profit or loss on disposal. This is the difference between the net sale price of the asset and its net book value at the time of disposal.

- You should also know how to handle the double entry bookkeeping for providing for depreciation, and for the disposal of fixed assets.

- You should be aware of the provisions of SSAP 12 *Accounting for depreciation.*

- Most organisations keep a fixed assets register. This is a listing of all fixed assets owned by the organisation broken down perhaps by department, location or asset type. This must be kept up to date.

- Discrepancies between the fixed assets register and the fixed assets present and between the fixed assets register and the nominal ledger must be investigated and either resolved or referred to the appropriate person.

Test your knowledge

1 Define a fixed asset. (see para 1.1)

2 What does depreciation measure? (1.7)

3 What is an asset's net book value? (1.10)

4 Give three common depreciation methods. (1.13)

5 How should a permanent fall in the value of a fixed asset be accounted for? (1.35)

6 Explain how the depreciation charge is adjusted when an asset's estimated useful life is increased. (1.40)

7 Define (in accounting terms) the profit or loss which arises on disposal of a fixed asset. (3.4)

8 What details about a fixed asset might be included in a fixed assets register? (5.3)

9 Why might the fixed assets register not reconcile with the fixed assets? (5.11)

Now try illustrative questions 17 and 18 at the end of the Study Text

Chapter 12

INTANGIBLE FIXED ASSETS

This chapter covers the following topics.

		Syllabus reference	Ability required
1	Goodwill	1(c)	Skill
2	Deferred development costs	1(c)	Skill

Introduction

Intangible fixed assets are fixed assets which have a value to the business because they have been paid for, but which do not have any physical substance. The most significant of such intangible assets are goodwill and deferred development costs.

The concept of goodwill might be familiar to you already, from common everyday knowledge. Goodwill is created by good relationships between a business and its customers, for example:

(a) by building up a reputation (by word of mouth perhaps) for high quality products or high standards of service;

(b) by responding promptly and helpfully to queries and complaints from customers;

(c) through the personality of the staff and their attitudes to customers.

In many companies, especially those which produce food or 'scientific' products such as medicines or 'high technology' products, the expenditure on *research and development* is considerable. When R & D is a large item of cost its accounting treatment may have a significant influence on the profits of a business and its balance sheet valuation. Because of this attempts have been made to standardise the treatment, and these are discussed in Section 2 of this chapter.

---

1 GOODWILL

1.1 The value of goodwill to a business might be extremely significant. However, goodwill is not usually valued in the accounts of a business at all, and we should not normally expect to find an amount for goodwill in its balance sheet. For example, the welcoming smile of the bar staff may contribute more to a pub's profits than the fact that a new electronic cash register has recently been acquired; even so, whereas the cash register will be recorded in the accounts as a fixed asset, the value of staff would be ignored for accounting purposes.

1.2 On reflection, this omission of goodwill from the accounts of a business might be easy to understand.

(a) The goodwill is inherent in the business but it has not been paid for, and it does not have an 'objective' value. We can guess at what such goodwill is worth, but such guesswork would be a matter of individual opinion, and not based on hard facts.

(b) Goodwill changes from day to day. One act of bad customer relations might damage goodwill and one act of good relations might improve it. Staff with a favourable personality might retire or leave to find another job, to be replaced by staff who need time to find their feet in the job, etc. Since goodwill is continually changing in value, it cannot realistically be recorded in the accounts of the business.

Purchased goodwill

1.3 There is one exception to the general rule that goodwill has no objective valuation. This is when a business is sold. People wishing to set up in business have a choice of how to do it - they can either buy their own fixed assets and stock and set up their business from scratch, or they can buy up an existing business from a proprietor willing to sell it. When a buyer purchases an existing business, he will have to purchase not only its fixed assets and stocks (and perhaps take over its creditors and debtors too) but also the goodwill of the business.

1.4 For example, suppose that Tony Tycoon agrees to purchase the business of Clive Dunwell for £30,000. Clive's business has net fixed assets valued at £14,000 and net current assets of £11,000, all of which are taken over by Tony. Tony will be paying more for the business than its tangible assets are worth, because he is purchasing the goodwill of the business too. The balance sheet of Tony's business when it begins operations (assuming that he does not change the value of the tangible fixed and current assets) will be:

TONY TYCOON
BALANCE SHEET AS AT THE START OF BUSINESS

	£
Intangible fixed asset: goodwill	5,000
Tangible fixed assets: net book value	14,000
Net current assets	11,000
Net assets	30,000
Capital	30,000

1.5 Purchased goodwill is shown in this balance sheet because it has been paid for. It has no tangible substance, and so it is an intangible fixed asset.

Purchased goodwill has been defined as 'the excess of the price paid for a business over the fair market value of the individual assets and liabilities acquired'.

Exercise

To make sure that you understand goodwill, try a solution to the following quick exercise.

Toad goes into business with £10,000 capital and agrees to buy Thrush's shoe-repair shop in the centre of a busy town for £6,500. Thrush's recent accounts show net assets of £3,500, which Toad values at £4,000.

Required

Prepare the balance sheet of Toad's business:

(a) before he purchases Thrush's business; and
(b) after the purchase.

Solution

(a)   Toad's balance sheet before the purchase is:

	£
Cash	10,000
Proprietor's interest	10,000

(b)   Thrush's valuation of the assets to be acquired is irrelevant to Toad who sees the situation thus:

	£
Consideration (cash to be paid)	6,500
Less net assets acquired (at Toad's valuation)	4,000
Difference (= goodwill)	2,500

Toad must credit his cash book with the £6,500 paid. He can only debit sundry assets with £4,000. A further debit of £2,500 is thus an accounting necessity and he must open up a goodwill account.

Toad's balance sheet immediately after the transfer would therefore be:

	£
Goodwill	2,500
Sundry assets	4,000
Cash (£10,000 - £6,500)	3,500
	10,000
Proprietor's interest	10,000

(Normally one would have more detail as to the breakdown of the sundry assets into fixed assets, current assets etc, but this is not relevant to the illustration. The main point is that the sundry assets acquired are tangible whereas the goodwill is not.)

This exercise highlights the difference between 'internally generated' goodwill, which (as in Thrush's case above) is not shown in the books and 'purchased' goodwill, which is. The purchased goodwill in this case is simply Thrush's internally generated goodwill, which has changed hands, bought by Toad at a price shown in Toad's accounts.

The accounting treatment of purchased goodwill

1.6   Once purchased goodwill appears in the accounts of a business, we must decide what to do with it. Purchased goodwill is basically a premium paid for the acquisition of a business as a going concern: indeed, it is often referred to as a 'premium on acquisition'. When a purchaser agrees to pay such a premium for goodwill, he does so because he believes that the true value of the business is worth more to him than the value of its tangible assets. One major reason why he might think so is that the business will earn good profits over the next few years, and so he will pay a premium now to get the business, in the expectation of getting his money back later. However, he pays for the goodwill at the time of purchase, and the value of the goodwill will eventually wear off. Goodwill, it was suggested earlier, is a continually changing thing. A business cannot last forever on its past reputation; it must create new goodwill as time goes on. Even goodwill created by a favourable location might suddenly disappear - for example, a newsagent's shop by a bus stop will lose its location value if the bus route is axed by the local transport authorities.

1.7   Since goodwill wears off, and is basically unstable anyway, it would be inadvisable to keep purchased goodwill indefinitely in the accounts of a business. The treatment of goodwill is the subject of an accounting standard, SSAP 22 *Accounting for goodwill*. SSAP 22 permits two alternative accounting treatments for *purchased* goodwill.

(a)   Write off goodwill immediately by treating it as a reduction in the retained profits of the business acquiring the goodwill.

(b)   Treat goodwill as an intangible fixed asset which, like all fixed assets, must be depreciated or amortised over its expected 'economic' life.

1.8 The advantage of immediately writing off goodwill is that it is prudent and it avoids goodwill ever appearing on the balance sheet. The disadvantage is that it ignores the fact that goodwill does have some longer-term value when first acquired (however difficult to quantify).

1.9 If goodwill is to be written off over a period of years it is shown in the balance sheet as an intangible fixed asset. The gradual 'write-off' approach is based on the idea that goodwill has a limited life and is a cost to be offset against future profits. The advantage of this approach is that it is probably a better representation of its gradual loss of value to the purchaser, as old goodwill is replaced by new goodwill. It is however less prudent than the immediate write-off and poses the problem of determining the estimated useful life of the goodwill, which tends to be subjective. An arbitrary figure such as five years is often used.

How is the value of purchased goodwill decided?

1.10 When a business is sold, there is likely to be some purchased goodwill in the selling price. But how is the amount of this purchased goodwill decided?

This is not really a problem for accountants, who must simply record the goodwill in the accounts of the new business. The value of the goodwill is a matter for the purchaser and seller to agree upon in fixing the purchase/sale price. However, two methods of valuation are worth mentioning here.

(a) The seller and buyer agree on a price without specifically quantifying the goodwill. The purchased goodwill will then be the difference between the price agreed and the value of the tangible assets in the books of the new business.

(b) However, the calculation of goodwill often precedes the fixing of the purchase price and becomes a central element of negotiation. There are many ways of arriving at a value for goodwill and most of them are related to the profit record of the business in question. Some of these ways are illustrated below.

1.11 For an illustration of a few possible methods, let us suppose that a business being sold on 31.12.X3 has recently generated profits as follows:

Year ending 31.12.X1 - £4,000
Year ending 31.12.X2 - £5,000
Year ending 31.12.X3 - £7,000
Capital employed £20,000

Goodwill might be valued at:

(a) twice the final year's profit - ie 2 × £7,000 = £14,000

or

(b) twice the average profit for the past three years

$$\text{ie } 2 \times \frac{£4,000 + £5,000 + £7,000}{3} = £10,667$$

or perhaps

(c) three times the average profit for the past two years

$$\text{ie } 3 \times \frac{£5,000 + £7,000}{2} = £18,000$$

(d) Alternatively the 'super profits' approach could be used. This relates the profit to the capital employed in one of a number of ways. Let us assume that in this particular business a reasonable return on capital employed would be 10% and that a reasonable salary for the proprietor would be £4,000. For the year 19X3 the return on the proprietor's funds, in excess of the salary that he could earn elsewhere, is therefore £3,000.

We could say:

(i)   the £3,000 represents a 10% return on the assets of the business; the assets must therefore be:

$$\frac{100}{10} \times £3,000 = \underline{£30,000}$$

Of the £30,000 we know that £20,000 exists in tangible form (net assets employed). Therefore the remaining £10,000 must be intangible, ie goodwill is £10,000.

In other words as well as our 10% return on tangible assets (£20,000 × 10% = £2,000) our intangible asset, goodwill, earns us a further £1,000 (£10,000 × 10%) which is the 'super profit';

(ii)   we could regard the intangible asset as having limited life and purchase, say seven years 'super profits'

Goodwill would therefore be 7 × £1,000 – $\underline{£7,000}$

Many other variations are possible. A formula may be agreed between vendor and purchaser in advance or there may be much haggling to reach agreement. The goodwill element of the purchase price is of course additional to the value of tangible assets acquired.

1.12   Any attempt to quantify goodwill in financial terms is purely arbitrary. Using the above methods we have calculated goodwill as high as £18,000 and as low as £7,000. Neither of these figures is the 'correct' figure because there is no correct figure; once a basis for the calculation has been agreed (eg two years purchase of average profits for the past three years) then a figure can be arrived at, but selection of the basis is entirely subjective. In practice, examination questions will always tell you the basis on which goodwill is to be calculated, and it will usually be some version of methods (a) to (c) above. The 'super profits' concept is generally considered rather old-fashioned, but it is mentioned for completeness.

1.13   No matter how goodwill is calculated within the total agreed purchase price, the goodwill shown by the purchaser in his accounts will be the difference between the purchase consideration and his own valuation of the tangible net assets acquired. If A values his tangible net assets at £40,000, goodwill is agreed at £21,000 and B agrees to pay £61,000 for the business but values the tangible net assets at only £38,000, then the goodwill in B's books will be £61,000 – £38,000 = £23,000.

2   DEFERRED DEVELOPMENT COSTS   *11/95*

2.1   This is the other intangible fixed asset you should know about. Large companies may spend significant amounts of money on research and development (R & D) activities. Obviously, any amounts so expended must be credited to cash and debited to an account for research and development expenditure. The accounting problem is how to treat the debit balance on R & D account at the balance sheet date.

2.2   There are two possibilities.

(a)   The debit balance may be classified as an expense and transferred to the profit and loss account. This is referred to as 'writing off' the expenditure.

(b)   The debit balance may be classified as an asset and included in the balance sheet. This is referred to as 'capitalising' or 'carrying forward' or 'deferring' the expenditure.

2.3   The argument for writing off R & D expenditure is that it is an expense just like rates or wages and its accounting treatment should be the same.

The argument for carrying forward R & D expenditure is based on the accruals concept. If R & D activity eventually leads to new or improved products which generate revenue, the costs should be carried forward to be matched against that revenue in future accounting periods.

2.4 Like goodwill, R & D expenditure is the subject of an accounting standard, SSAP 13 *Accounting for research and development*. SSAP 13 (and the Companies Act 1985) requires that *research* expenditure should always be written off in the period in which it is incurred. This is because the advantages derived from general research activities are too remote to justify carrying the expenditure forward.

2.5 Development expenditure is different. It usually relates to a specific project (eg the development of a new product) which can be profitably exploited in the foreseeable future. Provided the viability of the project has been carefully assessed, there is a strong argument for capitalising the development costs associated with it.

2.6 SSAP 13 allows companies to capitalise development expenditure in their accounts, provided that certain criteria are satisfied. Broadly, it is permissible to carry forward such expenditure in the circumstances described above. Even so, a company is never *obliged* to do so; it is always open to a company to take the most prudent view and write off development expenditure in the same way as research expenditure.

2.7 If a company capitalises development expenditure, it will appear in the balance sheet as an intangible asset. Like capitalised goodwill, it must be depreciated (amortised). The process of amortisation should begin when the development project is brought into commercial production.

2.8 Be sure to attempt illustrative question 19, which illustrates the accounting entries required in respect of goodwill and development expenditure.

Chapter roundup

- Intangible fixed assets are those which have a value to the business but which do not have any physical substance. The most significant intangible assets are goodwill and deferred development expenditure.

- If a business has goodwill, it means that the value of the business as a going concern is greater than the value of its separate tangible assets. The valuation of goodwill is extremely subjective and fluctuates constantly. For this reason, goodwill is not normally shown as an asset in the balance sheet.

- The exception to this rule is when someone purchases a business as a going concern. In this case the purchaser and vendor will fix an agreed price which includes an element in respect of goodwill. The way in which goodwill is then valued is not an accounting problem, but a matter of agreement between the two parties.

- Purchased goodwill may then either be immediately written off as an expense in the profit and loss account, or be retained in the balance sheet as an intangible asset. If it is retained in the balance sheet, it must be amortised over its estimated useful economic life.

- Expenditure on research activities must always be written off in the period in which it is incurred.

- Expenditure on development activities may also be written off in the same way. But if the criteria laid down by SSAP 13 are satisfied, such expenditure *may* be capitalised as an intangible asset. It must then be amortised, beginning from the time when the development project is brought into commercial production.

Test your knowledge

1   Why is it unusual to record goodwill as an asset in the accounts? (see para 1.2)

2   What is purchased goodwill? (1.3, 1.5)

3   What two methods of accounting for purchased goodwill are permitted by SSAP 22? (1.7)

4   How is the amount of purchased goodwill calculated? (1.13)

5   What is the required accounting treatment for expenditure on research? (2.4)

6   In what circumstances may development expenditure be capitalised? (2.5, 2.6)

Now try illustrative question 19 at the end of the Study Text

Chapter 13

BANK RECONCILIATIONS

This chapter covers the following topics.

		Syllabus reference	Ability required
1	The bank reconciliation	1(b)	Skill
2	Worked examples	1(b)	Skill

Introduction

The cash book of a business is the record of how much cash the business believes that it has in the bank. In the same way, you yourself might keep a private record of how much money you think you have in your own personal account at your bank, perhaps by making a note in your cheque book of income received and the cheques you write. If you do keep such a record you will probably agree that when your bank sends you a bank statement from time to time the amount it shows as being the balance in your account is rarely exactly the amount that you have calculated for yourself as being your current balance.

Why might your own estimate of your bank balance be different from the amount shown on your bank statement? There are three common explanations.

(a) *Error*. Errors in calculation, or recording income and payments, are more likely to have been made by you than by the bank, but it is conceivable that the bank has made a mistake too.

(b) *Bank charges or bank interest*. The bank might deduct charges for interest on an overdraft or for its services, which you are not informed about until you receive the bank statement.

(c) *Time differences*

   (i) There might be some cheques that you have received and paid into the bank, but which have not yet been 'cleared' and added to your account. So although your own records show that some cash has been added to your account, it has not yet been acknowledged by the bank - although it will be in a very short time when the cheque is eventually cleared.

   (ii) Similarly, you might have made some payments by cheque, and reduced the balance in your account accordingly in the record that you keep, but the person who receives the cheque might not bank it for a while. Even when it is banked, it takes a day or two for the banks to process it and for the money to be deducted from your account.

If you do keep a personal record of your cash position at the bank, and if you do check your periodic bank statements against what you think you should have in your account, you will be doing exactly the same thing that the bookkeepers of a business do when they make a bank reconciliation. A bank reconciliation is a comparison of a bank statement (sent monthly, weekly or even daily by the bank) with the cash book. Differences between the balance on the bank statement and the balance in the cash book will be errors or timing differences, and they should be identified and satisfactorily explained.

---

1   THE BANK RECONCILIATION

The bank statement

1.1   It is a common practice for a business to issue a monthly statement to each credit customer, itemising:

(a)   the balance he owed on his account at the beginning of the month;

(b) new debts incurred by the customer during the month;

(c) payments made by him during the month;

(d) the balance he owes on his account at the end of the month.

In the same way, a bank statement is sent by a bank to its short-term debtors and creditors - ie customers with bank overdrafts and customers with money in their account - itemising the balance on the account at the beginning of the period, receipts into the account and payments from the account during the period, and the balance at the end of the period.

1.2   It is necessary to remember, however, that if a customer has money in his account, the bank owes him that money, and the customer is therefore a creditor of the bank (hence the phrase 'to be in credit' means to have money in your account). This means that if a business has £8,000 cash in the bank, it will have a debit balance in its own cash book, but the bank statement, if it reconciles exactly with the cash book, will state that there is a credit balance of £8,000. (The bank's records are a 'mirror image' of the customer's own records, with debits and credits reversed.)

Why is a bank reconciliation necessary?

1.3   A bank reconciliation is needed to identify errors, either in the cash book of the business or errors made by the bank itself.

(a) *Errors*, once identified, must be corrected. Most errors are likely to be made by the business itself rather than the bank and they should be corrected in the cash book.

(b) *Bank charges* should be credited in the cash book of the business, and debited to the account for bank charges in the nominal ledger.

(c) *Time differences* should be listed and these ought to reconcile the balance on the bank statement with the balance on the corrected cash book.

What to look for when doing a bank reconciliation

1.4   The cash book and bank statement will rarely agree at a given date. If you are doing a bank reconciliation, you may have to look for the following items.

(a) *Corrections and adjustments to the cash book:*

(i)   payments made into the account or from the account by way of standing order, which have not yet been entered in the cash book;

(ii) dividends received (on investments held by the business), paid direct into the bank account but not yet entered in the cash book;

(iii) bank interest and bank charges, not yet entered in the cash book.

(b) *Items reconciling the correct cash book balance to the bank statement:*

(i)   cheques drawn (ie paid) by the business and credited in the cash book, which have not yet been presented to the bank, or 'cleared' and so do not yet appear on the bank statement;

(ii) cheques received by the business, paid into the bank and debited in the cash book, but which have not yet been cleared and entered in the account by the bank, and so do not yet appear on the bank statement.

2   WORKED EXAMPLES   *11/96*

Example: bank reconciliation

2.1   At 30 September 19X6, the balance in the cash book of Wordsworth Ltd was £805.15 (debit). A bank statement on 30 September 19X6 showed Wordsworth Ltd to be in credit by £1,112.30.

On investigation of the difference between the two sums, it was established that:

(a) the cash book had been undercast by £90.00 on the debit side*;

(b) cheques paid in not yet credited by the bank amounted to £208.20;

(c) cheques drawn not yet presented to the bank amounted to £425.35.

★ 'Casting' is an accountant's term for adding up.

Required

(a) Show the correction to the cash book.

(b) Prepare a statement reconciling the balance per bank statement to the balance per cash book.

Solution

2.2   (a)

	£
Cash book balance brought forward	805.15
Add	
Correction of undercast	90.00
Corrected balance	895.15

(b)

	£	£
Balance per bank statement		1,112.30
Add		
Cheques paid in, recorded in the cash book, but not yet credited to the account by the bank	208.20	
Less		
Cheques paid by the company but not yet presented to the company's bank for settlement	425.35	
		(217.15)
Balance per cash book		895.15

Example: more complicated bank reconciliation

2.3   On 30 June 19X0, Cook's cash book showed that he had an overdraft of £300 on his current account at the bank. A bank statement as at the end of June 19X0 showed that Cook was in credit with the bank by £65.

On checking the cash book with the bank statement you find the following.

(a) Cheques drawn, amounting to £500, had been entered in the cash book but had not been presented.

(b) Cheques received, amounting to £400, had been entered in the cash book, but had not been credited by the bank.

(c) On instructions from Cook the bank had transferred interest received on his deposit account amounting to £60 to his current account, recording the transfer on 5 July 19X0. This amount had, however, been credited in the cash book as on 30 June 19X0.

(d) Bank charges of £35 shown in the bank statement had not been entered in the cash book.

(e) The payments side of the cash book had been undercast by £10.

(f) Dividends received amounting to £200 had been paid direct to the bank and not entered in the cash book.

(g) A cheque for £50 drawn on deposit account had been shown in the cash book as drawn on current account.

(h) A cheque issued to Jones for £25 was replaced when out of date. It was entered again in the cash book, no other entry being made. Both cheques were included in the total of unpresented cheques shown above.

Required

(a) Indicate the appropriate adjustments in the cash book.

(b)   Prepare a statement reconciling the amended balance with that shown in the bank statement.

Solution

2.4   (a)   The errors to correct are given in notes (c) (e) (f) (g) and (h) of the problem. Bank charges (note (d)) also call for an adjustment.

	Adjustments in cash book	
	Debit	*Credit*
	(ie add to	*(ie deduct from*
	cash balance)	*cash balance)*
	£	£
Item		
(c) Cash book incorrectly *credited* with interest on 30 June It should have been *debited* with the receipt	60	
(c) Debit cash book (current a/c) with transfer of interest from deposit a/c (note 1)	60	
(d) Bank charges		35
(e) Undercast on payments (credit) side of cash book		10
(f) Dividends received should be debited in the cash book	200	
(g) Cheque drawn on deposit account, not current account. Add cash back to current account	50	
(h) Cheque paid to Jones is out of date and so cancelled. Cash book should now be debited, since previous credit entry is no longer valid (note 2)	25	
	395	45

	£	£
Cash book: balance on current account as at 30 June 19X0		(300)
Adjustments and corrections:		
Debit entries (adding to cash)	395	
Credit entries (reducing cash balance)	(45)	
Net adjustments		350
Corrected balance in the cash book		50

Notes

1   Item (c) is rather complicated. The transfer of interest from the deposit to the current account was presumably given as an instruction to the bank on or before 30 June 19X0. Since the correct entry is to debit the current account (and credit the deposit account) the correction in the cash book should be to debit the current account with $2 \times £60 = £120$ - ie to cancel out the incorrect credit entry in the cash book and then to make the correct debit entry. However, the bank does not record the transfer until 5 July, and so it will not appear in the bank statement.

2   Item (h). Two cheques have been paid to Jones, but one is now cancelled. Since the cash book is credited whenever a cheque is paid, it should be debited whenever a cheque is cancelled. The amount of cheques paid but not yet presented should be reduced by the amount of the cancelled cheque.

(b)   BANK RECONCILIATION STATEMENT AT 30 JUNE 19X0

	£	£
Balance per bank statement		65
Add: outstanding lodgements		
(ie cheques paid in but not yet credited)	400	
deposit interest not yet credited	60	
		460
		525
Less: unpresented cheques	500	
less cheque to Jones cancelled	25	
		475
Balance per corrected cash book		50

2.5 Notice that in preparing a bank reconciliation it is good practice to begin with the balance shown by the bank statement and end with the balance shown by the cash book. It is this corrected cash book balance which will appear in the balance sheet as 'cash at bank'. But examination questions sometimes ask for the reverse order: as always, read the question carefully.

2.6 You might be interested to see the adjustments to the cash book in part (a) of the problem presented in the 'debit and credit' account format, as follows:

CASH BOOK

19X0		£	19X0		£
Jun 30	Bank interest - reversal of incorrect entry	60	Jun 30	Balance brought down	300
	Bank interest account	60		Bank charges	35
	Dividends paid direct to bank	200		Correction of undercast	10
	Cheque drawn on deposit account written back	50		Balance carried down	50
	Cheque issued to Jones cancelled	25			
		395			395

Exercise

From the information given below relating to PWW Ltd you are required:

(a) to make such additional entries in the cash at bank account of PWW Ltd as you consider necessary to show the correct balance at 31 October 19X2;

(b) to prepare a statement reconciling the correct balance in the cash at bank account as shown in (a) above with the balance at 31 October 19X2 that is shown on the bank statement from Z Bank plc.

CASH AT BANK ACCOUNT IN THE LEDGER OF PWW LIMITED

19X2 October		£	19X2 October		£
1	Balance b/f	274	1	Wages	3,146
8	Q Manufacturing	3,443	1	Petty Cash	55
8	R Cement	1,146	8	Wages	3,106
11	S Limited	638	8	Petty Cash	39
11	T & Sons	512	15	Wages	3,029
11	U & Co	4,174	15	Petty Cash	78
15	V plc	1,426	22	A & Sons	929
15	W Electrical	887	22	B Limited	134
22	X and Associates	1,202	22	C & Company	77
26	Y Limited	2,875	22	D & E	263
26	Z Limited	982	22	F Limited	1,782
29	ABC plc	1,003	22	G Associates	230
29	DEE Corporation	722	22	Wages	3,217
29	GHI Limited	2,461	22	Petty Cash	91
31	Balance c/f	14	25	H & Partners	26
			26	J Sons & Co Ltd	868
			26	K & Co	107
			26	L, M & N	666
			28	O Limited	112
			29	Wages	3,191
			29	Petty Cash	52
			29	P & Sons	561
		21,759			21,759

Z BANK PLC - STATEMENT OF ACCOUNT WITH PWW LIMITED

19X2 October		Payments £	Receipts £			Balance £
1						1,135
1	cheque	55				
1	cheque	3,146				
1	cheque	421			O/D	2,487
2	cheque	73				
2	cheque	155			O/D	2,715
6	cheque	212			O/D	2,927
8	sundry credit		4,589			
8	cheque	3,106				
8	cheque	39			O/D	1,483
11	sundry credit		5,324			3,841
15	sundry credit		2,313			
15	cheque	78				
15	cheque	3,029				3,047
22	sundry credit		1,202			
22	cheque	3,217				
22	cheque	91				941
25	cheque	1,782				
25	cheque	134			O/D	975
26	cheque	929				
26	sundry credit		3,857			
26	cheque	230				1,723
27	cheque	263				
27	cheque	77				1,383
29	sundry credit		4,186			
29	cheque	52				
29	cheque	3,191				
29	cheque	26				
29	dividends on investments		2,728			
29	cheque	666				4,362
31	bank charges	936				3,426

Solution

(a)

CASH BOOK

		£				£
31 Oct	Dividends received	2,728	31 Oct	Unadjusted balance b/f (overdraft)		14
			31 Oct	Bank charges		936
			31 Oct	Adjusted balance c/f		1,778
		2,728				2,728

(b) BANK RECONCILIATION STATEMENT
AT 31 OCTOBER 19X2

	£	£
Corrected balance as per cash book		1,778
Cheques paid out but not yet presented	1,648	
Cheques paid in but not yet cleared by bank	0	
		1,648
Balance as per bank statement		3,426

Workings

1	Payments shown on bank statement but not in cash book*£(421 + 73 + 155 + 212)	£861

* Presumably recorded in cash book before 1 October 19X2
but not yet presented for payment as at 30 September 19X2

2	Payments in the cash book and on the bank statement £(3,146 + 55 + 3,106 + 39 + 78 + 3,029 + 3,217 + 91 + 1,782 + 134 + 929 + 230 + 263 + 77 + 52 + 3,191 + 26 + 666)		£20,111
3	Payments in the cash book but not on the bank statement = Total payments in cash book £21,759 minus £20,111 =		£1,648

		£
(Alternatively	J & Sons	868
	K & Co	107
	O Ltd	112
	P & Sons	561
		1,648)

4	Bank charges, not in the cash book	£936
5	Receipts recorded by bank statement but not in cash book: dividends on investments	£2,728
6	Receipts in the cash book and also bank statement (8 Oct £4,589; 11 Oct £5,324; 15 Oct £2,313; 22 Oct £1,202; 26 Oct £3,857; 29 Oct £4,186)	£21,471
7	Receipts recorded in cash book but not bank statement	None

Chapter roundup

- In theory, the entries appearing on a business's bank statement should be exactly the same as those in the business cash book. The balance shown by the bank statement as on a particular date should be the same as the cash book balance at the same date.

- It is common (and a very important financial control) to check this at regular intervals, say weekly or monthly. Invariably it will be found that the picture shown by the bank statement differs from that shown by the cash book. The reasons for this fall into three categories.

  o *Errors*. Entries on the bank statement may be incorrect, but more commonly, errors may be found in the cash book.

  o *Omissions*. Items may appear on the bank statement which have not yet been entered in the cash book. These may include bank changes and payments made by direct debit.

  o *Timing differences*. Cheques are entered in the cash book as soon as they are written, but there may be a delay before the payee receives them and a further delay while they are processed through the bank clearing system.

- When these discrepancies are noticed, appropriate adjustments must be made. Errors must be corrected; omissions from the cash book must be made good. The balance in the cash book will then be corrrect and up to date. Any remaining difference between the cash book balance and the statement balance should then be explained as the result of identifiable timing differences.

Test your knowledge

1   Name four common reasons for differences between the cash book, and the bank statements. (see para 1.4)

2   Show the standard layout of a bank reconciliation. (2.4 (b))

Now try illustrative questions 20 and 21 at the end of the Study Text

Chapter 14

CONTROL ACCOUNTS

<table>
<tr><td colspan="3">This chapter covers the following topics.</td></tr>
<tr><td></td><td>Syllabus
reference</td><td>Ability
required</td></tr>
<tr><td>1   What are control accounts?</td><td>1(b)</td><td>Skill</td></tr>
<tr><td>2   The operation of control accounts</td><td>1(b)</td><td>Skill</td></tr>
<tr><td>3   The purpose of control accounts</td><td>1(b)</td><td>Skill</td></tr>
</table>

Introduction

So far in this text we have assumed that the bookkeeping and double entry (and subsequent preparation of financial accounts) has been carried out by a business without any mistakes. This is not likely to be the case in real life: even the bookkeeper of a very small business with hardly any accounting entries to make will be prone to human error. If a debit is written as £123 and the corresponding credit as £321, then the books of the business are immediately out of balance by £198.

Once an error has been detected, it has to be corrected. In addition, a business is likely to have late adjustments to make to the figures in its accounts (eg depreciation; bad debt provision). A business needs to have some method available for making these corrections or adjustments.

In this chapter and in Chapter 17 we explain how errors can be detected, what kinds of error might exist, and how to post corrections and adjustments to produce final accounts.

1 WHAT ARE CONTROL ACCOUNTS?

1.1 A control account is an account in the nominal ledger in which a record is kept of the total value of a number of similar but individual items. Control accounts are used chiefly for debtors and creditors.

    (a) A debtors control account is an account in which records are kept of transactions involving all debtors in total. The balance on the debtors control account at any time will be the total amount due to the business at that time from its debtors.

    (b) A creditors control account is an account in which records are kept of transactions involving all creditors in total, and the balance on this account at any time will be the total amount owed by the business at that time to its creditors.

1.2 Although control accounts are used mainly in accounting for debtors and creditors, they can also be kept for other items, such as stocks of goods, wages and salaries. The first important idea to remember, however, is that a control account is an account which keeps a total record for a collective item (eg debtors) which in reality consists of many individual items (eg individual debtors).

1.3 A control account is an (impersonal) ledger account which will appear in the nominal ledger. Before we look at the reasons for having control accounts, we will first look at how they are made up.

Control accounts and personal accounts

1.4 The personal accounts of individual debtors are kept in the sales ledger, and the amount owed by each debtor will be a balance on his personal account. The amount owed by all the debtors together will be a balance on the debtors control account.

1.5 At any time the balance on the debtors control account should be equal to the sum of the individual balances on the personal accounts in the sales ledger.

1.6 For example, if a business has three debtors, A Arnold who owes £80, B Bagshaw who owes £310 and C Cloning who owes £200, the debit balances on the various accounts would be:

Sales ledger (personal accounts)

	£
A Arnold	80
B Bagshaw	310
C Cloning	200
Nominal ledger - debtors control account	590

1.7 What has happened here is that the three entries of £80, £310 and £200 were first entered into the sales day book. They were also recorded in the three personal accounts of Arnold, Bagshaw and Cloning in the sales ledger - but remember that this is not part of the double entry system.

1.8 Later, the *total* of £590 is posted from the sales day book into the debtors (control) account. It is fairly obvious that if you add up all the debit figures on the personal accounts, they also should total £590.

2 THE OPERATION OF CONTROL ACCOUNTS   *11/95, 5/97*

Example: accounting for debtors

2.1 You might still be uncertain why we need to have control accounts at all. Before turning our attention to this question, it will be useful first of all to see how transactions involving debtors are accounted for by means of an illustrative example. Folio numbers are shown in the accounts to illustrate the cross-referencing that is needed, and in the example folio numbers beginning:

(a) SDB, refer to a page in the sales day book;
(b) SL, refer to a particular account in the sales ledger;
(c) NL, refer to a particular account in the nominal ledger;
(d) CB, refer to a page in the cash book.

2.2 At 1 July 19X2, the Outer Business Company had no debtors at all. During July, the following transactions affecting credit sales and customers occurred.

(a) July 3:   invoiced A Arnold for the sale on credit of hardware goods: £100;

(b) July 11:   invoiced B Bagshaw for the sale on credit of electrical goods: £150;

(c) July 15:   invoiced C Cloning for the sale on credit of hardware goods: £250;

(d) July 10:   received payment from A Arnold of £90, in settlement of his debt in full, having taken a permitted discount of £10 for payment within seven days;

(e) July 18:   received a payment of £72 from B Bagshaw in part settlement of £80 of his debt. A discount of £8 was allowed for payment within seven days of invoice;

(f) July 28:   received a payment of £120 from C Cloning, who was unable to claim any discount.

Account numbers are as follows:

SL 4   Personal account: A Arnold
SL 9   Personal account: B Bagshaw
SL 13   Personal account: C Cloning
NL 6   Debtors control account
NL 7   Discounts allowed
NL 21   Sales: hardware
NL 22   Sales: electrical
NL 1   Cash control account

2.3   The accounting entries, suitably dated, would be as follows.

SALES DAY BOOK
SDB 35

Date 19X2	Name	Folio	Total £	Hardware £	Electrical £
July 3	A Arnold	SL 4 Dr	100.00	100.00	
11	B Bagshaw	SL 9 Dr	150.00		150.00
15	C Cloning	SL13 Dr	250.00	250.00	
			500.00	350.00	150.00
			NL 6 Dr	NL 21 Cr	NL 22 Cr

Note. The personal accounts in the sales ledger are debited on the day the invoices are sent out. The double entry in the ledger accounts might be made at the end of each day, week or month; here it is made at the end of the month, by posting from the sales day book as follows.

			£	£
DEBIT	NL 6	Debtors control account	500	
CREDIT	NL 21	Sales: hardware		350
	NL 22	Sales: electrical		150

CASH BOOK EXTRACT
RECEIPTS CASH BOOK - JULY 19X2

CB 23

Date 19X2	Narrative	Folio	Total £	Discount £	Debtors £
July 10	A Arnold	SL 4 Cr	90.00	10.00	100.00
18	B Bagshaw	SL 9 Cr	72.00	8.00	80.00
28	C Cloning	SL13 Cr	120.00	-	120.00
			282.00	18.00	300.00
			NL 1 Dr	NL 7 Dr	NL 6 Cr

The personal accounts in the sales ledger are memorandum accounts, because they are not a part of the double entry system.

MEMORANDUM SALES LEDGER
ARNOLD
A/c no: SL 4

Date 19X2	Narrative	Folio	£	Date 19X2	Narrative	Folio	£
July 3	Sales	SDB 35	100.00	July 10	Cash	CB 23	90.00
					Discount	CB 23	10.00
			100.00				100.00

B BAGSHAW
A/c no: SL 9

Date 19X2	Narrative	Folio	£	Date 19X2	Narrative	Folio	£
July 11	Sales	SDB 35	150.00	July 18	Cash	CB 23	72.00
					Discount	CB 23	8.00
				July 31	Balance	c/d	70.00
			150.00				150.00
Aug 1	Balance	b/d	70.00				

C CLONING

A/c no: SL 13

Date 19X2	Narrative	Folio	£	Date 19X2	Narrative	Folio	£
July 15	Sales	SDB 35	250.00	July 28	Cash	CB 23	120.00
				July 31	Balance	c/d	130.00
			250.00				250.00
Aug 1	Balance	b/d	130.00				

In the nominal ledger, the accounting entries can be made from the books of prime entry to the ledger accounts, in this example at the end of the month.

NOMINAL LEDGER (EXTRACT)
TOTAL DEBTORS (SALES LEDGER CONTROL ACCOUNT)

A/c no: NL 6

Date 19X2	Narrative	Folio	£	Date 19X2	Narrative	Folio	£
July 31	Sales	SDB 35	500.00	July 31	Cash and discount	CB 23	300.00
				July 31	Balance	c/d	200.00
			500.00				500.00
Aug 1	Balance	b/d	200.00				

Note. At 31 July the closing balance on the debtors control account (£200) is the same as the total of the individual balances on the personal accounts in the sales ledger (£0 + £70 + £130).

DISCOUNT ALLOWED

A/c no: NL 7

Date 19X2	Narrative	Folio	£	Date	Narrative	Folio	£
July 31	Debtors	CB 23	18.00				

CASH CONTROL ACCOUNT

A/c no: NL 1

Date 19X2	Narrative	Folio	£	Date	Narrative	Folio	£
July 31	Cash received	CB 23	282.00				

SALES - HARDWARE

A/c no: NL 21

Date	Narrative	Folio	£	Date 19X2	Narrative	Folio	£
				July 31	Debtors	SDB 35	350.00

SALES - ELECTRICAL

A/c no: NL 22

Date	Narrative	Folio	£	Date 19X2	Narrative	Folio	£
				July 31	Debtors	SDB 35	150.00

2.4   If we took the balance on the accounts shown in this example as at 31 July 19X2 the trial balance (insofar as it is appropriate to call these limited extracts by this name) would be as follows.

TRIAL BALANCE

	Debit £	Credit £
Cash (all receipts)	282	
Debtors	200	
Discount allowed	18	
Sales: hardware		350
Sales: electrical		150
	500	500

The trial balance is shown here to emphasise the point that a trial balance includes the balances on control accounts, but excludes the balances on the personal accounts in the sales ledger and purchase ledger.

Accounting for creditors

2.5 If you were able to follow the example above dealing with the debtors control account, you should have no difficulty in dealing with similar examples relating to purchases/creditors. If necessary refer back to revise the entries made in the purchase day book and purchase ledger personal accounts.

Entries in control accounts

2.6 Typical entries in the control accounts are listed below. Folio reference Jnl indicates that the transaction is first lodged in the journal before posting to the control account and other accounts indicated. References SRDB and PRDB are to sales returns and purchase returns day books.

SALES LEDGER (DEBTORS) CONTROL

	Folio	£		Folio	£
Opening debit balances	b/d	7,000	Opening credit balances		
Sales	SDB	52,390	(if any)	b/d	200
Dishonoured bills or	Jnl	1,000	Cash received	CB	52,250
cheques			Discounts allowed	CB	1,250
Cash paid to clear credit			Returns inwards from		
balances	CB	110	debtors	SRDB	800
Closing credit balances	c/d	120	Bad debts	Jnl	300
			Closing debit balances	c/d	5,820
		60,620			60,620
Debit balances b/d		5,820	Credit balances b/d		120

Note. Opening credit balances are unusual in the debtors control account. They represent debtors to whom the business owes money, probably as a result of the over payment of debts or for advance payments of debts for which no invoices have yet been sent.

BOUGHT LEDGER (CREDITORS) CONTROL

	Folio	£		Folio	£
Opening debit balances			Opening credit balances	b/d	8,300
(if any)	b/d	70	Purchases and other		
Cash paid	CB	29,840	expenses	PDB	31,000
Discounts received	CB	30	Cash received clearing		
Returns outwards to	PRDB		debit balances	CB	20
suppliers		60	Closing debit balances		
Closing credit balances	c/d	9,400	(if any)	c/d	80
		39,400			39,400
Debit balances	b/d	80	Credit balances	b/d	9,400

Note. Opening debit balances in the creditors control account would represent suppliers who owe the business money, perhaps because debts have been overpaid or because debts have been prepaid before the supplier has sent an invoice.

2.7   Posting from the journal to the memorandum sales or bought ledgers and to the nominal ledger may be effected as in the following example, where C Cloning has returned goods with a sales value of £50.

Journal entry	Folio	Dr £	Cr £
Sales	NL 21	50	
To debtors' control	NL 6		50
To C Cloning (memorandum)	SL 13	-	50

Return of electrical goods inwards.

2.8   It may help you to see how the debtors ledger and debtors (control) account are used set out in flowchart form.

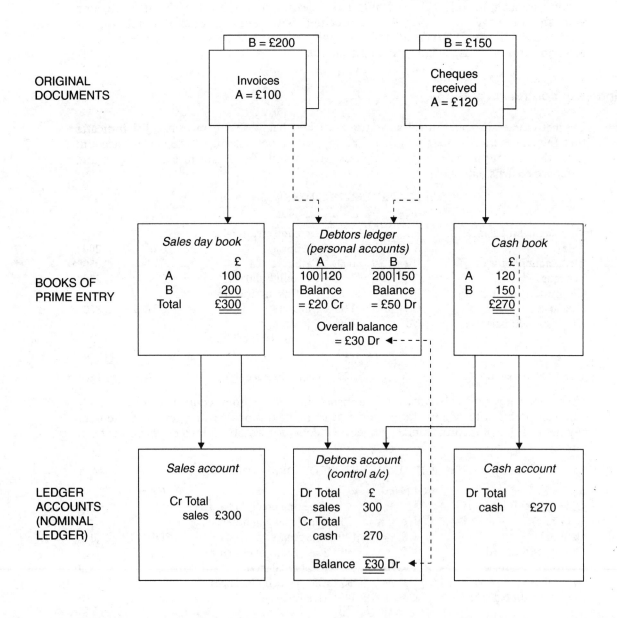

Notes

(a)   The debtors ledger is not part of the double entry system (it is not used to post the ledger accounts).

(b) Nevertheless, the total balance on the debtors ledger (ie all the personal account balances added up) should equal the balance on the debtors account (the debtors control account).

(c) This diagram implies that the memorandum accounts (sales or purchase ledger) are written up from the original invoices rather than from the sales day book. This is CIMA's official line on the treatment, although the other treatment is also possible in practice.

2.9 See now whether you can do the following exercise yourself.

Exercise

On examining the books of Exports Ltd, you ascertain that on 1 October 19X8 the debtors' ledger balances were £8,024 debit and £57 credit, and the creditors' ledger balances on the same date £6,235 credit and £105 debit.

For the year ended 30 September 19X9 the following particulars are available.

	£
Sales	63,728
Purchases	39,974
Cash received from debtors	55,212
Cash paid to creditors	37,307
Discount received	1,475
Discount allowed	2,328
Returns inwards	1,002
Returns outwards	535
Bad debts written off	326
Cash received in respect of debit balances in creditors' ledger	105
Amount due from customer as shown by debtors' ledger, offset against amount due to the same firm as shown by creditors' ledger (settlement by contra)	434
Cash received in respect of debt previously written off as bad	94
Allowances to customers on goods damaged in transit	212

On 30 September 19X9 there were no credit balances in the debtors' ledger except those outstanding on 1 October 19X8, and no debit balances in the creditors' ledger.

You are required to write up the following accounts recording the above transactions bringing down the balances as on 30 September 19X9.

(a) Debtors control account
(b) Creditors control account

Solution

(a)

DEBTORS CONTROL (OR TOTAL) ACCOUNT

19X8		£	19X8		£
Oct 1	Balances b/f	8,024	Oct 1	Balances b/f	57
19X9			19X9		
Sept 30	Sales	63,728	Sept 30	Cash received from debtors	55,212
	Balances c/f	57		Discount allowed	2,328
				Returns	1,002
				Bad debts written off	326
				Transfer creditors control account	434
				Allowances on goods damaged	212
				Balances c/f	12,238
		71,809			71,809

(b)

CREDITORS CONTROL (OR TOTAL) ACCOUNT

		£			£
19X8			*19X8*		
Oct 1	Balances b/f	105	Oct 1	Balances b/f	6,235
19X9			*19X9*		
Sept 30	Cash paid to		Sept 30	Purchases	39,974
	creditors	37,307		Cash	105
	Discount received	1,475			
	Returns outwards	535			
	Transfer debtors				
	control account	434			
	Balances c/f	6,458			
		46,314			46,314

Note. The double entry in respect of cash received for the bad debt previously written off is:

DEBIT	Cash	£94
CREDIT	Profit and loss account	£94

3   THE PURPOSE OF CONTROL ACCOUNTS

Reasons for having control accounts

3.1   The reasons for having control accounts are as follows.

(a)   They provide a check on the accuracy of entries made in the personal accounts in the sales ledger and purchase ledger. It is very easy to make a mistake in posting entries, because there might be hundreds of entries to make. Figures might get transposed. Some entries might be omitted altogether, so that an invoice or a payment transaction does not appear in a personal account as it should. By comparing:

(i)   the total balance on the debtors control account with the total of individual balances on the personal accounts in the sales ledger; and

(ii)   the total balance on the creditors control account with the total of individual balances on the personal accounts in the purchase ledger;

it is possible to identify the fact that errors have been made.

(b)   The control accounts could also assist in the location of errors, where postings to the control accounts are made daily or weekly, or even monthly. If a clerk fails to record an invoice or a payment in a personal account, or makes a transposition error, it would be a formidable task to locate the error or errors at the end of a year, say, given the hundreds or thousands of transactions during the year. By using the control account, a comparison with the individual balances in the sales or purchase ledger can be made for every week or day of the month, and the error found much more quickly than if control accounts did not exist.

(c)   Where there is a separation of clerical (bookkeeping) duties, the control account provides an *internal check*. The person posting entries to the control accounts will act as a check on a different person whose job it is to post entries to the sales and purchase ledger accounts.

(d)   To provide debtors and creditors balances more quickly for producing a trial balance or balance sheet. A single balance on a control account is obviously extracted more simply and quickly than many individual balances in the sales or purchase ledger. This means also that the number of accounts in the double entry bookkeeping system can be kept down to a manageable size, since the personal accounts are memorandum accounts only and the control accounts instead provide the accounts required for a double entry system.

3.2   However, particularly in computerised systems, it may be feasible to use sales and purchase ledgers without the need for operating separate control accounts. In such a system, the sales or purchase ledger printouts produced by the computer constitute the list of individual balances as well as providing a total balance which represents the control account balance.

Balancing and agreeing control accounts with sales and purchase (bought) ledgers

3.3   The control accounts should be balanced regularly (at least monthly), and the balance on the account agreed with the sum of the individual debtors' or creditors' balances extracted from the sales or bought ledgers respectively. It is one of the sad facts of an accountant's life that more often than not the balance on the control account does not agree with the sum of balances extracted, for one or more of the following reasons.

(a)   An incorrect amount may be posted to the control account because of a miscast of the total in the book of prime entry (ie adding up incorrectly the total value of invoices or payments). The nominal ledger debit and credit postings will then balance, but the control account balance will not agree with the sum of individual balances extracted from the (memorandum) sales ledger or purchase ledger. A journal entry must then be made in the nominal ledger to correct the control account and the corresponding sales or expense account.

(b)   A transposition error may occur in posting an individual's balance from the book of prime entry to the memorandum ledger, eg the sale to C Cloning of £250 might be posted to his account as £520. This means that the sum of balances extracted from the memorandum ledger must be corrected. No accounting entry would be required to do this, except to alter the figure in C Cloning's account.

(c)   A transaction may be recorded in the control account and not in the memorandum ledger, or vice versa. This requires an entry in the ledger that has been missed out which means a double posting if the control account has to be corrected, and a single posting if it is the individual's balance in the memorandum ledger that is at fault.

(d)   The sum of balances extracted from the memorandum ledger may be incorrectly extracted or miscast. This would involve simply correcting the total of the balances.

Example: agreeing control account balances with the sales and bought ledgers

3.4   Reconciling the control account balance with the sum of the balances extracted from the (memorandum) sales ledger or bought ledger should be done in two stages.

(a)   Correct the total of the balances extracted from the memorandum ledger. (The errors must be located first of course.)

	£	£
Sales ledger total		
Original total extracted		15,320
Add difference arising from transposition error (£95 written as £59)		36
		15,356
Less		
Credit balance of £60 extracted as a debit balance (£60 × 2)	120	
Overcast of list of balances	90	
		210
		15,146

(b)   Bring down the balance before adjustments on the control account, and adjust or post the account with correcting entries.

DEBTORS CONTROL

	£		£
Balance before adjustments	15,091	Petty cash - posting omitted	10
		Returns inwards - individual posting omitted from control account	35
Undercast of total invoices issued in sales day book	100	Balance c/d (now in agreement with the corrected total of individual balances in (a))	15,146
	15,191		15,191
Balance b/d	15,146		

Chapter roundup

- The two most important control accounts are those for debtors and creditors. They are part of the double entry system.

- Cash books and day books are totalled periodically (say once a month) and the appropriate totals are posted to the control accounts.

- The individual entries in cash and day books will have been entered one by one in the appropriate personal accounts contained in the sales ledger and purchase ledger. These personal accounts are not part of the double entry system: they are memorandum only.

- At suitable intervals the balances on personal accounts are extracted from the ledgers, listed and totalled. The total of the outstanding balances can then be reconciled to the balance on the appropriate control account and any errors located and corrected.

Test your knowledge

1 Name five accounting items for which control accounts may be used in the nominal ledger. (see para 1.2)

2 Give four reasons why a debtors control account is needed as well as a sales ledger. (3.1)

3 Why might the balance on the control account not agree with the total of the ledger account balances? (3.3)

Now try illustrative questions 22 and 23 at the end of the Study Text

Chapter 15

ACCOUNTING FOR VALUE ADDED TAX

This chapter covers the following topics.

		Syllabus reference	Ability required
1	The nature of VAT and how it is collected	1(b)	Skill
2	Accounting for VAT	1(b)	Skill

Introduction

As you will know from your own (unpleasant) experience, many business transactions involve VAT (value added tax). Many invoices and bills show any VAT charged separately.

VAT is charged on the supply of goods and services. It is a general consumer expenditure tax which hit the headlines recently with the controversial imposition of VAT on domestic fuel.

The basic principle is to add VAT at each stage of the production of goods (and services) with each supplier receiving credit for the VAT he has paid so that the total tax is actually borne by the final consumer. This is illustrated by means of an example in Section 1 of this chapter.

Section 2 deals with the accounting treatment of VAT. If you understand the principle behind the tax and how it is collected, you will understand the accounting treatment.

1 THE NATURE OF VAT AND HOW IT IS COLLECTED

1.1 Value added tax is an indirect tax levied on the sale of goods and services. It is administered by Customs and Excise rather than the Inland Revenue. Most of the work of collecting the tax falls on VAT-registered businesses and they remit the tax they collect to the authorities.

1.2 Before we look at how to account for VAT, it is first of all necessary to understand how VAT works.

Firstly, it is a cumulative tax, which might be collected at various stages of a product's life. In the illustrative example below, a manufacturer of a television buys materials and components to make the machine from suppliers, and then sells the television to a wholesaler, who in turn sells it to a retailer, who then sells it to a customer. It is assumed that the rate for VAT is 17.5% on all items. All the other figures given are hypothetical, for illustration only.

			Price net of VAT £	VAT 17.5% £	Total price £
(a)	(i)	Manufacturer purchases raw materials and components	40	7	47
	(ii)	Manufacturer sells the completed television to a wholesaler for, say	200	35	235
		The manufacturer hands over to Customs and Excise in VAT		28	

			Price net of VAT £	VAT 17.5% £	Total price £
(b)	(i)	Wholesaler purchases television for	200	35	235
	(ii)	Wholesaler sells television to a retailer for, say	320	56	376
		Wholesaler hands over to Customs and Excise in VAT		21	
(c)	(i)	Retailer purchases television for	320	56	376
	(ii)	Retailer sells television for, say	480	84	564
		Retailer hands over to Customs and Excise in VAT		28	
(d)		Customer purchases television for	480	84	564

1.3 The total tax of £84 is borne by the ultimate consumer. However, the tax is handed over to the authorities in stages. If we assume in the example that the VAT of £7 on the initial supplies to the manufacturer is paid by the supplier, Customs and Excise would collect the VAT as follows.

	£
Supplier of materials and components	7
Manufacturer	28
Wholesaler	21
Retailer	28
Total VAT paid	84

Input and output VAT

1.4 The example in Paragraphs 1.2 and 1.3 assumes that the supplier, manufacturer, wholesaler and retailer are all VAT-registered traders.

A VAT-registered trader must carry out the following tasks.

(a) Charge VAT on the goods and services sold at the rate prescribed by the government.

(b) Pay VAT on goods and services purchased from other businesses.

(c) Pay to Customs and Excise in VAT the difference between the VAT collected on sales and the VAT paid to suppliers for purchases. Payments are made at quarterly intervals.

1.5 VAT charged on goods and services sold by a business is referred to as output VAT; VAT paid on goods and services 'bought in' by a business is referred to as input VAT.

(a) If output VAT exceeds input VAT, the business pays the difference in tax to the authorities.

(b) If output VAT is less than input VAT in a period, Customs and Excise will refund the difference to the business.

Irrecoverable VAT

1.6 There are some circumstances in which traders are not allowed to reclaim VAT paid on their inputs. In these cases the trader must bear the cost of VAT and account for it accordingly. Three such cases need to be considered.

(a) Non-registered persons
(b) Registered persons carrying on exempted activities
(c) Non-deductible inputs

Non-registered persons

1.7 Traders whose sales (outputs) are below a certain minimum level need not register for VAT. Non-registered persons will pay VAT on their inputs and, because they are not registered, they cannot reclaim it. The VAT paid will effectively increase the cost of their P & L expenses and the cost of any fixed assets they may purchase. Non-registered persons do not charge VAT on their outputs.

Registered persons carrying on exempted activities

1.8 All outputs of registered traders are either taxable or exempt. Taxable outputs are charged to VAT either at zero per cent (zero-rated items) or at 17.5% (standard-rated items).

1.9 Traders carrying on exempt activities (such as banks) cannot reclaim VAT paid on their inputs, even though they may be VAT-registered. But some traders and companies carry on a mixture of taxable and exempt activities. Such traders need to apportion the VAT paid on inputs. Only VAT relating to taxable outputs may be reclaimed.

Non-deductible inputs

1.10 There are a few special cases where the input tax is not deductible even for a taxable person with taxable outputs. These are as follows

(a) VAT on motor cars, is never reclaimable unless a car is acquired new for resale, ie by a car dealer VAT on a car used wholly for business purposes is reclaimable. However, company cars are nearly always provided for at least some private use, so you should assume that the VAT is not reclaimable unless told otherwise. VAT on accessories such as car radios is deductible if ordered on a separate purchase order and fitted after delivery. The VAT charged when a car is hired is reclaimable if all use is business use. If there is some non-business use and the leasing company reclaimed VAT, the hirer can only reclaim 50% of the VAT on the hire charge.

(b) VAT on business entertaining is not deductible other than VAT on entertaining staff.

(c) VAT on expenses incurred on domestic accommodation for directors.

(d) VAT on non-business items passed through the business accounts with limited relief where the goods are used partly in the business.

(e) VAT which does not relate to the making of supplies by the buyer in the course of a business.

1.11 Where VAT is not recoverable, for any of the reasons described above, it must be regarded as an inherent part of the cost of the items purchased and included in the P & L charge or in the balance sheet as appropriate.

Relief for bad debts

1.12 Relief is available for VAT on bad debts if the debt is over six months old (measured from the date of the supply) and has been written off in the creditor's accounts. Where a supplier of goods or services has accounted for VAT on the supply and the customer does not pay, the supplier may claim a refund of VAT on the amount unpaid. Where payments on account have been received, they are attributed to debts in chronological order. The consideration must be money and not in excess of market value, and ownership of goods must have passed. If the debtor later pays all or part of the amount owed, a corresponding part of the VAT repaid must be paid back to HM Customs & Excise.

1.13 In order to claim the relief, the creditor must have a copy of the tax invoice, and records to show that the VAT in question has been accounted for and that the debt has been written off. The VAT is reclaimed on the creditor's VAT return.

2   ACCOUNTING FOR VAT   5/96, 5/97

Profit and loss account

2.1 A business does not make any profit out of the VAT it charges. It therefore follows that its sales should not include VAT. For example, if a business sells goods for £600 + VAT £105, ie for £705 total price, the sales account should only record the £600 excluding VAT. The accounting entries to record the sale would be as follows.

DEBIT	Cash or trade debtors	£705
CREDIT	Sales	£600
CREDIT	VAT creditor (output VAT)	£105

(The VAT creditor is the Customs and Excise authorities.)

2.2 The cost of purchases in the profit and loss account may or may not include the 'input' VAT paid, depending on whether or not the input VAT is recoverable.

(a) If input VAT is recoverable, the cost of purchases should exclude the VAT and be recorded net of tax. For example, if a business purchases goods on credit for £400 + VAT £70, the transaction would be recorded as follows.

DEBIT	Purchases	£400
DEBIT	VAT creditor (input VAT recoverable)	£70
CREDIT	Trade creditors	£470

(b) If the input VAT is not recoverable, the cost of purchases must include the tax, because it is the business itself which is at the 'end of the line' and which must bear the cost of the tax itself.

VAT in the cash book, sales day book and purchase day book

2.3 When a business makes a credit sale the total amount invoiced, including VAT, will be recorded in the sales day book. The analysis columns will then separate the VAT from the sales income of the business as follows.

		Sales	
Date	*Total*	*income*	*VAT*
	£	£	£
A Detter and Sons	235	200	35

2.4 When a business is invoiced by a supplier the total amount payable, including VAT, will be recorded in the purchase day book. The analysis columns will then separate the recoverable input VAT from the net purchase cost to the business as follows.

Date	*Total*	*Purchase*	*VAT*
	£	£	£
A Splier (Merchants)	188	160	28

2.5 When debtors pay what they owe, or creditors are paid, there is no need to show the VAT in an analysis column of the cash book, because input and output VAT arise when the sale is made, not when the debt is settled.

2.6 However, VAT charged on cash sales or VAT paid on cash purchases will be analysed in a separate column of the cash book. This is because output VAT having just arisen from the cash sale, must now be credited to the VAT creditor in the ledger accounts, and similarly input VAT paid on cash purchases, having just arisen, must be debited to the VAT creditor.

2.7 For example, the receipts side of a cash book might be written up as follows.

Date	Narrative	Folio	Total	Sales ledger (debtors)	Cash sales	Output VAT on cash sales
			£	£	£	£
	A Detter & Sons		235	235		
	Owen Ltd		660	660		
	Cash sales		329		280	49
	Newgate Merchants		184	184		
	Cash sales		94		80	14
			1,502	1,079	360	63

The payments side of a cash book might be written up as follows.

Date	Narrative	Folio	Total	Purchase ledger (creditors)	Cash purchases and sundry items	Input VAT on cash purchases
			£	£	£	£
	A Splier (Merchants)		188	188		
	Telephone bill paid		141		120	21
	Cash purchase of stationery		47		40	7
	VAT paid to Customs and Excise		1,400		1,400	
			1,776	188	1,560	28

Exercise

Are trade debtors and trade creditors shown in the accounts inclusive of VAT or exclusive of VAT?

Solution

Paragraph 2.2 will tell you.

Creditor for VAT

2.8 The VAT paid to the authorities each quarter is the difference between recoverable input VAT on purchases and output VAT on sales. For example, if a business is invoiced for input VAT of £8,000 and charges VAT of £15,000 on its credit sales and VAT of £2,000 on its cash sales, the VAT creditor account would be as follows.

VAT CREDITOR

	£		£
Creditors (input VAT)	8,000	Debtors (output VAT invoiced)	15,000
Cash (payment to authorities)	9,000	Cash (output VAT on cash sales)	2,000
	17,000		17,000

2.9 Payments to the authorities do not coincide with the end of the accounting period of a business, and so at the balance sheet date there will be a balance on the VAT creditor account. If this balance is for an amount payable to the authorities, the outstanding creditor for VAT will appear as a current liability in the balance sheet. Occasionally, a business will be owed money back by the authorities, and in such a situation, the VAT refund owed by the authorities would be a current asset in the balance sheet.

Chapter roundup

- VAT is an indirect tax levied on the sale of goods and services. Output VAT is charged on the sales made by a business. Input VAT is paid by a business on its purchases.

- The difference between input VAT and output VAT is paid to or reclaimed from Customs and Excise.

- If input VAT is recoverable it is excluded from the cost of purchases in the profit and loss account. VAT charged on sales to customers is also excluded from the profit and loss account.

- An outstanding creditor for VAT will appear as a current liability in the balance sheet.

- Some inputs are described as non-deductible, for example, cars unless they are bought for resale by a person trading in cars. Exam questions may try to catch you out with this.

Test your knowledge

1   If output VAT exceeds input VAT, the difference can be reclaimed from Customs and Excise. True or false? (see para 1.5)

2   What are the two rates of VAT which may be applicable to taxable outputs? (1.8)

3   Give two examples of expenditure on which input VAT is not recoverable. (1.10)

4   Under what circumstances is relief available for bad debts? (1.12)

5   A business purchases goods valued at £400. VAT is charged at 17.5%. What is the double entry to record the purchase? (2.2)

Now try illustrative question 24 at the end of the Study Text

Chapter 16

ACCOUNTING FOR WAGES AND SALARIES

		Syllabus reference	Ability required
This chapter covers the following topics.			
1	Gross pay and deductions	1(b)	Skill
2	Accounting for wages and salaries	1(b)	Skill

Introduction

If you keep an eye on what goes on in your bank account, you will notice, if you are like most people, that the items of income (which are few and far between) are mostly outnumbered by items of outgoings. The principal credit the bank posts to your bank statement is your salary or wage, every month (or week).

The credit entry to the bank or the jangle of coins in the wages packet is the final result of a long process of recording and calculation. This is often referred to as payroll processing and payroll accounting, a payroll being simply a list of employees and what they are to be paid. Being on the payroll of an organisation means that you are selling your labour to it for an agreed price.

From an employer's point of view, too, the wages and salaries bill is of great importance. It is usually one of the largest items of expenditure an employer has to incur.

Most people have to pay some of what they earn to the government as taxation, which pays for general social benefits, eg the Health Service. In addition, people pay National Insurance (NI) contributions, which, in practice, is similar to a tax. People pay tax on what they earn as Income Tax. The tax is collected by the employer when the employee is paid. The same is true for National Insurance. The system is called PAYE (Pay As You Earn). This system is the subject of Section 1.

While you might think that the employer is doing the government a favour by acting as a tax collector, the legal apparatus surrounding PAYE is quite strict. It is vital therefore, that proper accounting records are kept. This is covered in Section 2 of the chapter.

1 GROSS PAY AND DEDUCTIONS

1.1 The employees of a business are rewarded for their services by wages or salary payments. Such payments are commonly expressed in terms of a gross amount.

(a) An hourly-paid employee might have a wage rate of £5 per hour gross.

(b) A weekly-paid employee might have a wage rate of £150 per week gross, with additional payments for any overtime worked.

(c) A monthly-paid employee might have an annual salary of £12,000 gross. His gross monthly salary payment would be calculated as £12,000 ÷ 12 = £1,000.

1.2 A distinction is often made between wages staff and salaried staff. Wages staff are usually paid by reference to a weekly or hourly wage rate and receive their pay weekly. Salaried staff are usually paid by reference to an annual salary and receive their pay monthly. Traditionally, wages staff have tended to be paid in cash at the end of each week, while salaried staff have been paid monthly by automatic transfer from the business bank account to the employee's bank account. The distinction is now being eroded as more and more employees are paid by bank transfer.

1.3   For accounting purposes, there is no essential difference between wages procedures and salary procedures.

1.4   Although an employee's pay may be expressed as a gross amount, the amount of pay he actually receives will invariably be reduced by certain deductions. The most important of these are for income tax and National Insurance contributions.

1.5   The government requires that all employees (except those with very low incomes) should pay income tax on their earnings. Employees are also required to contribute to the cost of the welfare state by making contributions to a National Insurance fund.

1.6   You might think that these obligations of the employee are no concern of his employer. It can be argued that the employer should pay the agreed gross wage and leave the employee to settle his own liability with the Inland Revenue.

1.7   In practice, this is not the system that applies. The government requires that businesses should act as collecting agents on behalf of the Inland Revenue. When a business makes a wages or salary payment to an employee, it must calculate the amount of tax and National Insurance due from the employee. These amounts must be deducted from the employee's gross remuneration and paid by the business to the Inland Revenue. The employee receives only the net amount remaining after these deductions.

1.8   Because an employee effectively pays off his income tax liability in instalments, each time he receives a wages payment, this system of income tax collection is often referred to as PAYE or pay-as-you-earn.

1.9   Apart from these obligatory deductions which all businesses are required to operate, there may be other voluntary deductions from an employee's pay.

    (a)   Some businesses run savings schemes. An employee may agree to save £5 a week with the intention of withdrawing his savings at Christmas time. Each week the £5 would be deducted from his gross pay and held for him by his employer until such time as he decides to withdraw it.

    (b)   Some businesses encourage contributions to charity. An employee might agree to a weekly deduction of 50p from his wages as a contribution to Oxfam. The employer would deduct the agreed amount each week and at suitable intervals hand over the money collected to the charity.

    (c)   Some businesses run pension schemes to which employees contribute.

Example: accounting for deductions from gross pay

1.10   Suppose that Mr Little's gross pay for the week ending 31 October 19X6 is £140. His employer, Mr Big, calculates that income tax of £20 and National Insurance of £13 are due on that level of earnings. In addition, Little received a loan from the business in June 19X6 which he is repaying by means of weekly deductions of £5; he also voluntarily contributes 20p per week to a local charity, again by deduction from his gross wages.

    How should these amounts be accounted for?

Solution

1.11   The cost to Mr Big is the gross pay of £140 and this is the amount to be charged in his profit and loss account. The amount actually paid to Little is only £101.80 (£140 − £20 − £13 − £5 − 20p).

The deductions should be accounted for as follows.

(a) PAYE of £20 and National Insurance contribution of £13 must be handed over by Mr Big to the Inland Revenue. In practice, this payment would not be made every week. Mr Big would accumulate the amounts due in respect of all his employees and would make a single payment to Inland Revenue once a month.

(b) The £5 deduction is applied to reduce the amount of the loan outstanding from Little.

(c) The 20p deduction must be handed over by Mr Big to the local charity. Again, it would probably be convenient to accumulate these amounts for a number of weeks before making a payment.

Employer's National Insurance contributions

1.12 We have already seen that employees are normally obliged to pay National Insurance contributions which are deducted from their gross pay and paid over by their employer on their behalf. But employers also have to make a contribution themselves in respect of each of their employees. This is not a deduction from the employee's gross pay, it is an *extra* cost, borne by the employer. The employer's profit and loss account must show the total cost of employing staff and this includes not only the gross pay of each employee, but also the employer's National Insurance contributions.

1.13 When an employer is making his monthly payment to the Inland Revenue the amount paid must therefore include the following:

(a) PAYE income tax for each employee. This is deducted from the employees' gross pay;

(b) employees' National Insurance contributions, also deducted from the employees' gross pay;

(c) employer's National Insurance contributions, paid from the employer's own funds.

Calculating PAYE taxation and National Insurance contributions

1.14 Calculating National Insurance contributions is easy. An employee must pay a fixed percentage of his gross income and this amount is deducted from his pay. The percentage to apply depends on the level of the employee's income. For the employer's contribution, again a fixed percentage is applied to the employee's gross pay, but the percentage may differ from that used in calculating the employee's contribution.

1.15 Employees' NI contributions are subject to a maximum amount. There is no limit on the amount of an employer's contributions.

1.16 The government publishes tables detailing the amount of NI contributions payable at all levels of income. This means that employers never need to understand how NI is calculated: they simply extract the amounts from the tables.

1.17 PAYE contributions are more complicated, but again the use of Inland Revenue tables simplifies matters in practice. Briefly, it is necessary to do the calculations on a cumulative basis, rather than looking at each salary/wages payment in isolation.

1.18 First add up the amount of the employee's gross pay, up to and including his gross pay for the current week, to arrive at his gross pay for the tax year to date. (Tax years run from 6 April to 5 April.) Next calculate the amount of tax due for the year to date. This will depend on the employee's tax code, which reflects the value of tax allowances to which his personal circumstances entitle him.

1.19 The tax due for the year to date is then compared with the tax actually paid by the employee up to and including the previous week/month. The difference is the amount of tax due from the employee in the current week/month. This is the amount to be deducted from his gross wages.

1.20 It may sometimes be found that the tax due for the year to date is less than the tax already paid by the employee. In that case the employee will be entitled to a tax refund as an *addition* to his gross pay.

2   ACCOUNTING FOR WAGES AND SALARIES

2.1 It is now necessary to look at the double entry involved in accounting for wages and salaries. There are various ways of doing this but the method below involves the use of three control accounts as follows.

(a) Wages control account
(b) PAYE control account
(c) National Insurance contributions (NIC) control account

2.2 The first step is to calculate the total costs of employment to be borne by the business. These consist of employees' gross pay plus employer's National Insurance contributions. The following accounting entries would then be made.

DEBIT	P & L account - wages/salaries
CREDIT	Wages control account (gross pay)
CREDIT	NIC control account (employer's NIC)

2.3 The amount of deductions must be calculated for PAYE and employee's NIC. These amounts are debited to wages control account and credited to PAYE control account and NIC control account respectively.

2.4 The remaining credit balance on wages control account is then eliminated by paying employees their net pay: credit cash, debit wages control.

2.5 In due course, the credit balances on PAYE control and NIC control are eliminated by making payments to Inland Revenue.

2.6 Any voluntary deductions permitted by employees must be debited to wages control account and credited to a liability account until they are eventually paid over by the employer as appropriate.

Example: ledger accounts for wages and salaries

2.7 At 1 November 19X5 Netpay Ltd had the following credit balances on ledger accounts.

	£
PAYE control account	4,782
NIC control account	2,594
Employee savings account	1,373

The company's wages records for the month of November 19X5 showed the following.

	£
Total gross pay	27,294
PAYE	6,101
Employer's NIC	2,612
Employees' NIC	2,240
Employees' savings deductions	875
Net amounts paid to employees	18,078

The company paid £9,340 to Inland Revenue during the month, being £4,750 PAYE and £4,590 NIC.

You are required to show the ledger accounts recording these transactions.

Solution

2.8

WAGES CONTROL ACCOUNT

	£		£
PAYE control	6,101	Wages expense a/c - gross pay	27,294
NIC control - employees' contributions	2,240		
Employee savings a/c	875		
Bank - net pay	18,078		
	27,294		27,294

PAYE CONTROL ACCOUNT

	£		£
Bank	4,750	Balance b/f	4,782
Balance c/d	6,133	Wages control	6,101
	10,883		10,883
		Balance b/d	6,133

NIC CONTROL ACCOUNT

	£		£
Bank	4,590	Balance b/f	2,594
Balance c/d	2,856	Wages control - employees' NIC	2,240
		Wages expense a/c - employer's NIC	2,612
	7,446		7,446
		Balance b/d	2,856

EMPLOYEE SAVINGS ACCOUNT

	£		£
Balance c/d	2,248	Balance b/f	1,373
		Wages control	875
	2,248		2,248
		Balance	2,248

Note. This account shows the company's liability to employees, who may wish to withdraw their savings at any time.

Exercise

At 1 March 19X3 Brubeck Ltd had the following credit balances on ledger accounts.

	£
PAYE control account	23,000
NIC control account	12,500
Employee savings account	26,250

The company's wages records for the month of March 19X3 showed the following.

	£
PAYE	30,505
Employer's NIC	13,060
Employees' NIC	11,200
Employees' savings deductions	4,375
Net amounts paid to employees	90,390

The company paid £46,700 to the Inland Revenue during the month, being £23,750 PAYE and £22,950 NIC.

(a) How much was gross pay for the month?

(b) What is the balance c/d on the PAYE control account, if any?
(c) What is the balance c/d on the NIC control account, if any?
(d) What is the balance c/d on the Employee Savings account, if any?

Solution

(a) £136,470
(b) £29,755 credit
(c) £13,810 credit
(d) £30,625 credit

Chapter roundup

- The cost of employing staff must be shown in a business's profit and loss account. It comprises the gross pay earned by employees, plus employer's NIC.

- A business must deduct PAYE income tax and employees' NIC from employees' gross pay. Only the net amount is then paid to employees. The amounts deducted are paid over every month by the employer to the Inland Revenue.

Test your knowledge

1 What do the initials PAYE stand for? (see para 1.8)

2 List three voluntary deductions that an employee might permit from his gross pay. (1.9)

3 What is the total cost of employing staff shown in an employer's profit and loss account? (1.12)

4 Briefly summarise the principles of calculating PAYE income tax. (1.17 - 1.19)

5 What ledger accounting entries are necessary once the total payroll costs have been calculated? (2.2)

6 What ledger accounting entries are made in respect of voluntary deductions permitted by employees? (2.6)

Now try illustrative question 25 at the end of the Study Text

Chapter 17

CORRECTION OF ERRORS. PREPARATION OF FINAL ACCOUNTS

This chapter covers the following topics.

		Syllabus reference	Ability required
1	Types of error in accounting	1(b)	Skill
2	The correction of errors	1(b)	Skill
3	Preparation of final accounts	1(b)	Skill

Introduction

We have nearly reached our goal for this part of the text which is the preparation of the final accounts of a sole trader.

This chapter continues the subject of errors in accounts. You have already learned about errors which arise in the context of the cash book or the sales and purchase ledgers and debtors and creditors control account. Here we deal with errors that may be corrected by means of the journal or a suspense account.

1 TYPES OF ERROR IN ACCOUNTING

1.1 It is not really possible to draw up a complete list of all the errors which might be made by bookkeepers and accountants. Even if you tried, it is more than likely that as soon as you finished, someone would commit a completely new error that you had never even dreamed of! However, it is possible to describe five *types* of error which cover most of the errors which might occur. They are as follows.

    (a) Errors of transposition
    (b) Errors of omission
    (c) Errors of principle
    (d) Errors of commission
    (e) Compensating errors

1.2 Once an error has been detected, it needs to be put right.

    (a) If the correction involves a double entry in the ledger accounts, then it is done by using a journal entry in the journal.

    (b) When the error breaks the rule of double entry, then it is corrected by the use of a suspense account as well as a journal entry.

1.3. In this chapter we will:

    (a) look at the five common types of error;
    (b) review journal entries (which we briefly looked at earlier in this text); and
    (c) define a suspense account, and describe how it is used.

Errors of transposition

1.4   An error of transposition is when two digits in an amount are accidentally recorded the wrong way round. For example, suppose that a sale is recorded in the sales account as £6,843, but it has been incorrectly recorded in the total debtors account as £6,483. The error is the transposition of the 4 and the 8. The consequence is that total debits will not be equal to total credits. You can often detect a transposition error by checking whether the difference between debits and credits can be divided exactly by 9. For example, £6,843 – £6,483 = £360; £360 ÷ 9 = 40.

Errors of omission

1.5   An error of omission means failing to record a transaction at all, or making a debit or credit entry, but not the corresponding double entry.

(a)   If a business receives an invoice from a supplier for £250, the transaction might be omitted from the books entirely. As a result, both the total debits and the total credits of the business will be out by £250.

(b)   If a business receives an invoice from a supplier for £300, the purchase ledger control account might be credited, but the debit entry in the purchases account might be omitted. In this case, the total credits would not equal total debits (because total debits are £300 less than they ought to be).

Errors of principle

1.6   An error of principle involves making a double entry in the belief that the transaction is being entered in the correct accounts, but subsequently finding out that the accounting entry breaks the 'rules' of an accounting principle or concept. A typical example of such an error is to treat certain revenue expenditure incorrectly as capital expenditure.

(a)   For example, repairs to a machine costing £150 should be treated as revenue expenditure, and debited to a repairs account. If, instead, the repair costs are added to the cost of the fixed asset (capital expenditure) an error of principle would have occurred. As a result, although total debits still equal total credits, the repairs account is £150 less than it should be and the cost of the fixed asset is £150 greater than it should be.

(b)   Similarly, suppose that the proprietor of the business sometimes takes cash out of the till for his personal use and during a certain year these drawings amount to £280. The book-keeper states that he has reduced cash sales by £280 so that the cash book could be made to balance. This would be an error of principle, and the result of it would be that the drawings account is understated by £280, and so is the total value of sales in the sales account.

Errors of commission

1.7   Errors of commission are where the bookkeeper makes a mistake in carrying out his or her task of recording transactions in the accounts.

(a)   *Putting a debit entry or a credit entry in the wrong account.* For example, if telephone expenses of £540 are debited to the electricity expenses account, an error of commission would have occurred. The result is that although total debits and total credits balance, telephone expenses are understated by £540 and electricity expenses are overstated by the same amount.

(b)   *Errors of casting (adding up).* Suppose for example that the total daily credit sales in the sales day book of a business should add up to £28,425, but are incorrectly added up as £28,825. The total sales in the sales day book are then used to credit total sales and debit total debtors in the ledger accounts, so that total debits and total credits are still equal, although incorrect.

Compensating errors

1.8   Compensating errors are errors which are, coincidentally, equal and opposite to one another.

1.9   For example, two transposition errors of £540 might occur in extracting ledger balances, one on each side of the double entry. In the administration expenses account, £2,282 might be written instead of £2,822, while in the sundry income account, £8,391 might be written instead of £8,931. Both the debits and the credits would be £540 too low, and the mistake would not be apparent when the trial balance is cast. Consequently, compensating errors hide the fact that there are errors in the trial balance.

2   THE CORRECTION OF ERRORS   5/96

Journal entries

2.1   Some errors can be corrected by journal entries. To remind you, the format of a journal entry is:

Date	Folio	Debit	Credit
		£	£
Account to be debited		X	
Account to be credited			X
(Narrative to explain the transaction)			

2.2   The journal requires a debit and an equal credit entry for each 'transaction' - ie for each correction. This means that if total debits equal total credits before a journal entry is made then they will still be equal after the journal entry is made. This would be the case if, for example, the original error was a debit wrongly posted as a credit or vice versa.

2.3   Similarly, if total debits and total credits are unequal before a journal entry is made, then they will still be unequal (by the same amount) after it is made.

2.4   For example, suppose a bookkeeper accidentally posts a bill for £40 to the rates account instead of to the electricity account. A trial balance is drawn up, and total debits are £40,000 and total credits are £40,000. A journal entry is made to correct the misposting error as follows.

1.7.19X7

DEBIT	Electricity account	£40	
CREDIT	Rates account		£40

To correct a misposting of £40 from the rates account to electricity account.

2.5   After the journal has been posted, total debits will still be £40,000 and total credits will be £40,000. Total debits and totals credits are still equal.

2.6   Now suppose that, because of some error which has not yet been detected, total debits were originally £40,000 but total credits were £39,900. If the same journal correcting the £40 is put through, total debits will remain £40,000 and total credits will remain £39,900. Total debits were different by £100 *before* the journal, and they are still different by £100 *after* the journal.

2.7   This means that journals can only be used to correct errors which require both a credit and (an equal) debit adjustment.

Example: journal entries

2.8   Listed below are five errors which were used as examples earlier in this chapter. Write out the journal entries which would correct these errors.

(a)   A business receives an invoice for £250 from a supplier which was omitted from the books entirely.

(b)   Repairs worth £150 were incorrectly debited to the fixed asset (machinery) account instead of the repairs account.

(c)   The bookkeeper of a business reduces cash sales by £280 because he was not sure what the £280 represented. In fact, it was drawings.

(d)   Telephone expenses of £540 are incorrectly debited to the electricity account.

(e)   A page in the sales day book has been added up to £28,425 instead of £28,825.

Solution

2.9   (a)   DEBIT   Purchases   £250
              CREDIT   Creditors   £250

       A transaction previously omitted.

       (b)   DEBIT   Repairs account   £150
              CREDIT   Fixed asset (machinery) a/c   £150

       The correction of an error of principle. Repairs costs incorrectly added to fixed asset costs.

       (c)   DEBIT   Drawings account   £280
              CREDIT   Sales   £280

       An error of principle, in which sales were reduced to compensate for cash drawings not accounted for.

       (d)   DEBIT   Telephone expenses   £540
              CREDIT   Electricity expenses   £540

       Correction of an error of commission. Telephone expenses wrongly charged to the electricity account.

       (e)   DEBIT   Debtors   £400
              CREDIT   Sales   £400

       The correction of a casting error in the sales day book.
       (£28,825 – £28,425 = £400)

Use of journal entries in examinations

2.10   Occasionally an examination question might ask you to 'journalise' a transaction (ie write it out in the form of a journal entry), even though the transaction is perfectly normal and nothing to do with an error. This is just the examiner's way of finding out whether you know your debits and credits. For example:

Question: A business sells £500 of goods on credit. Journalise the transaction.

Answer:

DEBIT   Debtors   £500
CREDIT   Sales   £500

Goods to the value of £500 sold on credit.

2.11   No error has occurred here, just a normal credit sale of £500. But by asking you to put it in the form of a journal, the examiner can see that you understand the double-entry bookkeeping involved.

Suspense accounts

2.12   A suspense account is a *temporary* account which can be opened for a number of reasons. The most common reasons are as follows.

(a) A trial balance is drawn up which does not balance (ie total debits do not equal total credits).

(b) The bookkeeper of a business knows where to post the credit side of a transaction, but does not know where to post the debit (or vice versa). For example, a cash payment might be made and must obviously be credited to cash. But the bookkeeper may not know what the payment is for, and so will not know which account to debit.

2.13 In both these cases, a temporary suspense account is opened up until the problem is sorted out. The next few paragraphs explain exactly how this works.

Use of suspense account: when the trial balance does not balance

2.14 When an error has occurred which results in an imbalance between total debits and total credits in the ledger accounts, the first step is to open a suspense account. For example, suppose an accountant draws up a trial balance and finds that, for some reason he cannot immediately discover, total debits exceed total credits by £162.

2.15 He knows that there is an error somewhere, but for the time being he opens a suspense account and enters a credit of £162 in it. This serves two purposes.

(a) Because the suspense account now exists, the accountant will not forget that there is an error (of £162) to be sorted out.

(b) Now that there is a credit of £162 in the suspense account, the trial balance balances.

2.16 When the cause of the £162 discrepancy is tracked down, it is corrected by means of a journal entry. For example, suppose it turned out that the accountant had accidentally failed to make a credit of £162 to purchases. The journal entry would be:

DEBIT	Suspense a/c	£162	
CREDIT	Purchases		£162

To close off suspense a/c and correct error.

2.17 Whenever an error occurs which results in total debits not being equal to total credits, the first step an accountant makes is to open up a suspense account. Three more examples are given below.

Example: transposition error

2.18 The bookkeeper of Mixem Gladly Ltd made a transposition error when entering an amount for sales in the sales account. Instead of entering the correct amount of £37,453.60 he entered £37,543.60, transposing the 4 and 5. The debtors were posted correctly, and so when total debits and credits on the ledger accounts were compared, it was found that credits exceeded debits by £(37,543.60 − 37,453.60) = £90.

2.19 The initial step is to equalise the total debits and credits by posting a debit of £90 to a suspense account.

2.20 When the cause of the error is discovered, the double entry to correct it should be logged in the journal as:

DEBIT	Sales	£90	
CREDIT	Suspense a/c		£90

To close off suspense a/c and correct transposition error.

Example: error of omission

2.21 When Guttersnipe Builders paid the monthly salary cheques to its office staff, the payment of £5,250 was correctly entered in the cash account, but the bookkeeper omitted to debit the office salaries account. As a consequence, the total debit and credit balances on the ledger accounts were not equal, and credits exceeded debits by £5,250.

2.22 The initial step in correcting the situation is to debit £5,250 to a suspense account, to equalise the total debits and total credits.

2.23 When the cause of the error is discovered, the double entry to correct it should be logged in the journal as:

DEBIT	Office salaries account	£5,250
CREDIT	Suspense account	£5,250

To close off suspense account and correct error of omission.

Example: error of commission

2.24 A bookkeeper might make a mistake by entering what should be a debit entry as a credit, or vice versa. For example, suppose that a credit customer pays £460 of the £660 he owes to Ashdown Tree Felling Contractors, but Ashdown's bookkeeper has debited £460 on the debtors account in the nominal ledger by mistake instead of crediting the payment received.

2.25 The total debit balances in Ashdown's ledger accounts would now exceed the total credits by 2 × £460 = £920. The initial step in correcting the error would be to make a credit entry of £920 in a suspense account. When the cause of the error is discovered, it should be corrected as follows.

DEBIT	Suspense account	£920
CREDIT	Debtors	£920

To close off suspense account and correct error of commission.

2.26 In the debtors account in the nominal ledger, the correction would appear therefore as follows.

DEBTORS ACCOUNT

	£		£
Balance b/f	660	Suspense account: error corrected	920
Payment incorrectly debited	460	Balance c/f	200
	1,120		1,120

Use of suspense account: not knowing where to post a transaction

2.27 Another use of suspense accounts occurs when a bookkeeper does not know in which account to post one side of a transaction. Until the mystery is sorted out, the credit entry can be recorded in a suspense account. A typical example is when the business receives cash through the post from a source which cannot be determined. The double entry in the accounts would be a debit in the cash book, and a credit to a suspense account.

2.28 Similarly, when the bookkeeper knows in which account to make one entry, but for some reason does not know where to make the corresponding entry, this can be posted to a suspense account. A very common example is to credit proceeds on disposal of fixed assets to the suspense account instead of working out the profit or loss on disposal.

Example: not knowing where to post a transaction

2.29   Windfall Garments received a cheque in the post for £620. The name on the cheque is R J Beasley Esq, but Windfall Garments have no idea who this person is, nor why he should be sending £620. The bookkeeper decides to open a suspense account, so that the double entry for the transaction is:

DEBIT	Cash	£620	
CREDIT	Suspense account		£620

2.30   Eventually, it transpires that the cheque was in payment for a debt owed by the Haute Couture Corner Shop and paid out of the proprietor's personal bank account. The suspense account can now be cleared, as follows.

DEBIT	Suspense account	£620	
CREDIT	Debtors		£620

Suspense accounts might contain several items

2.31   If more than one error or unidentifiable posting to a ledger account arises during an accounting period, they will all be merged together in the same suspense account. Indeed, until the causes of the errors are discovered, the bookkeepers are unlikely to know exactly how many errors there are. An examination question might give you a balance on a suspense account, together with enough information to make the necessary corrections, leaving a nil balance on the suspense account and correct balances on various other accounts. In practice, of course, finding these errors is far from easy!

Suspense accounts are temporary

2.32   It must be stressed that a suspense account can only be temporary. Postings to a suspense account are only made when the bookkeeper doesn't know yet what to do, or when an error has occurred. Mysteries must be solved, and errors must be corrected. Under no circumstances should there still be a suspense account when it comes to preparing the balance sheet of a business. The suspense account must be cleared and all the correcting entries made before the final accounts are drawn up.

3   PREPARATION OF FINAL ACCOUNTS   *5/95, 11/95, 5/97*

3.1   You have already had practice at preparing a profit and loss account and balance sheet from a simple trial balance. Now see if you can do the same thing but at a more advanced level, taking account of adjustments for depreciation, stock, accruals, prepayments and bad and doubtful debts. Have a go at the following exercise.

Exercise

The following trial balance was extracted from the ledger of Stephen Chee, a sole trader, as at 31 May 19X1 - the end of his financial year.

STEPHEN CHEE
TRIAL BALANCE AS AT 31 MAY 19X1

	Dr £	Cr £
Property, at cost	120,000	
Equipment, at cost	80,000	
Provisions for depreciation (as at 1 June 19X0)		
- on property		20,000
- on equipment		38,000
Purchases	250,000	
Sales		402,200
Stock, as at 1 June 19X0	50,000	
Discounts allowed	18,000	
Discounts received		4,800
Returns out		15,000
Wages and salaries	58,800	
Bad debts	4,600	
Loan interest	5,100	
Other operating expenses	17,700	
Trade creditors		36,000
Trade debtors	38,000	
Cash in hand	300	
Bank	1,300	
Drawings	24,000	
Provision for bad debts		500
17% long term loan		30,000
Capital, as at 1 June 19X0		121,300
	667,800	667,800

The following additional information as at 31 May 19X1 is available.

(a)   Stock as at the close of business has been valued at cost at £42,000.
(b)   Wages and salaries need to be accrued by £800.
(c)   Other operating expenses are prepaid by £300.
(d)   The provision for bad debts is to be adjusted so that it is 2% of trade debtors.
(e)   Depreciation for the year ended 31 May 19X1 has still to be provided for as follows:

Property: 1.5% per annum using the straight line method; and
Equipment: 25% per annum using the diminishing balance method.

Required

Prepare Stephen Chee's trading and profit and loss account for the year ended 31 May 19X1 and his balance sheet as at that date.

Solution

STEPHEN CHEE
TRADING AND PROFIT AND LOSS ACCOUNT
FOR THE YEAR ENDED 31 MAY 19X1

	£	£
Sales		
Cost of sales		402,200
Opening stock	50,000	
Purchases	250,000	
Purchases returns	(15,000)	
	285,000	
Closing stock	42,000	
		243,000
Gross profit		159,200
Other income - discounts received		4,800
		164,000
Expenses		
Operating expenses		
Wages and salaries (£58,800 + £800)	59,600	
Discounts allowed	18,000	
Bad debts (W1)	4,860	
Loan interest	5,100	
Depreciation	12,300	
Other operating expenses (£17,700 - £300)	17,400	
		117,260
Net profit for the year		46,740

STEPHEN CHEE
BALANCE SHEET AS AT 31 MAY 19X0

	Cost £	Accumu- lated depn. £	Net book value £
Fixed assets			
Property	120,000	21,800	98,200
Equipment	80,000	48,500	31,500
	200,000	70,300	129,700
Current assets			
Stock		42,000	
Trade debtors net of provision for bad debts (£38,000 less 2%)		37,240	
Prepayments		300	
Bank		1,300	
Cash in hand		300	
		81,140	
Current liabilities			
Trade creditors		36,000	
Accruals		800	
		36,800	
Net current assets			44,340
Less 17% loan			30,000
Net assets			144,040
Capital			
Balance at 1 June 19X0			121,300
Net profit for the year			46,740
			168,040
Drawings			24,000
			144,040

Workings

		£
1	*Provision for bad debts*	
	Previous provision	500
	New provision (2% × 38,000)	760
	Increase	260
	Per trial balance	4,600
	Profit and loss account	4,860

		£
2	*Depreciation*	
	Property	
	Opening provision	20,000
	Provision for the year (1.5% × 120,000)	1,800
	Closing provision	21,800
	Equipment	
	Opening provision	38,000
	Provision for the year (25% × 42,000)	10,500
	Closing provision	48,500

Tips for final accounts questions

3.2 The examination paper will contain a compulsory question involving preparation of final accounts, Such a question may involve a sole trader, which is the type of organisation you have dealt with so far. Alternatively, you may have to prepare the final accounts of a limited company or a not-for-profit organisation, and the accounts may have to be prepared from incomplete records, all topics you will cover in this Study Text.

3.3 Whatever form the final accounts question takes, you should bear in mind the following tips.

(a) *Annotate the trial balance* If you are given a trial balance, note the final destination of each item, for example:

T = Trading account

P/L = Profit and loss account

M = Manufacturing account

I/E = Income and expenditure account

B/S = Balance sheet

(b) *Show workings clearly.* The workings should be clearly referenced to the final accounts and should enable the marker to follow through your calculations. This is particularly important because if, as often happens under time pressure, you make minor arithmetical mistakes, you will not be heavily penalised if the marker can see that you have used the right method.

(c) *Present a clear, logical layout of financial accounts.* Allow plenty of space, better too much than too little. For example if you have to do a profit and loss account and balance sheet you should allow at least one page for the Profit and Loss account, one for the balance sheet and one or more for your workings. Underline any totals for columns and figures, and if you make a mistake, cross it out neatly and clearly. You do not have time to wait for Tippex to dry.

Chapter roundup

- There are five types of error.

  - Errors of transposition
  - Errors of omission
  - Errors of principle
  - Errors of commission
  - Compensating errors

- Errors which leave total debits and total credits on the ledger accounts in balance can be corrected by using journal entries. Otherwise, a suspense account has to be opened first (and a journal entry used later to record the correction of the error, clearing the suspense account in the process).

- Suspense accounts, as well as being used to correct some errors, are also opened when it is not known immediately where to post an amount. When the mystery is solved, the suspense account is closed and the amount correctly posted using a journal entry.

- Suspense accounts are only temporary. None should exist when it comes to drawing up the financial statements at the end of the accounting period.

- You should now be able to prepare a set of final accounts for a sole trader from a trial balance after incorporating period end adjustments for depreciation, stock, prepayments, accruals and bad and doubtful debts.

Test your knowledge

1   List five types of error made in accounting. (see para 1.1)

2   What is the format of a journal entry? (2.1)

3   Explain what a suspense account is. (2.12)

4   What must be done with a suspense account before preparing a balance sheet? (2.32)

Now try illustrative questions 26 to 29 at the end of the Study Text

Chapter 18

COMPUTER APPLICATIONS IN ACCOUNTING

This chapter covers the following topics.

		Syllabus reference	*Ability required*
1	Accounting packages	1(b)	Knowledge
2	Accounting modules	1(b)	Knowledge
3	Databases	1(b)	Knowledge
4	Spreadsheets	1(b)	Knowledge
5	Practical experience	1(b)	Knowledge

Introduction

We referred briefly to computerised accounting systems in Chapter 14 on control accounts. These days, most accounting systems are computerised and anyone training to be an accountant should be able to work with them.

The most important point to remember is that the principles of computerised accounting are the same as those of manual accounting. You should by now have a good grasp of these principles.

The first section of this chapter talks about accounting *packages*. This is a rather general term, but most of us can probably name the accounting package that we use at work.

An accounting package consists of several accounting *modules*, eg sales ledger, cash book. An exam question may take one of these modules and ask you to describe inputs, processing and outputs. Alternatively, you may be asked to outline the advantages of computer processing over manual processing, for example, for debtors or payroll.

Questions may ask you to discuss the advantages and disadvantages of databases and spreadsheets. These are discussed in Sections 3 and 4. It is likely that you will have used a spreadsheet in your workplace.

1   ACCOUNTING PACKAGES   *11/95*

1.1   The syllabus for this paper requires you to know about the use of computers in financial accounting practice. Questions will *not* be set on the technical aspects of how computers work.

1.2   We shall assume, therefore, that you know that a modern computer generally consists of a keyboard, a television-like screen, a box-like disk drive which contains all the necessary electronic components for data processing, and a printer. This is the computer hardware.

1.3   Computer programs are the instructions that tell the electronics how to process data. The general term used for these is software. Software is what we are concerned with in this text, and in particular 'applications software', that is packages of computer programs that carry out specific tasks.

(a)   Some applications are devoted specifically to an accounting task, for example a payroll package, a fixed asset register or a stock control package.

(b)   Other applications have many uses in business, including their use for accounting purposes. Packages of this sort that we shall describe are databases and spreadsheets.

Accounting packages

1.4   One of the most important facts to remember about computerised accounting is that *in principle, it is exactly the same as manual accounting*.

1.5   Accounting functions retain the same names in computerised systems as in more traditional written records. Computerised accounting still uses the familiar ideas of day books, ledger accounts, double entry, trial balance and financial statements. The principles of working with computerised sales, purchase and nominal ledgers are exactly what would be expected in the manual methods they replace. The only difference is that these various books of account have become invisible. Ledgers are now computer files which are held in a computer-sensible form, ready to be called upon.

1.6   However, the *advantages* of accounting packages compared with a manual system are as follows.

(a)   The packages can be used by non-specialists.

(b)   A large amount of data can be processed very quickly.

(c)   Computerised systems are more accurate than manual systems.

(d)   A computer is capable of handling and processing large volumes of data.

(e)   Once the data has been input, computerised systems can analyse data rapidly to present useful control information for managers such as a trial balance or a debtors schedule.

1.7   The advantages of computerised accounting system far outweigh the disadvantages, particularly for large businesses. However, the following may be identified as possible disadvantages.

(a)   The initial time and costs involved in installing the system, training personnel and so on.

(b)   The need for security checks to make sure that unauthorised personnel do not gain access to data files.

(c)   The necessity to develop a system of coding (see below) and checking.

(d)   Lack of 'audit trail'. It is not always easy to see where a mistake has been made.

(e)   Possible resistance on the part of staff to the introduction of the system.

Coding

1.8   Computers are used more efficiently if vital information is expressed in the form of codes. For example, nominal ledger accounts will be coded individually, perhaps by means of a two-digit code: eg

00   Ordinary share capital
01   Share premium
05   Profit and loss account
15   Purchases
22   Debtors ledger control account
41   Creditors ledger control account
42   Interest
43   Dividends etc

In the same way, individual accounts must be given a unique code number in the sales ledger and purchase ledger.

1.9 When an invoice is received from a supplier (code 1234) for £3,000 for the purchase of raw materials, the transaction might be coded for input to the computer as:

	Nominal ledger			*Stock*	
Supplier Code	*Debit*	*Credit*	*Value*	*Code*	*Quantity*
1234	15	41	£3,000	56742	150

Code 15 might represent purchases and code 41 the creditors control account. This single input could be used to update the purchase ledger, the nominal ledger, and the stock ledger. The stock code may enable further analysis to be carried out, perhaps allocating the cost to a particular department or product. Thus the needs of both financial accounting and cost accounting can be fulfilled at once.

Using an accounting package

1.10 When a user begins to work with an accounting package he will usually be asked to key in a password. Separate passwords can be used for different parts of the system, for example for different ledgers if required. The user will then be presented with a 'menu' of options such as 'enter new data' or 'print report' or a Windows-type screen with buttons and icons. By selecting the appropriate option the user will then be guided through the actions needed to enter the data or generate the report.

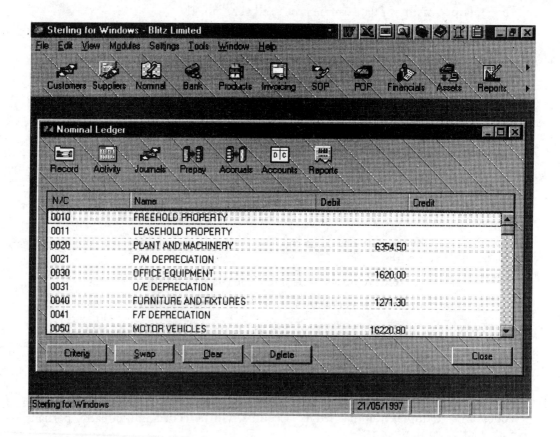

Modules

1.11 An accounting package will consist of several modules. A module is a program which deals with one particular part of a business accounting system. A simple accounting package might consist of only one module (in which case it is called a stand-alone module), but more often it will consist of several modules. The name given to a set of several modules is a *suite*. An accounting package, therefore, might have separate modules for:

(a) invoicing;
(b) stock;
(c) sales ledger;
(d) purchase ledger;
(e) nominal ledger;
(f) payroll;
(g) cash book;
(h) job costing;
(i) fixed asset register;
(j) report generator;

and so on.

Integrated software

1.12 Each module may be integrated with the others, so that data entered in one module will be passed automatically or by simple operator request through into any other module where the data is of some relevance. For example, if there is an input into the invoicing module authorising the despatch of an invoice to a customer, there might be *automatic links*:

(a) to the sales ledger, to update the file by posting the invoice to the customer's account;

(b) to the stock module, to update the stock file by:

   (i) reducing the quantity and value of stock in hand;
   (ii) recording the stock movement;

(c) to the nominal ledger, to update the file by posting the sale to the sales account;

(d) to the job costing module, to record the sales value of the job on the job cost file;

(e) to the report generator, to update the sales analysis and sales totals which are on file and awaiting inclusion in management reports.

1.13 A diagram of an integrated accounting system is given below.

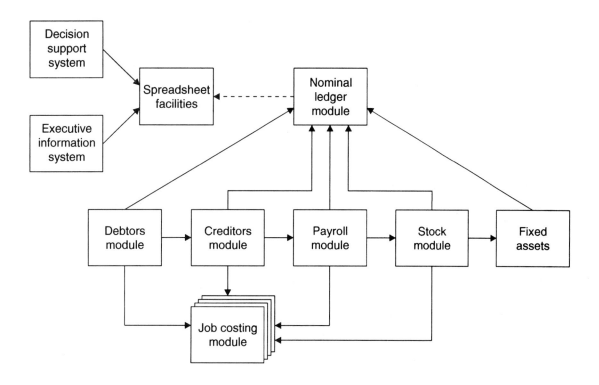

1.14   The *advantages* of integrated software are as follows.

(a)   It becomes possible to make just one entry in one of the ledgers which automatically updates the others.

(b)   Users can specify reports, and the software will automatically extract the required data from *all* the relevant files.

(c)   Both of the above simplify the workload of the user, and the irritating need to constantly load and unload disks is eliminated.

1.15   There are some *disadvantages* of integrated software.

(a)   Usually, it requires more computer memory than separate (stand-alone) systems - which means there is less space in which to store actual data.

(b)   Because one program is expected to do everything, the user may find that an integrated package has fewer facilities than a set of specialised modules. In effect, an integrated package could be 'Jack of all trades but master of none'.

2   ACCOUNTING MODULES

2.1   In this section we shall look at some of the accounting modules in more detail, starting with the sales ledger.

Accounting for debtors

2.2   A computerised sales ledger will be expected to keep the sales ledger up-to-date, and also it should be able to produce certain output (eg statements, sales analysis reports, responses to file interrogations etc). The output might be produced daily (eg day book listings), monthly (eg statements), quarterly (eg sales analysis reports) or periodically (eg responses to file interrogations, or customer name and address lists printed on adhesive labels for despatching circulars or price lists).

2.3   What we need to do is to have a closer look at the forms that input, output and processing take within a sales ledger. We will begin by thinking about what data we would expect to see in a sales ledger.

Data held on a sales ledger file

2.4   The sales ledger *file* will consist of individual *records* for each customer account. Some of the data held on the record will be *standing data* (ie it will change infrequently). Typical items of standing data are:

(a)   customer account number,

(b)   customer name;

(c)   address;

(d)   credit limit;

(e)   account sales analysis code;

(f)   account type (there are two different types of account - open item or balance forward - which we will look at shortly).

Each of these items is referred to as a *field* of information.

2.5   Other data held on a customer record will change as the sales ledger is updated. Such data is called *variable data*, and will include:

(a)   transaction data;
(b)   transaction description (eg sale, credit note etc);
(c)   transaction code (eg to identify payment period allowed);
(d)   debits;

(e) credits;

(f) balance.

2.6 The file which contains these customer records - the sales ledger - is sometimes called a *master file*. If it is updated from another file containing various transactions, then that file is called a *transactions file*. Developments in the way computers store information mean that you are not likely to see these terms much any more - people more often talk about 'databases' of information.

Exercise 1

What is the relationship between a file, a field and a record?

Solution

A file is made up of records which are made up of fields. Make sure you learn any new terminology like this, because it will make your answers to examination questions far more convincing.

Input to a sales ledger system

2.7 Bearing in mind what we expect to find in a sales ledger, we can say that typical data input into sales ledger system is as follows.

(a) *Amendments:*

    (i) amendments to customer details, eg change of address, change of credit limit, etc;

    (ii) insertion of new customers;

    (iii) deletion of old 'non-active' customers.

(b) *Transaction data relating to:*

    (i) sales transactions, for invoicing;

    (ii) customer payments;

    (iii) credit notes;

    (iv) adjustments (debit or credit items).

2.8 Some computerised sales ledgers produce invoices, so that basic sales data is input into the system. But other businesses might have a specialised invoicing module, so that the sales ledger package is not expected to produce invoices. The invoice details are already available (as output from the specialised module) and are input into the sales ledger system rather than basic sales data. So item (b)(i) of the list of typical data should read as follows.

    '(b) (i) Sales transactions, for invoicing (if the sales ledger is expected to produce invoices) or invoice details (if already available from a specialised invoicing module).'

Processing in a sales ledger system

2.9 The primary action involved in updating the sales ledger is modifying the amount outstanding on the customer's account. How the amount is modified depends on what data is being input (ie whether it is an invoice, credit note, remittance etc).

2.10 When processing starts, the balance on an account is called the *brought-forward* balance. When processing has finished, the balance on the account is called the *carried-forward* balance. These terms are often abbreviated to b/f and c/f.

2.11 What a computer does is to add or subtract whatever you tell it to from the b/f balance, and end up with a c/f balance.

	£	£
Brought forward account balance		X
Add:		
Invoice value	X	
Adjustments (+)	X	
		X
		X
Deduct:		
Credit note value	X	
Adjustments (-)	X	
Remittances	X	
		X
Carried forward account balance		X

This method of updating customer accounts is called the balance forward method.

2.12 Most systems also offer users the *open item* method of processing the data, which is much neater. Under this method, the user identifies specific invoices, and credits individual payments against specific invoices. Late payments of individual invoices can be identified and chased up. The customer's outstanding balance is the sum of the unpaid open items. The open item method follows best accounting practice, but it is more time consuming than the balance forward method.

Outputs from a sales ledger system

2.13 Typical outputs in a computerised sales ledger are as follows.

(a) *Day book listing*. A list of all transactions posted each day. This provides an audit trail - ie it is information which the auditors of the business can use when carrying out their work. Batch and control totals will be included in the listing.

(b) *Invoices* (if the package is one which is expected to produce invoices.)

(c) *Statements*. End of month statements for customers.

(d) *Aged debtors list*. Probably produced monthly.

(e) *Sales analysis reports*. These will analyse sales according to the sales analysis codes on the sales ledger file.

(f) *Debtors reminder letters*. Letters can be produced automatically to chase late payers when the due date for payment goes by without payment having been received.

(g) *Customer lists* (or perhaps a selective list). The list might be printed on to adhesive labels, for sending out customer letters or marketing material.

(h) *Responses to enquiries*, perhaps output on to a VDU screen rather than as printed copy, for fast response to customer enquiries.

(i) *Output onto disk file for other modules* - eg to the stock control module and the nominal ledger module, if these are also used by the organisation, and the package is not an integrated one.

The advantages of a computerised debtor system

2.14 The advantages of such a system, in addition to the advantages of computerised accounting generally, are its ability to assist in sales administration and marketing by means of outputs such as those listed above.

Purchase ledger

2.15 A computerised purchase ledger will certainly be expected to keep the purchase ledger up-to-date, and also it should be able to output various reports requested by the user. In fact, a computerised purchase ledger is much the same as a computerised sales ledger, except that it is a sort of mirror image as it deals with purchases rather than sales.

Exercise 2

What sort of data would you expect to be held on a purchase ledger file?

Solution

The purchase ledger will consist of individual records for each supplier account. Just as for customer accounts, some of the data held on record will be *standing* data, and some will be *variable* data. Standing data will include:

(a)   account number;
(b)   name;
(c)   address;
(d)   credit details;
(e)   bank details (eg method of payment);
(f)   cash discount details, if appropriate.

Variable data will include:

(a)   transaction date;
(b)   transaction description;
(c)   transaction code;
(d)   debits;
(e)   credits;
(f)   balance.

Inputs to a purchase ledger system

2.16   Bearing in mind what we expect to see held on a purchase ledger, typical data input into a purchase ledger system is:

(a)   details of purchases recorded on invoices;
(b)   details of returns to suppliers for which credit notes are received;
(c)   details of payments to suppliers;
(d)   adjustments.

Processing in a purchase ledger system

2.17   The primary action involved in updating the purchase ledger is adjusting the amounts outstanding on the supplier accounts. These amounts will represent money owed to the suppliers. This processing is identical to updating the accounts in the sales ledger, except that the sales ledger balances are debits (debtors) and the purchase ledger balances are credits (creditors). Again, the open item approach is the best.

Outputs from a purchase ledger system

2.18   Typical outputs in a computerised purchase ledger are as follows.

(a)   Lists of transactions posted - produced every time the system is run.

(b)   An analysis of expenditure for nominal ledger purposes. This may be produced every time the system is run or at the end of each month.

(c)   List of creditors balances together with a reconciliation between the total balance brought forward, the transactions for the month and the total balance carried forward.

(d)   Copies of creditors' accounts. This may show merely the balance b/f, current transactions and the balance c/f. If complete details of all unsettled items are given, the ledger is known as an *open-ended ledger*. (This is similar to the open item or balance forward methods with a sales ledger system.)

(e)   Any purchase ledger system can be used to produce details of payments to be made. For example:

(i)   remittance advices (usually a copy of the ledger account);
(ii)   cheques;

(iii)   credit transfer listings.

(f)   Other special reports may be produced for:

(i)   costing purposes;
(ii)   updating records about fixed assets;
(iii)   comparisons with budget;
(iv)   aged creditors list.

Payroll

2.19   The purpose of a payroll system is to compute the gross wages and salaries of employees and produce payslips, cheques and/or listings sent to banks instructing them to make payments. A computerised payroll system will be expected to carry out these tasks in accordance with how much employees should receive, how they should receive it and when it should be paid. The system should also be able to calculate tax deductions, national insurance deductions, savings, loan repayments etc, as well as printing various other outputs connected with employees' pay.

Data held on a payroll file

2.20   Payroll files will consist of an individual record for each employee.

(a)   *Standing* data on each employee will include:

(i)   personal details (eg name, employee number, job grade, address etc);
(ii)   rate of pay;
(iii)   details of deductions (including tax code);
(iv)   holidays;

(b)   *Variable* (transaction) data will include:

(i)   gross pay to date;
(ii)   tax to date;
(iii)   pension contributions etc.

Inputs to a payroll system

2.21   The main inputs into a *wages* system (ie into a weekly-paid payroll) are as follows.

(a)   Clock cards or time sheets (sometimes both are used). Details of overtime worked will normally be shown on these documents. Sometimes payroll might be directly linked to an electronic time recording system.

(b)   Amount of bonus, or appropriate details if the bonus is calculated by the computer.

2.22   *Salary* systems (ie a monthly-paid payroll) are similar to those for wages but it is usual for the monthly salary to be generated by the computer from details held on the master file and therefore (with the exception of overtime, bonuses etc) there is no need for any transaction input. So the inputs for a salary system are just overtime, bonuses etc (because the basic salary is already on the master file).

Processing in a payroll system

2.23   The primary action involved in processing a payroll is calculating an employee's gross pay, calculating and implementing the various deductions in order to find net pay, and then making payment by the appropriate method.

2.24   In the case of wages, this means taking the input data on hours worked and pay details, and calculating the weekly wage due to the employee. The same calculation is carried out every week.

2.25   In the case of salaries, payroll processing might just mean picking an option to pay all the monthly-paid employees the same amount as they received the previous month

This could happen in theory, but in practice there are usually some amendments to make to the monthly pay details, and these are implemented during payroll processing.

Outputs from a payroll system

2.26   Typical outputs in a payroll system are:

(a)   payslips;

(b)   payroll (this is often a copy of the payslips);

(c)   payroll analysis, including analysis of deductions (tax, national insurance etc) and details for costing purposes;

(d)   various forms required for PAYE (Pay As You Earn) tax purposes;

(e)   coin analysis, cheques, credit transfer forms, as appropriate;

(f)   in some cases, a floppy disk with payment details for despatch to the bank and payment through the BACS system.

Nominal ledger

2.27   The nominal ledger (or general ledger) is an accounting record which summarises the financial affairs of a business. It is the nucleus of an accounting system. It contains details of assets, liabilities and capital, income and expenditure and so profit or loss. It consists of a large number of different accounts, each account having its own purpose or 'name' and an identity or code.

2.28   A nominal ledger will consist of a large number of coded accounts. For example, part of a nominal ledger might be as follows.

Account code	*Account name*
100200	Plant and machinery (cost)
100300	Motor vehicles (cost)
100201	Plant and machinery depreciation
100301	Vehicles depreciation
300000	Total debtors
400000	Total creditors
500130	Wages and salaries
500140	Rent and rates
500150	Advertising expenses
500160	Bank charges
500170	Motor expenses
500180	Telephone expenses
600000	Sales
700000	Cash

2.29   A business will, of course, choose its own codes for its nominal ledger accounts. The codes given in this table are just for illustration.

2.30   It is important to remember that a computerised nominal ledger works in exactly the same way as a manual nominal ledger, although there are some differences in terminology. For instance, in a manual system, the sales and debtors accounts were posted from the sales day book (not the sales ledger). But in a computerised system, the sales day book is automatically produced as part of the 'sales ledger module'. So it may *sound* as if you are posting directly from the sales ledger, but in fact the day book is part of a computerised sales ledger.

Inputs to the nominal ledger

2.31   Inputs depend on whether the accounting system is integrated or not.

(a)   If the system is integrated, then as soon as data is put into the sales ledger module (or anywhere else for that matter), the relevant nominal ledger accounts are updated. There is nothing more for the system user to do.

(b)   If the system is not integrated then the output from the sales ledger module (and anywhere else) has to be input into the nominal ledger. This is done by using journal entries. For instance.

DEBIT	A/c 300000	£3,000	
CREDIT	A/c 600000		£3,000

Where 600000 is the nominal ledger code for sales, and 300000 is the code for debtors.

2.32   Regardless of whether the system is integrated or not, the actual data needed by the nominal ledger package to be able to update the ledger accounts includes:

(a)   date;
(b)   description;
(c)   amount;
(d)   account codes (sometimes called distinction codes).

Outputs from the nominal ledger

2.33   The main outputs apart from listings of individual nominal ledger accounts are:

(a)   the trial balance;
(b)   financial statements.

3   DATABASES

3.1   A database may be described as a 'pool' of data, which can be used by any number of applications. Its use is not restricted to the accounts department. A stricter definition is provided in the CIMA's *Computing Terminology*.

'Frequently a much abused term. In its strict sense a database is a file of data structured in such a way that it may serve a number of applications without its structure being dictated by any one of those applications, the concept being that programs are written around the database rather than files being structured to meet the needs of specific programs. The term is also rather loosely applied to simple file management software.'

3.2   The software that runs the database is called the database management system (DBMS). The CIMA's definition is as follows.

'Technically, a system which uses a database philosophy for the storage of information. In practice this term is often used to describe any system which enables the definition, storage and retrieval of information from discrete files within a system. Thus many simple file-handling systems are frequently referred to as "database systems".'

3.3   The database approach can also be summarised diagrammatically.

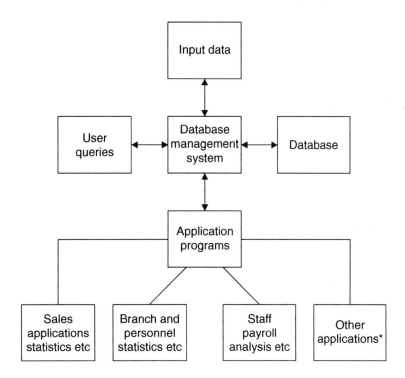

* The range of applications which make use of a database will vary widely, depending on what data is held on the database files.

3.4   Note the following from the diagram.

(a)   Data is input, and the DBMS software organises it into the database. If you like, you can think of the database as a vast library of fields and records, waiting to be used.

(b)   Various application programs (sales, payroll etc) are 'plugged into' the DBMS software so that they can use the database, or the same application used by different departments can all use the database.

(c)   As there is only one pool of data, there is no need for different departments to keep many different files with duplicated information.

Objectives of a database

3.5   The main virtues of a database are as follow.

(a)   There is common data for all users to share.
(b)   The extra effort of keeping duplicate files in different departments is avoided.
(c)   Conflicts between departments who use inconsistent data are avoided.

3.6   A database should have four major objectives.

(a)   It should be *shared*. Different users should be able to access the *same data* in the database for their own processing applications (and at the *same time* in some systems) thus removing the need for duplicating data on different files.

(b)   The *integrity* of the database must be preserved. This means that one user should not be allowed to alter the data on file so as to spoil the database records for other users. However, users must be able to update the data on file, and so make valid alterations to the data.

(c) The database system should provide for the needs of different users, who each have their own processing requirements and data access methods. In other words, the database should provide for the operational requirements of all its users.

(d) The database should be capable of *evolving*, both in the short term (it must be kept updated) and in the longer term (it must be able to meet the future data processing needs of users, not just their current needs).

Example: fixed assets and databases

3.7 An organisation, especially a large one, may possess a large quantity of fixed assets. Before computerisation these would have been kept in a manual fixed asset register. A database enables this fixed asset register to be stored in an electronic form. A database file for fixed assets might contain most or all of the following categories of information.

(a) Code number to give the asset a unique identification in the database

(b) Type of asset (for example motor car, leasehold premises), for published accounts purposes

(c) More detailed description of the asset (for example serial number, car registration number, make)

(d) Physical location of the asset (for example address)

(e) Organisational location of the asset (for example accounts department)

(f) Person responsible for the asset (for example in the case of a company-owned car, the person who uses it)

(g) Original cost of the asset

(h) Date of purchase

(i) Depreciation rate and method applied to the asset

(j) Accumulated depreciation to date

(k) Net book value of the asset

(l) Estimated residual value

(m) Date when the physical existence of the asset was last verified

(n) Supplier

Obviously, the details kept about the asset would depend on the type of asset it is.

3.8 Any kind of computerised fixed asset record will improve efficiency in accounting for fixed assets because of the ease and speed with which any necessary calculations can be made. Most obvious is the calculation of the depreciation provision which can be an extremely onerous task if it is done monthly and there are frequent acquisitions and disposals and many different depreciation rates in use.

3.9 The particular advantage of using a database for the fixed asset function is its flexibility in generating reports for different purposes. Aside from basic cost and net book value information a database with fields such as those listed above in the record of each asset could compile reports analysing assets according to location say, or by manufacturer. This information could be used to help compare the performance of different divisions, perhaps, or to assess the useful life of assets supplied by different manufacturers. There may be as many more possibilities as there are permutations of the individual pieces of data.

4 SPREADSHEETS

4.1 A *spreadsheet* appears to the user like a flat piece of paper divided into columns and rows to resemble a sheet of accountant's analysis paper. The intersection of each column and row is referred to as a cell. A cell can contain text, numbers or formulae. Use of a formula means that the cell which contains the formula will display the results of a calculation based on data in other cells. If the numbers in those other cells change, the result displayed in the formula cell will also change accordingly. With this facility, a spreadsheet is used to create financial models.

The use of spreadsheets

4.2   Spreadsheets have many uses, both for accounting and for other purposes. It is perfectly possible, for example, to create proforma balance sheets and P&L accounts on a spreadsheet, or set up the notes for financial accounts, like the fixed assets note.

5   PRACTICAL EXPERIENCE

5.1   The CIMA Guidance Notes state:

> 'Questions will *not* be set on the technical aspects of how computers work, but candidates may benefit from having practical experience in using computer packages and, in particular, using the controls and interpreting outputs from such accounting systems.'

5.2   It is thus clear that reading about computer systems and packages is no substitute for using them, and you should make every effort to gain experience in using an accounting package.

Chapter roundup

- Computer software used in accounting may be divided into two types.
    - o   Dedicated accounting packages
    - o   General software, the uses of which include accounting amongst many others

- In principle computerised accounting is the same as manual accounting, but a computerised approach has certain advantages which you should learn thoroughly.

- An accounting package consists of a number of 'modules' which perform all the tasks needed to maintain a normal accounting function like purchase ledger or payroll. In modern systems the modules are usually integrated with each other.

- A database is a file of data structured in such a way that it can serve a number of applications without its structure being dictated by any particular function.

- Spreadsheets, too, are often useful both in financial accounting and cost accounting.

- Reading about accounting packages is no substitute for using one.

Test your knowledge

1   What are the advantages of computerised accounting? (see para 1.6)

2   What are the disadvantages? (1.7)

3   What is an accounting suite? (1.11)

4   What are the advantages of integrated software? (1.14)

5   What sort of data is input into a sales ledger system? (2.7)

6   What is the open item method of processing? (2.12)

7   What sort of data might be held on a payroll file? (2.20)

8   What should be the four major objectives of a database? (3.6)

9   What are the advantages of using a database to maintain fixed asset records? (3.7,3.8)

10   Distinguish between a database and a spreadsheet. (4.1)

Now try illustrative question 30 at the end of the Study Text

Part C
Final accounts and audit

Chapter 19

THE ACCOUNTS OF UNINCORPORATED ORGANISATIONS

This chapter covers the following topics.

		Syllabus reference	Ability required
1	The accounts of a non-trading organisation	1(c)	Skill
2	The receipts and payments account	1(c)	Skill
3	Preparing income and expenditure accounts	1(c)	Skill

Introduction

This part of the Study Text is concerned with the preparation of final accounts for a variety of organisations.

So far you have dealt with the accounts of businesses. This chapter considers non-trading organisations, that is organisations which are not incorporated under the Companies Act and whose objectives are to provide services to their members or the pursuit of one or a number of activities rather than the earning of profit.

Such entities may be, and often are, very small in both membership and wealth. However, they can also be very large like the Automobile Association, which in 1994 had over 8 million members and net assets with a book value of over £400 million.

So long as subscriptions are charged, there will be a need for some financial records, the minimum possible being a cash book and petty cash book. Clubs which rely on this minimum package often confine their annual accounts to a *receipts and payments account*. This is simply a summary of cash received and paid for a period, and is discussed in Section 2 of this chapter.

A receipts and payments account may be adequate for some clubs but has important deficiencies when used by clubs which have substantial assets (in addition to cash) and liabilities. The arguments in favour of accruals based accounting apply to clubs as well as profit making entities, and most large clubs do produce financial statements based on accruals accounting. In particular many clubs produce what is basically a profit and loss account but they call it an *income and expenditure account*. This is the subject of Section 3 of this chapter.

1 THE ACCOUNTS OF A NON-TRADING ORGANISATION

1.1 Since a non-trading organisation does not exist to make a profit, it is inappropriate to refer to its 'profit and loss' account. However, a non-trading organisation must be able to pay its way, and so it is still important to ensure that income covers expenses. For this reason, an 'income and expenditure' account, together with a balance sheet, is an important report for judging the financial affairs of the organisation. The principles of 'accruals' accounting (the matching concept) are applied to income and expenditure accounts in the same way as for profit and loss accounts.

1.2 An income and expenditure account is simply the name that is given to what is effectively the profit and loss account of a non-trading organisation, such as sports clubs, social clubs, societies and other associations, charities and so on.

1.3   There are one or two differences between the final accounts of a non-trading organisation and those of a business.

(a)   Since non-trading organisations do not exist to make profits, the difference between income and matching expenditure in the *income and expenditure account* is referred to as a *surplus* or a *deficit* rather than a profit or loss.

(b)   The capital or proprietorship of the organisation is referred to as the *accumulated fund*, rather than the capital account. In addition, other separate funds might be kept by the organisation (see Paragraph 1.7).

(c)   There is usually no separate trading account. Instead, it is usual to net off expenditure against income for like items. To explain this point further, it will be useful to consider the sources of income for a non-trading organisation in further detail.

Sources of income for non-trading organisations

1.4   Non-trading organisations differ in purpose and character, but we shall concentrate here on sports clubs, social clubs or societies. These will obtain their income from various sources which include the following.

(a)   Membership subscriptions for annual membership of the club (and initial joining subscriptions for first year members)

(b)   Payments for life membership

(c)   'Profits' from bar sales

(d)   'Profits' from the sale of food in the club restaurant or cafeteria

(e)   'Profits' from social events, such as dinner-dances

(f)   Interest received on investments

1.5   Netting off expenditure against income for like items means that where some sources of income have associated costs, the net surplus or deficit should be shown in the income and expenditure account.

(a)   If a club holds an annual dinner-dance, for example, the income and expenditure account will net off the costs of the event against the revenue to show the surplus or deficit.

(b)   Similarly, if a club has a bar, the income and expenditure account will show the surplus or deficit on its trading. Although the organisation itself does not trade, the bar within the organisation does, and so it is in fact correct to refer to 'profits' from the bar.

1.6   Where there is trading activity within a non-trading organisation (eg bar sales, cafeteria sales etc) so that the organisation must hold stocks of drink or food etc it is usual to prepare a trading account for that particular activity, and then to record the surplus or deficit from trading in the income and expenditure account. An example is shown below.

FOOLSMATE CHESS CLUB
BAR TRADING ACCOUNT FOR THE YEAR TO 31 DECEMBER 19X5

	£	£
Sales		18,000
Less cost of goods sold		
Bar stocks 1 January 19X5	1,200	
Purchases	15,400	
	16,600	
Less bar stocks at 31 December 19X5	1,600	
		15,000
Bar profit (taken to income and expenditure account)		3,000

Funds of non-trading organisations

1.7   Although the capital of a non-trading organisation is generally accounted for as the accumulated fund, some separate funds might be set up for particular purposes.

(a)   A life membership fund is a fund for the money subscribed for life membership by various members of the organisation. The money paid for life membership is commonly invested outside the organisation (for example in a building society account). The investment then earns interest for the organisation.

(b)   A building fund might be set up whereby the organisation sets aside money to save for the cost of a new building extension. The money put into the fund will be invested outside the organisation, earning interest, until it is eventually needed for the building work. It might take several years to create a fund large enough for the building work planned.

1.8   The basic principles of accounting for special funds are as follows.

(a)   When money is put into the fund:

DEBIT   Cash
CREDIT   Special-purpose fund

(b)   When the cash is invested:

DEBIT   Investments (eg building society account)
CREDIT   Cash

(c)   When the investments earn interest:

DEBIT   Cash
CREDIT   Interest received account (and subsequently, the income and expenditure account, or possibly the fund account itself).

2   THE RECEIPTS AND PAYMENTS ACCOUNT

2.1   Many charities and clubs have little, if any, accounting expertise and keep records only of cash paid and received. The receipts and payments account is effectively a summary of an organisation's cash book. To facilitate the production of such a financial statement an analysed cash book will probably be used. No balance sheet is produced with a receipts and payments account.

Example: receipts and payments account

2.2

HIGH LEE STRONG TENNIS CLUB
RECEIPTS AND PAYMENTS ACCOUNT
FOR THE YEAR ENDED 30 APRIL 19X0

Receipts	£	*Payments*	£
Balance b/f	16	Bar expenses	106
Bar takings	160	Rent	50
Subscriptions	328	Wages	140
		Postage	10
		Printing	12
		Affiliation fees to LTS	18
		Lawn mower★	50
		Heat and light	60
		Balance c/f	58
	504		504

★Item of capital expenditure

2.3   The *advantages* of this type of financial statement are as follows.

(a)   It is very easy to produce and understand.

(b)   It serves as a basis for the preparation of the income and expenditure account and balance sheet.

2.4   In isolation, the receipts and payments account has some *disadvantages*.

(a)   It takes no account of any amounts owing or prepaid.

(b)   It includes items of capital expenditure and makes no distinction between capital and revenue items.

(c)   It takes no account of depreciation of fixed assets.

2.5   For the layman, however, particularly in the case of small clubs where the transactions are simple and straightforward, a receipts and payments account will be sufficient.

3   PREPARING INCOME AND EXPENDITURE ACCOUNTS

3.1   Examination questions often provide a receipts and payments account, balances of assets and liabilities at the beginning of the period, and details of accruals and prepayments at the end of the period. You would be required typically to perform the following tasks.

(a)   Calculate the balance on the accumulated fund at the beginning of the period.
(b)   Prepare a trading account for a particular activity for the period.
(c)   Prepare an income and expenditure account for the period.
(d)   Prepare a balance sheet at the end of the period.

3.2   Before looking at an example of an income and expenditure account we need to look at each of the following items in some detail.

(a)   Membership subscriptions
(b)   Bar trading account
(c)   Life membership

These are items which we have not yet come across in previous chapters of this Study Text, because they are not found in the accounts of businesses. We must not forget, however, that in many respects the accounts of non-trading organisations are similar to those of businesses with fixed assets, a provision for depreciation, current assets and current liabilities, expense accounts (eg electricity, telephone, stationery etc) accruals and prepayments.

Membership subscriptions

3.3   Annual membership subscriptions of clubs and societies are usually payable one year in advance.

A club or society therefore receives payments from members for benefits which the members have yet to enjoy, and so payments in advance by members, being receipts in advance to the club or society, will be shown in the balance sheet of the society as a current liability, to the extent that the year's membership has still to run as at the balance sheet date.

3.4   A numerical example might help to clarify this point.

The Mudflannels Cricket Club charges an annual membership of £50 payable in advance on 1 October each year. All 40 members pay their subscriptions promptly on 1 October 19X4. If the club's accounting year ends on 31 December total subscriptions of $40 \times £50 = £2,000$ would be treated as follows.

(a) $40 \times \dfrac{9 \text{ months}}{12 \text{ months}} \times £50 = £1,500$ will appear in the balance sheet of the club as at 31 December 19X4 as a current liability 'subscriptions in advance'. These subscriptions relate to the period 1 January to 30 September 19X5.

(b) $40 \times \dfrac{3 \text{ months}}{12 \text{ months}} \times £50 = £500$ will appear as income in the income and expenditure account for the period 1 October to 31 December 19X4.

3.5 When members are in arrears with subscriptions and owe money to the club or society, they are 'debtors' of the organisation and so appear as current assets in the balance sheet 'subscriptions in arrears'. These should be shown as a separate item in the balance sheet, and should not be netted off against subscriptions in advance.

3.6 For example, suppose that the Bluespot Squash Club has 100 members, each of whom pays an annual membership of £60 on 1 November. Of those 100 members, 90 pay their subscriptions before 31 December 19X5 (for the 19X5/X6 year) but 10 have still not paid. If the club's accounting year ends on 31 December, then as at 31 December 19X5 the balance sheet of the club would include the following items.

(a) *Subscriptions in advance (current liability)*

$90 \text{ members} \times \dfrac{10 \text{ months}}{12 \text{ months}} \times £60 = £4,500$

(b) *Subscriptions in arrears (current asset)*

$10 \text{ members} \times \dfrac{2 \text{ months}}{12 \text{ months}} \times £60 = £100$

It is not uncommon, however, for clubs to take no credit for subscription income until the money is received. In such a case, any subscriptions in arrears are not credited to income and *not* shown as a current asset. It is essential to read the question carefully.

Example: subscriptions

3.7 At 1 January 19X8, the Little Blithering Debating Society had membership subscriptions paid in advance of £1,600, and subscriptions in arrears of £250. During the year to 31 December 19X8 receipts of subscription payments amounted to £18,400. At 31 December 19X8 subscriptions in advance amounted to £1,750 and subscriptions in arrears to £240.

What is the income from subscriptions to be shown in the income and expenditure account for the year to 31 December 19X8?

Solution

3.8 The question does not say that subscriptions are only accounted for when received. You may therefore assume that the society takes credit for subscriptions as they become due, whether or not they are received.

The income for the income and expenditure account would be calculated as follows.

		£	£
Payments received in the year			18,400
Add:	subscriptions due but not yet received (ie subscriptions in arrears 31 Dec 19X8)	240	
	subscriptions received last year relating to current year (ie subscriptions in advance 1 Jan 19X8)	1,600	
			1,840
			20,240
Less:	subscriptions received in current year relating to last year (ie subscriptions in arrears 1 Jan 19X8)	250	
	subscriptions received in current year relating to next year (ie subscriptions in advance 31 Dec 19X8)	1,750	
			2,000
Income from subscriptions for the year			18,240

3.9   You may find it simpler to do this calculation as a ledger account.

SUBSCRIPTIONS ACCOUNT

	£		£
Subscriptions in arrears b/f	250	Subscriptions in advance b/f	1,600
I & E a/c (balancing figure)	18,240	Cash	18,400
Subscriptions in advance c/d	1,750	Subscriptions in arrears c/d	240
	20,240		20,240
Subscriptions in arrears b/d	240	Subscriptions in advance b/d	1,750

Exercise

The following information relates to a sports club.

	£
19X4 subscriptions unpaid at beginning of 19X5	410
19X4 subscriptions received during 19X5	370
19X5 subscriptions received during 19X5	6,730
19X6 subscriptions received during 19X5	1,180
19X5 subscriptions unpaid at end of 19X5	470

The club takes credit for subscription income when it becomes due, but takes a prudent view of overdue subscriptions. What amount should be credited to the income and expenditure account for 19X5?

Solution

SUBSCRIPTIONS

	£		£
Balance b/f	410	Bank: 19X4	370
		19X5	6,730
∴ I & E account	7,200	19X6	1,180
		19X4 subs written off	40
Balance c/f	1,180	Balance c/f	470
	8,790		8,790

Bar trading account

3.10   If a club has a bar or cafeteria a separate trading account will be prepared for its trading activities. A bar trading account will contain the following items.

(a) Bar takings

(b) Opening stocks of goods, purchases and closing stocks of goods, to give the cost of bar sales

(c) A gross profit item (a) minus item (b)

(d) Other expenses directly related to the running of the bar, if any

(e) A net profit item (c) minus item (d)

The net bar profit is then included under income in the income and expenditure account. A loss on the bar would be included under expenditure.

Life membership

3.11   Some clubs offer membership for life in return for a given lump sum subscription. Life members, having paid this initial lump sum, do not have to pay any further annual subscriptions. In return the club receives a sum of money, which it can then invest, with the annual interest from these investments being accounted for as income in the income and expenditure account.

The 'once-and-for-all' payments from life members are not income relating to the year in which they are received by the club, because the payment is for the life of the members, which can of course be a very long time to come. Because they are long-term payments, they are recorded in the club accounts as an addition to a life membership fund as follows.

DEBIT   Cash
CREDIT   Life membership fund

3.12   The life membership fund is shown in the balance sheet of the club or society immediately after the accumulated fund.

3.13   Life members enjoy the benefits of membership over their life, and so their payment to the club is 'rewarded' as time goes by. Accounting for life membership over time can be explained with an example.

Suppose that Annette Cord pays a life membership fee of £300 to the Tumbledown Tennis Club. The £300 will initially be put into the club's life membership fund. We will suppose that this money is invested by the club, and earns interest of £30 per annum.

3.14   There are two ways of accounting for the life membership fee.

(a)   To keep the £300 in the life membership fund until Annette Cord dies. (Since the £300 earns interest of £30 pa this interest can be said to represent income for the club in lieu of an annual subscription.)

When Annette eventually dies (in five years, or 50 years, or whenever) the £300 she contributed can then be transferred (on death of the life member) out of the life membership fund and directly into the accumulated fund.

(b)   To write off subscriptions to the life membership fund by transferring a 'fair' amount from the fund into the income and expenditure account. A 'fair' amount will represent the proportion of the total life membership payment which relates to the current year. We do not know how long any life member will live, but if an estimated average life from becoming a life member until death is, say, 20 years, it might seem reasonable to write off payments to the fund over a 20 year period. In each year, one-twentieth of life membership fees would be deducted from the fund and added as income in the income and expenditure account.

In the case of Annette Cord, the annual transfer would be £15, and after 20 years, her contribution to the fund would have been written off in full from the fund and transferred to the income and expenditure accounts of those 20 years.

This transfer of £15 to the income and expenditure account will of course be supplementary to the annual interest of £30 earned by the club each year from investing the fee of £300.

3.15   If method (b) is selected in preference to method (a), the life membership fund could be written down by either a straight line method or a reducing balance method, in much the same way as fixed assets are depreciated - with the exception that it is a capital fund being written off, and the amount of the annual write-off is income to the club, and not an expense like depreciation.

3.16   A further feature of method (b) is that there is no need to record the death of individual members (unlike method (a)). The annual write off is based on an average expected life of members, and it does not matter when any individual member dies. The same average write off each year will be used.

3.17   A possible reason for preferring method (b) to method (a) is that life membership subscriptions eventually pass through the income and expenditure account as income of the club, which is logically reasonable, since life members although they pay a long time in advance, do eventually enjoy the benefits of membership in return for their payment. Why therefore, should life membership fees be essentially different from ordinary annual membership subscriptions? It is fair that in due course of time, life membership fees should be accounted for as income of the club, to boost the annual surpluses, or reduce the annual deficits.

3.18   In spite of the logical reasons why method (b) should perhaps be preferable, method (a) is still commonly used. In an examination question, unless you are told about a rate for 'writing off' the life membership fund annually, you should assume that method (a) should be used, where the question gives you information about the death of club life members.

Example: life membership fund

3.19   The Coxless Rowing Club has a scheme whereby as an alternative to paying annual subscriptions, members can at any time opt to pay a lump sum which gives them membership for life. Lump sum payments received for life membership are held in a life membership fund but then credited to the income and expenditure account in equal instalments over a ten year period, beginning in the year when the lump sum payment is made and life membership is acquired.

The treasurer of the club, Beau Trace, establishes the following information.

(a)   At 31 December 19X4, the balance on the life membership fund was £8,250.

(b)   Of this opening balance, £1,220 should be credited as income for the year to 31 December 19X5.

(c)   During the year to 31 December 19X5, new life members made lump sum payments totalling £1,500.

Required

Show the movements in the life membership fund for the year to 31 December 19X5, and in doing so, calculate how much should be transferred as income from life membership fund to the income and expenditure account.

Solution

3.20

LIFE MEMBERSHIP FUND

	£	£
As at 31 December 19X4		8,250
New life membership payments received in 19X5		1,500
		9,750
Less transfer to income and expenditure account:		
out of balance as at 31 December 19X4	1,220	
out of new payments in 19X5 (10% of £1,500)	150	
		1,370
Fund as at 31 December 19X5		8,380

The income and expenditure account for the year would show:

Income from life membership		1,370

Accounting for the sale of investments and fixed assets

3.21   In accounting for clubs and societies, the income and expenditure account is used to record the surplus or deficit in the transactions for the year. Occasionally a club or society might sell off some of its investments or fixed assets, and in doing so might make a profit or loss on the sale.

(a)   The profit/loss on the sale of an investment is simply the difference between the sale price and the balance sheet value (usually cost) of the investment.

(b)   The profit/loss on the sale of a fixed asset is the difference between the sale price and the net book value of the asset at the date of sale.

3.22   There is nothing different or unusual about the accounts of non-trading organisations in computing the amount of such profits or losses. What is different, however, is how the profit or losses should be recorded in the accounts.

(a)   The profit or loss on the sale of investments is not shown in the income and expenditure account. Instead, the profit is directly added to (or loss subtracted from) the accumulated fund.

(b)   The profit or loss on the sale of a fixed asset which is not subject to depreciation charges in the income and expenditure account, is also taken directly to the accumulated fund.

(c)   The profit or loss on the sale of fixed assets which have been subject to depreciation charges is recorded in the income and expenditure account.

3.23   The point of difference in (c) compared with (a) and (b) is that since depreciation on the asset has been charged in the income and expenditure account in the past, it is appropriate that a profit or loss on sale should also be reported through the account.

Income and expenditure accounts: an example

3.24   The preceding explanations might be sufficient to enable you to prepare an income and expenditure account yourself. A lengthy example is given below. If you think you understand the explanations given in it, you should go on to attempt the illustrative questions recommended at the end of the chapter.

3.25   The assets and liabilities of the Berley Sports Club at 31 December 19X4 were as follows.

	£
Pavilion at cost less depreciation	13,098
Bank and cash	1,067
Bar stock	291
Bar debtors	231
Rates prepaid	68
Contributions owing to sports club by users of sports club facilities	778
Bar creditors	427
Loans to sports club	1,080
Accruals: water	13
electricity	130
miscellaneous	75
loan interest	33
Contributions paid in advance by users of sports club facilities	398

A receipts and payments account for the year ended 31 December 19X5 was produced as follows.

	£		£
Opening balance	1,067	Bar purchases	2,937
Bar sales	4,030	Repayment of loan capital	170
Telephone	34	Rent of ground	79
Contributions from users of club		Rates	320
facilities	1,780	Water	38
Socials	177	Electricity	506
Miscellaneous	56	Insurance	221
		Repairs to equipment	326
		Expenses of socials	67
		Maintenance of ground	133
		Wages of groundsman	140
		Telephone	103
		Bar sundries	144
		Loan interest	97
		Miscellaneous	163
		Closing balance	1,700
	7,144		7,144

The following information as at 31 December 1985 was also provided.

	£
Bar stock	394
Bar debtors	50
Bar creditors	901
Rent prepaid	16
Water charges owing	23
Electricity owing	35
Creditors for bar sundries	65
Contributions by users of sports club facilities:	
owing to sports club	425
paid in advance to sports club	657
Rates prepaid	76

Depreciation on the pavilion for the year was £498.

You are asked to prepare a statement showing the gross and net profits earned by the bar, an income and expenditure account for the year ended 31 December 19X5 and a balance sheet as at that date.

Approach to a solution

3.26   We are not given the size of the accumulated fund as at the beginning of the year, but it can be calculated as the balancing figure to make total liabilities plus capital equal to total assets (as at 31 December 19X4).

Calculation of accumulated fund at 1 January 19X5

	£	£
Assets		
Pavilion at cost less depreciation		13,098
Bank and cash		1,067
Bar stock		291
Bar debtors		231
Rates prepaid		68
Contributions in arrears		778
		15,533
Liabilities		
Bar creditors	427	
Loans	1,080	
Accrued charges £(13 + 130 + 75 + 33)	251	
Contributions received in advance	398	
		2,156
∴ Accumulated fund at 1 January 19X5		13,377

3.27   The next step is to analyse the various items of income and expenditure.

(a)   There is a bar, and so a bar trading account can be prepared.

(b)   Income from the telephone (presumably from members paying the club for calls they make) can be netted off against telephone expenditure.

(c)   The revenue from socials has associated expenses to net off against it.

(d)   There is also miscellaneous income and contributions from club members.

3.28   The bar trading account can only be put together after we have calculated bar sales and purchases.

(a)   We are given bar debtors as at 1 January 19X5 and 31 December 19X5 and also cash received from bar sales. The bar sales for the year can therefore be calculated.

BAR DEBTORS

		£			£
1.1.19X5	Balance b/f	231	31.12.19X5	Cash	4,030
31.12.19X5	∴ Bar sales	3,849	31.12.19X5	Balance c/f	50
		4,080			4,080

(b) Similarly, purchases for the bar are calculated from opening and closing amounts for bar creditors, and payments for bar purchases.

BAR CREDITORS

		£			£
31.12.19X5	Cash	2,937	1.1.19X5	Balance b/f	427
31.12.19X5	Balance c/f	901	31.12.19X5	∴ Bar purchases	3,411
		3,838			3,838

(c) Be clear in your own mind that cash receipts from bar sales and cash payments for bar supplies are not the bar sales and cost of bar sales that we want. Cash receipts and payments in the year are not for matching quantities of goods, nor do they relate to the actual goods sold in the year.

(d) Other bar trading expenses are bar sundries.

	£
Cash payments for bar sundries	144
Add creditors for bar sundries as at 31.12.19X5	65
	209
Less creditors for bar sundries as at 1.1.19X5	0
Expenses for bar sundries for the year	209

3.29 BAR TRADING ACCOUNT
FOR THE YEAR ENDED 31 DECEMBER 19X5

	£	£
Sales		3,849
Cost of sales		
Opening stock	291	
Purchases	3,411	
	3,702	
Less closing stock	394	
		3,308
Gross profit		541
Sundry expenses		209
Net profit		332

3.30 Contributions to the sports club for the year should be calculated in the same way as membership subscriptions. Using a T account format below, the income from contributions (for the income and expenditure account) is the balancing figure. Contributions in advance brought forward are liabilities (credit balance b/f) and contributions in arrears brought forward are assets (debit balance b/f).

CONTRIBUTIONS

		£			£
1.1.19X5	Balance in arrears b/f	778	1.1.19X5	Balance in advance b/f	398
31.12.19X	∴ Income and expenditure	1,168	31.12.19X5	Cash	1,780
31.12.19X5	Balance in advance c/f	657	31.12.19X5	Balance in arrears c/f	425
		2,603			2,603

3.31   BERLEY SPORTS CLUB - INCOME AND EXPENDITURE ACCOUNT
        FOR THE YEAR ENDED 31 DECEMBER 19X5

	£	£
Income		
Contributions		1,168
Net income from bar trading		332
Income from socials: receipts	177	
less expenses	67	
		110
Miscellaneous		56
		1,666
Expenses		
Ground rent (79 – 16)	63	
Rates (320 + 68 – 76)	312	
Water (38 – 13 + 23)	48	
Electricity (506 – 130 + 35)	411	
Insurance	221	
Equipment repairs	326	
Ground maintenance	133	
Wages	140	
Telephone (103 – 34)	69	
Loan interest (97 –33)	64	
Miscellaneous expenses (163 – 75)	88	
Depreciation	498	
		2,373
		(707)

BERLEY SPORTS CLUB
BALANCE SHEET AS AT 31 DECEMBER 19X5

	£	£
Fixed assets		
Pavilion at NBV £(13,098 – 498)		12,600
Current assets		
Bar stock	394	
Bar debtors	50	
Contributions in arrears	425	
Prepayments £(16+76)	92	
Cash at bank	1,700	
	2,661	
Current liabilities		
Bar creditors £(901+65)	966	
Accrued charges	58	
Contributions in advance	657	
	1,681	
Net current assets		980
		13,580
Long-term liability		
Loan £(1,080-170)		910
		12,670
Accumulated fund		
Balance at 1 January 19X5		13,377
Less deficit for year		(707)
		12,670

Chapter roundup

- The *receipts and payments account* is, in effect, a summary of the cash book. For small clubs with a few straightforward transactions, this statement may be sufficient. For larger concerns, however, the receipts and payments account will form the basis for the preparation of the income and expenditure account and balance sheet.

- *Income and expenditure accounts* are the equivalent of profit and loss accounts for non-trading organisations. In the examination it is usually easy to recognise such questions because they always refer to the accounts of a club or society.

- You should remember to do the following when presenting income and expenditure accounts.

  - Match the sources of revenue with related costs to show net income from the organisation's various activities.

  - Treat subscriptions received in advance as a current liability and (unless the question states the contrary) treat subscriptions in arrears as a current asset.

  - Describe the result for the year as surplus or deficit, not as profit or loss.

  - Describe the capital of the organisation as the accumulated fund but remember that capital may also include other funds such as a life membership fund.

Test your knowledge

1   List three differences between the accounts of a non-trading organisation and those of a business. (see para 1.3)

2   List five sources of income for a non-trading organisation. (1.4)

3   Describe two ways of accounting for income from life membership fees. (3.14)

4   The profit or loss on the sale of a fixed asset which has been subject to depreciation charges is taken directly to the accumulated fund. True or false? (3.22)

Now try illustrative questions 31 and 32 at the end of the Study Text

Chapter 20

INCOMPLETE RECORDS

This chapter covers the following topics.

		Syllabus reference	Ability required
1	Incomplete records questions	1(c)	Skill
2	The opening balance sheet	1(c)	Skill
3	Credit sales and debtors	1(c)	Skill
4	Purchases and trade creditors	1(c)	Skill
5	Establishing cost of sales	1(c)	Skill
6	Stolen goods or goods destroyed	1(c)	Skill
7	The cash book	1(c)	Skill
8	Accruals and prepayments	1(c)	Skill
9	Drawings	1(c)	Skill
10	Dealing with incomplete records problems in the examination	1(c)	Skill

Introduction

So far in your work on preparing the final accounts for a sole trader we have assumed that a full set of records are kept. In practice many sole traders do not keep a full set of records and you must apply certain techniques to arrive at the necessary figures.

Incomplete records questions are a very good test of your understanding of the way in which a set of accounts is built up.

Limited companies are obliged by law to keep proper accounting records. They will be considered in Chapter 21.

1 INCOMPLETE RECORDS QUESTIONS   *11/95, 11/96*

1.1 Incomplete records problems occur when a business does not have a full set of accounting records, either because:

(a) the proprietor of the business does not keep a full set of accounts; or

(b) some of the business accounts are accidentally lost or destroyed.

1.2 The problem for the accountant is to prepare a set of year-end accounts for the business; ie a trading, profit and loss account, and a balance sheet. Since the business does not have a full set of accounts, preparing the final accounts is not a simple matter of closing off accounts and transferring balances to the trading, P&L account, or showing outstanding balances in the balance sheet. The task of preparing the final accounts involves:

(a) establishing the cost of purchases and other expenses;

(b) establishing the total amount of sales;

(c) establishing the amount of creditors, accruals, debtors and prepayments at the end of the year.

1.3 Examination questions often take incomplete records problems a stage further, by introducing an 'incident' - such as fire or burglary- which leaves the owner of the business uncertain about how much stock has been destroyed or stolen.

1.4 The great merit of incomplete records problems is that they focus attention on the relationship between cash received and paid, sales and debtors, purchases and creditors, and stocks, as well as calling for the preparation of final accounts from basic principles.

1.5 The final accounts you are asked to prepare a may include a 'statement of affairs'. This simply means a balance sheet produced from incomplete records where some of the figures have to be deduced, a balance sheet in summary form because there is insufficient data for a full one, or one which is not in a standard format.

1.6 To understand what incomplete records are about, it will obviously be useful now to look at what exactly might be incomplete. The items we shall consider in turn are:

(a) the opening balance sheet;
(b) credit sales and debtors;
(c) purchases and trade creditors;
(d) purchases, stocks and the cost of sales;
(e) stolen goods or goods destroyed;
(f) the cash book;
(g) accruals and prepayments;
(h) drawings.

2 THE OPENING BALANCE SHEET

2.1 In practice there should not be any missing item in the opening balance sheet of the business, because it should be available from the preparation of the previous year's final accounts. However, an examination problem might provide information about the assets and liabilities of the business at the beginning of the period under review, but then leave the balancing figure - ie the proprietor's business capital - unspecified.

Example: opening balance sheet

2.2 Suppose a business has the following assets and liabilities as at 1 January 19X3.

	£
Fixtures and fittings at cost	7,000
Provision for depreciation, fixtures and fittings	4,000
Motor vehicles at cost	12,000
Provision for depreciation, motor vehicles	6,800
Stock in trade	4,500
Trade debtors	5,200
Cash at bank and in hand	1,230
Trade creditors	3,700
Prepayment	450
Accrued rent	2,000

You are required to prepare a balance sheet for the business, inserting a balancing figure for proprietor's capital.

Solution

2.3 Balance sheet as at 1 January 19X3

	£	£
Fixed assets		
Fixtures and fittings at cost	7,000	
Less accumulated depreciation	4,000	
		3,000
Motor vehicles at cost	12,000	
Less accumulated depreciation	6,800	
		5,200
		8,200
Current assets		
Stock in trade	4,500	
Trade debtors	5,200	
Prepayment	450	
Cash	1,230	
	11,380	
Current liabilities		
Trade creditors	3,700	
Accrual	2,000	
	5,700	
Net current assets		5,680
		13,880
Proprietor's capital as at 1 January 19X3 (balancing figure)		13,880

3 CREDIT SALES AND DEBTORS

3.1 If a business does not keep a record of its sales on credit, the value of these sales can be derived from the opening balance of trade debtors, the closing balance of trade debtors, and the payments received from trade debtors during the period.

	£
Credit sales are:	
Payments received from trade debtors	X
Plus closing balance of trade debtors (since these represent sales in the current	
period for which cash payment has not yet been received)	X
Less opening balance of trade debtors (unless these become bad debts, they will pay	
what they owe in the current period for sales in a previous period)	(X)
	X

3.2 For example, suppose that a business had trade debtors of £1,750 on 1 April 19X4 and trade debtors of £3,140 on 31 March 19X5. If payments received from trade debtors during the year to 31 March 19X5 were £28,490, and if there are no bad debts, then credit sales for the period would be:

	£
Cash received from debtors	28,490
Plus closing debtors	3,140
Less opening debtors	(1,750)
Credit sales	29,880

If there are bad debts during the period, the value of sales will be increased by the amount of bad debts written off, no matter whether they relate to opening debtors or credit sales during the current period.

3.3 The same calculation could be made in a T account, with credit sales being the balancing figure to complete the account.

DEBTORS

	£		£
Opening balance b/f	1,750	Cash received	28,490
Credit sales (balancing fig)	29,880	Closing balance c/f	3,140
	31,630		31,630

3.4 The same interrelationship between credit sales, cash from debtors, and opening and closing debtors balances can be used to derive a missing figure for cash from debtors, or opening or closing debtors, given the values for the three other items. For example, if we know that opening debtors are £6,700, closing debtors are £3,200 and credit sales for the period are £69,400, then cash received from debtors during the period would be:

DEBTORS

	£		£
Opening balance	6,700	Cash received (balancing figure)	72,900
Sales (on credit)	69,400	Closing balance c/f	3,200
	76,100		76,100

An alternative way of presenting the same calculation would be as follows.

	£
Opening balance of debtors	6,700
Credit sales during the period	69,400
Total money owed to the business	76,100
Less closing balance of debtors	3,200
Equals cash received during the period	72,900

4 PURCHASES AND TRADE CREDITORS

4.1 A similar relationship exists between purchases of stock during a period, the opening and closing balances for trade creditors, and amounts paid to trade creditors during the period.

If we wish to calculate an unknown amount for purchases, the amount would be derived as follows.

	£
Payments to trade creditors during the period	X
Plus closing balance of trade creditors	X
(since these represent purchases in the current period for which payment has not yet been made)	
Less opening balance of trade creditors	(X)
(these debts, paid in the current period, relate to purchases in a previous period)	
Purchases during the period	X

4.2 For example, suppose that a business had trade creditors of £3,728 on 1 October 19X5 and trade creditors of £2,645 on 30 September 19X6. If payments to trade creditors during the year to 30 September 19X6 were £31,479, then purchases during the year would be:

	£
Payments to trade creditors	31,479
Plus closing balance of trade creditors	2,645
Less opening balance of trade creditors	(3,728)
Purchases	30,396

4.3 The same calculation could be made in a T account, with purchases being the balancing figure to complete the account.

CREDITORS

	£		£
Cash payments	31,479	Opening balance b/f	3,728
Closing balance c/f	2,645	Purchases (balancing figure)	30,396
	34,124		34,124

5   ESTABLISHING COST OF SALES

5.1   When the value of purchases is not known, a different approach might be required to find out what they were, depending on the nature of the information given to you.

5.2   One approach would be to use information about the cost of sales, and opening and closing stocks, in other words, to use the trading account rather than the trade creditors account to find the cost of purchases.

		£
Since	opening stocks	X
	plus purchases	X
	less closing stocks	(X)
	equals the cost of goods sold	X
then	the cost of goods sold	X
	plus closing stocks	X
	less opening stocks	(X)
	equals purchases	X

5.3   Suppose that the stock in trade of a business on 1 July 19X6 has a balance sheet value of £8,400, and a stock taking exercise at 30 June 19X7 showed stock to be valued at £9,350. Sales for the year to 30 June 19X7 are £80,000, and the business makes a gross profit of $33^1/3\%$ on cost for all the items that it sells. What were the purchases during the year?

5.4   The cost of goods sold can be derived from the value of sales, as follows.

		£
Sales	$(133^1/3\%)$	80,000
Gross profit	$(33^1/3\%)$	20,000
Cost of goods sold	(100%)	60,000

The cost of goods sold is 75% of sales value.

	£
Cost of goods sold	60,000
Plus closing stock	9,350
Less opening stocks	(8,400)
Purchases	60,950

6   STOLEN GOODS OR GOODS DESTROYED

6.1   A similar type of calculation might be required to derive the value of goods stolen or destroyed. When an unknown quantity of goods is lost, whether they are stolen, destroyed in a fire, or lost in any other way such that the quantity lost cannot be counted, then the cost of the goods lost is the difference between:

(a)   the cost of goods sold; and

(b)   opening stock of the goods (at cost) plus purchases less closing stock of the goods (at cost).

In theory (a) and (b) should be the same. However, if (b) is a larger amount than (a), it follows that the difference must be the cost of the goods purchased and neither sold nor remaining in stock - ie the cost of the goods lost.

Example: cost of goods destroyed

6.2   Orlean Flames is a shop which sells fashion clothes. On 1 January 19X5, it had stock in trade which cost £7,345. During the 9 months to 30 September 19X5, the business purchased goods from suppliers costing £106,420. Sales during the same period were £154,000. The shop makes a gross profit of 40% on cost for everything it sells. On 30 September 19X5, there was a fire in the shop which destroyed most of the stock in it. Only a small amount of stock, known to have cost £350, was undamaged and still fit for sale.

How much stock was lost in the fire?

Solution

6.3 (a)

	£
Sales (140%)	154,000
Gross profit (40%)	44,000
Cost of goods sold (100%)	110,000

(b)

	£
Opening stock, at cost	7,345
Plus purchases	106,420
	113,765
Less closing stock, at cost	350
Equals cost of goods sold and goods lost	113,415

(c)

	£
Cost of goods sold and lost	113,415
Cost of goods sold	110,000
Cost of goods lost	3,415

Example: cost of goods stolen

6.4 Beau Gullard runs a jewellery shop in the High Street. On 1 January 19X9, his stock in trade, at cost, amounted to £4,700 and his trade creditors were £3,950.

During the six months to 30 June 19X9, sales were £42,000. Beau Gullard makes a gross profit of $33^1/_3\%$ on the sales value of everything he sells.

On 30 June, there was a burglary at the shop, and all the stock was stolen.

In trying to establish how much stock had been taken, Beau Gullard was only able to say that:

(a) he knew from his bank statements that he had paid £28,400 to creditors in the 6 month period to 30 June 19X9;

(b) he currently owed creditors £5,550.

Required

(a) Calculate the amount of stock stolen.
(b) Prepare a trading account for the 6 months to 30 June 19X9.

Solution

6.5 (a) The first 'unknown' is the amount of purchases during the period. This is established by the method previously described in this chapter.

CREDITORS

	£		£
Payments to creditors	28,400	Opening balance b/f	3,950
Closing balance c/f	5,550	Purchases (balancing figure)	30,000
	33,950		33,950

(b) The cost of goods sold is also unknown, but this can be established from the gross profit margin and the sales for the period.

		£
Sales	(100%)	42,000
Gross profit	$(33^1/_3\%)$	14,000
Cost of goods sold	$(66^2/_3\%)$	28,000

(c)   The cost of the goods stolen is:

	£
Opening stock at cost	4,700
Purchases	30,000
	34,700
Less closing stock (after burglary)	0
Cost of goods sold and goods stolen	34,700
Cost of goods sold (see (b) above)	28,000
Cost of goods stolen	6,700

(d)   The cost of the goods stolen will not be a charge in the trading account, and so the trading account for the period is as follows:

BEAU GULLARD
TRADING ACCOUNT FOR THE SIX MONTHS TO 30 JUNE 19X9

	£	£
Sales		42,000
Less cost of goods sold		
Opening stock	4,700	
Purchases	30,000	
	34,700	
Less stock stolen	6,700	
		28,000
Gross profit		14,000

Accounting for stock destroyed, stolen or otherwise lost

6.6   When stock is stolen, destroyed or otherwise lost, the loss must be accounted for somehow. The procedure was described briefly in the earlier chapter on accounting for stocks. Since the loss is not a trading loss, the cost of the goods lost is not included in the trading account, as the previous example showed. The accounting double entry is therefore

DEBIT   See below
CREDIT   Trading account (although instead of showing the cost of the loss as a credit, it is usually shown as a deduction on the debit side of the trading account, which is the same as a 'plus' on the credit side).

6.7   The account that is to be debited is one of two possibilities, depending on whether or not the lost goods were insured against the loss.

(a)   If the lost goods were not insured, the business must bear the loss, and the loss is shown in the P & L account: ie

DEBIT   Profit and loss
CREDIT   Trading account

(b)   If the lost goods were insured, the business will not suffer a loss, because the insurance will pay back the cost of the lost goods. This means that there is no charge at all in the P&L account, and the appropriate double entry is:

DEBIT   Insurance claim account (debtor account)
CREDIT   Trading account

with the cost of the loss. The insurance claim will then be a current asset, and shown in the balance sheet of the business as such. When the claim is paid, the account is then closed by

DEBIT   Cash
CREDIT   Insurance claim account

7   THE CASH BOOK

7.1   The construction of a cash book, largely from bank statements showing receipts and payments of a business during a given period, is often an important feature of incomplete records problems. In an examination, the purpose of an incomplete records question is largely to test the understanding of candidates about how various items of receipts or payments relate to the preparation of a final set of accounts for a business.

7.2   We have already seen in this chapter that information about cash receipts or payments might be needed to establish:

(a)   the amount of purchases during a period; or
(b)   the amount of credit sales during a period.

Other items of receipts or payments might be relevant to establishing:

(a)   the amount of cash sales; or
(b)   the amount of certain expenses in the P & L account; or
(c)   the amount of drawings by the business proprietor.

7.3   It might therefore be helpful, if a business does not keep a cash book day-to-day, to construct a cash book at the end of an accounting period. A business which typically might not keep a day-to-day cash book is a shop, where:

(a)   many sales, if not all sales, are cash sales (ie with payment by notes and coins, cheques, or credit cards at the time of sale);

(b)   some payments are made in notes and coins out of the till rather than by payment out of the business bank account by cheque.

7.4   Where there appears to be a sizeable volume of receipts and payments in cash (ie notes and coins), then it is also helpful to construct a two column cash book. This is a cash book with one column for receipts and payments, and one column for money paid into and out of the business bank account.

An example will illustrate the technique and the purpose of a two column cash book.

Example: two column cash book

7.5   Jonathan Slugg owns and runs a shop selling fishing tackle, making a gross profit of 25% on the cost of everything he sells. He does not keep a cash book.

On 1 January 19X7 the balance sheet of his business was as follows.

	£	£
Net fixed assets		20,000
Stock	10,000	
Cash in the bank	3,000	
Cash in the till	200	
	13,200	
Trade creditors	1,200	
		12,000
		32,000
Proprietor's capital		32,000

In the year to 31 December 19X7:

(a)   there were no sales on credit;
(b)   £41,750 in receipts were banked;
(c)   the bank statements of the period show the payments:

		£
(i)	to trade creditors	36,000
(ii)	sundry expenses	5,600
(iii)	in drawings	4,400

(d)   payments were also made in cash out of the till:

		£
(i)	to trade creditors	800
(ii)	sundry expenses	1,500
(iii)	in drawings	3,700

At 31 December 19X7, the business had cash in the till of £450 and trade creditors of £1,400. The cash balance in the bank was not known and the value of closing stock has not yet been calculated. There were no accruals or prepayments. No further fixed assets were purchased during the year. The depreciation charge for the year is £900.

Required

(a) Prepare a two column cash book for the period;

(b) Prepare the trading, profit and loss account for the year to 31 December 19X7 and the balance sheet as at 31 December 19X7.

Discussion and solution

7.6   A two column cash book is completed as follows.

(a) Enter the opening cash balances.

(b) Enter the information given about cash payments (and any cash receipts, if there had been any such items given in the problem).

(c) The cash receipts banked are a 'contra' entry, being both a debit (bank column) and a credit (cash in hand column) in the same account.

(d) Enter the closing cash in hand (cash in the bank at the end of the period is not known).

CASH BOOK

	Cash in hand £	Bank £		Cash in hand £	Bank £
Balance b/f	200	3,000	Trade creditors	800	36,000
Cash receipts banked			Sundry expenses		
(contra)		41,750		1,500	5,600
Sales*	48,000		Drawings	3,700	4,400
			Cash receipts banked		
			(contra)	41,750	
Balance c/f		*1,250	Balance c/f	450	
	48,200	46,000		48,200	46,000

* Balancing figure

(e) The closing balance of money in the bank is a balancing figure.

(f) Since all sales are for cash, a balancing figure that can be entered in the cash book is sales, in the cash in hand (debit) column.

7.7   It is important to notice that since not all receipts from cash sales are banked, the value of cash sales during the period is:

	£
Receipts banked	41,750
Plus expenses and drawings paid out of the till in cash	
£(800 + 1,500 + 3,700)	6,000
Plus any cash stolen (here there is none)	0
Plus the closing balance of cash in hand	450
	48,200
Less the opening balance of cash in hand	(200)
Equals cash sales	48,000

7.8   The cash book constructed in this way has enabled us to establish both the closing balance for cash in the bank and also the volume of cash sales. The trading, profit and loss account and the balance sheet can also be prepared, once a value for purchases has been calculated.

CREDITORS

	£		£
Cash book:		Balance b/f	1,200
Payments from bank	36,000	Purchases (balancing figure)	37,000
Cash book:			
Payments in cash	800		
Balance c/f	1,400		
	38,200		38,200

The gross profit margin of 25% on cost indicates that the cost of the goods sold is £38,400, ie:

	£
Sales (125%)	48,000
Gross profit (25%)	9,600
Cost of goods sold (100%)	38,400

The closing stock amount is now a balancing figure in the trading account.

JONATHAN SLUGG
TRADING, PROFIT AND LOSS ACCOUNT
FOR THE YEAR ENDED 31 DECEMBER 19X7

	£	£
Sales		48,000
Less cost of goods sold		
Opening stock	10,000	
Purchases	37,000	
	47,000	
Less closing stock (balancing figure)	8,600	
		38,400
Gross profit (25/125 × £48,000)		9,600
Expenses		
Sundry £(1,500 + 5,600)	7,100	
Depreciation	900	
		8,000
Net profit		1,600

JONATHAN SLUGG
BALANCE SHEET AS AT 31 DECEMBER 19X7

	£	£
Net fixed assets £(20,000 – 900)		19,100
Stock	8,600	
Cash in the till	450	
	9,050	
Bank overdraft	1,250	
Trade creditors	1,400	
	2,650	
Net current assets		6,400
		25,500
Proprietor's capital		
Balance b/f		32,000
Net profit for the year		1,600
		33,600
Drawings £(3,700 + 4,400)		(8,100)
Balance c/f		25,500

Theft of cash from the till

7.9   When cash is stolen from the till, the amount stolen will be a credit entry in the cash book, and a debit in either the P&L account or insurance claim account, depending on whether the business is insured. The missing figure for cash sales, if this has to be calculated, must not ignore cash received but later stolen - see above.

8   ACCRUALS AND PREPAYMENTS

8.1   Where there is an accrued expense or a prepayment, the charge to be made in the P&L account for the item concerned should be found from the opening balance b/f, the closing balance c/f, and cash payments for the item during the period. The charge in the P&L account is perhaps most easily found as the balancing figure in a T account.

8.2   For example, suppose that on 1 April 19X6 a business had prepaid rent of £700 which relates to the next accounting period. During the year to 31 March 19X7 it pays £9,300 in rent, and at 31 March 19X7 the prepayment of rent is £1,000. The cost of rent in the P&L account for the year to 31 March 19X7 would be the balancing figure in the following T account. (Remember that a prepayment is a current asset, and so is a debit balance b/f.)

RENT

	£		£
Prepayment: balance b/f	700	P & L account (balancing figure)	9,000
Cash	9,300	Prepayment: balance c/f	1,000
	10,000		10,000
Balance b/f	1,000		

8.3   Similarly, if a business has accrued telephone expenses as at 1 July 19X6 of £850, pays £6,720 in telephone bills during the year to 30 June 19X7, and has accrued telephone expenses of £1,140 as at 30 June 19X7, then the telephone expense to be shown in the P&L account for the year to 30 June 19X7 is the balancing figure in the following T account. (Remember that an accrual is a current liability, and so is a credit balance b/f.)

TELEPHONE EXPENSES

	£		£
Cash	6,720	Balance b/f (accrual)	850
Balance c/f (accrual)	1,140	P&L a/c (balancing figure)	7,010
	7,860		7,860
		Balance b/f	1,140

9   DRAWINGS

9.1   Drawings would normally represent no particular problem at all in preparing a set of final accounts from incomplete records, but it is not unusual for examination questions to introduce a situation in which:

(a)   the business owner pays income into his bank account which has nothing whatever to do with the business operations. For example, the owner might pay dividend income, or other income from investments into the bank, from stocks and shares which he owns personally, separate from the business itself. (In other words, there are no investments in the business balance sheet, and so income from investments cannot possibly be income of the business);

(b)   the business owner pays money out of the business bank account for items which are not business expenses, such as life insurance premiums or a payment for his family's holidays etc.

9.2   Where such personal items of receipts or payments are made:

(a)   receipts should be set off against drawings. For example, if a business owner receives £600 in dividend income and pays it into his business bank account, although the dividends are from investments not owned by the business, then the accounting entry is:

DEBIT   Cash
CREDIT   Drawings;

(b) payments should be charged to drawings; ie

    DEBIT   Drawings
    CREDIT Cash

Drawings: beware of the wording in an examination question

9.3 You should note that:

(a) if a question states that a proprietor's drawings during a given year are 'approximately £40 per week' then you should assume that drawings for the year are £40 × 52 weeks = £2,080;

(b) however, if a question states that drawings in the year are 'between £35 and £45 per week', do not assume that the drawings average £40 per week and so amount to £2,080 for the year. You could not be certain that the actual drawings did average £40, and so you should treat the drawings figure as a missing item that needs to be calculated.

10 DEALING WITH INCOMPLETE RECORDS PROBLEMS IN THE EXAMINATION

10.1 A suggested approach to dealing with incomplete records problems brings together the various points described so far in this chapter. The nature of the 'incompleteness' in the records will vary from problem to problem, but the approach, suitably applied, should be successful in arriving at the final accounts whatever the particular characteristics of the problem might be.

10.2 The approach is as follows.

(a) *Step 1*. If possible, and if it is not already known, establish the opening balance sheet and the proprietor's interest.

(b) *Step 2*. Open up four accounts.

    (i)   Trading account (if you wish, leave space underneath for entering the P&L account later)

    (ii)   A cash book, with two columns if cash sales are significant and there are payments in cash out of the till

    (iii) A debtors account

    (iv) A creditors account

(c) *Step 3*. Enter the opening balances in these accounts.

(d) *Step 4*. Work through the information you are given line by line; and each item should be entered into the appropriate account if it is relevant to one or more of these four accounts.

You should also try to recognise each item as a 'P&L account income or expense item' or a 'closing balance sheet item'.

It may be necessary to calculate an amount for drawings and an amount for fixed asset depreciation.

(e) *Step 5*. Look for the balancing figures in your accounts. In particular you might be looking for a value for credit sales, cash sales, purchases, the cost of goods sold, the cost of goods stolen or destroyed, or the closing bank balance. Calculate these missing figures, and make any necessary double entry (eg to the trading account from the creditors account for purchases, to the trading account from the cash book for cash sales, and to the trading account from the debtors account for credit sales).

(f) *Step 6*. Now complete the P&L account and balance sheet. Working T accounts might be needed where there are accruals or prepayments.

10.3 An example will illustrate this approach.

Example: an incomplete records problem

10.4 John Snow is the sole distribution agent in the Branton area for Diamond floor tiles. Under an agreement with the manufacturers, John Snow purchases the Diamond floor tiles at a trade discount of 20% off list price and annually in May receives an agency commission of 1% of his purchases for the year ended on the previous 31 March.

For several years, John Snow has obtained a gross profit of 40% on all sales. In a burglary in January 19X1 John Snow lost stock costing £4,000 as well as many of his accounting records. However, after careful investigations, the following information has been obtained covering the year ended 31 March 19X1.

(a) Assets and liabilities at 31 March 19X0 were as follows:

		£
Buildings:	at cost	10,000
	provision for depreciation	6,000
Motor vehicles:	at cost	5,000
	provision for depreciation	2,000
Stock: at cost		3,200
Trade debtors (for sales)		6,300
Agency commission due		300
Prepayments (trade expenses)		120
Balance at bank		4,310
Trade creditors		4,200
Accrued vehicle expenses		230

(b) John Snow has been notified that he will receive an agency commission of £440 on 1 May 19X1.

(c) Stock, at cost, at 31 March 19X1 was valued at an amount £3,000 more than a year previously.

(d) In October 19X0 stock costing £1,000 was damaged by damp and had to be scrapped as worthless.

(e) Trade creditors at 31 March 19X1 related entirely to goods received whose list prices totalled £9,500.

(f) Discounts allowed amounted to £1,620 whilst discounts received were £1,200.

(g) Trade expenses prepaid at 31 March 19X1 totalled £80.

(h) Vehicle expenses for the year ended 31 March 19X1 amounted to £7,020.

(i) Trade debtors (for sales) at 31 March 19X1 were £6,700.

(j) All receipts are passed through the bank account.

(k) Depreciation is provided annually at the following rates.

Buildings 5% on cost
Motor vehicles 20% on cost.

(l) Commissions received are paid directly to the bank account.

(m) In addition to the payments for purchases, the bank payments were:

	£
Vehicle expenses	6,720
Drawings	4,300
Trade expenses	7,360

(n) John Snow is not insured against loss of stock owing to burglary or damage to stock caused by damp.

Required

Prepare John Snow's trading and profit and loss account for the year ended 31 March 19X1 and a balance sheet on that date.

Discussion and solution

10.5 This is an incomplete records problem because we are told that John Snow has lost many of his accounting records. In particular we do not know sales for the year, purchases during the year, or all the cash receipts and payments.

10.6 The first step is to find the opening balance sheet, if possible. In this case, it is. The proprietor's capital is the balancing figure.

JOHN SNOW
BALANCE SHEET AS AT 31 MARCH 19X0

	Cost	*Dep'n*	*NBV*
	£	£	£
Fixed assets			
Buildings	10,000	6,000	4,000
Motor vehicles	5,000	2,000	3,000
	15,000	8,000	7,000
Current assets			
Stock		3,200	
Trade debtors		6,300	
Commission due		300	
Prepayments		120	
Balance at hand		4,310	
		14,230	
Current liabilities			
Trade creditors		4,200	
Accrued expenses		230	
		4,430	
			9,800
			16,800
Proprietor's capital as at 31 March 19X0			16,800

10.7 The next step is to open up a trading account, cash book, debtors account and creditors account and to insert the opening balances, if known. Cash sales and payments in cash are not a feature of the problem, and so a single column cash book is sufficient.

10.8 The problem should then be read line by line, identifying any transactions affecting those accounts.

TRADING ACCOUNT

	£	£
Sales (note (f))		60,000
Opening stock	3,200	
Purchases (note (a))	44,000	
	47,200	
Less: damaged stock written off (note (c))	(1,000)	
stock stolen (note (e))	(4,000)	
	42,200	
Less closing stock (note (b))	6,200	
Cost of goods sold		36,000
Gross profit (note (f))		24,000

CASH BOOK

	£		£
Opening balance	4,310	Trade creditors	
Trade debtors (see below)	57,980	(see creditors a/c)	39,400
Agency commission (note (g))	300	Trade expenses	7,360
		Vehicle expenses	6,720
		Drawings	4,300
		Balance c/f	4,810
	62,590		62,590

TRADE DEBTORS

	£		£
Opening balance b/f	6,300	Discounts allowed (note (d))	1,620
Sales (note (f))	60,000	Cash received (balancing figure)	57,980
		Closing balance c/f	6,700
	66,300		66,300

TRADE CREDITORS

	£		£
Discounts received (note (d))	1,200	Opening balance b/f	4,200
Cash paid (balancing figure)	39,400	Purchases (note (a))	44,000
Closing balance c/f	7,600		
	48,200		48,200

VEHICLE EXPENSES

	£		£
Cash	6,720	Accrual b/f	230
Accrual c/f (balancing figure)	530	P & L account	7,020
	7,250		7,250

10.9   The trading account is complete already, but now the P&L account and balance sheet can be prepared. Remember not to forget items such as the stock losses, commission earned on purchases, discounts allowed and discounts received.

JOHN SNOW
TRADING, PROFIT AND LOSS ACCOUNT
FOR THE YEAR ENDED 31 MARCH 19X1

	£	£
Sales (note (f))		60,000
Opening stock	3,200	
Purchases (note (a))	44,000	
	47,200	
Less: damaged stock written off (note (c))	(1,000)	
stock stolen	(4,000)	
	42,200	
Less closing stock (note (b))	6,200	
Cost of goods sold		36,000
Gross profit (note (f))		24,000
Add: commission on purchases		440
discounts received		1,200
		25,640
Expenses		
Trade expenses (note (h))	7,400	
Stock damaged	1,000	
Stock stolen	4,000	
Vehicle expenses	7,020	
Discounts allowed	1,620	
Depreciation		
Buildings	500	
Motor vehicles	1,000	
		22,540
Net profit (to capital account)		3,100

JOHN SNOW
BALANCE SHEET AS AT 31 MARCH 19X1

	Cost £	Dep'n £	NBV £
Fixed assets			
Buildings	10,000	6,500	3,500
Motor vehicles	5,000	3,000	2,000
	15,000	9,500	5,500
Current assets			
Stock		6,200	
Trade debtors		6,700	
Commission due		440	
Prepayments (trade expenses)		80	
Balance at bank		4,810	
		18,230	
Current liabilities			
Trade creditors		7,600	
Accrued expenses		530	
		8,130	
			10,100
			15,600
Proprietor's capital			
As at 31 March 19X0			16,800
Net profit for year to 31 March 19X1		3,100	
Less drawings		(4,300)	
Retained deficit			(1,200)
As at 31 March 19X1			15,600

Notes

(a)   The agency commission due on 1 May 19X1 indicates that purchases for the year to 31 March 19X1 were

   100%/1% × £440 = £44,000

(b)   Closing stock at cost on 31 March 19X1 was £(3,200 + 3,000) = £6,200.

(c)   Stock scrapped (£1,000) is accounted for by:

   CREDIT   Trading account
   DEBIT   P&L account

(d)   Discounts allowed are accounted for by:

   DEBIT   Discounts allowed account
   CREDIT   Debtors

   Similarly, discounts received are:

   DEBIT   Creditors
   CREDIT   Discounts received

   Note. Discounts received represents settlement discounts, not *trade* discounts, which are not usually accounted for as they are given automatically at source.

(e)   Stocks lost in the burglary are accounted for by:

   CREDIT   Trading account
   DEBIT   P&L account

(f)   The trade discount of 20% has already been deducted in arriving at the value of the purchases. The gross profit is 40% on sales, so with cost of sales = £36,000

		£
Cost	(60%)	36,000
Profit	(40%)	24,000
Sales	(100%)	60,000

   (It is assumed that trade expenses are not included in the trading account, and so should be ignored in this calculation.)

(g)   The agency commission of £300 due on 1 May 19X0 would have been paid to John Snow at that date.

(h) The P&L account expenditure for trade expenses and closing balance on vehicle expenses account are as follows:

TRADE EXPENSES

	£		£
Prepayment	120	P&L account (balancing figure)	7,400
Cash	7,360	Prepayment c/f	80
	7,480		7,480

Using a debtors account to calculate both cash sales and credit sales

10.10 A final point which needs to be considered is how a missing value can be found for cash sales and credit sales, when a business has both, but takings banked by the business are not divided between takings from cash sales and takings from credit sales.

Example: using a debtors account

10.11 Suppose, for example, that a business had, on 1 January 19X8, trade debtors of £2,000, cash in the bank of £3,000, and cash in hand of £300.

During the year to 31 December 19X8 the business banked £95,000 in takings.

It also paid out the following expenses in cash from the till:

Drawings	£1,200
Sundry expenses	£800

On 29 August 19X8 a thief broke into the shop and stole £400 from the till.

At 31 December 19X8 trade debtors amounted to £3,500, cash in the bank £2,500 and cash in the till £150.

What was the value of sales during the year?

Solution

10.12 If we tried to prepare a debtors account and a two column cash book, we would have insufficient information, in particular about whether the takings which were banked related to cash sales or credit sales.

DEBTORS

	£		£
Balance b/f	2,000	Payments from debtors (credit sales)	*Unknown*
Credit sales	*Unknown*		
		Balance c/f	3,500

CASH BOOK

	Cash £	Bank £		Cash £	Bank £
Balance b/f	300	3,000	Drawings	1,200	
			Sundry expenses	800	
Debtors-payments		*Unknown*	Cash stolen	400	
Cash sales	*Unknown*		Balance c/f	150	2,500

All we do know is that the combined sums from debtors and cash takings banked is £95,000.

The value of sales can be found instead by using the debtors account, which should be used to record cash takings banked as well as payments by debtors. The balancing figure in the debtors account will then be a combination of credit sales and some cash sales. The cash book only needs to be a single column.

DEBTORS

	£		£
Balance b/f	2,000	Cash banked	95,000
Sales-to trading account	96,500	Balance c/f	3,500
	98,500		98,500

CASH (EXTRACT)

	£		£
Balance in hand b/f	300	Payments in cash:	
Balance in bank b/f	3,000	Drawings	1,200
Debtors a/c	95,000	Expenses	800
		Other payments	?
		Cash stolen	400
		Balance in hand c/f	150
		Balance in bank c/f	2,500

The remaining 'undiscovered' amount of cash sales is now found as follows.

	£	£
Payments in cash out of the till		
Drawings	1,200	
Expenses	800	
		2,000
Cash stolen		400
Closing balance of cash in hand		150
		2,550
Less opening balance of cash in hand		(300)
Further cash sales		2,250

(This calculation is similar to the one described above for calculating cash sales.)

Total sales for the year are:

	£
From debtors account	96,500
From cash book	2,250
Total sales	98,750

Exercise

Mary Grimes, retail fruit and vegetable merchant, does not keep a full set of accounting records. However, the following information has been produced from the business's records.

(a)   Summary of the bank account for the year ended 31 August 19X8

	£		£
1 Sept 19X7 balance brought forward	1,970	Payment to suppliers	72,000
		Purchase of motor van (E471 KBR)	13,000
Receipts from trade debtors	96,000	Rent and rates	2,600
Sale of private yacht	20,000	Wages	15,100
Sale of motor van (A123 BWA)	2,100	Motor vehicle expenses	3,350
		Postages and stationery	1,360
		Drawings	9,200
		Repairs and renewals	650
		Insurances	800
		31 August 19X8 balance c/fwd	2,010
	120,070		120,070
1 Sept 19X8 balance b/fwd	2,010		

(b) Assets and liabilities, other than balance at bank as at:

			1 Sept 19X7 £	31 Aug 19X8 £
Trade creditors			4,700	2,590
Trade debtors			7,320	9,500
Rent and rates accruals			200	260
Motor vans:				
	A123 BWA:	At cost	10,000	-
		Provision for depreciation	8,000	-
	E471 KBR:	At cost	-	13,000
		Provision for depreciation	-	To be determined
Stock in trade			4,900	5,900
Insurance prepaid			160	200

(c) All receipts are banked and all payments are made from the business bank account.

(d) A trade debt of £300 owing by John Blunt and included in the trade debtors at 31 August 19X8 (see (b) above), is to be written off as a bad debt.

(e) It is Mary Grimes' policy to provide depreciation at the rate of 20% on the cost of motor vans held at the end of each financial year; no depreciation is provided in the year of sale or disposal of a motor van.

(f) Discounts received during the year ended 31 August 19X8 from trade creditors amounted to £1,100.

Required

(a) Prepare Mary Grimes' trading and profit and loss account for the year ended 31 August 19X8.

(b) Prepare Mary Grimes' balance sheet as at 31 August 19X8.

Solution

(a) TRADING AND PROFIT AND LOSS ACCOUNT
FOR THE YEAR ENDED 31 AUGUST 19X8

	£	£
Sales (W1)		98,180
Opening stock	4,900	
Purchases (W2)	70,990	
	75,890	
Less closing stock	5,900	
		69,990
Gross profit		28,190
Discounts received		1,100
Profit on sale of motor vehicle £2,100 - £(10,000 - 8,000)		100
		29,390
Rent and rates (W3)	2,660	
Wages	15,100	
Motor vehicle expenses	3,350	
Postages and stationery	1,360	
Repairs and renewals	650	
Insurances (W4)	760	
Bad debt	300	
Depreciation of van (20% × £13,000)	2,600	
		26,780
		2,610

(b) BALANCE SHEET AS AT 31 AUGUST 19X8

	£	£
Fixed assets		
Motor van: cost	13,000	
depreciation	2,600	
		10,400
Current assets		
Stock	5,900	
Debtors (£9,500 - £300 bad debt)	9,200	
Prepayment	200	
Cash at bank	2,010	
	17,310	
Current liabilities		
Creditors	2,590	
Accrual	260	
	2,850	
Net current assets		14,460
		24,860
Capital account		
Balance at 1 September 19X7 (W5)		11,450
Additional capital: proceeds on sale of yacht		20,000
Net profit for the year	2,610	
Less drawings	9,200	
Retained loss for the year		(6,590)
Balance at 31 August 19X8		24,860

Workings

1 Sales

	£
Cash received from customers	96,000
Add debtors balances at 31 August 19X8	9,500
	105,500
Less debtors balances at 1 September 19X7	7,320
Sales in year	98,180

2 Purchases

	£	£
Payments to suppliers		72,000
Add: creditors balances at 31 August 19X8	2,590	
discounts granted by creditors	1,100	
		3,690
		75,690
Less creditors balances at 1 September 19X7		4,700
		70,990

3 Rent and rates

	£
Cash paid in year	2,600
Add accrual at 31 August 19X8	260
	2,860
Less accrual at 1 September 19X7	200
Charge for the year	2,660

4 Insurances

	£
Cash paid in year	800
Add prepayment at 1 September 19X7	160
	960
Less prepayment at 31 August 19X8	200
	760

Workings 1-4 could also be presented in ledger account format as follows.

TOTAL DEBTORS

	£		£
Balance b/f	7,320	Bank	96,000
∴ Sales	98,180	Balance c/f	9,500
	105,500		105,500

TOTAL CREDITORS

	£		£
Bank	72,000	Balance b/f	4,700
Discounts received	1,100	∴ Purchases	70,990
Balance c/f	2,590		
	75,690		75,690

RENT AND RATES

	£		£
Bank	2,600	Balance b/f	200
Balance c/f	260	∴ P & L charge	2,660
	2,860		2,860

INSURANCES

	£		£
Balance b/f	160	∴ P & L charge	760
Bank	800	Balance c/f	200
	960		960

5   *Capital at 1 September 19X7*

	£	£
Assets		
Bank balance		1,970
Debtors		7,320
Motor van £(10,000 - 8,000)		2,000
Stock		4,900
Prepayment		160
		16,350
Liabilities		
Trade creditors	4,700	
Accrual	200	
		4,900
		11,450

Chapter roundup

- Incomplete records questions may test your ability to prepare accounts in the following situations.

    o A trader does not maintain a ledger and therefore has no continuous double entry record of transactions.

    o Accounting records are destroyed by accident, such as fire.

    o Some essential figure is unknown and must be calculated as a balancing figure. This may occur as a result of stock being damaged or destroyed, or because of misappropriation of assets.

- The approach to incomplete records questions is to build up the information given so as to complete the necessary double entry. This may involve reconstructing control accounts for:

    o cash and bank (often in columnar format);
    o debtors and creditors

- Where stock, sales or purchases is the unknown figure it will be necessary to use information on gross profit percentages so as to construct a trading account in which the unknown figure can be inserted as a balance.

Test your knowledge

1   In the absence of a sales account or sales day book, how can a figure of sales for the year be computed? (see para 3.1)

2   In the absence of a purchase account or purchases day book, how can a figure of purchases for the year be computed? (4.1)

3   What is the accounting double entry to record the loss of stock by fire or burglary? (6.6, 6.7)

4   If a business proprietor pays his personal income into the business bank account, what is the accounting double entry to record the transaction? (9.2)

Now try illustrative questions 33 to 35 at the end of the Study Text

Chapter 21

LIMITED COMPANIES

This chapter covers the following topics.

		Syllabus reference	Ability required
1	The statutory framework of limited company accounts	1(c)	Skill
2	Share capital and reserves	1(c)	Skill
3	The final accounts of limited companies	1(c)	Skill
4	The ledger accounts of limited companies	1(c)	Skill

Introduction

So far, this Study Text has dealt mainly with the accounts of businesses in general. In this chapter we shall turn our attention to the accounts of *limited companies.* As we should expect, the accounting rules and conventions for recording the business transactions of limited companies and then preparing their final accounts, are much the same as for sole traders. For example, companies will have a cash book, sales day book, purchase day book, journal, sales ledger, purchase ledger and nominal ledger etc. They also prepare a profit and loss account annually, and a balance sheet at the end of the accounting year.

We shall see in this chapter that, in the balance sheet, the treatment of assets and liabilities is basically the same but the particular nature of limited companies calls for changes in the owners' equity section. Similarly, in the profit and loss account, the principal differences are found in the appropriation account - that part of the profit and loss account which shows how the profit or loss for the period has been divided.

One important difference is the legal requirement that limited companies must publish their accounts. The relevant legislation specifies certain information which must be included in the published financial statements of a limited company.

It should be stressed that, while you do not have to learn the published accounts formats by heart at this stage, it is important for you to have an overall awareness of the form of company accounts. In Chapter 24 you will learn about interpretation of accounts and this will include items in company accounts formats.

---

1   THE STATUTORY FRAMEWORK OF LIMITED COMPANY ACCOUNTS

1.1   The following are the most significant differences between the accounts of limited companies and those of unincorporated organisations.

(a)   The legislation governing the activities of limited companies is very extensive. Amongst other things, the Companies Acts define certain minimum accounting records which must be maintained by companies. The filing of accounts with the Registrar of Companies, normally once a year, is one such duty. This is so accounts are available for public inspection. They contain detailed requirements on the minimum information which must be disclosed in a company's accounts. Businesses which are not limited companies (non-incorporated businesses) enjoy comparative freedom from statutory regulation.

(b)   The owners of a company (its *members or shareholders*) may be very numerous. Their capital is shown differently from that of a sole trader; and similarly the appropriation account of a company is different.

(c) In the case of a sole trader, day-to-day management of the business is usually in the hands of the owner. With companies, the owners (members or shareholders) appoint directors to be responsible for management. The fact that in small companies shareholders and directors are often the same people should not obscure the legal distinction between the two roles. If a director receives a salary it is an employee payroll cost chargeable as an expense against profit. If the director is also a shareholder and receives a *dividend* (see 2.4), that is an appropriation of profit, similar to *drawings* in a sole trader's accounts.

Limited liability

1.2 Sole traders and partnerships are, with some significant exceptions, generally fairly small concerns. The amount of capital involved may be modest, and the proprietors of the business usually participate in managing it. Their liability for the debts of the business is unlimited, which means that if the business runs up debts that it is unable to pay, the proprietors will become personally liable for the unpaid debts, and would be required, if necessary, to sell their private possessions in order to repay them. For example, if a sole trader has some capital in his business, but the business now owes £40,000 which it cannot repay, the trader might have to sell his house to raise the money to pay off his business debts.

1.3 Limited companies offer *limited liability* to their owners. This means that the maximum amount that an owner stands to lose in the event that the company becomes insolvent and cannot pay off its debts, is the capital in the business. This limited liability is therefore a major advantage of turning a business into a limited company. For example, if a limited company becomes insolvent owing large sums of money to its creditors, the owners of the company will not be required to pay the company's debts from their own personal resources.

1.4 As a business grows, it needs more capital to finance its operations, and significantly more than the people currently managing the business can provide themselves. One way of obtaining more capital is to invite investors from outside the business to invest in the ownership or 'equity' of the business. These new co-owners would not usually be expected to help with managing the business. To such investors, limited liability is very attractive. Investments are always risky undertakings, but with limited liability the investor knows the maximum amount that he stands to lose when he puts some capital into a company.

1.5 There are two classes of limited company.

(a) *Private companies*. These have the word 'limited' at the end of their name. Being private, they cannot invite members of the public to invest in their equity (ownership).

(b) *Public companies*. These are much fewer in number than private companies, but are generally much larger in size. They have the words 'public limited company' - shortened to PLC or plc (or the Welsh language equivalent) at the end of their name. Public limited companies can invite members of the general public to invest in their equity, and the 'shares' of these companies are traded on the Stock Exchange.

2   SHARE CAPITAL AND RESERVES   *S/96, S/97*

The capital of limited companies

2.1 The proprietors' capital in a limited company consists of share capital. When a company is set up for the first time, it issues shares, which are paid for by investors, who then become shareholders of the company. Shares are denominated in units of 25 pence, 50 pence, £1 or whatever seems appropriate. The 'face value' of the shares is called their nominal value.

2.2   For example, when a company is set up with a *share capital* of, say, £100,000, it may be decided to issue:

(a)   100,000 shares of £1 each nominal value; or
(b)   200,000 shares of 50p each; or
(c)   400,000 shares of 25p each; or
(d)   250,000 shares of 40p each etcetera.

The nominal value is not the same as the market value, which is the price someone is prepared to pay for the share.

2.3   A distinction is made between authorised, issued, called up and paid up share capital. This will be covered in detail in your later studies. For now you should note that the *authorised* share capital is the maximum amount of share capital that the company is empowered to issue. *Issued* share capital is the nominal amount of share capital that has been issued to shareholders. This cannot exceed the authorised share capital.

Dividends

2.4   Profits paid out to shareholders are called *dividends*. Dividends are appropriations of profit after tax. A company might pay dividends in two stages during the course of their accounting year.

(a)   In mid year, after the half-year financial results are known, the company might pay an interim dividend.

(b)   At the end of the year, the company might pay a further final dividend.

The total dividend for the year is the sum of the interim and the final dividend. (Not all companies by any means pay an interim dividend. Interim dividends are, however, commonly paid out by public limited companies.)

At the end of an accounting year, a company's directors will have proposed a final dividend payment, but this will not yet have been paid. This means that the final dividend should be appropriated out of profits and shown as a current liability in the balance sheet.

2.5   The terminology of dividend payments can be confusing, since they may be expressed either in the form, as 'x pence per share' or as 'y per cent'. In the latter case, the meaning is always 'y per cent of the *nominal* value of the shares in issue'. For example, suppose a company's issued share capital consists of 100,000 50p ordinary shares which were issued at a premium of 10p per share. The company's balance sheet would include the following.

| Called up share capital: | 100,000 50p ordinary shares | £50,000 |
| Share premium account | $(100,000 \times 10p)$ | £10,000 |

If the directors wish to pay a dividend of £5,000, they may propose either:

(a)   a dividend of 5p per share $(100,000 \times 5p = £5,000)$; or
(b)   a dividend of 10% $(10\% \times £50,000 = £5,000)$.

Ordinary shares and preference shares

2.6   At this stage it is relevant to distinguish between the two types of shares most often encountered, preference shares and ordinary shares.

Preference shares carry the right to a final dividend which is expressed as a percentage of their nominal value: eg a 6% £1 preference share carries a right to an annual dividend of 6p. Preference dividends have priority over ordinary dividends. If the directors of a company wish to pay a dividend (which they are not obliged to do) they must pay any preference dividend first. Otherwise, no ordinary dividend may be paid.

2.7   *Ordinary shares* are by far the most common. They carry no right to a fixed dividend but are entitled to all profits left after payment of any preference dividend. Generally however, only a part of such remaining profits is distributed, the rest being kept in reserve (see below). The amount of ordinary dividends fluctuates although there is a general expectation that it will increase from year to year. Should the company be wound up, any surplus is shared between the ordinary shareholders. Ordinary shares normally carry voting rights, and in effect ordinary shareholders are the owners of the company.

Reserves

2.8 The ordinary shareholders' total investment in a limited company is called the *equity* and consists of share capital plus *reserves*. You will also meet the term *shareholders' funds*, which is used to describe the total of all share capital, both ordinary and preference, and the reserves. The important point to note is that all reserves are owned by the ordinary shareholders.

2.9 A distinction should be made between the two types of reserves.

(a) Statutory reserves are reserves which a company is required to set up by law and which are not available for the distribution of dividends.

(b) Non-statutory reserves are reserves consisting of profits which are distributable as dividends, if the company so wishes.

Profit and loss reserve (retained profits)

2.10 This is the most significant non-statutory reserve, and it is described in many different ways:

(a) revenue reserve;
(b) retained profits;
(c) retained earnings;
(d) undistributed profits;
(e) profit and loss account;
(f) unappropriated profits.

2.11 These are profits earned by the company and not appropriated by dividends, taxation or transfer to another reserve account. This reserve generally increases from year to year, as most companies do not distribute all their profits as dividends. Dividends can be paid from it: even if a loss is made in one particular year, a dividend can be paid from previous years' retained profits. For example, if a company makes a loss of £100,000 in one year, yet has unappropriated profits from previous years totalling £250,000, it can pay a dividend not exceeding £150,000. One reason for retaining some profit each year is to enable the company to pay dividends even when profits are low (or non-existent). Another reason is usually shortage of cash. Very occasionally, you might come across a debit balance on the profit and loss account. This would indicate that the company has accumulated losses.

Other non-statutory reserves

2.12 The company directors may choose to set up other reserves. These may have a specific purpose (for example plant and machinery replacement reserve) or not (for example general reserve). The creation of these reserves usually indicates a general intention not to distribute the profits involved at any future date, although legally any such reserves, being non-statutory, remain available for the payment of dividends.

2.13 Profits are transferred to these reserves by making an appropriation out of profits, usually profits for the year. Typically, you might come across the following.

	£	£
Profit after taxation		100,000
Appropriations of profit		
Dividend	60,000	
Transfer to general reserve	10,000	
		70,000
Retained profits for the year		30,000
Profit and loss reserve b/f		250,000
Profit and loss reserve c/f		280,000

2.14   There is no real significance about the creation of separate non-statutory reserves. After all, there is little difference between the following two balance sheet extracts.

		£	£
(a)	Net assets		3,500
	Financed by		
	Share capital		2,000
	Reserves: general (distributable as dividend)	1,000	
	retained profits (distributable)	500	
			1,500
			3,500

		£
(b)	Net assets	3,500
	Financed by	
	Share capital	2,000
	Reserves: retained profit (distributable)	1,500
		3,500

2.15   The establishment of a 'plant and machinery replacement reserve' (or something similar) indicates an intention by a company to keep funds in the business to replace its plant and machinery (over and above the provision for depreciation, perhaps because inflation is pushing up replacement costs). However, the reserve would still, legally, represent distributable profits, and the existence of such a reserve no more guarantees the company's ability to replace its fixed assets in the future than the depreciation charge in the P & L account, or accumulated provision for depreciation in the balance sheet.

The share premium account

2.16   There are a number of statutory (or capital) reserves, the most important of which at this stage is the share premium account. A share premium arises when a company sells shares for a price which is higher than their nominal value. By 'premium' is meant the difference between the issue price of the share and its nominal value. When a company is first incorporated (set up) the issue price of its shares will probably be the same as their nominal value and so there would be no share premium. If the company does well the market value of its shares will increase, but not the nominal value. The price of any new shares issued will be approximately their market value. The difference between cash received by the company and the nominal value of the new shares issued is transferred to the share premium account. For example, if X Ltd issues 1,000 £1 ordinary shares at £2.60 each the book entry will be as follows.

		£	£
DEBIT	Cash	2,600	
CREDIT	Ordinary share capital		1,000
CREDIT	Share premium account		1,600

A share premium account only comes into being when a company issues shares at a price in excess of their nominal value. The market price of the shares, once they have been issued, has no bearing at all on the company's accounts, and so if their market price goes up or down, the share premium account would remain unaltered.

Revaluation reserve

2.17 A revaluation reserve must be created when a company revalues one or more of its fixed assets. Revaluations frequently occur with freehold property, as the market value of property rises. The company's directors might wish to show a more 'reasonable' value of the asset in their balance sheet, to avoid giving a misleading impression about the financial position of the company.

2.18 When an asset is revalued the revaluation reserve is credited with the difference between the revalued amount of the asset, and its net book value before the revaluation took place. Depreciation is subsequently charged on the revalued amount.

Example: revaluation reserve

2.19 X Ltd bought freehold land and buildings for £20,000 ten years ago; their net book value (after depreciation of the buildings) is now £19,300. A professional valuation of £390,000 has been given, and the directors wish to reflect this in the accounts.

2.20 The revaluation surplus is £390,000 – £19,300 = £370,700. The entry to be made is thus:

		£	£
DEBIT	Freehold property	370,700	
CREDIT	Revaluation reserve		370,700

The balance sheet will then include the following.

	£
Reserves	
Revaluation reserve	370,700
Fixed assets	
Freehold property (at valuation)	390,000

2.21 An unrealised capital profit (such as the £370,700 above) is generally not distributable, whereas a realised capital profit (ie if the property is actually sold for £390,000) usually is distributable.

Distinction between reserves and provisions

2.22 A reserve is an appropriation of distributable profits for a specific purpose (eg plant replacement) while a provision is an amount charged against revenue as an expense. A provision relates either to a diminution in the value of an asset (eg doubtful debtors) or a known liability (eg audit fees), the amount of which cannot be established with any accuracy. Provisions (for depreciation, doubtful debts etc) are dealt with in company accounts in the same way as in the accounts of other types of business.

Exercise

(a) How do the Companies Acts influence the contents of accounts?

(b) Name two differences between the accounts of a sole trader and the accounts of an owner-managed limited company.

(c) A public company has 10,000,000 25p shares in issue and their current value on the stock market is £4.97 per share. What is the value of share capital in the company's nominal ledger?

(d) Is the profit and loss reserve of a limited company the same thing as the trading account of a sole trader?

(e) When is a revaluation reserve created?

Solution

(a) See 1.1 (a).
(b) See Paragraph 1.1 (b) and (c).
(c) £2.5m.

(d)   No: the reserve is for *retained* profits, not profits of the current year only.

(e)   See Paragraph 2.17.

3   THE FINALE ACCOUNTS OF LIMITED COMPANIES

3   **THE FINAL ACCOUNTS OF LIMITED COMPANIES**   *5/95, 5/97*

3.1   The preparation and publication of the final accounts of limited companies in the UK are governed by the Companies Act 1985 as amended by the Companies Act 1989. At this stage in your studies, you do not have to learn the detailed regulations laid down by these Acts. However, the general format of the balance sheet and profit and loss account of a limited company will be shown with some simplifications, in order to introduce certain assets and liabilities which we have not come across before in earlier chapters of this Study Text.

3.2   TYPICAL COMPANY LIMITED BALANCE SHEET AS AT.....

	£	£	£
Fixed assets			
Intangible assets			
Development costs		X	
Concessions, patents, licences, trademarks		X	
Goodwill		X̲	
			X
Tangible assets			
Land and buildings		X	
Plant and machinery		X	
Fixtures, fittings, tools and equipment		X	
Motor vehicles		X̲	
			X
Investments			X̲
			X̄
Current assets			
Stocks		X	
Debtors and prepayments		X	
Investments		X	
Cash at bank and in hand		X̲	
		X̄	
Creditors: amounts falling due within one year (ie current liabilities)			
Debenture loans (nearing their redemption date)	X		
Bank loans and overdrafts	X		
Trade creditors	X		
Bills of exchange payable	X		
Taxation	X		
Accruals	X		
Proposed dividend	X̲		
		(X̲)	
Net current assets			X̲
Total assets less current liabilities			X̄
Creditors : amounts falling due after more than one year			
Debenture loans		X	
Taxation		X̲	
			(X̲)
			X̄̄

Capital and reserves	£	£
Called up share capital		
Ordinary shares	X	
Preference shares	X	
		X
Reserves		
Share premium account	X	
Revaluation reserve	X	
Other reserves	X	
Profit and loss account (retained profits)	X	
		X
		X

3.3 TYPICAL COMPANY LIMITED
PROFIT AND LOSS ACCOUNT FOR THE YEAR ENDED...

	£	£
Turnover		X
Cost of sales		(X)
Gross profit		X
Distribution costs	X	
Administrative expenses	X	
		(X)
		X
Other operating income	X	
Income from fixed asset investments	X	
Other interest receivable and similar income	X	
		X
		X
Interest payable		(X)
Profit before taxation		X
Tax		(X)
Profit after tax		X
Dividends: preference	X	
ordinary	X	
		(X)
Retained profit for the year		X
Profit and loss account as at the beginning of the year		X
Profit and loss account as at the end of the year		X

Investments

3.4 Investments are fixed assets if the company intends to hold on to them for a long time, and current assets if they are only likely to be held for a short time before being sold.

Creditors: amounts falling due within one year

3.5 The term 'creditors: amounts falling due within one year' was introduced by the Companies Act 1981 as an alternative phrase meaning 'current liabilities'.

Debenture loans

3.6 Limited companies may issue debenture stock ('debentures') or loan stock. These are long-term liabilities described on the balance sheet as loan capital. They are different from share capital for the following reasons.

(a) Shareholders are members of a company, while providers of loan capital are creditors.

(b) Shareholders receive dividends (appropriations of profit) whereas the holders of loan capital are entitled to a fixed rate of interest (an expense charged against revenue).

(c) Loan capital holders can take legal action against a company if their interest is not paid when due, whereas shareholders cannot enforce the payment of dividends.

(d) Debentures or loan stock are often secured on company assets, whereas shares are not.

3.7   Interest is calculated on the nominal value of loan capital, regardless of its market value. If a company has £700,000 (nominal value) 12% debentures in issue, interest of £84,000 will be charged in the profit and loss account per year. Interest is usually paid half-yearly and examination questions often require an accrual to be made for interest due at the year end. Accrued interest is shown as a current liability in the year-end balance sheet.

3.8   For example, if a company has £700,000 of 12% debentures in issue, pays interest on 30 June and 31 December each year, and ends its accounting year on 30 September, there would be an accrual of three months' unpaid interest $(3/12 \times £84,000) = £21,000$ at the end of each accounting year that the debentures are still in issue.

Taxation

3.9   Companies pay *corporation tax* on the profits they earn. The charge for corporation tax on profits for the year is shown as a deduction from net profit, before appropriations. In the balance sheet, tax payable to the government is generally shown as a current liability.

3.10   When corporation tax on profits is calculated for the profit and loss account the calculation is only an estimate of what the company thinks its tax liability will be. In subsequent dealings with the Inland Revenue, a different corporation tax charge might eventually be agreed. Any difference is adjusted in the estimated taxation charge for the following year.

Example: taxation

3.11   Urals Ltd made a profit before tax of £150,000 in the year to 30 September 19X3 and of £180,000 in the following year (to 30 September 19X4).

The estimated corporation tax for the first year was £60,000 and in the second year was £75,000. The actual tax charge in the year to 30 September 19X3 was finally agreed with the Inland Revenue at £55,000.

Required

Compute the charge for taxation in the year to 30 September 19X4.

Solution

3.12

	To 30 September	
	19X3	*19X4*
	£	£
Estimate of tax on profits	60,000	75,000
Actual tax charge	55,000	
Overestimate of tax in 19X3	5,000	
		(5,000)
Tax charge in year to 30 September 19X4		70,000

The effect of this adjustment will be to increase profits in 19X4 by £5,000, to correct the 'error' in 19X3 when profits were reduced by £5,000 because of the overestimate of the tax charge.

3.13 Most companies pay tax within 12 months of their accounting year end. However, the tax on profits in the P & L account and the tax payable in the balance sheet are not usually the same amount, for reasons which will be covered in your later studies.

Examination question on company accounts

3.14 We can now draw together several of the items described in this chapter into an illustrative example. Study it carefully because it is typical of the type of problems encountered in the examination.

3.15 The accountant of Wislon Ltd has prepared the following trial balance as at 31 December 19X7.

	£'000
50p ordinary shares (fully paid)	350
7% £1 preference shares (fully paid)	100
10% debentures (secured)	200
Retained profit 1 January 19X7	242
General reserve 1 January 19X7	171
Freehold land and buildings 1 January 19X7 (cost)	430
Plant and machinery 1 January 19X7 (cost)	830
Provision for depreciation	
Freehold buildings 1 January 19X7	20
Plant and machinery 1 January 19X7	222
Stock 1 January 19X7	190
Sales	2,695
Purchases	2,152
Preference dividend	7
Ordinary dividend (interim)	8
Debenture interest	10
Wages and salaries	254
Light and heat	31
Sundry expenses	113
Suspense account	135
Debtors	179
Creditors	195
Cash	126

Notes

(a) Sundry expenses include £9,000 paid in respect of insurance for the year ending 1 September 19X8. Light and heat does not include an invoice of £3,000 for electricity for the three months ending 2 January 19X8, which was paid in February 19X8. Light and heat also includes £20,000 relating to salesmen's commission.

(b) The suspense account is in respect of the following items.

	£'000
Proceeds from the issue of 100,000 ordinary shares	120
Proceeds from the sale of plant	300
	420
Less consideration for the acquisition of Mary & Co	285
	135

(c) The net assets of Mary & Co were purchased on 3 March 19X7. Assets were valued as follows.

	£'000
Investments	230
Stock	34
	264

All the stock acquired was sold during 19X7. The investments were still held by Wislon at 31 December 19X7.

(d) The freehold property was acquired some years ago. The buildings element of the cost was estimated at £100,000 and the estimated useful life of the assets was fifty years at the time of purchase. As at 31 December 19X7 the property is to be revalued at £800,000.

(e) The plant which was sold had cost £350,000 and had a net book value of £274,000 as on 1 January 19X7. £36,000 depreciation is to be charged on plant and machinery for 19X7.

(f) The debentures have been in issue for some years. The 50p ordinary shares all rank for dividends at the end of the year.

(g) The directors wish to provide for:

(i)   debenture interest due;
(ii) a final ordinary dividend of 2p per share;
(iii) a transfer to general reserve of £16,000;
(iv) audit fees of £4,000.

(h) Stock as at 31 December 19X7 was valued at £220,000 (cost).

(i) Taxation is to be ignored.

Required

Prepare the final accounts of Wislon Ltd.

Approach and suggested solution

3.16 (a) The usual adjustments are needed for accruals and prepayments (insurance, light and heat, debenture interest and audit fees). The debenture interest accrued is calculated as follows.

	£'000
Charge needed in P & L account (10% × £200,000)	20
Amount paid so far, as shown in trial balance	10
Accrual - presumably six months' interest now payable	10

The accrued expenses shown in the balance sheet comprise:

	£'000
Debenture interest	10
Light and heat	3
Audit fee	4
	17

(b) The misposting of £20,000 to light and heat is also adjusted, by reducing the light and heat expense, but charging £20,000 to salesmen's commission.

(c) Depreciation on the freehold building is calculated as $\dfrac{£100,000}{50} = £2,000$.

The net book value of the freehold property is then £430,000 – £20,000 – £2,000 = £408,000 at the end of the year. When the property is revalued a reserve of £800,000 – £408,000 = £392,000 is then created.

(d) The profit on disposal of plant is calculated as proceeds £300,000 (per suspense account) less NBV £274,000 ie £26,000. The cost of the remaining plant is calculated at £830,000 – £350,000 = £480,000. The depreciation provision at the year end is made up of the following.

	£'000
Balance 1 January 19X7	222
Charge for 19X7	36
Less depreciation on disposals (350 – 274)	(76)
	182

(e)   Goodwill arising on the purchase of Mary & Co is calculated as follows.

	£'000
Consideration (per suspense account)	285
Assets at valuation	264
Goodwill	21

In the absence of other instructions, this is shown as an asset on the balance sheet. The investments, being owned by Wislon at the year end, are also shown on the balance sheet, whereas Mary's stock, acquired and then sold, is added to the purchases figure for the year.

(f)   The other item in the suspense account is dealt with as follows.

	£'000
Proceeds of issue of 100,000 ordinary shares	120
Less nominal value 100,000 × 50p	50
Excess of consideration over nominal value (= share premium)	70

(g)   Appropriations of profit must be considered. The final ordinary dividend, shown as a current liability in the balance sheet, is calculated as follows.

(700,000 + 100,000 ordinary shares) × 2p = £16,000

(h)   The transfer to general reserve increases that reserve to £171,000 + £16,000 = £187,000.

3.17   WISLON LIMITED
TRADING AND PROFIT AND LOSS ACCOUNT
FOR THE YEAR ENDING 31 DECEMBER 19X7

	£'000	£'000	£'000
Sales			2,695
Less cost of sales			
Opening stock		190	
Purchases		2,186	
		2,376	
Less closing stock		220	
			2,156
Gross profit			539
Profit on disposal of plant			26
			565
Less expenses			
Wages, salaries and commission		274	
Sundry expenses		107	
Light and heat		14	
Depreciation: freehold buildings		2	
plant		36	
Audit fees		4	
Debenture interest		20	
			457
Net profit			108
Appropriations			
Transfer to general reserve		16	
Dividends			
Preference (paid)	7		
Ordinary: interim (paid)	8		
final (proposed)	16		
		31	
			47
Retained profit for the year			61
Retained profit brought forward			242
Retained profit carried forward			303

3.18   WISLON LIMITED
        BALANCE SHEET AS AT 31 DECEMBER 19X7

			£'000
Fixed assets			
Intangible assets			
Goodwill			21
Tangible assets	Cost/ val'n £'000	Dep'n £'000	
Freehold property	800	-	800
Plant and machinery	480	182	298
	1,280	182	
Investments			230
			1,349
Current assets			
Stock		220	
Debtors		179	
Prepayment		6	
Cash		126	
		531	
Creditors: amounts falling due within one year			
Creditors	195		
Accrued expenses	17		
Proposed dividend	16		
		228	
Net current assets			303
Total assets less current liabilities			1,652
Creditors: amounts falling due after more than one year			
10% debentures (secured)			(200)
			1,452
Capital and reserves			
Called up share capital			
50p ordinary shares		400	
7% £1 preference shares		100	
			500
Reserves			
Share premium		70	
Revaluation reserve		392	
General reserve		187	
Profit and loss account		303	
			952
			1,452

4   THE LEDGER ACCOUNTS OF LIMITED COMPANIES

4.1   Limited companies keep ledger accounts and the only difference between the ledger accounts of companies and sole traders is the nature of some of the accounts which need to be kept.

For example, there will be an account for each of the following items.

(a)   *Taxation*

(i)   Tax charged against profits will be accounted for as follows.

DEBIT   P & L account
CREDIT   Taxation account

(ii)   The outstanding balance on the taxation account will be a liability in the balance sheet, until eventually paid, when the accounting entry would be as follows.

DEBIT   Taxation account
CREDIT   Cash

(b) *Dividends*

A separate account will be kept for the dividends for each different class of shares (eg preference, ordinary).

(i)   Dividends declared out of profits will be accounted for as follows.

DEBIT   P & L appropriation account
CREDIT   Dividends payable account

Dividends payable (but not yet paid) are a current liability.

(ii) When dividends are paid the following entries would be made.

DEBIT   Dividends payable account
CREDIT   Cash

(c) *Debenture loans*

Debenture loans are a long term liability and will be shown as a credit balance in a debenture loan account. Interest payable on such loans is not credited to the loan account, but is credited to a separate creditors account for interest until it is eventually paid.

DEBIT   Interest account (an expense, chargeable against profits)
CREDIT   Interest payable (a current liability until eventually paid).

(d) *Share capital and reserves*

There will be a separate account for each different class of share capital and for each different type of reserve. The balance on the share capital account will always be a credit and the balance on the reserve account will nearly always be a credit.

Chapter roundup

- This chapter has explained some important differences between the accounts of a limited company and those of sole traders.

- The accounting records and financial statements of a limited company are strictly regulated by statute.

- A company is recognised in law as a person, with its own identity quite separate from that of its owners. One important consequence of this is the concept of limited liability: a company's shareholders have no liability for the company's debts, beyond what they have contributed as capital.

- To reflect the difference in ownership, the capital of companies is shown differently from that of sole traders.

- Profits paid out to shareholders are called *dividends*.

- *Preference shares* carry the right to a fixed dividend which is expressed as a percentage of their nominal value.

- *Ordinary shares* normally carry voting rights. They carry no right to a fixed dividend but are entitled to all profits left after payment of any preference dividend.

- Statutory reserves are reserves which a company must set up by law. They are not distributable.

- Non statutory reserves are distributable.

- The difference between the price paid for a new issue of shares and their nominal value is the *premium*, which is credited to a share premium account.

- A revaluation reserve must be created when a company revalues one or more of its fixed assets.

- The preparation and publication of final accounts of limited companies is governed by the Companies Act 1985.

Test your knowledge

1   What is the meaning of limited liability? (see para 1.3)

2   What are the differences between ordinary shares and preference shares?   (2.7)

3   How does a share premium account arise? (2.16)

4   What is the difference between a reserve and a provision? (2.22)

5   What are the differences between debentures and share capital? (3.6)

Now try illustrative question 36 at the end of the Study Text

Chapter 22

MANUFACTURING ACCOUNTS AND CASH FLOW STATEMENTS

This chapter covers the following topics.

		Syllabus reference	*Ability required*
1	Manufacturing accounts	1(c)	Skill
2	Profits and cash flow	1(c)	Skill
3	Cash flow statements	1(c)	Skill

Introduction

So far in our studies of accounts preparation we have confined ourselves to the accounts of trading organisations. Britain has been called a nation of shopkeepers, but we would be a very hungry nation if no one actually made things. In Section 1 of this chapter we consider the problems of preparing accounting statements for manufacturing firms.

The most obvious difference between a manufacturing and a trading firm is that the former has many more different types of expense. The *purchases* of the trading firm are replaced by the myriad expenses that arise when, for example, a willow tree is converted into a cricket bat. The traditional way of showing the cost of goods produced is the *manufacturing account*.

Yet another type of statement is introduced in Sections 2 and 3: the cash flow statement.

In the long run, a profit will result in an increase in the company's cash balance but, as Keynes observed, 'in the long run we are all dead'. In the short run, the making of a profit will not necessarily result in an increased cash balance. This observation leads us to two questions. The first relates to the importance of the distinction between cash and profit. The second is concerned with the usefulness of the information provided by the balance sheet and profit and loss account in the problem of deciding whether the company has, or will be able to generate, sufficient cash to finance its operations.

The importance of the distinction between cash and profit and the scant attention paid to this by the profit and loss account has resulted in the development of cash flow statements.

---

1 MANUFACTURING ACCOUNTS

5/96

1.1 A company's trading account will usually include a cost of goods sold derived as the total of opening stock plus purchases, less closing stock. This is particularly suitable for a retail business which buys in goods and sells them on to customers without altering their condition. But for a manufacturing company it would be truer to say that the cost of goods sold is as follows.

	£
Opening stock of finished goods	X
Plus cost of finished goods produced in the period	X
	X
Less closing stock of finished goods	(X)
Cost of finished goods sold	X

1.2   A manufacturing account is an account in which the costs of producing finished goods are accumulated. Eventually the 'cost of finished goods produced in the period' is transferred to the trading account as part of the cost of goods sold; this is illustrated above.

1.3   The costs accumulated in a manufacturing account are as follows.

(a)   The cost of raw materials consumed in the period. This is the opening stock of raw materials, plus purchases of raw materials less closing stock of raw materials.

(b)   The cost of direct factory wages. We have seen that the total of (a) and (b) is often referred to as the prime cost.

(c)   Production overheads or factory overheads.

1.4   A pro-forma manufacturing account is set out below with illustrative figures.

MANUFACTURING ACCOUNT
FOR THE YEAR ENDED 31 DECEMBER 19X6

	£	£
Raw materials		
Opening stock	4,000	
Purchases (net of returns)	207,000	
	211,000	
Less closing stock	23,000	
		188,000
Factory wages		21,000
Prime cost		209,000
Production overhead		
Factory power	4,000	
Plant depreciation	3,000	
Plant maintenance	1,500	
Rates and insurance	2,500	
Light and heat	3,000	
Sundry expenses	5,000	
Factory manager's salary	9,000	
Building depreciation	1,000	
		29,000
Production cost of resources consumed		238,000
Work in progress		
Opening stocks	8,000	
Closing stocks	(17,000)	
Increase in work in progress stocks		(9,000)
Production cost of finished goods produced		229,000

1.5   You may need to think carefully about the adjustment for work in progress near the end of the statement. When a business purchases raw materials they are issued to production departments as required. Employees in the production departments will work on the raw materials in order to convert them eventually into finished goods ready for sale. At the balance sheet date, there will be work in progress in the production departments, ie work which has been partly converted but which has not yet reached the stage of being finished goods.

1.6   The value of this work in progress will include not only the cost of the raw materials, but also the wages of employees who have worked on it plus any attributable overheads. It follows that the prime cost and factory overheads shown in the manufacturing account will not all have resulted in the production of finished goods, because some of the costs may have gone to increase the stocks of work in progress. To arrive at the cost of finished goods produced, any such increase must be deducted from the total costs incurred.

1.7   Of course, if the value of work in progress had *fallen* during the period, this fall would be an *increase* in the cost of finished goods produced.

Example: manufacturing, trading and profit and loss account

1.8   A manufacturing company has its factory and offices at the same site. Its results for the year to 31 December 19X5 were as follows.

	£
Sales	179,000
Purchases of raw materials	60,000
Direct labour	70,000
Depreciation of equipment	10,000
Uniform Business Rate	5,000
Depreciation of building	2,000
Heating and lighting	3,000
Telephone	2,000
Other manufacturing overheads	2,300
Other administration expenses	2,550
Other selling expenses	1,150

Shared overhead costs are to be apportioned as follows.

	Manufacturing	*Administration*	*Selling*
Depreciation of equipment	80%	5%	15%
Rates	50%	30%	20%
Depreciation of building	50%	30%	20%
Heating and lighting	40%	35%	25%
Telephone	-	40%	60%

The values of stocks are as follows.

	At 1 January 19X5 £	*At 31 December 19X5* £
Raw materials	5,000	3,000
Work in progress	4,000	3,000
Finished goods	16,000	18,000

Required

Prepare the manufacturing, trading and profit and loss account of the company for the period to 31 December 19X5.

Solution

1.9   MANUFACTURING ACCOUNT FOR THE YEAR ENDED 31 DECEMBER 19X5

	£	£
Opening stock of raw materials		5,000
Purchases		60,000
		65,000
Closing stock of raw materials		3,000
Raw materials used in production		62,000
Direct labour		70,000
Prime cost		132,000
Manufacturing overheads		
Depreciation of equipment (80% of £10,000)	8,000	
UBR (50% of £5,000)	2,500	
Depreciation of building (50% of £2,000)	1,000	
Heating and lighting (40% of £3,000)	1,200	
Other expenses	2,300	
		15,000
Manufacturing costs during the year		147,000
Add opening stock of work in progress	4,000	
Less closing stock of work in progress	(3,000)	
Reduction in stock of work in progress		1,000
Cost of finished goods fully produced,		
transferred to trading account		148,000

TRADING AND PROFIT AND LOSS ACCOUNT
FOR THE YEAR ENDED 31 DECEMBER 19X5

	£	£	£
Sales			179,000
Opening stock of finished goods		16,000	
Cost of finished goods produced		148,000	
		164,000	
Closing stock of finished goods		18,000	
Cost of goods sold			146,000
Gross profit			33,000
Selling expenses			
Depreciation of equipment (15% of £10,000)	1,500		
UBR (20% of £5,000)	1,000		
Depreciation of building (20% of £2,000)	400		
Heating and lighting (25% of £3,000)	750		
Telephone (60% of £2,000)	1,200		
Other expenses	1,150		
		6,000	
Administration expenses			
Depreciation of equipment (5% of £10,000)	500		
Rates (30% of £5,000)	1,500		
Depreciation of building (30% of £2,000)	600		
Heating and lighting (35% of £3,000)	1,050		
Telephone (40% of £2,000)	800		
Other expenses	2,550		
		7,000	
			13,000
Net profit			20,000

1.10   The CIMA examiner has confirmed that the more advanced aspects of manufacturing accounts, specifically transfer pricing and provisions for unrealised profit will not be examined.

Exercise 1

The following information has been extracted from the books of account of the Marsden Manufacturing Company for the year to 30 September 19X4.

	£
Advertising	2,000
Depreciation for the year to 30 September 19X4	
Factory equipment	7,000
Office equipment	4,000
Direct wages	40,000
Factory: insurance	1,000
heat	15,000
indirect materials	5,000
power	20,000
salaries	25,000
Finished goods (at 1 October 19X3)	24,000
Office: electricity	15,000
general expenses	9,000
postage and telephones	2,900
salaries	70,000
Raw material purchases	202,000
Raw material stock (at 1 October 19X3)	8,000
Sales	512,400
Work in progress (at 1 October 19X3)	12,000

Notes

(a)   At 30 September 19X4 the following stocks were on hand.

	£
Raw materials	10,000
Work in progress	9,000
Finished goods	30,000

(b)   At 30 September 19X4 there was an accrual for advertising of £1,000, and it was estimated that £1,500 had been paid in advance for electricity. These items had not been included in the books of account for the year to 30 September 19X4.

You are required to prepare Marsden's manufacturing, trading and profit and loss account for the year to 30 September 19X4.

Solution

MANUFACTURING, TRADING AND PROFIT AND LOSS ACCOUNT
FOR THE YEAR ENDED 30 SEPTEMBER 19X4

	£	£
Raw materials		
Opening stock	8,000	
Purchases	202,000	
	210,000	
Less closing stock	10,000	
		200,000
Factory wages		40,000
Prime cost		240,000
Indirect production expenses		
Insurance	1,000	
Heat	15,000	
Indirect materials	5,000	
Power	20,000	
Salaries	25,000	
Depreciation of factory equipment	7,000	
		73,000
		313,000
Work in progress		
Opening stock	12,000	
Less closing stock	9,000	
		3,000
Factory cost of goods produced		316,000

	£	£
Sales		512,400
Less cost of goods sold		
Opening stock of finished goods	24,000	
Factory cost of goods produced	316,000	
	340,000	
Less closing stock of finished goods	30,000	
		310,000
Gross profit		202,400
Expenses		
Advertising £(2,000 + 1,000)	3,000	
Depreciation of office equipment	4,000	
Electricity £(15,000 – 1,500)	13,500	
General expenses	9,000	
Postage and telephones	2,900	
Salaries	70,000	
		102,400
Net profit		100,000

* It is assumed that the finished goods valuations are at transfer price from the factory, not at cost.

2 PROFITS AND CASH FLOW

2.1 To be successful in business, an enterprise must make a profit. Profits are needed to pay dividends to shareholders (and shareholders expect to receive dividends as a return on their investment in ownership of the business) and to reward partners or proprietors. Some profits are retained within the business as reserves or as proprietor's funds, to finance the development and growth of the business. We can therefore say that although a firm may be able to bear occasional losses, it must be profitable in the long term. A loss means that the value of sales in a period is less than the value of resources used up in making the sales, so that a loss causes a reduction in the overall value of a business. Long-term losses will lead to the eventual collapse of a firm.

2.2   In addition to being *profitable* in order to survive and grow, it is also necessary for a firm to 'pay its way': to *pay in cash* for the goods and services and capital equipment it buys, the workforce it employs and the other expenses (such as rent, rates and taxation) that it incurs. If a firm does not pay its bills when they are due, it will first of all lose the goodwill of its suppliers or workforce and may then be driven into liquidation. It is therefore necessary to be not just profitable, but also capable of obtaining cash to meet demand for payment.

2.3   Profits and cash surpluses are not the same thing, for a number of reasons.

(a)   Cash may be obtained from a transaction which has nothing to do with profit or loss. For example, an issue of shares or loan stock for cash has no effect on profit (except for subsequent interest charges on a loan) but is obviously a source of cash. Similarly, an increase in bank overdraft provides a source of cash for payments, but it is not reported in the profit and loss account.

(b)   Cash may be paid for the purchase of fixed assets, but the charge in the profit and loss account is depreciation, which is only a part of an asset's cost. For example, a company may have existing fixed assets which originally cost £300,000. If it buys a new asset for £20,000 on 1 January and if depreciation is charged at a rate of 10% of cost:

(i)   the charge for depreciation for the year to 31 December would be 10% of £320,000 or £32,000;

(ii)   the cash payments during the year would be £20,000 - the purchase cost of the new asset.

(c)   When a fixed asset is sold there is a profit or loss on sale equal to the difference between the sale proceeds and the 'net book value' of the asset in the balance sheet at the time it is sold. For example, if an asset originally cost £50,000 and depreciation of £35,000 has been charged since its purchase, its net book value will be £15,000. If it is now sold for £11,000, there will be a loss on disposal of £4,000. This loss would be recorded in the profit and loss account, but the effect of the sale would be to increase the firm's cash by £11,000 (the sale price).

(d)   The profit and loss account reports the total value of sales in a year. If goods are sold on credit, the cash receipts will differ from the value of sales. The relationship between sales and receipts is as follows (excluding increases or decreases in the provision for doubtful debts and writing-off bad debts).

	£
Debtors owing money at the start of the year	X
Sales during the year	X
Total money due from customers	X
Less debtors owing money at the end of the year	(X)
Cash receipts from debtors during the year	X

(e)   Similarly, the profit and loss account reports the cost of goods sold during the year. However:

(i)   if materials are bought on credit, the cash payments to suppliers will be different from the value of materials purchased;

(ii)   if some materials are bought and added to stocks rather than sold (ie if there is an increase in stocks during the year) total purchases will be different from the materials cost of sales. (In the same way, a firm may decide to run down its stocks and sell goods without making good the stocks used up by purchasing replacement items.)

The relationship between the cost of materials in the materials cost of sales and cash payments for materials purchased is as follows:

	£
Opening stocks (at the start of the year)	X
Add purchases during the year	X
	X̄
Less closing stocks at the end of the year	(X)
Equals materials cost in the cost of sales	Ȳ
Payments still owing to creditors at the start of the year	X
Add materials cost in the cost of sales	Y
	X̄
Less payments still owing to creditors at the end of the year	(X)
Equals cash payments to creditors during the year	X̄

The need for information about cash flow

2.4   It has been suggested to you in the previous paragraphs that:

(a)   a firm must not only be profitable, but must also obtain cash receipts (or an overdraft facility) to pay its way;

(b)   profits and cash surpluses are not the same.

Information about cash receipts and payments can therefore add to our understanding of a firm's operations and financial stability. Whereas a profit and loss statement reports on profitability, cash flow statements report on liquidity.

3   CASH FLOW STATEMENTS   *5/95, 11/96*

3.1   It follows from the above discussion that 'profit' does not always give a useful or meaningful picture of a company's operations. Readers of a company's financial statements might even be misled by a reported profit figure.

(a)   Shareholders might believe that if a company makes a profit after tax, of say, £100,000 then this is the amount which it could afford to pay as a dividend. Unless the company has sufficient cash available to stay in business and also to pay a dividend, the shareholders' expectations would be wrong.

(b)   Employees might believe that if a company makes profits, it can afford to pay higher wages next year. This opinion may not be correct: the ability to pay wages depends on the availability of cash.

(c)   Creditors might consider that a profitable company is a going concern. However:

(i)   if a company builds up large amounts of unsold stocks of goods, their cost would not be chargeable against profits, but cash would have been used up in making them, thus weakening the company's liquid resources;

(ii)   a company might capitalise large development costs, having spent considerable amounts of money on R & D, but only charge small amounts against current profits. As a result, the company might show reasonable profits, but get into severe difficulties with its liquidity position. (This is roughly the problem that led to the collapse of the old Rolls Royce company in 1971.)

(d)   Management might suppose that if their company makes a profit, and reinvests some of those profits, then the company must be expanding. This is not the case: in a period of inflation, a company might have insufficient retained profits to prevent the operating capability of the firm from declining.

(e)   Survival of a business entity depends not so much on profits as on its ability to pay its debts when they fall due. Such payments might include 'profit and loss' items such as material purchases, wages, interest and taxation etc, but also capital payments for new fixed assets and the repayment of loan capital when this falls due (eg on the redemption of debentures).

3.2   From these examples, it may be apparent that a company's performance and prospects depend not so much on the 'profits' earned in a period, but more realistically on liquidity: cash flows. A statement of cash flows is unambiguous and provides information which is additional to that provided in the rest of the accounts. It also lends itself to organisation by activity and not by balance sheet classification. In September 1991 the Accounting Standards Board (ASB) published FRS 1 *Cash flow statements*. You do not need to know the prescribed format in detail, but you should know how to construct a cash flow statement and what its aims are.

3.3   The aim of a cashflow statement should be to assist users:

(a)   to assess the enterprise's ability to generate positive net cash flows in the future;
(b)   to assess its ability to meet its obligations to service loans, pay dividends etc;
(c)   to assess the reasons for difference between reported profit and related cash flows;
(d)   to assess the effect on its finances of major transactions in the year.

The statement should therefore show changes in cash and cash equivalents. The opening and closing figures given for cash etc should be those shown in the balance sheet. Receipts and payments should not be netted off. Non-cash transactions should be reported separately by note (eg purchasing an asset with lease finance) and a reconciliation of net income to net cash flow from operating activities should be given.

3.4   The statement should classify cash receipts and payments as resulting from investing, financing or operating activities. Examples of each are:

(a)   investing: making loans, acquiring/disposing of fixed assets;

(b)   financing: borrowing/repaying money, making an issue of shares, paying dividends;

(c)   operating: receipts from customers, payments to employees and suppliers, any other cash flows from transactions not classified as investing or financing.

3.5   A cash flow statement can be a historical statement or a forecast. It shows the sources and uses of cash over a period of time, whereas a cash budget shows expected sources and uses of cash daily, weekly or monthly, to help in management of working capital.

Example: cash flow statement

3.6   Flail Ltd commenced trading on 1 January 19X1 with a medium-term loan of £21,000 and a share issue which raised £35,000. The company purchased fixed assets for £21,000 cash, and during the year to 31 December 19X1 entered into the following transactions.

(a)   Purchases from suppliers were £19,500, of which £2,550 was unpaid at the year end.

(b)   Wages and salaries amounted to £10,500, of which £750 was unpaid at the year end.

(c)   Interest on the loan of £2,100 was fully paid in the year and a repayment of £5,250 was made.

(d)   Sales turnover was £29,400, including £900 debtors at the year end.

(e)   Interest on cash deposits at the bank amounted to £75.

(f)   A dividend of £4,000 was proposed as at 31 December 19X1.

You are required to prepare a historical cash flow statement for the year ended 31 December 19X1.

Solution

3.7   FLAIL LIMITED
       STATEMENT OF CASH FLOWS FOR
       THE YEAR ENDED 31 DECEMBER 19X1

	£	£
Operating activities		
Cash received from customers	28,500	
(£29,400 – £900)		
Cash paid to suppliers (£19,500 – £2,550)	(16,950)	
Cash paid to and on behalf of employees (£10,500 – £750)	(9,750)	
Cash flow from operating activities		1,800
Returns on investment and servicing of finance		
Interest paid	(2,100)	
Interest received	75	
		(2,025)
Capital expenditure		
Purchase of fixed assets	(21,000)	
Cash flow from investing activities		(21,000)
Financing		
Issue of shares	35,000	
Proceeds from medium-term loan	21,000	
Repayment of medium-term loan	(5,250)	
Cash flow from financing activities		50,750
Net increase in cash		29,525
Cash at 1 January 19X1		-
Cash at 31 December 19X1		29,525

Note that the dividend is only proposed and so there is no related cash flow in 19X1.

Exercise 2

The directors of Flail Ltd obtain the following information in respect of projected cash flows for the year to 31 December 19X2.

(a)   Fixed asset purchases for cash will be £3,000.

(b)   Further expenses will be:

   (i)   purchases from suppliers - £18,750 (£4,125 owed at the year end);

   (ii)   wages and salaries - £11,250 (£600 owed at the year end);

   (iii) loan interest - £1,575.

(c)   Turnover will be £36,000 (£450 debtors at the year end).

(d)   Interest on bank deposits will be £150.

(e)   A further capital repayment of £5,250 will be made on the loan.

(f)   A dividend of £5,000 will be proposed and last year's final dividend paid.

(g)   Corporation tax of £2,300 will be paid in respect of 19X1.

Prepare the cash flow forecast for the year to 31 December 19X2.

Solution

FLAIL LIMITED
STATEMENT OF FORECAST CASH FLOWS FOR
THE YEAR ENDING 31 DECEMBER 19X2

	£	£
Operating activities		
Cash received from customers	36,450	
(£36,000 + £900 – £450)		
Cash paid to suppliers (£18,750 + £2,550 – £4,125)	(17,175)	
Cash paid to and on behalf of employees		
(£11,250 + £750 – £600)	(11,400)	
Net cash flow from operating activities		7,875
Returns on investments and servicing of finance		
Interest paid	(1,575)	
Interest received	150	
		(1,425)
Taxation		(2,300)
Capital expenditure		
Purchase of fixed assets		(3,000)
		1,150
Equity dividends paid		(4,000)
Financing		
Repayment of medium-term loan		(5,250)
Forecast net decrease in cash at 31 December 19X2		(8,100)
Cash as at 31 December 19X1		29,525
Forecast cash as at 31 December 19X2		21,425

Indirect method

3.8 Another way of arriving at net cash flows from operating activities is to start from operating profit and adjust for non-cash items, such as depreciation, debtors etc. This is known as the *indirect method*. A proforma calculation is given below.

	£
Operating profit (P&L)	X
Add depreciation	X
Loss (profit) on sale of fixed assets	X
(Increase)/decrease in stocks	(X)/X
(Increase)/decrease in debtors	(X)/X
Increase/(decrease) in creditors	X/(X)
Net cash flow from operating activities	X

3.9 It is important to understand why certain items are added and others subtracted. Note the following points.

(a) Depreciation is not a cash expense, but is deducted in arriving at the profit figure in the profit and loss account. It makes sense, therefore, to eliminate it by adding it back.

(b) By the same logic, a loss on a disposal of a fixed asset (arising through underprovision of depreciation) needs to be added back and a profit deducted.

(c) An increase in stocks means less cash - you have spent cash on buying stock.

(d) An increase in debtors means debtors have not paid as much, therefore less cash.

(e) If we pay off creditors, causing the figure to decrease, again we have less cash.

3.10 It is important that you familiarise yourself with the indirect method by practising illustrative question 38 at the end of the Study Text. It is the indirect method which will generally be needed, particularly in more advanced cash flow statements, where you will be required to follow the FRS 1 format.

3.11 Note that, in an examination question, you may not be given the profit figure; instead you may be required to calculate it by finding the difference between the capital figures in two consecutive years' balance sheets.

The advantages of cash flow accounting

3.12 The advantages of cash flow accounting are as follows.

(a) Survival in business depends on the ability to generate cash. Cash flow accounting directs attention towards this critical issue.

(b) Cash flow is more comprehensive than 'profit' which is dependent on accounting conventions and concepts.

(c) Creditors (long and short-term) are more interested in an entity's ability to repay them than in its profitability. Whereas 'profits' might indicate that cash is likely to be available, cash flow accounting is more direct with its message.

(d) Cash flow reporting provides a better means of comparing the results of different companies than traditional profit reporting.

(e) Cash flow reporting satisfies the needs of all users better.

 (i) For management, it provides the sort of information on which decisions should be taken: (in management accounting, 'relevant costs' to a decision are future cash flows); traditional profit accounting does not help with decision-making.

 (ii) For shareholders and auditors, cash flow accounting can provide a satisfactory basis for stewardship accounting.

 (iii) As described previously, the information needs of creditors and employees will be better served by cash flow accounting.

(f) Cash flow forecasts are easier to prepare, as well as more useful, than profit forecasts.

Exercise 3

You should give some thought to the possible *disadvantages* of cashflow accounting which are essentially the advantages of accruals accounting. There is also the practical problem that few businesses keep historical cash flow information in the form needed to prepare a historical cash flow statement and so extra record keeping is likely to be necessary.

Chapter roundup

- Manufacturing accounts are prepared for internal management use only. Their purpose is to distinguish between the costs and profitability associated with manufacturing operations and those associated with trading (which are shown in the trading account).

- Manufacturing accounts highlight the following.

  o *Prime cost*. The cost of raw materials and direct labour employed in production.

  o *Factory cost of goods produced*. Equal to prime cost plus indirect factory expenses and plus or minus any movement over the period in the cost of work in progress.

- Profit does not always give a useful or meaningful picture of a company's operations.

- Survival in business depends on the ability to generate cash. Cash flow accounting directs attention towards this critical issue.

- Cash flow statements concentrate on the sources and uses of cash, and are a useful indicator of a company's liquidity and solvency.

Test your knowledge

1   What is the formula for the cost of finished goods sold by a manufacturing company? (see para 1.1)

2   Describe the categories of cost which are accumulated in a manufacturing account (1.3)

3   Why is it argued that users of accounts can be misled by the reported profit figure? (3.1)

4   Differentiate between a cash flow statement and a cash budget. (3.5)

5   How is net cash flow from operating activities calculated using the indirect method? (3.8)

6   What are the advantages of cash flow accounting? (3.12)

Now try illustrative questions 37 and 38 at the end of the Study Text

Chapter 23

INTERNAL AND EXTERNAL AUDIT

This chapter covers the following topics.

		Syllabus reference	Ability required
1	Ownership v stewardship	1(b)	Knowledge
2	External audit	1(b)	Appreciation
3	Internal audit	1(b)	Appreciation
4	Internal control systems	1(b)	Appreciation
5	Audit trail	1(b)	Appreciation
6	The detection and prevention of fraud	1(b)	Appreciation

Introduction

So far in your studies you have been mainly concerned with the preparation of accounts. Your syllabus also requires you to have an appreciation of the purpose of external and internal audit.

It is a requirement of the Companies Act that all companies must appoint *external auditors* who will report to the *members* of the company on whether in their opinion, the annual statutory accounts give a true and fair view. The duties of the external auditor are imposed by statute and cannot be limited, either by the directors or by the members of the company. External auditors are not employees of the company.

Internal auditors are employees of the company whose duties are fixed by management, and who report ultimately to *management*. In recent years it has become increasingly common for large companies to set up internal audit departments and for the external auditors to alter their audit approach to take account of the work done by the internal auditors.

1   OWNERSHIP V STEWARDSHIP   5/95

1.1   Stewardship when applied to an organisation refers to the primary function of the managers who are responsible for the running of the business on a day to day basis. As proprietors became further and further removed from the day to day management of the business they owned, the stewardship role encompassed the safeguarding and accounting for the business's assets.

1.2   The development of external auditing was based on the 'stewardship' concept of company management. The function of the auditor was to assure the proprietors that the stewardship of the organisation was effectively carried out.

1.3   However, the stewardship concept is wider than the requirement to ensure that the assets of an organisation are properly recorded, valued and insured. It should also include the control of costs, the improvement of efficiency and the optimisation of profits. Additionally whilst management's stewardship responsibilities extend primarily to the owners of the business it also includes all other users of the accounts.

2   EXTERNAL AUDIT

What is external audit?

2.1   An external audit is an independent examination of, and expression of opinion on the financial statements of an enterprise.

2.2   By 'enterprise' we generally mean limited company, and by 'external audit' we generally mean statutory audit, that is, under the Companies Act 1985. The statutory audit requirement, arose as discussed in Section 1, because of the separation of owners (shareholders) and managers (directors).

2.3   External auditors are generally firms of chartered or certified accountants. They summarise their conclusions on the company's financial statements by issuing an audit report. The report must state whether in the auditors opinion:

(a)   the balance sheet gives a true and fair view of the state of affairs of the company at the end of the financial year;

(b)   the profit and loss account gives a true and fair view of the profit or loss of the company for the financial year; and

(c)   the financial statements have been properly prepared in accordance with the Companies Act 1985.

2.4   The term 'true and fair' is not defined in company law or accounting standards. The words are used together rather than separately and the term is generally taken to mean 'reasonably accurate and free from bias or distortion'.

2.5   Although there is no official definition of 'true and fair', the Companies Act 1985 states that the directors may depart from any provisions of company law or accounting standards if these are inconsistent with the requirement to give a true and fair view. This 'true and fair override' has been treated as an important loophole in the law and has been the cause of much argument and dissatisfaction within the accounting profession.

2.6   In June 1993 Mary Arden QC stated that the Courts are more likely than ever to rule that compliance with accounting standards is necessary for accounts to give a true and fair view as required by the Companies Act 1985.

Other statutory audits

2.7   Limited company audits are by far the most important external audits for your purposes. However you should be aware that audits are compulsory under statute in the case of a large number of undertakings. Examples include the following.

(a)   Building societies must be audited under the Building Society Act 1986

(b)   Trade unions and employers' associations must be audited under the Trade Union and Labour Relations Act 1974.

(c)   Various acts, including the Housing Association Act 1985 set out requirements for the audit of housing associations.

Non-statutory audits

2.8   Non-statutory audits are performed by independent auditors because the owners, members, trustees, governing bodies or other interested parties desire them, not because the law requires them. Auditing may therefore extend to any kind of undertaking which produces accounts (eg clubs, sole traders, charities, partnerships), and may extend to forms of financial statements other than the annual report and accounts. An example might be an audit of a statement of expenditure in support of an application for a regional development grant

2.9   The term 'audit' is often applied to non-financial matters. Examples include the following.

     (a)   The circulation figures of a newspaper or magazine used when soliciting advertising

     (b)   Environmental audit reports, for example those produced by the Body Shop

2.10   The remainder of this chapter will be concerned with *internal* audit unless otherwise stated.

Exercise 1

James Johnson is a sole trader. His business has grown rapidly over the last few years and he has asked John Jameson to become a partner in his firm. Jameson has agreed, but he has said that he will only become a partner if the books are properly audited every year. James asks you why John might want an audit and what advantages it could bring to the business.

Required

Answer the queries raised by James Johnson.

Solution

     (a)   John might decide that an audit is desirable because James has been in charge alone for a long time. John needs someone who is objective and can understand the accounting records to reassure him that the business is producing the results claimed by James. The other reasons for such a request are reflected in part (b).

     (b)   The advantages of an audit for a partnership include the following.

         (i)   Any weaknesses in the accounting system of the business would be highlighted and improvements to the system would be suggested by the auditor. These could save both time and money.

         (ii)   Arguments between the partners would be avoided if the accounts are checked by an independent auditor. This will be case particularly in the calculation of the partners' profit shares.

         (iii)   Third parties who have an interest in the accounts will find them more convincing if they are audited. Examples of such third parties will include Customs and Excise, the Inland Revenue and bankers and other potential sources of finance or credit.

---

3   INTERNAL AUDIT

3.1   There are several 'official' definitions of an internal audit. The Institute of Internal Auditors, the professional body of internal auditors, defines the process as follows.

> 'Internal auditing is an independent appraisal function established within an organisation to examine and evaluate its activities as a service to the organisation. The objective of internal auditing is to assist members of the organisation in the effective discharge of their responsibilities. To this end internal auditing furnishes them with analysis, appraisals, recommendations, counsel and information concerning the activities reviewed.'

3.2   The CIMA's Official Terminology defines an audit as a systematic examination of the activities and status of an entity based primarily on investigation and analysis of its systems, controls and records. Internal audit is now defined as per the Institute of Internal Auditors, but the CIMA's own definition used to be:

> 'an independent appraisal activity established within a organisation as a service to it. It is a control which functions by examining and evaluating the adequacy and effectiveness of other controls'. It analyses 'the effectiveness of all parts of an entity's operations and management'.

3.3   You should note that these definitions suggest that internal audit has a much wider scope than external audit. External auditors need *only* consider whether a company's accounts give a true and fair view of its financial position. They need not comment in their audit reports on ways in which the company's results or controls could be improved. Contrary to popular belief, it is also not their responsibility to detect fraud; they are merely obliged to plan their audit tests so that they have a reasonable expectation of detecting fraud. It is the responsibility of the *directors* to set up an adequate system of internal control, which should deter and expose fraud. Internal audit is one type of internal control.

3.4   The functions of an internal audit department are well summarised in a Statement of Auditing Standards *Considering the Work of Internal Audit,* issued by the Auditing Practices Board in March 1995.

'The scope and objectives of internal audit vary widely and depend on the size and structure of the entity and the requirements of its management and directors. Generally internal audit activities include one or more of the following:

(a)   review of the accounting and internal control systems: the establishment of adequate accounting and internal control systems is a responsibility of management and the directors which demands proper attention on a continuous basis. Often, internal audit is assigned specific responsibility for reviewing the design of the systems, monitoring their operation and recommending improvements thereto;

(b)   examination of financial and operating information: this may include review of the means used to identify, measure, classify and report such information and specific enquiry into individual items including detailed testing of transactions, balances and procedures;

(c)   review of the economy, efficiency and effectiveness of operations including non-financial controls of an organisation;

(d)   review of compliance with laws, regulations and other external requirements and with internal policies and directives and other requirements including appropriate authorisation of transactions; and

(e)   special investigations into particular areas, for example suspected fraud.'

3.5   From the definitions of the internal audit the two main features of internal audit emerge.

(a)   *Independence*. Although an internal audit department is part of an organisation, it should be independent of the line management whose sphere of authority it may audit. The department should therefore report to the board or to a special internal audit committee and not to the finance director. The reason for this is best seen by thinking about what could happen if the internal audit department reported some kind of irregularity to a finance director without realising that the finance director was actually involved. The director would take the report and decide that it was all very interesting, but not worth pursuing. A very different line might be taken by another, independent director!

It is also important that internal auditors should have appropriate scope in carrying out their responsibilities, and unrestricted access to records, assets and personnel.

'In the ideal situation, the internal audit function reports to the highest level of management but also has a direct line of communication to the entity's main board or audit committee and is free of any other operating responsibility.'

(b)   *Appraisal*. Internal audit is concerned with the appraisal of work done by other people in the organisation, and internal auditors should not carry out any of the work themselves. The appraisal of operations provides a service to management, providing information on strengths and weaknesses throughout the organisation. Such information is invaluable to management when it comes to taking action to improve performance, or planning future activities of the company.

3.6   However, these broad descriptions are fairly vague: what is missing is a definition of just what 'a review of activities as a service to all levels of management' entails - in other words, what exactly are the *objectives* of internal audit?

Objectives of internal audit

3.7   After giving its broad definition, the Institute of Internal Auditors goes on to state the following.

> 'The objective of internal auditing is to assist members of the organisation in the effective discharge of their responsibilities. To this end internal auditing furnishes them with analyses, appraisals, recommendations, counsel and information concerning the activities reviewed.'

3.8   Internal audit is an important element of management control, as it is a tool used to ensure that all financial and any other internal controls are working satisfactorily. Internal auditors will investigate systems within the organisation, identify any weaknesses or scope for improvement, and make recommendations to the 'line' managers responsible for the system that they have audited.

Differences between internal and external audit

3.9   There are three main differences between internal and external audit.

(a)   *Appointment.* External auditors are appointed by the shareholders (although they are usually only ratifying the directors' choice) and must be independent of the company, whereas internal auditors are employees of the organisation.

(b)   *Responsibility.* External auditors are responsible to the owners (ie shareholders, the public or Parliament), whereas internal auditors are responsible to senior management.

(c)   *Objectives.* The objectives for external auditors are defined by statute, whereas those for internal auditors are set by management. In other words, management - perhaps the internal auditors themselves - decide what parts of the organisation or what systems they are going to look at, and what type of audit should be carried out for example a systems audit, or a value for money audit.

Essential elements of internal audit

3.10   In addition to the need for *independence* several other essential elements of internal audit have been identified.

(a)   *Staffing and training*

(i)   The internal audit department should possess or have access to all the necessary skills for performing its function. It must be adequately staffed, and staff are likely to be drawn from a variety of disciplines.

(ii)   Internal audit staff should be given the training to carry out their work competently.

(b)   *Relationships*

Without surrendering their objectivity, internal auditors should try to establish good working relationships and mutual understanding with:

(i)   management;
(ii)   external auditors;
(iii) if there is one, the organisation's auditing committee.

Internal audit plans should be discussed with senior management, individual audits should be arranged in consultation with the management concerned, and audit reports should be discussed with the management when they are being prepared.

Internal auditors should have regular meetings with the external auditors (who may be able to place reliance on some of the work done by the internal auditors). They should discuss their audit plans, so as to avoid unnecessary overlaps in their work.

(c) *Due care*

Internal auditors should exercise due care in fulfilling their responsibilities. The chief internal auditor should ensure that his staff maintain standards of integrity and of adequate quality in their work.

(d) *Planning, controlling and recording*

Internal auditors should plan, control and record their work.

(e) *Evidence*

Internal auditors should obtain sufficient, relevant and reliable evidence on which to base reasonable conclusions and recommendations.

Deciding just what evidence will be needed for any particular audit work calls for judgement by the auditors, with their judgement having regard to:

(i)   the scope of the audit assignment;
(ii)   the significance of the matters under review;
(iii) just what evidence is available and obtainablc;
(iv)   what it would cost and how long it would take to obtain.

(f) *Reporting*

Internal auditors should report their findings, conclusions and recommendations promptly to management.

'The chief internal auditor should ensure that reports are sent to managers who have a direct responsibility for the unit or function being audited and who have the authority to take corrective action.'

If the internal auditors find evidence of a serious weakness or malpractice, this should be reported immediately, orally or in writing, as soon as it is discovered, in an 'interim report'.

The internal auditors, having made recommendations in their report, should subsequently follow up their work by checking to see whether their recommendations have been implemented by management.

Auditing standards and guidelines

3.11 In the remainder of this chapter we will occasionally refer to auditing standards and guidelines. These have been issued by the Auditing Practices Board (APB) and its forerunner the Auditing Practices Committee (APC), largely for the benefit of external auditors. However, many can be applied to internal audit and used to define 'best practice'. For example, a guideline on internal control will tell a business what type of internal control they should have, and external auditors what type of internal control they should expect to find.

3.12 Do not worry about remembering the names of specific auditing standards or guidelines, or whether they were produced by the APB or the APC. The examiner has said quite categorically that you do not need to know the detailed content of auditing standards and guidelines. However, to understand internal auditing you will need a general understanding of the principles contained in such standards and guidelines.

4   INTERNAL CONTROL SYSTEMS   5/96

4.1 One of the main tasks of the internal auditors is to check the operational 'systems' within their organisation, to find out whether the system's *internal controls* are sufficient and are working properly. If they are not, it is the auditors' task to recommend improvements.

4.2 Internal audit thus acts as an internal control over other internal controls in the systems that are audited.

So what are the other 'internal controls' in a system that the internal auditors may wish to investigate?

4.3   An internal control system is defined by guidance of the Committee on the Financial Aspects of Corporate Governance (Cadbury Committee) as:

'the whole system of controls, financial and otherwise, established in order to provide reasonable assurance of:

(a)   effective and efficient operations;

(b)   internal financial control; and

(c)   compliance with laws and regulations.'

4.4   The Cadbury Code is concerned with the financial aspects of corporate governance and thus principally with 'internal financial control'. This is defined as:

'the internal controls established in order to provide reasonable assurance of:

(a)   the safeguarding of assets against unauthorised use or disposition; and

(b)   the maintenance of proper accounting records and the reliability of financial information used within the business or for publication.'

4.5   These definitions are fairly broad, and a more comprehensive list of the range of internal controls which may exist in an organisation is given in the appendix to the old guideline of the Auditing Practices Committee *Internal Controls*. There are eight types of control listed (one way of remembering them is to use the mnemonic SPAM SOAP).

S egregation of duties
P hysical
A uthorisation and approval
M anagement
S upervision
O rganisation
A rithmetical and accounting
P ersonnel

4.6   *Segregation of duties*. The APC stated: 'one of the prime means of control is the separation of those responsibilities or duties which would, if combined, enable one individual to record and process a complete transaction. Segregation of duties reduces the risk of intentional manipulation or error and increases the element of checking. Functions which should be separated include those of authorisation, execution, custody, recording and, in the case of a computer-based accounting system, systems development and daily operations.'

4.7   A classic example of segregation of duties, which both internal and external auditors look for, concerns the receipt, recording and banking of cash. It is not a good idea for the person who opens the post (and 'receives' the cash) to be the person responsible for recording that the cash has arrived - and even poorer practice for him to be the person responsible for taking the cash to the bank. If these duties are not segregated, there is always the chance that he will simply pocket the cash, and nobody would be any the wiser. Dividing the duties so that no one person carries all these responsibilities is therefore a form of internal control, in this case helping to safeguard cash receipts.

4.8   *Physical*. These internal controls were defined by the APC as being 'concerned mainly with the custody of assets and involve procedures and security measures designed to ensure that access to assets is limited to authorised personnel. This includes both direct access and indirect access via documentation. These controls assume importance in the case of valuable, portable, exchangeable or desirable assets.'

4.9   *Authorisation and approval*. The APC stated: 'all transactions should require authorisation or approval by an appropriate responsible person. The limits for these authorisations should be specified.'

4.10   For example, a company might set the rule that the head of a particular department may authorise revenue expenditure up to £500, but that for anything more expensive he must seek the approval of a director. Such authorisation limits will vary from company to company: £500 could be quite a large amount for a small company, but seem insignificant to a big one.

4.11   *Management*. The APC stated: 'these are the controls exercised by management outside the day-to-day routine of the system. They include the overall supervisory controls exercised by management, the review of management accounts and comparison thereof with budgets, the internal audit function and any other special review procedures.'

4.12   *Supervision*. The APC stated: 'any system of internal control should include the supervision by responsible officials of day-to-day transactions and the recording thereof.'

4.13   *Organisation*. As stated by the APC: 'enterprises should have a plan of their organisation, defining and allocating responsibilities and identifying lines of reporting for all aspects of the enterprise's operations, including the controls. The delegation of authority and responsibility should be clearly specified.'

4.14   For example, it could happen that an employee in a company finds himself working for two masters, say a product manager (who is responsible for the production, marketing and profitability of one particular product) and a sales manager (who supervises the company sales policy for all products). A company which is organised in this overlapping fashion is said to have a matrix organisation. The point here is that the employee might be confused. He might not know who he is supposed to be working for at any one time; he might not know his priorities; he might work harder for one manager at the expense of the other. Such a state of affairs would be detrimental to the company, so it is sensible to set clear lines of authority and responsibility - in short, the company should utilise organisational controls.

4.15   *Arithmetical and accounting*. The APC stated: 'these are the controls within the recording function which check that the transactions to be recorded and processed have been authorised, that they are all included and that they are correctly recorded and accurately processed. Such controls include checking the arithmetical accuracy of the records, the maintenance and checking of totals, reconciliations, control accounts and trial balances, and accounting for documents.'

4.16   *Personnel*. This last type of internal control was defined by APC as:

> 'procedures to ensure that personnel have capabilities commensurate with their responsibilities. Inevitably, the proper functioning of any system depends on the competence and integrity of those operating it. The qualifications, selection and training as well as the innate personal characteristics of the personnel involved are important features to be considered in setting up any control system.'

4.17   As an example, a company accountant should be suitably qualified. It is no good asking somebody to produce a set of financial statements if he does not know a profit and loss account from a balance sheet. Nowadays, 'qualified' tends to mean someone who possesses a professional qualification of some sort, but it is important to remember that others are still able to do a job because of work experience - they are 'qualified' through that experience.

Internal control system

4.18   A company's operational systems (eg its purchasing system, its stock control system, its sales system, its capital expenditure planning system, its computerised management information systems etc etc) will incorporate some internal controls from the SPAM SOAP list above. The controls that there are will depend on the particular circumstances of the company, but the range of internal controls it ends up with is called the company's or the system's *internal control system*.

4.19 An operational system need not possess *all* of the SPAM SOAP internal controls - or indeed the organisation may not be able to implement all of them, perhaps because they would be too expensive and so not worth having. For example, a very small organisation may have insufficient staff to be able to organise a desirable level of segregation of duties.

4.20 Management has the responsibility for deciding what internal controls there should be. The internal auditors contribute to internal controls by measuring and evaluating the other internal controls installed by management and reporting to management on their effectiveness.

Administrative controls and accounting controls

4.21 It may also be useful to distinguish between administrative controls and accounting controls.

(a) *Administrative controls* are concerned with achieving the objectives of the organisation and with implementing policies. The controls relate to:

(i)   establishing a suitable organisation structure;
(ii)   the division of managerial authority;
(iii) reporting responsibilities;
(iv)   channels of communication.

(b) *Accounting controls* aim to provide accurate accounting records and to achieve accountability. They apply to:

(i)   the recording of transactions;
(ii)   establishing responsibilities for records, transactions and assets.

Accounting controls are applied to procedures/assets and liabilities such as cash and cheques, stocks, sales and debtors, purchases and creditors, fixed assets, investments, capital expenditure, and debt capital and equity.

Detect controls and prevent controls

4.22 Yet another way of analysing internal controls is to distinguish between detect controls and prevent controls.

(a) *Detect controls* are controls that are designed to detect errors once they have happened.

(b) *Prevent controls* are controls that are designed to prevent errors from happening in the first place.

4.23 Examples of detect controls in an accounting system are bank reconciliations and regular checks of physical stocks against book records of stocks.

4.24 Examples of prevent controls are as follows.

(a) Checking invoices from suppliers against goods received notes before paying the invoices.

(b) Regular checking of delivery notes against invoices, to ensure that all deliveries have been invoiced.

(c) Signing of goods received notes, credit notes, overtime records etc, to confirm that goods have actually been received, credit notes properly issued, overtime actually authorised and worked etc.

Auditing internal controls

4.25 Internal auditors should check internal controls in two ways.

(a) First, they should establish what internal controls there are, and whether these are sufficient or whether they should be improved.

(b) Secondly, they should check whether the internal controls that exist are working properly. They will obtain evidence that controls exist and are working properly by means of verification procedures.

4.26 If an internal auditors notice that a control is absent or weak or not properly applied, then the should report it to senior management, who will probably ask for an assessment of the risk involved. It is then the responsibility of management to decide whether the risk is acceptable, or whether to take action on the missing or inadequate control.

4.27 Conversely, no internal control system is foolproof. In fact, Statement of Auditing Standards 300, issued by the APB in March 1995, specifically makes this point.

'An internal control system can only provide the directors with reasonable confidence that their objectives are reached because of inherent limitations such as:

(a) the usual requirement that the cost of an internal control is not disproportionate to the potential loss which may result from its absence;

(b) most systematic internal controls tend to be directed at routine transactions rather than non-routine transactions;

(c) the potential for human error due to carelessness, distraction, mistakes of judgement and the misunderstanding of instructions;

(d) the possibility of circumvention of internal controls through collusion with parties outside or inside the entity;

(e) the possibility that a person responsible for exercising an internal control could abuse that responsibility, for example by overriding an internal control; and

(f) the possibility that procedures may become inadequate due to changes in conditions or that compliance with procedures may deteriorate over time.'

Practical aspects of internal control

4.28 For the purpose of your examination, you might need to specify the types of controls you would expect to find in certain areas of operations, for example:

(a) cash and cheques;
(b) wages and salaries;
(c) purchases and creditors;
(d) sales and debtors;
(e) fixed assets;
(f) investments.

These are all financial systems, but internal audit can apply to any other system, eg management information systems or decision making systems. Controls over sales/debtors and purchases/creditors will be considered below.

Controls over sales and debtors

4.29 There are three separate elements into which accounting controls may be divided. They are selling (authorisation), goods outwards (custody) and accounting (recording).

4.30 *Selling:* considerations include the following.

(a) What arrangements are to be made to ensure that goods are sold at their correct price and to deal with and check exchanges, discounts and special reductions including those in connection with cash sales.

(b) Who is to be responsible for, and how control is to be maintained over, the granting of credit terms to customers.

(c)   Who is to be responsible for accepting customers' orders and what procedure is to be adopted for issuing production orders and despatch notes.

(d)   Who is to be responsible for the preparation of invoices and credit notes and what controls are to be instituted to prevent errors and irregularities (for instance, how selling prices are to be ascertained and authorised, how the issue of credit notes is to be controlled and checked, what checks there should be on prices, quantities, extensions and totals shown on invoices and credit notes, and how such documents in blank or completed form are to be protected against loss or misuse).

(e)   What special controls are to be exercised over the despatch of goods free of charge or on special terms.

4.31   *Goods outwards:* factors to be considered include the following.

(a)   Who may authorise the despatch of goods and how is such authority evidenced.

(b)   What arrangements are to be made to examine and record goods outwards (preferably this should be done by a person who has no access to stocks and has no accounting or invoicing duties).

(c)   The procedure to be instituted for agreeing goods outwards records with customers' orders, despatch notes and invoices.

4.32   *Accounting:* so far as possible sales ledger staff should have no access to cash, cash books or stocks, and should not be responsible for invoicing and other duties normally assigned to sales staff. The following are amongst matters which should be considered.

(a)   The appointment of persons as far as possible separately responsible for:

(i)   recording sales and sales returns;
(ii)   maintaining customers' accounts;
(iii)   preparing debtors' statements.

(b)   The establishment of appropriate control procedures in connection with sales returns, price adjustments and similar matters

(c)   Arrangements to ensure that goods dispatched but not invoiced (or vice versa) during an accounting period are properly dealt with in the accounts of the periods concerned (cut-off procedures).

(d)   The establishment of arrangements to deal with sales to companies or branches forming part of the same group.

(e)   What procedures are to be adopted for the preparation, checking and despatch of debtors' statements and for ensuring that they are not subject to interference before despatch.

(f)   How discounts granted and special terms are to be authorised and evidenced.

(g)   Who is to deal with customers' queries arising in connection with statements.

(h)   What procedure is to be adopted for reviewing and following up overdue accounts.

(i)   Who is to authorise the writing off of bad debts, and how such authority is to be evidenced.

(j)   The institution of a sales control account and its regular checking preferably by an independent official against customers' balances on the sales ledger.

Controls over purchases and creditors

4.33   There are also three separate elements into which accounting controls may be divided in the consideration of purchase procedures. They are buying (authorisation), receipt of goods (custody) and accounting (recording).

4.34   *Buying:* factors to be considered include the following.

(a) The procedure to be followed when issuing requisitions for additions to and replacement of stocks, and the persons to be responsible for such requisitions.

(b) The preparation and authorisation of purchase orders (including procedures for authorising acceptance where tenders have been submitted or prices quoted).

(c) The institution of checks for the safe-keeping of order forms and safeguarding their use.

(d) As regards capital items, any special arrangements as to authorisations required.

4.35   *Goods inwards:* factors to be considered include the following.

(a) Arrangements for examining goods inwards as to quantity, quality and condition; and for evidencing such examination.

(b) The appointment of a person responsible for accepting goods, and the procedure for recording and evidencing their arrival and acceptance.

(c) The procedure to be instituted for checking goods inwards records against authorised purchase orders.

4.36   *Accounting:* factors to be considered include the following.

(a) The appointment of persons so far as possible separately responsible for:

    (i)   checking suppliers' invoices;
    (ii)   recording purchases and purchase returns;
    (iii)   maintaining suppliers' ledger accounts or similar records;
    (iv)   checking suppliers' statements;
    (v)   authorising payment.

(b) Arrangements to ensure that before accounts are paid:

    (i)   the goods concerned have been received, accord with the purchase order, are properly priced and correctly invoiced;

    (ii)   the expenditure has been properly allocated; and

    (iii)   payment has been duly authorised by the official responsible.

Exercise 2

You should get into the habit of thinking about the accounting and other systems you have come across at work (or which your friends and colleagues have worked with) and trying to spot the internal controls.

Ask yourself two questions.

(a) What could go wrong?

(b) How could these problems be prevented and, if not prevented, detected (cost-effectively)?

Evaluation of internal controls

4.37   The evaluation of internal controls within a system comes from the following sources.

(a) *System documentation:* ie deciding how the system works, and describing this 'on paper'.

(b) *Identification of potential errors:* ie recognising what can go wrong in this system.

Potential errors can arise whenever there is a chance that one of the following objectives might not be achieved or satisfied.

    (i)   Existence or occurrence - ie proof that something exists or has happened

    (ii)   Completeness - ie that an account balance contains every item that it should

(iii)   Valuation or measurement - ie that a proper system of valuation has been used

(iv)   Ownership - ie proof of ownership of assets

(v)   Disclosure - ie that items are disclosed whenever disclosure is appropriate

(c)   *Identification of controls:* ie recognising the controls within the system that are designed to detect or prevent errors in the system.

4.38   Having identified potential errors and the controls to detect or prevent them, the auditors can assess whether the controls appear to be good enough to do their job sufficiently well.

4.39   When a control is evaluated, the auditors must assess the level of 'risk' that the control is inadequate or might not be properly applied. Factors to consider include the following.

(a)   The nature of the control itself

(b)   The timing and frequency of the control check

(c)   Who performs the control, taking into consideration the competence, experience and integrity of staff, and the degree of supervision

(d)   What errors the control has succeeded in identifying and eliminating in the past

(e)   Whether there have been changes in the system or in staff, bearing in mind that control procedures might weaken and become slack in the early period of a new system or just after a change of staff

5   AUDIT TRAIL

5.1   In general terms an audit trail is a means by which an auditor can follow through a transaction from its origin to its ultimate location or vice versa. In a manual accounting system an audit trail is created by preserving hard copy evidence of transactions with the hard copy of various documents being preserved and stored for future checking or evidence if required.

5.2   An example of and audit trail for purchases would be a collection of documents and records beginning with the purchase order issued by a business and allowing the auditors to trace that order through all the records into the purchases or cost of sales figure in the profit and loss account. The intermediate records might include the goods received note, the purchase invoice, the purchase day book and the purchases account.

5.3   An audit trail such as that described above can be used by both internal and external auditors 'in both directions', depending on the auditors' objective. Thus the auditors can start with a sales order and trace it through to 'sales' in the profit and loss account or can trace a sale from the profit and loss account back through the sales account, the sales day book, the sales invoice and the despatch note to the sales order.

5.4   Special considerations apply to computerised accounting systems which are, of course, the majority. For the purposes of computerised systems an audit trail may be defined slightly differently as:

'...a record of the file updating which takes place during a specific transaction. It enables a trace to be kept of all operations on files' *(Glossary of Computing Terms of the British Computer Society)*

5.5   An audit trail should ideally be provided so that every transaction on a file contains a unique reference back to the original source of the input, for example, a sales system transaction record should hold a reference to the customer order, delivery note and invoice. Where master file records are updated several times, or from several sources, the provision of a satisfactory audit trail is more difficult but some attempt should nevertheless be made to provide one.

5.6   CIPFA, in its *Computer audit guidelines*, comments as follows.

> 'In a computer system the audit trail will not always be apparent as it would be in a manual system, as the data is often retained only on magnetic media and is a form that is intelligible only to the computer programs designed to access it.
>
> There may be occasions when the audit trail is not readily visible.
>
> (a)   Output may be limited to a summary of items processed, thus making it impossible to trace an individual transaction right through the system from input to final resting place.
>
> (b)   Magnetic storage devices may be updated by over-writing the equivalent record with the result brought about by the newly input data, thus making visible reconciliation of start, change and finish position impossible.
>
> (c)   Reports may be on an exception basis only.
>
> Though such occasions may arise it should be remembered that though individual transactions are not visibly traceable through the system, the existence of adequate processing controls will ensure that at least an overall reconciliation of records/transactions input and processed can be made....
>
> The auditor may therefore have to be satisfied with a trail which, while not visible in detail, is nevertheless reconcilable throughout the system.'

6   THE DETECTION AND PREVENTION OF FRAUD

6.1   Give an employee responsibility, and he may manage the resources under his control dishonestly. The incidence of financial fraud, particularly in a computer environment, is increasing fast. This trend, together with the increasing sophistication of fraudsters, creates difficult problems for management and for internal auditors.

6.2   The mere presence of internal auditors will serve to discourage fraudsters for fear of being discovered, but the public's expectations go much further. Recently the Minister for Corporate and Consumer Affairs called on the whole accountancy profession to be 'the front line of the public's defences against fraud'.

6.3   The profession has responded in a number of ways, not least the issue of the Auditing Practices Board's Statement of Auditing Standards *Fraud and error* (January 1995).

6.4   Everyone has their own idea of where an acceptable bending of the rules ends and fraud begins, so it is appropriate to start with a definition of fraud. In *Derry v Peek*, fraud was defined as: 'a false representation of fact made with the knowledge of its falsity, or without belief in its truth, or recklessly careless, whether it be true or false'.

6.5   The auditing guideline concerns financial fraud, and the definition runs as follows.

> 'The word 'irregularities' is used to refer to intentional distortions of financial statements, for whatever purpose, and to misappropriations of assets, whether or not accompanied by distortions of financial statements. Fraud is one type of irregularity. The word 'fraud' is used to refer to irregularities involving the use of criminal deception to obtain an unjust or illegal advantage.'

6.6   The auditors will best be able to detect frauds if they are knowledgeable (not experienced!) in the most common methods of fraud. These are as follows.

(a)   Ghost employees on the payroll
(b)   Miscasting of the payroll
(c)   Stealing unclaimed wages
(d)   Collusion with external parties

(e)   Teeming and lading
(f)   Altering cheques after signature
(g)   Inflating expense claims
(h)   Using the company's assets for personal gain
(i)   Stealing fully depreciated assets
(j)   Issuing false credit notes or fraudulently writing off debts
(k)   Failing to record all sales

6.7   *Ghost employees.* These are imaginary employees for whom the wages department prepare wage packets which are distributed amongst the fraudsters. This type of fraud arises when there is extensive reliance on casual workers, and minimal record keeping for such workers. Inflated overtime claims can also result from poor time recording systems. Such frauds can be detected from a review of the numbers of employees required to achieve a standard amount of work. If at some times of the year, a larger number appear to be required, there may be something amiss. Scrutiny of signatures given as proof of receipt of wages should also be made.

6.8   *Miscasting of the payroll.* This fraud often succeeds due to its simplicity. If there are twenty employees, each to be paid £100, then the computer program for the payroll could be adjusted so that an extra £50 is added to the total added up for the amounts to be paid. Thus management approve a payment of £2,050 for the period's wages, each employee gets his £100 and the fraudster collects his extra £50. Manual payroll systems can be manipulated in a similar way. When employees are paid in cash, this type of fraud can be hard to trace and all too easy to perpetrate.

6.9   Stealing *unclaimed wages* is also common. This is effectively confined to wages paid in cash and can occur when an employee leaves without notice or is away sick. In the case of a subsequent claim for unpaid wages, it could be claimed that the cash in the original pay packet was paid back into the bank.

6.10 *Collusion with external parties* could involve suppliers, customers or their staff. Possible frauds are overcharging on purchase invoices, undercharging on sales invoices or the sale of confidential information (eg customer lists, expansion plans) to a competitor. Management should watch out for unusual discounts or commissions being given or taken, or for an excessive zeal on the part of an employee to handle all business with a particular company.

6.11 *Teeming and lading* is a 'rolling' fraud rather than a 'one-off' fraud. It occurs when a clerk has the chance to misappropriate payments from debtors or to creditors. Cash received by the company is borrowed by the cashier rather than being kept as petty cash or banked. (It is also possible, although riskier and more difficult to organise, to misappropriate cheques made payable to the company.) When the cashier knows that a reconciliation is to be performed, or audit visit planned, he pays the money back so that everything appears satisfactory at that point, but after the audit the teeming and lading starts again. Surprise visits by auditors and independent checking of cash balances should discourage this fraud.

6.12 A common fraud arising when one employee has sole control of the sales ledger and recording debtors' cheques is to pay cheques into a separate bank account, either by forged endorsement or by opening an account in a name similar to the employer's.

6.13 The clerk has to allocate cheques or cash received from other debtors against the account of the debtor whose payment was misappropriated. This prevents other staff from asking why the account is still overdue or from sending statements etc to the debtors. However, the misallocation has to continue as long as the money is missing. This fraud, therefore, never really stops. It can be detected by independent verification of debtors balances (eg by writing to them) and by looking at unallocated payments, if the sales ledger is organised to show this. In addition, sending out itemised monthly statements to debtors should act as a deterrent, although in a really elaborate fraud the clerk may be keeping two sets of books, so that the statements show the debtor's own analysis of amounts due and paid off in the month, but do not agree with the books.

6.14   *Altering cheques* and *inflating expense claims* are self-explanatory.

6.15   *Using the company's assets for personal gain* and *stealing fully depreciated assets* are both encountered in practice. Whether or not the private use of company telephones and photocopiers is a serious matter is up to the company to judge, but it may still be fraudulent. More serious examples include the sale by employees of unused time on the computer, which is a growing fraud.

6.16   Another way of avoiding detection when cash and cheques received from debtors have been misappropriated is to *issue a credit note* which is not sent to the customer (who has paid his account) but is recorded in the books. Again, the issue of itemised statements monthly should show this up, as the customer would query the credit note. However, any company with sufficiently lax controls to allow one clerk both to receive and record cash and additionally to authorise and issue credit notes is unlikely to ensure that someone else issues and follows up statements. A similar tactic is to *write a debt off* as bad to cover up the disappearance of the payment.

6.17   A very elaborate fraud may be perpetrated in a business with extremely poor controls over sales recording and minimal segregation of duties. In such circumstances, a dishonest bookkeeper may invoice customers but fail to record the invoices so that the customer's payments never have to be recorded and the misappropriation is not missed. This type of fraud can occur where a customer is receiving large numbers of invoices from the business every month and so the bookkeeper's failure to record one or two invoices (if detected by auditors or his superiors) is simply put down to incompetence rather than fraud. A warning sign here is the perception by customers that 'your accounts department is a mess ... always getting things wrong ... we've given up trying to get out account right...'.

The role of the internal auditors

6.18   The internal auditors should start their work by identifying the areas of the business most susceptible to fraud. These will include areas where cash is involved, and the other areas where the auditors' judgement is that the internal controls are insufficient to safeguard the assets. The existence of a properly functioning system of internal controls will diminish the incidence of frauds, so the auditors' opinion on the internal control system is of fundamental importance.

6.19   Whenever a fraud is discovered, they should judge whether a weakness in internal controls has been highlighted, and if so what changes are needed.

Prevention of fraud

6.20   Fraud will only be prevented successfully if potential fraudsters perceive the risk of detection as being high, and if personnel are adequately screened before employment and given no incentive to turn against the company once employed. The following safeguards should therefore be implemented.

(a)   A good internal control system
(b)   Continuous supervision of all employees
(c)   Surprise audit visits
(d)   Thorough personnel procedures

6.21   The work of employees must be monitored as this will increase the perceived risk of being discovered. Actual results must regularly be compared against budgeted results, and employees should be asked to explain significant variances.

6.22   Surprise audit visits are a valuable contribution to preventing fraud. If a cashier is carrying out a teeming and lading fraud and is told that an audit visit is due the following week, he may be able to square up the books before the visit so that the auditors will find nothing wrong. But if the threat of a surprise visit is constantly present, the cashier will not be able to carry out a teeming and lading fraud without the risk of being discovered, and this risk is usually sufficient to prevent the fraud. The auditors do not need to carry out any sophisticated audit tests during their surprise visit. There are stories of internal auditors arriving without warning, and taking all the books into a room of their own to read the newspaper for an hour - but the fraud deterrent effect on the employee is highly significant, because the employee thinks that every figure is being checked.

6.23   Finally, personnel procedures must be adequate to prevent the occurrence of frauds.

(a)   Whenever a fraud is discovered, the fraudster should be dismissed and the police should be informed. Too often an employee is 'asked to resign' and then moves on to a similar job where the fraud is repeated, often because management fear loss of face or investor confidence. This is a self-defeating policy.

(b)   All new employees should be required to produce adequate references from their previous employers.

(c)   If an employee's lifestyle changes dramatically, explanations should be sought.

(d)   Every employee must be made to take his annual holiday entitlement. Often in practice the employee who is 'so dedicated that he never takes a holiday' is in fact not taking his leave for fear of his fraud being discovered by his replacement worker while he is away.

(e)   Pay levels should be adequate and working conditions of a reasonable standard. If employees feel that they are being paid an unfairly low amount or 'exploited', they may look for ways to supplement their pay dishonestly.

Management fraud

6.24   So far, this chapter has concentrated on employee fraud. However, arguably more serious (and very much more difficult to prevent and detect) is the growing problem of management fraud. While employee fraud is usually undertaken purely for the employee's financial gain, management fraud is often undertaken to improve the company's apparent performance, to reduce tax liabilities or to improve manager's promotion prospects. Managers are often in a position to override internal controls and to intimidate their subordinates into collusion or turning a blind eye. This makes it difficult to detect such frauds. In addition, where the company is benefiting financially rather than the manager, it can be difficult to persuade staff that any dishonesty is involved. This clash of interest between loyalty to an employer and professional integrity can be difficult to resolve and can compromise an internal auditor's independence. Management fraud often comes to light after a take-over or on a change of audit staff or practices. Its consequences can be far reaching for the employing company in damaging its reputation or because it results in legal action. Because management usually have access to much larger sums of money than more lowly employees, the financial loss to the company can be immense.

Chapter roundup

- It is important to distinguish between external and internal auditors.

- *External auditors* report to the members of the company on whether in their opinion, the annual statutory accounts give a true and fair view. Their duties are imposed by statute and they are not employees of the company.

- *Internal auditors* are employees of the company whose duties are fixed by management and who report to management.

- Financial statements are obliged by the Companies Act 1985 to give a true and fair view. This phrase has proved problematic on occasions and is not clearly defined.

- The scope of an internal audit varies widely and may range from systems review to implementation of corporate policies, plans and processes.

- The essential elements of internal audit are as follows.

  - Independence
  - Staffing and training
  - Relationships
  - Due care
  - Planning, controlling and recording
  - Reporting

- Eight types of internal control have been identified. They can be remembered by using the mnemonic SPAM SOAP.

- An audit trail enables auditors to trace a transaction from beginning to end to verify that it has been processed completely and correctly.

- In auditing, detection of fraud is an important objective (but by no means the only objective). Auditors should be aware of the common types of fraud and should be particularly watchful when internal controls are poor, especially if an employee's expenditure appears to be inconsistent with his salary or if a department is performing unexpectedly badly.

Test your knowledge

1. What is meant by 'stewardship'? (see paras 1.1 - 1.3)

2. What is meant by 'true and fair'? (2.5, 2.6)

3. Internal auditors should not report to the finance director. Why not? (3.5)

4. The directors are the recipients of the external auditors' report. True or false? (3.9)

5. What is an internal control system? (4.3)

6. Why aim for segregation of duties? (4.6)

7. Give examples of detect and prevent controls and distinguish between the two terms.(4.22 - 4.24)

8. What is an audit trail? (5.1)

9. What controls over accounting would you (ideally) expect to find in a sales system?

10. What is teeming and lading? (6.11)

Now try illustrative question 39 at the end of the Study Text

Part D
Interpretation of accounts

Chapter 24

INTERPRETING COMPANY ACCOUNTS

This chapter covers the following topics.

		Syllabus reference	Ability required
1	The uses of ratio analysis	1(d)	Knowledge
2	Profit margin, asset turnover and return on capital employed	1(d)	Knowledge
3	Working capital	1(d)	Knowledge
4	Liquidity	1(d)	Knowledge
5	Gearing	1(d)	Knowledge
6	Items in company accounts formats	1(d)	Appreciation
7	Planning your answers	1(b),(d)	Appreciation

Introduction

So far your studies have concentrated on the *preparation* of accounts. This chapter focuses on *interpretation* primarily by means of ratio analysis.

The purpose of financial statement analysis is to provide data for decision making. The financial statements disclose the results of the activities of an entity and are prepared to help interested persons decide on questions such as whether to lend it money or invest in its shares. Financial statement analysis can be seen as part of the link between the financial statements and the decision making process.

It has already been mentioned (in Chapter 1) that the users of financial statements extend beyond present and potential shareholders and creditors and include such groups as employees, government bodies and society at large. We will not attempt to deal with the possible decision needs of each class of user - such a discussion would require a book of its own. Instead we will concentrate on two aspects of the entity that are relevant to all groups of users, namely its profitability, liquidity and gearing. The topics will be discussed in terms of limited companies, but it should be realised that most of the points will be relevant when examining the accounts of other business entries.

The penultimate section of this chapter is entitled 'items in company accounts formats'. This is not a topic in itself, but arises from your study and practice of limited company accounts and interpretation questions. Finally Section 7 gives advice on planning your answers.

1 THE USES OF RATIO ANALYSIS

1.1 The profit and loss account and the balance sheet are both sources of useful information about the condition of a business. The analysis and interpretation of these statements can be done by calculating certain ratios, between one item and another, and then using the ratios for *comparison*, in terms of profitability, liquidity and efficiency, either:

(a) between one year and the next for a particular business, in order to identify any trends, or significantly better or worse results than before; or

(b) between one business and another, to establish which business has performed better, and in what ways.

The most important ratios are described in this chapter.

1.2   When ratio analysis is used to assess the relative strength of a particular business, by comparing its profitability and financial stability with another business, the two businesses should be largely similar:

(a)   in size;

(b)   in their line of activities.

1.3   If the businesses are not broadly similar in size or in what they do, then differences revealed by ratio analysis might merely arise as a natural consequence of the size difference, or the varying lines of business they operate in. We do not need ratios to tell us that one business is larger, or that two businesses operate in entirely different industries!

1.4   Suppose for example, that we compared the results of a manufacturing company with the results of a company which operates a chain of hairdressing salons and beauty parlours.

(a)   The manufacturing company might specialise in undertaking large-scale contracts for major customers (eg shipbuilding, building telephone exchange equipment, defence contracts with the Ministry of Defence etc). These companies might operate so as to make a small profit percentage on a very large turnover - eg a profit of £1 million on a contract with a sales value of £20 million, say. In contrast, a service industry such as hairdressing and beautician service, might be more likely to derive a higher profit percentage, but on a lower total sales turnover.

(b)   The assets of the two companies would differ. Both might own freehold property, but the manufacturing company would have much larger amounts of fixed assets (plant and machinery, for example) and also much more stock-in-trade and debtors - since much shop business is paid for in cash.

1.5   Comparing the accounting ratios of the two businesses would be pointless, since the ratios would merely serve to inform us that the businesses are different, not that either business is less profitable or less financially stable than it should be.

2   PROFIT MARGIN, ASSET TURNOVER AND RETURN ON CAPITAL EMPLOYED   *11/95, 5/96*

2.1   There are three principal ratios which can be used to measure how the operations of a business have been managed. These are:

(a)   profit margin;

(b)   asset turnover;

(c)   return on capital employed.

2.2   *Profit margin.* This is the ratio of profit to sales, and may also be called 'profit percentage'. For example, if a company makes a profit of £20,000 on sales of £100,000 its profit percentage or profit margin is 20%. This also means that its costs are 80% of sales. A high profit margin indicates that:

(a)   *either* costs are being kept well under control because if the ratio of costs:sales goes down, the profit margin will automatically go up. For example, if the costs:sales ratio changes from 80% to 75%, the profit margin will go up from 20% to 25%.

(b)   *or* sales prices are high. For example, if a company sells goods for £100,000 and makes a profit of £16,000 costs would be £84,000 and the profit margin is 16%. Now if the company can raise selling prices by 20% to £120,000 without affecting the volume of goods sold or their costs, profits would rise by the amount of revenue increase (£20,000) to £36,000 and the profit margin would also rise (from 16% to 30%).

2.3   *Asset turnover*. This is the ratio of sales in a year to the amount of net assets (capital) employed. For example, if a company has sales in 19X4 of £720,000 and has assets of £360,000, the asset turnover will be:

$$\frac{£720,000}{£360,000} = 2 \text{ times.}$$

This means that for every £1 of assets employed, the company can generate sales turnover of £2 per annum. To utilise assets more efficiently, managers should try to create a higher volume of sales and so a higher asset turnover ratio. For example, suppose that our firm with assets of £360,000 can increase its sales turnover from £720,000 to £900,000 per annum. The asset turnover would improve to:

$$\frac{£900,000}{£360,000} = 2.5 \text{ times.}$$

The significance of this improvement is that if a business can create more sales turnover from the same amount of assets it should make larger profits (because of the increase in sales) without having to increase the size of its investment.

2.4   *Return on capital employed (ROCE)* is the amount of profit as a percentage of capital employed. If a company makes a profit of £30,000, we do not know how good or bad this profit is until we look at the amount of capital which has been invested to achieve the profit. £30,000 might be a good-sized profit for a small firm, but it would not be good enough for a 'giant' firm such as Marks and Spencer. For this reason, it is helpful to measure performance by relating profits to the amount of capital employed, and because this seems to be the *only* satisfactory ratio or percentage which judges profits in relation to the size of the business, it is sometimes called the *primary ratio* in financial analysis.

2.5   You may already have realised that there is a mathematical connection between return on capital employed, profit margin and asset turnover, since sales in the right-hand side of the equation below cancel out.

$$\frac{\text{Profit}}{\text{Capital employed}} = \frac{\text{Profit}}{\text{Sales}} \times \frac{\text{Sales}}{\text{Capital employed}}$$

$$\text{ROCE} = \text{Profit margin} \times \text{Asset turnover}$$

This is important. If we accept that ROCE is the most important single measure of business performance, comparing profit with the amount of capital invested, we can go on to say that business performance is dependent on two separate 'subsidiary' factors, each of which contributes to ROCE:

(a)   profit margin;
(b)   asset turnover.

For this reason, just as ROCE is sometimes called the *primary ratio*, the profit margin and asset turnover ratios are sometimes called the *secondary ratios*.

2.6   The implications of this relationship must be understood. Suppose that a return on capital employed of 20% is thought to be a good level of business performance in the retail trade for electrical goods.

(a)   Company A might decide to sell its products at a fairly high price and make a profit margin on sales of 10%. It would then need only an asset turnover of 2.0 times to achieve a ROCE of 20%:

$$20\% = 10\% \times 2$$

(b)   Company B might decide to cut its prices so that its profit margin is only 2½%. Provided that it can achieve an asset turnover of 8 times a year, attracting more customers with its lower prices, it will still make the desired ROCE:

$$20\% = 2\frac{1}{2}\% \times 8$$

2.7   Company A might be a department store and company B a discount warehouse. Each will have a different selling price policy, but each, in its own way, can be effective in achieving a target ROCE. In this example, if we supposed that both companies had capital employed of £100,000 and a target return of 20% or £20,000:

(a) Company A would need annual sales of £200,000 to give a profit margin of 10% and an asset turnover of 2 times:

$$\frac{£20,000}{£100,000} = \frac{£20,000}{£200,000} \times 2$$

(b) Company B would need annual sales of £800,000 to give a profit margin of only 2½% but an asset turnover of 8 times.

$$\frac{£20,000}{£100,000} = \frac{£20,000}{£800,000} \times 8$$

The inter-relationship between profit margin and asset turnover

2.8   A higher return on capital employed can be obtained by increasing the profit margin or the asset turnover ratio. The profit margin can be increased by reducing costs or by raising selling prices. However, if selling prices are raised, it is likely that sales demand will fall, with the possible consequence that the asset turnover will also decline. If higher prices mean lower sales turnover, the increase in profit margin might be offset by the fall in asset turnover, so that total return on capital employed might not improve.

Example: profit margin and asset turnover

2.9   Suppose that Swings and Roundabouts Ltd achieved the following results in 19X6.

Sales	£100,000
Profit	£5,000
Capital employed	£20,000

The company's management wish to decide whether to raise its selling prices. They think that if they do so, they can raise the profit margin to 10% and by introducing extra capital of £55,000, sales turnover would be £150,000.

Evaluate the decision in terms of the effect on ROCE, profit margin and asset turnover.

Solution

2.10   The current ratios are:

Profit margin (5/100)	5%
Asset turnover (100/20)	5 times
ROCE (5/20)	25%

With the proposed changes, the profit would be 10% × £150,000 = £15,000, and the asset turnover would be

$$\frac{£150,000}{£(20,000+55,000)} = 2 \text{ times, so that the ratios would be:}$$

Profit margin	×	Asset turnover	= ROCE
10%	×	2 times	$= 20\% \left(\dfrac{£15,000}{£75,000}\right)$

In spite of increasing the profit margin and raising the total volume of sales, the extra assets required (£55,000) only raise total profits by £(15,000 – 5,000) = £10,000.

The return on capital employed falls from 25% to 20% because of the sharp fall in asset turnover from 5 times to 2 times.

Whose return and whose capital employed?

2.11 Most of the providers of finance to a business expect some return on their investment.

(a) Trade creditors and most other current liabilities merely expect to be paid what they are owed.

(b) A bank charges interest on overdrafts.

(c) Interest must be paid to the holders of loan stock and debentures.

(d) Preference shareholders expect a dividend at a fixed percentage rate of the nominal value of their shares.

(e) Ordinary shareholders also expect a dividend. However, any retained profits kept in the business also represent funds 'owned' or 'provided' by them.

2.12 So when we refer to 'return' we must be clear in our mind about which providers of finance we are concerned with, and we should relate the return earned for those providers of finance to the amount of capital they are providing.

(a) If 'return' is the net profit of the sole trader, it is earned by the average capital invested by him over the accounting period.

(b) If 'return' is the net profit of a partnership, it is earned by the capital employed by the partners over the accounting period. However a partner's return might be his share of partnership profit earned by his own average capital employed over the accounting period (capital plus current account).

(c) If 'return' is profit after tax, it is return earned by ordinary and preference shareholders.

The capital employed by these investors is:

(i) the nominal value of preference shares;

(ii) the nominal value of ordinary shares;

(iii) the amount in the various reserves, because reserves are surpluses or profits retained in a business and 'owned' by the equity investors - the ordinary shareholders in a company.

(d) If 'return' is profit after tax and preference dividend, the left-over return is for ordinary shareholders, and is called '*earnings*'. The return on equity capital is:

$$\frac{\text{Earnings}}{\text{Ordinary share capital plus reserves}}$$

(e) If we prefer to consider the business as a whole, we need to measure capital employed as the value of all its assets, or as fixed assets plus net current assets (current assets minus current liabilities, which is the amount of *working capital employed*). Since some of those assets are financed by debt capital, the return on those assets must recognise the return earned for the providers of debt capital. For this reason, ROCE is often calculated, for the business entity as a whole, as:

$$\frac{\text{Profit before interest and tax}}{\text{Fixed assets plus net current assets}}$$

Example: ROCE

2.13 For example, suppose that Draught Ltd reports the following profit and loss account and balance sheet.

PROFIT AND LOSS ACCOUNT FOR 19X4 (EXTRACT)

	£
Profit before interest and tax	120,000
Interest	(20,000)
Profit before tax	100,000
Taxation	(40,000)
Profit after tax (earnings)	60,000
Ordinary dividend	(50,000)
Retained profits	10,000

BALANCE SHEET AT 31 DECEMBER 19X4

	£	£
Fixed assets: tangible assets		350,000
Current assets	400,000	
Less: current liabilities	(150,000)	
Net current assets		250,000
Total assets less current liabilities		600,000
Creditors: amounts falling due after more than one year:		
10% debenture loans		200,000
		400,000
Capital and reserves		
Called up share capital (ordinary shares of £1)		100,000
Profit and loss account		300,000
		400,000

2.14 The return on capital employed would usually be measured in one of two ways:

(a) $$\frac{\text{Profits after tax}}{\text{Assets financed by shareholders}} \times 100\%$$

Here, this would be $\dfrac{£60,000}{£400,000} \times 100\% = 15\%$

(b) $$\frac{\text{Profits before interest and tax}}{\text{Total assets less current liabilities}} \times 100\%$$

If assets financed by debt capital are included below the line, it is thought to be more appropriate to show profits before interest above the line because interest is the return on debt capital. Here we have:

$\dfrac{£120,000}{£600,000} \times 100\% = 20\%$

Examination formula

2.15 The CIMA *Guidance Notes* 1997-98 for the *Financial Accounting Fundamentals* paper make the following statement with regard to ROCE.

'In the examination candidates may be required to calculate the return on capital employed using the formula:

Net profit before tax and interest/average capital employed

where average capital employed includes long-term finance, but does not include short-term finance such as bank overdrafts. As additional guidance where questions do not include any long-term finance, then any mention of interest payable can be assumed to relate to short-term finance. Where questions include both short-term and long-term finance, the Examiner will clarify the content of any figure for interest payable.'

Exercise 1

Using the formula given in 2.15 above, calculate ROCE. Relevant figures as at 31 December 19X3 are as follows.

	£
10% debenture loans	200,000
Ordinary share capital	100,000
Profit and loss account	290,000
	590,000

Solution

Average capital employed = (590 + 600) ÷ 2 = £595,000

$$\text{ROCE} = \frac{120,000}{595,000} = 20.2\%$$

Earnings per share

2.16 In the previous example it is possible to calculate the return on each ordinary share in the year. This is the earnings per share (EPS). Earnings are profits after tax and preference dividend, which can either be paid out as a dividend to ordinary shareholders or retained in the business. Earnings are the total return for ordinary shareholders and for Draught Ltd in 19X4, the EPS is:

$$\frac{\pounds 60,000}{100,000 \text{ shares}} = 60 \text{ pence}$$

Capital employed: conclusion

2.17 Since capital employed can be defined in a variety of ways, you are advised to answer questions on ROCE with care. It is important to compare like with like.

Profitability and asset turnover

2.18 The profit:sales ratio and asset turnover ratio (assets:capital employed) can be analysed in more depth from information given in financial statements.

(a) Profitability can be analysed by measuring the ratio of various cost items to sales. For example:

(i) $\dfrac{\text{cost of sales}}{\text{sales}}$ and $\dfrac{\text{gross profit}}{\text{sales}}$

(ii) $\dfrac{\text{distribution costs}}{\text{sales}}$

and

(iii) $\dfrac{\text{administrative expenses}}{\text{sales}}$

Changes in these ratios over time, from year to year, might indicate that a certain aspect of the business operations (eg cost of sales, distribution costs, administration expenses) are becoming too expensive and so squeezing profits.

(b) Asset turnover can be further analysed, taking fixed assets and working capital separately.

(i) The fixed asset turnover ratio is:

$$\frac{\text{Sales}}{\text{Fixed assets}}$$

(ii) Working capital ratios are described separately later in the chapter.

3   WORKING CAPITAL

3.1   Working capital is the difference between current assets (mainly stocks, debtors and cash) and current liabilities (such as trade creditors and a bank overdraft).

Current assets are items which are either cash already, or which will soon lead to the receipt of cash. Stocks will be sold to customers and create debtors; and debtors will soon pay in cash for their purchases.

Current liabilities are items which will soon have to be paid for with cash. Trade creditors will have to be paid and bank overdraft is usually regarded as a short-term borrowing which may need to be repaid fairly quickly (or on demand, ie immediately).

In balance sheets, the word 'current' is applied to stocks, debtors, short-term investments and cash (current assets) and amounts due for payment within one year's time (current liabilities).

Working capital and trading operations

3.2   Current assets and current liabilities are a necessary feature of a firm's trading operations. There is a repeated cycle of buying and selling which is carried on all the time. For example, suppose that on 1 April a firm has the following items.

	£
Stocks	3,000
Debtors	0
Cash	2,000
	5,000
Creditors	0
Working capital	5,000

3.3   It might sell all the stocks for £4,500, and at the same time obtain more stock from suppliers at a cost of £3,500. The balance sheet items would now be:

	£
Stocks	3,500
Debtors	4,500
Cash	2,000
	10,000
Creditors	(3,500)
Working capital	6,500

(The increase in working capital to £6,500 from £5,000 is caused by the profit of £1,500 on the sale of the stocks.)

3.4   The debtors for £4,500 will eventually pay in cash and the creditors for £3,500 must also be paid. This would give us:

	£
Stocks	3,500
Debtors	0
Cash (2,000 + 4,500 – 3,500)	3,000
	6,500
Creditors	0
Working capital	6,500

3.5   However, if the stocks are sold on credit for £5,500 and further purchases of stock costing £6,000 are made, the cycle of trading will continue as follows:

	£
Stocks	6,000
Debtors	5,500
Cash	3,000
	14,500
Creditors	(6,000)
Working capital (boosted by further profit of £2,000)	8,500

From this basic example you might be able to see that working capital items are part of a continuous flow of trading operations. Purchases add to stocks and creditors at the same time, creditors must be paid and debtors will pay for their goods. The cycle of operations always eventually comes back to cash receipts and cash payments.

The operating cycle or cash cycle

3.6   The operating cycle (or cash cycle) is a term used to describe the connection between working capital and cash movements in and out. The cycle is usually measured in days or months.

3.7   A firm buys raw materials, probably on credit. The raw materials might be held for some time in stores before being issued to the production department and turned into an item of finished goods. The finished goods might be kept in a warehouse for some time before they are eventually sold to customers. By this time, the firm will probably have paid for the raw materials purchased. If customers buy the goods on credit, it will be some time before the cash from the sales is eventually received.

3.8   The cash cycle, or operating cycle, measures the period of time:

(a)   between the purchase of raw materials and the receipt of cash from debtors for goods sold; and

(b)   between the time cash is paid out for raw materials and the time cash is received in from debtors.

3.9   This cycle of repeating events may be shown diagramatically.

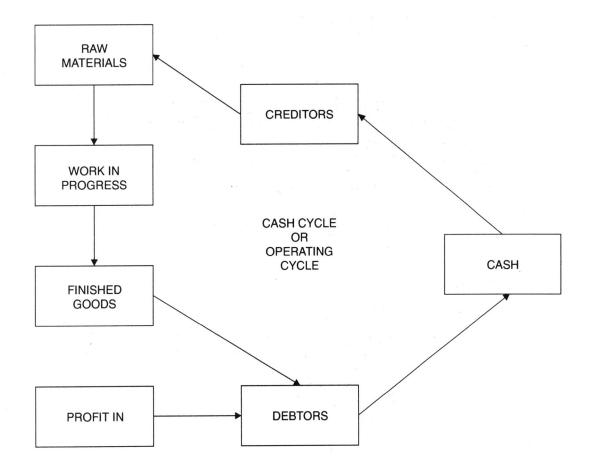

3.10 Suppose that a firm buys raw materials on 1½ months' credit, holds them in store for 1 month and then issues them to the production department. The production cycle is very short, but finished goods are held for 1 month before they are sold. Debtors take two months' credit. The cash cycle would be:

	Months
Raw material stock turnover period	1.0
Less: credit taken from suppliers	(1.5)
Finished goods stock turnover period	1.0
Debtor's payment period	2.0
Cash cycle	2.5

There would be a gap of 2½ months between paying cash for raw materials and receiving cash (including profits) from debtors.

3.11 A few dates might clarify this point. Suppose the firm purchases its raw materials on 1 January. The sequence of events would then be as follows.

	Date
Purchase of raw materials	1 Jan
Issue of materials to production (one month after purchase)	1 Feb
Payment made to suppliers (1½ months after purchase)	15 Feb
Sale of finished goods (one month after production begins)	1 Mar
Receipt of cash from debtors (two months after sale)	1 May

The cash cycle is the period of 2½ months from 15 February, when payment is made to suppliers, until 1 May, when cash is received from debtors.

Turnover periods

3.12 A 'turnover' period is an (average) length of time.

(a) In the case of stock turnover, it is the length of time an item of stock is held in stores before it is used.

  (i) A raw materials stock turnover period is the length of time raw materials are held before being issued to the production department.

  (ii) A work in progress turnover period is the length of time it takes to turn raw materials into finished goods in the factory.

  (iii) A finished goods stock turnover period is the length of time that finished goods are held in a warehouse before they are sold.

  (iv) When a firm buys goods and re-sells them at a profit, the stock turnover period is the time between their purchase and their resale.

(b) The debtors' turnover period, or debt collection period, is the length of the credit period taken by customers - it is the time between the sale of an item and the receipt of cash for the sale from the customer.

(c) Similarly, the creditors' turnover period, or period of credit taken from suppliers, is the length of time between the purchase of materials and the payment to suppliers.

3.13 Turnover periods can be calculated from information in a firm's profit and loss account and balance sheet.

Stock turnover periods are calculated as follows.

(a) Raw materials: $\dfrac{\text{(Average) raw material stocks held}}{\text{Total raw materials consumed in one year}} \times 12 \text{ months}$

(b) Work in progress (the length of the production period):

$$\dfrac{\text{(Average) finished goods stocks held}}{\text{Total cost of production in the year}} \times 12 \text{ months}$$

(c) Finished goods: $\dfrac{\text{(Average) stocks}}{\text{Total cost of goods sold in one year}} \times 12 \text{ months}$

(d)   Stocks of items bought for re-sale:

$$\frac{\text{(Average) stocks}}{\text{Total (materials) cost of goods bought and sold in one year}} \times 12 \text{ months}$$

The word 'average' is put in brackets because although it is strictly correct to use average values, it is more common to use the value of stocks shown in a balance sheet - at one point in time - to estimate the turnover periods. But you could use opening and closing balances in a period divided by two.

3.14   For example, if a company buys goods costing £620,000 in one year but uses goods costing £600,000 in production (in regular monthly quantities) and the cost of material in stock at 1 January is £100,000, the stock turnover period could be calculated as:

$$\frac{£100,000}{£600,000} \times 12 \text{ months} = 2 \text{ months}$$

In other words, stocks are bought two months before they are eventually re-sold.

3.15   The debt collection period is calculated as:

$$\frac{\text{Average debtors}}{\text{Annual credit sales}} \times 12 \text{ months}$$

For example, if a company sells goods for £1,200,000 per annum in regular monthly quantities, and if debtors in the balance sheet are £150,000, the debt collection period is:

$$\frac{£150,000}{£1,200,000} \times 12 \text{ months} = 1.5 \text{ months}$$

In other words, debtors will pay for goods $1^{1}/_{2}$ months on average after the time of sale.

3.16   The period of credit taken from suppliers is calculated as:

$$\frac{\text{Average trade creditors}}{\text{Total purchases in one year}} \times 12 \text{ months}$$

(Notice that the creditors are compared with materials bought whereas for raw material stock turnover, raw material stocks are compared with materials used in production. This is a small, but very significant difference.)

For example, if a company sells goods for £600,000 and makes a gross profit of 40% on sales, and if the amount of trade creditors in the balance sheet is £30,000, the period of credit taken from the suppliers is:

$$\frac{£30,000}{(60\% \text{ of } £600,000)} \times 12 \text{ months} = 1 \text{ month}$$

In other words, suppliers are paid in the month following the purchase of goods.

Exercise 2

Legion Ltd's 19X4 accounts show the following.

	£
Sales	360,000
Cost of goods sold	180,000
Stocks	30,000
Debtors	75,000
Trade creditors	45,000

Calculate the length of the cash cycle.

Solution

Stock turnover	Debt collection period	Credit taken from suppliers
$\dfrac{30,000}{180,000} \times 12$	$\dfrac{75,000}{360,000} \times 12$	$\dfrac{45,000}{180,000} \times 12$
= 2 months	= $2\frac{1}{2}$ months	= 3 months

The cash cycle is:

	Months
Stock turnover period	2.0
Credit taken from suppliers	(3.0)
Debt collection period	2.5
Cash cycle	1.5

In this example, Legion Ltd pays its suppliers one month after the stocks have been sold, since the stock turnover is two months but credit taken is three months.

Turnover periods and the total amount of working capital

3.17   If the stock turnover period gets longer or if the debt collection period gets longer, the total amount of stocks or of debtors will increase. Similarly, if the period of credit taken from the suppliers gets shorter, the amount of creditors will become smaller. The effect of these changes would be to increase the size of working capital (ignoring bank balances or overdrafts).

3.18   Suppose that a company has annual sales of £480,000 (in regular monthly quantities, all on credit) and a materials cost of sales of £300,000. (*Note.* A 'materials cost of sales' is the cost of materials in the cost of sales.)

(a)   If the stock turnover period is 2 months, the debt collection period 1 month and the period of credit taken from suppliers is 2 months, the company's working capital (ignoring cash) would be:

		£
Stocks	(2/12 × £300,000)	50,000
Debtors	(1/12 × £480,000)	40,000
		90,000
Creditors	(2/12 × £300,000)	(50,000)
		40,000

The cash cycle would be (2 + 1 – 2) = 1 month.

(b)   Now if the stock turnover period is extended to 3 months and the debt collection period to 2 months, and if the payment period for purchases from suppliers is reduced to one month, the company's working capital (ignoring cash) would be:

		£
Stocks	(3/12 × £300,000)	75,000
Debtors	(2/12 × £480,000)	80,000
		155,000
Creditors	(1/12 × £300,000)	(25,000)
		130,000

and the cash cycle would be (3 + 2 – 1) = 4 months.

3.19   If we ignore the possible effects on the bank balance or bank overdraft, (which are themselves included in working capital) it should be seen that a lengthening of the cash cycle will result in a larger volume of working capital.

3.20   If the volume of working capital required by a business varies with the length of the cash cycle, it is worth asking the question: 'Is there an ideal length of cash cycle and an ideal volume of working capital?'

3.21 Obviously, stocks, debtors and creditors should be managed efficiently, and:

(a) stocks should be sufficiently large to meet the demand for stock items when they are needed, but they should not be allowed to become excessive;

(b) debtors should be allowed a reasonable credit period, but overdue payments should be 'chased up', to obviate the risk of bad debts;

(c) suppliers should be asked to allow a reasonable period of credit and the firm should make use of the credit periods offered by them.

4   LIQUIDITY   *5/95, 5/96, 11/96*

4.1 Another important aspect of the size of working capital, however, is liquidity. The word 'liquid' means 'readily converted into cash' and a firm's liquidity is its ability to convert its assets into cash to meet all the demands for payments when they fall due.

4.2 The most liquid asset, of course, is cash itself (or a bank balance). The next most liquid assets are short-term investments (stocks and shares) because these can be sold quickly for cash should this be necessary. Debtors are fairly liquid assets because they should be expected to pay their bills in the near future. Stocks are the least liquid current asset because they must first be sold (perhaps on credit) and the customers given a credit period in which to pay before they can be converted into cash.

4.3 Current liabilities are items which must be paid for in the near future. When payment becomes due, enough cash must be available. The managers of a business must therefore make sure that a regular supply of cash comes in (from current assets) at all times to meet the regular flow of payments it is necessary to provide for.

4.4 As the previous description of the cash cycle might suggest, the amount of current assets and current liabilities for any business will affect its liquidity. In other words, the volume of working capital helps us to judge the firm's ability to pay its bills. To understand this more clearly, it may help to begin by looking at the capital structure of a business and at how current assets and working capital are financed.

The financing of working capital and business assets

4.5 BALANCE SHEET AS AT 31 DECEMBER 19X6

	£'000	£'000
Fixed assets		
Goodwill		50
Premises		700
Plant and machinery		300
		1,050
Current costs		
Stocks	99	
Debtors	50	
Cash in hand	1	
	150	
Current liabilities		
Bank overdraft	20	
Trade creditors	50	
Taxation due	30	
	100	
Net current assets (= working capital)		50
Total assets less current liabilities		1,100
Long-term liabilities		
Loan stock		200
		900

	£'000
Capital and reserves	
Share capital	400
Reserves	500
	900

4.6   The *long-term funds* of the business are share capital and reserves of £900,000 and loan stock of £200,000, making £1,100,000 in total. These funds help to finance the business and we can calculate that these funds are being used as follows.

	£
To 'finance' goodwill	50,000
To finance premises	700,000
To finance plant and machinery	300,000
To finance working capital	50,000
	1,100,000

Working capital is therefore financed by the long-term funds of the business.

4.7   If a company has more current liabilities than current assets, it has *negative* working capital. This means that to some extent, current liabilities are helping to finance the fixed assets of the business. In the following balance sheet, working capital is negative (net current liabilities of £20,000).

BALANCE SHEET AS AT ....

	£	£
Fixed assets		220,000
Current assets	60,000	
Current liabilities	80,000	
Net current liabilities		(20,000)
Total assets less current liabilities		200,000
Capital and reserves		200,000

The fixed assets of £220,000 are financed by share capital and reserves (£200,000), but also by current liabilities (£20,000). Since current liabilities are debts which will soon have to be paid, the company is faced with more payments than it can find the cash from liquid assets to pay for. This means that the firm will either have to:

(a)   sell off some fixed assets to get the cash; or

(b)   borrow money to overcome its cash flow problems, by offering any unmortgaged property as security for the borrowing;

(c)   be forced into 'bankruptcy' or 'liquidation' by the creditors who cannot be paid.

4.8   Clearly, a business must be able to pay its bills on time and this means that to have negative working capital would be financially unsound and dangerous. To be safe, a business should have current assets in excess of current liabilities, not just equality with current assets and current liabilities exactly the same amount.

4.9   The next question to ask then is whether there is an 'ideal' amount of working capital which it is prudent to have. In other words, is there an ideal relationship between the amount of current assets and the amount of current liabilities? Should a minimum proportion of current assets be financed by the long-term funds of a business?

4.10   These questions cannot be answered without a hard-and-fast rule, but the relative size of current assets and current liabilities are measured by so-called *liquidity ratios*.

Liquidity ratios

4.11   There are two common liquidity ratios.

(a)   The current ratio or working capital ratio
(b)   The quick ratio or liquidity ratio

4.12   The *current ratio* or *working capital ratio* is the more commonly used and is the ratio of current assets to current liabilities.

A 'prudent' current ratio is sometimes said to be 2:1. In other words, current assets should be twice the size of current liabilities. This is a rather simplistic view of the matter, because particular attention needs to be paid to certain matters.

(a)   Bank overdrafts: these are technically repayable on demand, and therefore must be classified as current liabilities. However, many companies have semi-permanent overdrafts in which case the likelihood of their having to be repaid in the near future is remote. It would also often be relevant to know a company's overdraft limit - this may give a truer indication of liquidity than a current or quick ratio.

(b)   Are the year-end figures typical of the year as a whole? This is particularly relevant in the case of seasonal businesses. For example, many large retail companies choose an accounting year end following soon after the January sales and their balance sheets show a higher level of cash and lower levels of stock and creditors than would be usual at any other time in the year.

4.13   In practice, many businesses operate with a much lower current ratio and in these cases, the best way to judge their liquidity would be to look at the current ratio at different dates over a period of time. If the trend is towards a lower current ratio, we would judge that the liquidity position is getting steadily worse.

For example, if the liquidity ratios of two firms A and B are as follows:

	1 Jan	*1 Apr*	*1 July*	*1 Oct*
Firm	A1.2 : 1	1.2 : 1	1.2 : 1	1.2 : 1
Firm	B1.3 : 1	1.2 : 1	1.1 : 1	1.0 : 1

we could say that firm A is maintaining a stable liquidity position, whereas firm B's liquidity is deteriorating. We would then begin to question firm B's continuing ability to pay its bills. A bank for instance, would need to think carefully before granting any request from firm B for an extended overdraft facility.

4.14   It is dangerous however to leap to conclusions when analysing ratios. As well as seasonal variations, it is possible that there is not so much overtrading as deliberately selling hard in order to build up business over time. What looks like a poor balance sheet in one year may develop later into a much bigger and better one.

4.15   The *quick ratio* is used when we take the view that stocks take a long time to get ready for sale, and then there may be some delay in getting them sold, so that stocks are not particularly liquid assets. If this is the case, a firm's liquidity depends more heavily on the amount of debtors, short-term investments and cash that it has to match its current liabilities. The quick ratio is the ratio of current assets *excluding stocks* to current liabilities.

4.16   A 'prudent' quick ratio is 1 : 1. In practice, many businesses have a lower quick ratio (eg 0.5 : 1), and the best way of judging a firm's liquidity would be to look at the trend in the quick ratio over a period of time. The quick ratio is also known as the *liquidity ratio* and as the *acid test ratio*.

Example: working capital ratios

4.17   The cash balance of Wing Ltd has declined significantly over the last 12 months. The following financial information is provided:

	Year to 31 December	
	19X2	*19X3*
	£	£
Sales	573,000	643,000
Purchases of raw materials	215,000	264,000
Raw materials consumed	210,000	256,400
Cost of goods manufactured	435,000	515,000
Cost of goods sold	420,000	460,000
Debtors	97,100	121,500
Creditors	23,900	32,500
Stocks: raw materials	22,400	30,000
work in progress	29,000	34,300
finished goods	70,000	125,000

All purchases and sales were made on credit.

Required

(a) Analyse the above information, which should include calculations of the cash operating cycle (the time lag between making payment to suppliers and collecting cash from customers) for 19X2 and 19X3.

(b) Prepare a brief report on the implications of the changes which have occurred between 19X2 and 19X3.

Notes

(a) Assume a 360 day year for the purpose of your calculations and that all transactions take place at an even rate.

(b) All calculations are to be made to the nearest day.

Solution

4.18 (a) The information should be analysed in as many ways as possible, and you should not omit any important items. The relevant calculations would seem to be as follows:

(i)

	19X2	*19X3*
	£	£
Sales	573,000	643,000
Cost of goods sold	(420,000)	(460,000)
Gross profit	153,000	183,000
Gross profit percentage	26.7%	28.5%

(ii) Size of working capital and liquidity ratios, ignoring cash/bank overdrafts:

	£	£
Debtors	97,100	121,500
Stocks: raw materials	22,400	30,000
work in progress	29,000	34,300
finished goods	70,000	125,000
	218,500	310,800
Creditors	(23,900)	(32,500)
Working capital (ignoring cash or overdraft)	194,600	278,300
Current ratio	218,500	310,800
	23,900	32,500
	= 9.1:1	= 9.6:1

(iii) *Turnover periods*

	19X2			19X3		
			days			*days*
Raw materials in stock	$\dfrac{22,400}{210,000} \times 360 =$		38.4	$\dfrac{30,000}{256,400} \times 360 =$		42.1
Work in progress	$\dfrac{29,000}{435,000} \times 360 =$		24.0	$\dfrac{34,300}{515,000} \times 360 =$		23.9
Finished goods stock	$\dfrac{70,000}{420,000} \times 360 =$		60.0	$\dfrac{125,000}{460,000} \times 360 =$		97.8
Debtors' collection period	$\dfrac{97,100}{573,000} \times 360 =$		61.0	$\dfrac{121,500}{643,000} \times 360 =$		68.0
Creditors' payment period	$\dfrac{23,900}{215,000} \times 360 =$		(40.0)	$\dfrac{32,500}{264,000} \times 360 =$		(44.3)
Cash cycle			143.4			187.5

(b) Sales were about 12% higher in 19X3 than in 19X2 and the cost of sales was about 9% higher. The investments in stocks and debtors minus creditors rose from £194,600 to £278,300, ie by £83,700 or nearly 44%. This is completely out of proportion to the volume of increase in trade, which indicates that working capital turnover periods are not being properly controlled.

The increase in working capital of £83,700 means that the net cash receipts from profits in 19X3 were £83,700 less than they would have been if there had been no increase at all in stocks and debtors (less creditors) during 19X3. The company might therefore have an unnecessary bank overdraft, although we are not given enough information to comment on this point fully.

Current assets must be financed by a combination of long-term funds and current liabilities. Working capital (current assets minus current liabilities) is the amount of this finance provided by long-term funds. A large and unnecessary increase in working capital will mean that too many long-term funds are invested in current assets (and they are obviously being invested wastefully if trading operations can be sustained with less working capital). A current ratio (ignoring cash and bank overdraft) of over 9:1 would appear excessive, both in 19X2 and 19X3.

The causes of the increase in working capital in 19X3 are:

(i) the increase in sales; but mainly
(ii) the increased length of turnover periods.

Raw materials stock turnover has risen from 38 to 42 days, although this increase was 'cancelled out' by an extension of the credit taken from suppliers, from 40 to 44 days. Debtors, already allowed 61 days to pay in 19X2, were allowed 68 days in 19X3 and this would seem to be an excessive length of time. The most serious change, however, is the increase in the finished goods stock turnover period from 60 days (2 months) to 98 days (over 3 months) and it is difficult to see an obvious reason why this should have occurred, although there may have been a temporary build-up at the end of 19X3 in preparation for a big sales drive.

5 GEARING *11/95*

5.1 Companies are financed by different types of capital and that each type expects a return in the form of interest or dividend.

Gearing is a method of comparing how much of the long-term capital of a business is provided by equity (ordinary shares and reserves) and how much is provided by investors who are entitled to interest or dividend before ordinary shareholders can have a dividend themselves. These sources of capital are loans and preference shares, and are sometimes known collectively as 'prior charge capital'.

5.2   The two most usual methods of measuring gearing are:

(a) $$\frac{\text{Prior charge capital (long - term loans and preference shares)}}{\text{Equity (ordinary share plus reserves)}} \times 100\%$$

(i)   A business is low-geared if the gearing is less than 100%.
(ii)   It is neutrally-geared if the gearing is exactly 100%.
(iii) It is high-geared if the gearing is more than 100%.

(b) $$\frac{\text{Prior charge capital (long - term loans and preference shares)}}{\text{Total long - term capital}}$$

A business is now low-geared if gearing is less than 50% (calculated under method (b)), neutrally-geared if gearing is exactly 50% and high-geared if it exceeds 50%.

5.3   Low gearing means that there is more equity finance in the business than there is prior charge capital. High gearing means the opposite - prior charge capital exceeds the amount of equity.

5.4   A numerical example might be helpful.

Draught Ltd, the company in paragraph 2.13, has a gearing of

$$\frac{£200,000}{£400,000} \quad \begin{array}{l}\text{(debenture loans plus preference shares)}\\\text{(ordinary shares plus reserves)}\end{array} \times 100\% = 50\%$$

Why is gearing important?

5.5   Gearing can be important when a company wants to raise extra capital, because if its gearing is already too high, we might find that it is difficult to raise a loan. Would-be lenders might take the view that ordinary shareholders should provide a fair proportion of the total capital for the business and that at the moment they are not doing so. Unless ordinary shareholders are prepared to put in more money themselves (either by issuing new shares or by retaining more profits), the company might be viewed as a bad business risk.

5.6   If excessive gearing indicates that more loans should not be made to a company, what is excessive gearing?

Unfortunately, there is no hard and fast answer to this question. The 'acceptable' level of gearing varies according to the country (eg average gearing is higher among companies in Japan than in Britain), the industry, and the size and status of the individual company within the industry. The more stable the company is, the more 'safe' higher gearing should be.

5.7   The advantages of gearing (ie of using debt capital) are as follows.

(a)   Debt capital is cheaper.

(i)   The reward (interest or preference dividend) is fixed permanently, and therefore diminishes in real terms if there is inflation. Ordinary shareholders, on the other hand, usually expect dividend growth.

(ii)   The reward required by debt-holders is usually lower than that required by equity holders, because debt capital is often secured on company assets, whereas ordinary share capital is a more risky investment.

(iii) Payments of interest attract tax relief, whereas ordinary (or preference) dividends do not.

(b)   Debt capital does not normally carry voting rights, but ordinary shares usually do. The issue of debt capital therefore leaves pre-existing voting rights unchanged.

(c)   If profits are rising, ordinary shareholders will benefit from gearing (see example below).

5.8   The main disadvantage of gearing is that if profits fall even slightly, the profit available to shareholders will fall at a greater rate.

6 ITEMS IN COMPANY ACCOUNTS FORMATS

6.1 Your syllabus requires you to:

'demonstrate an appreciation of the types of headings which appear in company accounts and the general contents of each heading.'   *(CIMA Guidance Notes 1997/98)*

6.2 By far the most effective way to acquire such an appreciation is to look at as many examples as possible. A 'feel' for the headings will come from practice at company accounts preparation questions. You also need to be able to *interpret* the information, a skill which you will acquire by practising ratio analysis questions.

Exercise 3

You are given summarised results of an electrical engineering business, as follows.

PROFIT AND LOSS ACCOUNT

	Year ended	
	31.12.X7	31.12.X6
	£'000	£'000
Turnover	60,000	50,000
Cost of sales	42,000	34,000
Gross profit	18,000	16,000
Operating expenses	15,500	13,000
	2,500	3,000
Interest payable	2,200	1,300
Profit before taxation	300	1,700
Taxation	350	600
(Loss) profit after taxation	(50)	1,100
Dividends	600	600
Transfer (from) to reserves	(650)	500

BALANCE SHEET

	£'000	£'000
Fixed assets		
Intangible	850	–
Tangible	12,000	11,000
	12,850	11,000
Current assets		
Stocks	14,000	13,000
Debtors	16,000	15,000
Bank and cash	500	500
	30,500	28,500
Creditors due within one year	24,000	20,000
Net current assets	6,500	8,500
Total assets less current liabilities	19,350	19,500
Creditors due after one year	6,000	5,500
	13,350	14,000
Capital and reserves		
Share capital	1,300	1,300
Share premium	3,300	3,300
Revaluation reserve	2,000	2,000
Profit and loss	6,750	7,400
	13,350	14,000

Required

(a) Prepare a table of the following 12 ratios, calculated for both years, clearly showing the figures used in the calculations.

Current ratio
Quick assets ratio
Stock turnover in days
Debtors turnover in days
Creditors turnover in days
Gross profit %
Net profit % (before taxation)
ROCE
Gearing

(b) Making full use of the information given in the question, of your table of ratios, and your common sense, comment on the apparent position of the business and on the actions of the management.

Solution

(a)

	19X7	19X6
Current ratio	$\frac{30,500}{24,000} = 1.27$	$\frac{28,500}{20,000} = 1.43$
Quick assets ratio	$\frac{16,500}{24,000} = 0.69$	$\frac{15,500}{20,000} = 0.78$
Stock (number of days held)	$\frac{14,000}{42,000} \times 365 = 122$ days	$\frac{13,000}{34,000} \times 365 = 140$ days
Debtors (number of days outstanding	$\frac{16,000}{60,000} \times 365 = 97$ days	$\frac{15,000}{50,000} \times 365 = 109$ days
Creditors (number of days outstanding)	$\frac{24,000}{42,000} \times 365 = 209$ days	$\frac{20,000}{34,000} \times 365 = 215$ days
Gross profit	$\frac{18,000}{60,000} = 30\%$	$\frac{16,000}{50,000} = 32\%$
Net profit % (before taxation)	$\frac{300}{60,000} = 0.5\%$	$\frac{1,700}{50,000} = 3.4\%$
ROCE	$\frac{2,500}{19,350} = 13\%$	$\frac{3,000}{19,500} = 15\%$
Gearing	$\frac{6,000}{19,350} = 31\%$	$\frac{5,500}{19,500} = 28\%$

(b) Turnover has increased by 20%, but cost of sales has increased at a faster rate (23%) with the result that gross profit percentage has fallen by 2%. This trend may well be due to forces beyond the company's control such as the recession and the actions of suppliers and competitors.

Interest expense has increased significantly, and this is one of the main factors contributing to the after tax loss shown in 19X7. In view of the loss it was perhaps imprudent of the company to maintain the dividend at its 19X6 level although this may be a deliberate device to maintain shareholder confidence. Borrowing has increased, leading to a worsening of the gearing ratio.

As regards current assets, there is a welcome improvement in stock, debtors and creditors turnover which have all fallen. This is linked to a fall in the current and quick ratios neither of which, however, appears dangerously low.

An encouraging sign is that the company has invested in fixed assets which, it is to be hoped, will pay off in future years.

Exercise 4

Try to get hold of as many sets of published accounts as possible. Study them carefully to familiarise yourself with the format. Try to form your own opinions on how well the companies are doing.

As a morale booster you should repeat this exercise at later stages in your studies. You may be pleasantly surprised at the progress you make!

7   PLANNING YOUR ANSWERS

7.1   Questions on interpreting company accounts generally call for discursive or 'wordy' answers, as do questions on internal and external audit. While you may feel like breathing a sigh of relief after all that number crunching, you should not be tempted to waffle. The best way to avoid going off the point is to prepare an answer plan. This has the advantage of making you think before you write and structure your answer logically.

7.2   The following approach may be adopted when preparing an answer plan.

   (a)   Read the question requirements

   (b)   Skim through the question to see roughly what it is about.

   (c)   Read through the question carefully, underlining any key words.

   (d)   Set out the headings for the main parts of your answer. Leave space to insert points within the headings.

   (e)   Jot down points to make within the main sections, underlining points on which you wish to expand.

   (f)   Write your full answer.

7.3   You should allow yourself the full time allocation for written answers, that is 1.8 minutes per mark. If, however, you run out of time, a clear answer plan with points in note form will earn you more marks than an introductory paragraph written out in full.

Chapter roundup

- The profit and loss account and balance sheet provide useful information about the condition of a business. Ratios can be calculated and trends identified so that different businesses can be compared or the performance of a business over time can be judged.

- The ratios which you need to be able to calculate for your examinations are as follows.

  o Return on capital employed

  o Gross profit percentage

  o Net profit percentage

  o Cost to sales ratios (eg cost of sales/sales, distribution costs/ sales, administrative expenses/sales)

  o Asset turnover

  o Debtors collection period

  o Creditors payment period

  o Gearing

- Return on capital employed may be calculated in a number of ways. The examiner proposes to use the formula:

$$\frac{\text{Net profit before tax and interest}}{\text{Average capital employed}}$$

  where average capital employed includes long-term, but not short-term finance.

- You also need to be able to interpret the ratios and suggest reasons for the results obtained.

- The interpretation of financial statements requires a large measure of common sense. For example:

  o you should not expect a firm of solicitors (say) to have substantial plant and machinery;

  o you should not expect a chain of supermarkets to make many sales on credit; you should expect it to turn over its (perishable) stock quickly;

  o you should expect a business that 'piles 'em high and sells 'em cheap' to have a low gross profit margin;

  o you should expect a more upmarket organisation to have higher selling and administrative costs, reflecting the level of service given to customers.

- You should familiarise yourself with published accounts formats as much as possible both by exam question practice and if possible by looking at real life examples.

Test your knowledge

1 Define 'profit margin' and 'asset turnover'. (see paras 2.2, 2.3)

2 What is the relationship which links ROCE, profit margin and asset turnover? (2.5, 2.8)

3 How is the ratio 'return on total long-term capital' calculated? (2.12)

4 What is the 'cash cycle'? (3.6)

5 What is (a) a finished goods stock turnover period; and (b) a debtors turnover period? How are they calculated? (3.13, 3.15)

6 A lengthening of the cash cycle will result in a smaller volume of working capital. True or false? (3.19)

7 Define (a) the current ratio and (b) the quick ratio. (4.12, 4.15)

8 A decrease in creditors has the effect of increasing the cash balance. True or false? (4.18)

9 Describe two methods of calculating a gearing ratio. (5.2)

10 List three advantages of debt capital over equity capital. (5.7)

Now try question 40 at the end of the Study Text

Multiple choice questions and suggested solutions

Multiple choice questions account for 30% of the marks for Paper 1. There are fifteen questions worth two marks each. It is important, therefore, that you practise them.

The questions contain one right answer and three wrong answers (called distractors). The distractors will often be 'nearly right'; for example they may show a result which a candidate would have obtained if he had got three quarters of the way through the appropriate working. Some 'wordy' questions will also have very plausible distractors.

You will be able to do some questions in a couple of seconds while others will require workings. Use your answer book for these workings but remember to cross them out before you hand it in.

While with written questions you get credit for method and for getting part way through the question, MCQ answers are just right or wrong. Do not, therefore, spend a long time on one MCQ. If you cannot do it, just guess and go on to the next one.

1 At 31 December 19X4 the ledger of X Ltd included a £1,270 provision for doubtful debts. During the year bad debts of £ 680 were written off. Debtors balances at 31 December 19X5 totalled £60,500 and the company wished to carry forward a general provision of 2%. The charge for bad and doubtful debts in the profit and loss account for 19X5 is:

    A   £620
    B   £740
    C   £1,800
    D   £1,890

2 A company wished to purchase a delivery van costing £8,250. The van dealer agrees to accept £6,900 cash together with the company's existing van in part-exchange. The existing van originally cost £ 6,400 and has a net book value of £1,750.

How should the trade-in value of the existing van be reflected in the company's ledger?

A	DEBIT	motor vans account	£1,350	
	CREDIT	motor vans disposal account		£1,350
B	DEBIT	cash	£1,350	
	CREDIT	motor vans disposal account		£1,350
C	DEBIT	motor vans disposal account	£1,350	
	CREDIT	motor vans account		£1,350
D	DEBIT	cash	£4,650	
	CREDIT	motor vans account		£4,650

3 The only entries in a company's sales ledger control account are: balance b/f £2,750; purchase ledger contra £380; sales £37,210; bank £33,240; returns inwards £420. The balance carried forward will be:

    A   £420
    B   £5,920
    C   £6,680
    D   £6,760

4 The balance on a company's sales ledger control account differs from the total of the balances in the sales ledger. Which one of the following circumstances could have caused the discrepancy?

    A   A settlement discount was incorrectly calculated
    B   Returns inwards were not recorded
    C   There was an error of addition in the sales daybook
    D   A bad debt was written off

5 A bank reconciliation revealed the following differences between the cash book and the bank statement.

    (i)   Outstanding lodgements of £369
    (ii)   Unpresented cheques of £743
    (iii)   A direct debit of £27 not entered in the cash book

If the balance shown by the bank statement is £514 overdrawn, what is the unadjusted balance in the cash book?

    A   £113 credit
    B   £167 debit
    C   £861 credit
    D   £915 credit

6   On 1 April 19X5 a company pays £4,950 in rent for the year ended 31 March 19X6. This was an increase of 10% on the charge for the previous year. In the company's profit and loss account for the year ended 31 December 19X5 what would be the charge for rent?

   A   £4,613
   B   £4,827
   C   £4,838
   D   £4,950

7   Mr X buys 1,000 50p shares in Y plc at a price of 70p each. If the company declares a dividend of 5% Mr X will receive:

   A   £25
   B   £35
   C   £50
   D   £70

8   A sole trader's stock at the beginning of his accounting period is £7,350. During the period he purchases goods for resale amounting to £48,390. He withdraws goods costing £350 for his own use. Sales for the period are £90,000 and his gross profit is a constant 80% on cost. What is the cost of his closing stock?

   A   £5,390
   B   £5,740
   C   £37,390
   D   £37,740

9   A credit balance has arisen on a trade debtors account. Which of the following could not account for it?

   A   A sales invoice has been paid twice.
   B   A sales invoice has been posted to another customer's account in error.
   C   Returns outwards have not been taken into account.
   D   A cheque from the customer was made out in the wrong amount.

10   At 1 January 19X1, the accounts of John Smith show accrued rent payable of £500. During the year he pays rent bills totalling £2,550, including one bill for £750 in respect of the quarter ending 31 January 19X2.

   What is the profit and loss charge for rent payable for the year ended 31 December 19X1?

   A   £1,800
   B   £2,300
   C   £2,800
   D   £3,300

11   Jones purchases goods with a list price of £16,000. The supplier grants a trade discount of 5% on list price and Jones also takes advantage of a settlement discount amounting to 2% of list price.

   In Jones' balance sheet the value of this stock should be

   A   £14,880
   B   £15,200
   C   £15,680
   D   £16,000

12 The total cost of wages and salaries debited in a business's profit and loss account is equal to:

A the total net pay received by all employees
B the total gross pay earned by all employees
C the total gross pay earned by all employees plus employer's NI contributions
D the total net pay received by all employees plus employer's NI contributions

13 If sales are £8,000 and the gross profit percentage is 20%, what is the cost of sales?

A £1,600
B £2,000
C £6,000
D £6,400

14 A toy shop makes purchases of £20,248 and sales of £26,520. The proprietor's children take goods costing £486 without paying for them. Closing stock was valued at its cost of £2,240 and the gross margin achieved was a constant 30% on sales.

What was the cost of the opening stock?

A £556
B £1,042
C £2,392
D £2,878

15 On checking the list of balances on the creditors ledger accounts, it is found that the total is £2,250 more than the balance on the creditors control account.

Which of the following errors could, by itself, account for this difference?

A The total of contra entries against debtor accounts is overstated by £1,125.

B Purchases day book has been overcast by £2,250.

C A credit note to the value of £1,125 has been omitted from a creditors ledger account.

D A creditors ledger account with a debit balance of £1,125 has been treated as a credit balance.

16 Waverly Products acquired a new mainframe computer system for £50,000 on 1 November 19X1. The computer's estimated useful life is five years, at the end of which it is expected to have a scrap value of £4,550.

If the company's financial year ends on 31 March, and straight line depreciation is applied on a time-apportioned basis, what is the depreciation charge on the computer in the profit and loss account for the year to 31 March 19X2?

A £3,788
B £4,167
C £9,090
D £10,000

17 On 30 November, Hayman Services Ltd receives a $3,500 (US dollar) cheque from a customer in Florida, enters this cheque as £3,500 in his accounting records and lodges the cheque in its usual bank account (£ sterling). On 2 December, the bank discovers this error and adjusts the company's bank account with the sterling equivalent of £1,950.

In order to correct the company's records, which of the following is the sole adjusting journal entry?

		£	£
A	Bank: current account	1,950	
	Debtors		1,950
B	Bank: current account	1,950	
	Losses on exchange		1550
	Debtors		400
C	Debtors	1550	
	Bank: current account		1550

The following information relates to questions 18 and 19.

The Tufty Club makes up its accounts to 31 December each year and has an accounting policy for subscription income of recognising subscriptions in arrears only when the cash is actually received, but recognising subscriptions in advance in the accounting period they relate to.

Information for the year ending 31 December 19X8 is as follows.

Total cash received from subscriptions (including £200 outstanding from the previous year)	£5,800
Subscriptions received in advance as at 31 December 19X7	£160
Subscriptions received in advance as at 31 December 19X8	£180

---

18 What amount will be included in the income and expenditure account of the club in respect of subscriptions for the year ending 31 December 19X8?

A £5,960
B £5,780
C £5,800
D £5,980

19 In respect of its policy for recognising subscriptions in arrears, which of the four fundamental accounting concepts of SSAP 2 is the club following?

A Accruals (matching)
B Going concern
C Consistency
D Prudence

20 On 31 January 19X8 a company's cash book showed a credit balance of £150 on its current account which did not agree with the bank statement balance. In performing the reconciliation the following points come to light.

	£
Not recorded in the cash book	
Bank charges	36
Transfer from deposit account to current account	500
Not recorded on the bank statement	
Unpresented cheques	116
Outstanding lodgements	630

It was also discovered that the bank had debited the company's account with a cheque for £400 in error. What was the original balance on the bank statement?

A £200 Cr
B £600 Dr
C £564 Dr
D £1,600 Dr

21 At 30 September 19X7 the balance on Giorgio Ltd's provision for doubtful debts was £6,400.

During the year ended 30 September 19X8 bad debts, previously provided for of £250 were written off. At 30 September 19X8 debtors balances are £156,000 and the company wishes to have a provision of 5% of this amount in its year end balance sheet.

The profit and loss account charge for bad and doubtful debts for the year ended 30 September 19X8 is

A   £250
B   £1,400
C   £1,650
D   £1,900

The following information relates to questions 22 and 23.

A company purchases a machine costing £24,000. It has an expected life of five years and an expected residual value of £5,000. The company uses the straight line method of depreciation.

At the beginning of year 3, the company spends £8,000 on major technical improvements to the machine. This has the effect of extending its useful life by three years, with an expected residual value of £2,300 at the end of year 8.

22 What is the depreciable amount of the asset after the technical improvements have been made?

A   £16,700
B   £18,300
C   £20,100
D   £22,100

23 What is the amount of the depreciation charge in year 4?

A   £2,762
B   £3,683
C   £3,712
D   £4,950

24 Jehu's accounts showed a gross profit for the year of £27,200. After the accounts were prepared it was found that the opening stock had been overstated by £1,200 while closing stock had been understated by £1,700.

What is the amount of Jehu's corrected gross profit for the year?

A   £24,300
B   £26,700
C   £27,700
D   £30,100

25 A creditors control account contains the following entries:

	£
Bank	79,500
Credit purchases	83,200
Discounts received	3,750
Contra with debtors control account	4,000
Balance c/f at 31 December 19X8	12,920

There are no other entries in the account. What was the opening balance brought forward at 1 January 19X8?

A   £8,870
B   £8,970
C   £16,970
D   £24,370

26 After you have paid a creditor £1,000 he informs you that you were entitled to a settlement discount of 5% which you forgot to deduct. What is the correct double entry to rectify this error in your books?

    A   DEBIT   Discount allowed
            CREDIT   Creditors account

    B   DEBIT   Creditors account
            CREDIT   Discount received

    C   DEBIT   Bank account
            CREDIT   Discount received

    D   DEBIT   Discount received
            CREDIT   Creditors account

27 The total of the balances in a company's sales ledger is £800 more than the debit balance on its debtors control account. Which one of the following errors could by itself account for the discrepancy?

    A   The sales day book has been undercast by £800.

    B   Settlement discounts totalling £800 have been omitted from the nominal ledger.

    C   One sales ledger account with a credit balance of £800 has been treated as a debit balance.

    D   The cash receipts book has been undercast by £800.

28 A company's bank statement shows £715 direct debits and £353 investment income not recorded in the cash book. The bank statement does not show a customer's cheque for £875 entered in the cash book on the last day of the accounting period. If the cash book shows a credit balance of £610 what balance appears on the bank statement?

    A   £97 overdrawn
    B   £627 overdrawn
    C   £1,123 overdrawn
    D   £1,847 overdrawn

29 Harry has budgeted sales for the coming year of £175,000. He achieves a constant gross mark-up of 40% on cost. He plans to reduce his stock level by £13,000 over the year.

What will Harry's purchases be for the year?

    A   £92,000
    B   £112,000
    C   £118,000
    D   £138,000

30 An item of stock has a cost of £4 and a net realisable value of £3. Which of the following concepts dictates the amount at which it should be stated in the balance sheet?

    A   Going concern
    B   Accruals
    C   Consistency
    D   Prudence

31 A company has authorised share capital of 1,000,000 50p ordinary shares and an issued share capital of 800,000 50p ordinary shares. If an ordinary dividend of 5% is declared, the amount payable to shareholders is:

    A   £50,000
    B   £25,000
    C   £40,000
    D   £20,000

32 A rates prepayment of £370 was treated as an accrual in preparing a trader's profit and loss account. As a result, his profit was:

A understated by £740
B overstated by £740
C understated by £370
D overstated by £370

33 On the last day of a company's accounting period goods costing £570 and invoiced to a customer for £780 were awaiting collection by the customer. They were erroneously counted as stock in the annual stock take. As a result, the company's profit for the year was:

A overstated by £570
B overstated by £780
C overstated by £210
D correctly stated

34 A company achieves a constant 20% gross profit margin. An amount of £2,400, taken from a proforma invoice relating to goods sent to a customer on a sale or return basis, has been credited to sales in the company's accounts. As a result, profit is overstated by:

A £400
B £480
C £2,000
D £2,400

35 Mr Harmon does not keep full accounting records, but the following information is available in respect of his accounting year ended 31 December 19X9.

	£
Cash purchases in year	3,900
Cash paid for goods supplied on credit	27,850
Creditors at 1 January 19X9	970
Creditors at 31 December 19X9	720

In his trading account for 19X9, what will be Harmon's figure for purchases?

A £27,600
B £31,500
C £31,750
D £32,000

36 Company Z has 85 units of stock in hand at its year end. They originally cost £60 each and now can not be sold until they are modified at a cost of £15 each. The selling price of the modified units will then be £80 each. Z's selling costs are 15% of selling price. What is the balance sheet valuation of this stock?

A £4,505
B £5,100
C £5,355
D £6,375

37 Which one of the following costs would be classified as revenue expenditure on the invoice for a new company car?

A Delivery costs
B Number plates
C Road tax
D A stereo radio

38 Under SSAP 13 which of the following can normally be treated as research and development expenditure?

A Costs of patent registration
B Market research costs to confirm demand for a new product
C Costs of development to be reimbursed by a client
D Design of a pre-production prototype

39   Goodwill generated by a business could be valued with reasonable certainty by estimating the business's current market value and the value of its separable net assets. How should such goodwill be treated in a company's financial statements?

    A   It should be capitalised, revalued each year and amortised over its estimated economic life

    B   It should be written off in full against reserves or capitalised and amortised over its estimated economic life

    C   It should not be capitalised but should be disclosed in a note to the balance sheet

    D   It should neither be capitalised nor disclosed in the financial statements

40   Tennyson plc runs the Shalott chain of greengrocers. Stock turnover is very high and Tennyson plc would like to value its stock at sales price less estimated gross profit. Is this an acceptable method of stock valuation under SSAP 9 and the Companies Act 1985?

	SSAP 9	*CA 1985*
A	Yes	No
B	Yes	Yes
C	No	Yes
D	No	No

1   A   The charge is made up as follows.

	£
Bad debts written off	680
Less decrease in provision for doubtful debts £1,270 – (2% × £60,500)	(60)
	620

2   A

3   B

DEBTORS

	£		£
Balance b/f	2,750	Purchase ledger contra	380
Sales	37,210	Bank	33,240
		Returns inwards	420
		Balance c/f	5,920
	39,960		39,960

4   C

5   C

	£	£
Balance per bank statement		(514)
Unpresented cheques		(743)
		(1,257)
Outstanding lodgements	369	
Direct debit omitted	27	
		396
Balance per cash book		(861)

Don't forget that an overdrawn balance is a credit balance in the cash book.

6   C

	£
1 January 19X5 to 31 March 19X5 (3/12 × 10/11 × £4,950)	1,125
1 April 19X5 to 31 December 19X5 (9/12 × £4,950)	3,713
	4,838

7   A   Mr X owns shares with a nominal value of £500. His dividend is 5% × £500 = £25.

8   A

TRADING ACCOUNT

	£	£
Sales		90,000
Opening stock	7,350	
Purchases	48,390	
	55,740	
Less drawings	350	
	55,390	
Less closing stock (balancing figure)	5,390	
Cost of sales (100/180 × £90,000)		50,000
Gross profit		40,000

9   C   Returns outwards relate to purchases and creditors, and could not affect a debtors account in any way.

10   A   £(2,550 – 500 – ($^{1}/3$ × 750))

11   B   The stock valuation should take account of trade discounts but not of settlement discounts.

12   C   The total P & L charge is the cost borne by the employer. This includes gross pay and the employer's own contribution to National Insurance.

13   D   Gross profit percentage is a percentage of sales. In this case gross profit = 20% × £8,000 = £1,600 and therefore cost of sales = £6,400.

14   B   The trading account looks like this.

	£	£
Sales		26,520
Opening stock (balancing figure)	1,042	
Purchases £(20,248 – 486)	19,762	
	20,804	
Closing stock	2,240	
		18,564
Gross profit (30% of sales)		7,956

15   D   Option A is rejected because the difference would then be only £1,125. Option B does not work because when this error is corrected the difference is even greater. Option C accounts for a difference of only £1,125.

16   A   Annual depreciation charge $£\dfrac{50,000 - 4,550}{5}$

= £9,090

For five months charge   = £9,090 × ^{5}/12

= £3,788

17   C   The original (incorrect) entry was

DEBIT	Bank: current account	£3,500
CREDIT	Debtors	£3,500

The entry should have been

DEBIT	Bank current account	£1,950
CREDIT	Debtors	£1,950

The adjustment required is therefore the difference of £(3,500 – 1,950) = £1,550.

18   B

SUBSCRIPTIONS ACCOUNT

	£		£
∴ To income and expenditure a/c	5,780	Balance b/d	160
Balance c/d	180	Cash	5,800
	5,960		5,960

19   D

20   B

CASH ACCOUNT

	£		£
		Balance b/d	150
Transfer from deposit account	500	Charges	36
		Balance c/d	314
	500		500

		£
Balance per cash book		314
Add unpresented cheques		116
Less uncleared lodgements		(630)
Less error by bank		(400)
Balance per bank statement		(600)

Note that on the bank statement Dr is overdrawn

21   C   PROVISION FOR DOUBTFUL DEBTS

	£		£
Debtors account	250	Balance b/d	6,400
Balance c/d (5% × £156,000)	7,800	∴ To P & L a/c (answer C)	1,650
	8,050		8,050

22   D

	£
Original depreciable amount	19,000
Less amount already depreciated ($2/5 \times £19,000$)	7,600
	11,400
Add: further capital expenditure	8,000
fall in residual value	2,700
New depreciable amount	22,100

	£	£
Alternatively:		
Total capital cost £(24,000 + 8,000)		32,000
Less: estimated residual value	2,300	
already depreciated	7,600	
		9,900
		22,100

23   B   The new depreciable amount of £22,100 must be written off over the revised remaining life of six years. In each of years 3 to 8 the annual charge is therefore $1/6 \times £22,100$ or £3,683.

24   D   The effect of each error is to overstate cost of sales and therefore understate profit. The total understatement is therefore £2,900 which means that corrected profit is £(27,200 + 2,900) = £30,100.

25   C

	£	£
Amounts due to creditors at 1 January (balancing figure)		16,970
Purchases in year		83,200
		100,170
Less: cash paid to creditors in year	79,500	
discounts received	3,750	
contra with debtors control	4,000	
		87,250
Amounts still unpaid at 31 December		12,920

26   B   To record discount received we credit the discount received account. But no cash is actually received from the creditor (we merely reduce any later liabilities to him that may arise). So do not debit bank account (option C); instead debit creditors account (option B).

27   A   The total of sales invoices in the day book is debited to the control account. If the total is understated by £800, the debits in the control account will also be understated by £800. Options B and D would have the opposite effect: credit entries in the control account would be understated. Option C would lead to a discrepancy of 2 × £800 = £1,600.

			£	£
28	**D**	Balance per cash book		(610)
		Items on statement, not in cash book:		
		Direct debits	(715)	
		Investment income	353	
				(362)
		Corrected balance per cash book		(972)
		Item in cash book not on statement:		
		Customer's cheque		(875)
		Balance per bank statement		(1,847)

29   **B**   Cost of sales $= 100/140 \times £175,000$
                       $= £125,000$

Since the stock level is being allowed to fall, it means that purchases will be £13,000 less than £125,000.

30   **D**   Prudence

31   **D** $800,000 \times 50p \times 5\% = £20,000$.

32   **A**   The amount of £370 has effectively been debited twice in error.

33   **A**   The sale was valid. The stock was overstated by £570 reducing the reported cost of sales by that amount.

34   **B** $£2,400 \times 20\% = £480$.

35   **B**   Credit purchases $= £(27,850 + 720 - 970) = £27,600$. Therefore total purchases $= £(27,600 + 3,900) = £31,500$.

36   **A**   Stock is valued at the lower of cost or net realisable value. In this case, net realisable value is

$£80 - £15 - £12 (= 80\% \times 15) = £53$ NRV.
$£53 \times 85 = £4,505$.

37   **C**

38   **D**   SSAP 13 (revised) gives several examples of activities which would normally be included in R & D and several which wouldn't. Market research and costs of patent registration are in the second list. Design of pre-production prototypes is in the first. It also specifically says that reimbursable development work should be dealt with as contract WIP.

39   **D**   Inherent goodwill can *never*, under any circumstances, be capitalised. Although it always exists and is no different in character from purchased goodwill, purchased goodwill 'is established as a fact at a particular point in time by a market transaction; this is not true of non-purchased goodwill' (SSAP 22). A *purchase* of goodwill provides an objective valuation which is lacking in *estimates* of a business's market value.

40   **B**   The CA 85 allows any method the directors think appropriate so long as, under the historical cost accounting rules, stock is stated at production cost or purchase price. This would appear to be satisfied here. SSAP 9 states that 'in the case of retail stores holding a large number of rapidly changing individual items, stock on the shelves has often been stated at current selling prices less the normal gross profit margin. In these particular circumstances, this may be acceptable as being the only practical method of arriving at a figure which approximates to cost'.

Illustrative questions and suggested solutions

Examination standard questions are indicated by marks and time allocations.

1   USERS OF ACCOUNTING INFORMATION

The Corporate Report identified many different user groups of accounting information. Identify those who might be interested in financial information about a large public company and describe their information needs.

2   DEFINITIONS

The observance each of the following concepts is presumed in financial statements unless otherwise stated.

(a) Going concern
(b) Accruals
(c) Consistency
(d) Prudence

Required

Explain each of the above concepts giving examples of how each is observed in conventional financial statements.

3   FINANCIAL REPORTING   *27 mins*

The Corporate Report identified many different user groups of accounting information.

With regard to the particular needs of shareholders:

(a) describe their information needs;   **6 Marks**

(b) explain how changing price levels affect the information provided and discuss the steps which may be taken to ensure that their information needs continue to be satisfied despite such changes.   **9 Marks**

Total Marks = 15

4   THE ACCOUNTING EQUATION

Peter Reid decides he is going to open a bookshop called Easyread, which he does by investing £5,000 on 1 January 19X7. During the first month of Easyread's existence, the following transactions occur.

(a) Bookshelves are purchased for £1,800.
(b) Books are purchased for £2,000.
(c) Half of the books are sold for £1,500 cash.
(d) Peter draws £200 out of the business for himself.
(e) Peter's brother John loans £500 to the business.
(f) Carpets are purchased for £1,000 on credit (to be paid in two months time).
(g) A bulk order of books worth £400 is sold on credit (to be paid in one month's time) for £600.

Required

Write down the accounting equation after each transaction has occurred.

5   FINANCIAL STATEMENTS

What is the difference between the balance sheet and the trading, profit and loss account? What is the difference between capital and revenue expenditure? Which of the following transaction is capital expenditure and which revenue expenditure?

(a) A bookseller buys a car for its director for £9,000.
(b) In the first year, the car is depreciated by £900.
(c) The business buys books for £1,500.
(d) The business builds an extension for £7,600.

(e) The original building is repainted, a job costing £1,200.

(f) A new sales assistant is taken on and his salary in the first year is £10,000.

6   BUSINESS TRANSACTIONS

The following is a list of typical business transactions.

(a) The purchase of goods on credit.

(b) Allowance to credit customers upon the return of faulty goods.

(c) Refund from petty cash to an employee of an amount spend on entertaining a client.

(d) Credit card sales.

Required

For each transaction identify clearly

(i)   the original document(s) for the data; and

(ii) the book of original entry for the transaction.

7   BEECHFIELD   *36 mins*

Beechfield Ltd make use of a petty cash book as part of their book-keeping system. The following is a summary of the petty cash transactions for the month of November 19X9.

			£
November	1	Opening petty cash book float received from cashier	350
	2	Cleaning materials	5
	3	Postage stamps	10
	6	Envelopes	12
	8	Taxi fare	32
	10	Petrol for company car	17
	14	Typing paper	25
	15	Cleaning materials	4
	16	Bus fare	2
	20	Visitors' lunches	56
	21	Mops and brushes for cleaning	41
	23	Postage stamps	35
	27	Envelopes	12
	29	Visitors' lunches	30
	30	Photocopying paper	40

Required

(a) Draw up the petty cash book for the month using analysis columns for stationery, cleaning, entertainment, travelling and postages. Show clearly the receipt of the amount necessary to restore the float and the balance brought forward for the start of the following month. Folio numbers are not required.

12 Marks

(b) Show how the stationery and postages accounts would appear in the nominal ledger.

8 Marks

Total Marks = 20

8   JOCKFIELD

The following is a summary of the petty cash transactions of Jockfield Ltd for May 19X2.

May   1   Received from cashier £300 as petty cash float

			£
2	Postages		18
3	Travelling		12
4	Cleaning		15
7	Petrol for delivery van		22
8	Travelling		25
9	Stationery		17
11	Cleaning		18
14	Postage		5
15	Travelling		8
18	Stationery		9
	Cleaning		23
20	Postage		13
24	Delivery van 5,000 miles service		43
26	Petrol		18
27	Cleaning		21
29	Postage		5
30	Petrol		14

Required

(a) Rule up a suitable petty cash book with analysis columns for expenditure on cleaning, motor expenses, postage, stationery, travelling.

(b) Enter the month's transactions.

(c) Enter the receipt of the amount necessary to restore the imprest and carry down the balance for the commencement of the following month.

(d) State how the double entry for the expenditure is completed.

9   J OCKEY   *27 mins*

Mr J Ockey commenced trading as a wholesale stationer on 1 May 19X4 with a capital of £5,000 with which he opened a bank account for his business.

During May the following transactions took place.

May   1   Bought shop fittings and fixtures for cash form Store Fitments Ltd for £2,000
       2   Purchased goods on credit from Abel £650
       4   Sold goods on credit to Bruce £700
       9   Purchased goods on credit from Green £300
      11   Sold goods on credit to Hill £580
      13   Cash sales paid intact into bank £200
      16   Received cheque from Bruce in settlement of his account
      17   Purchased goods on credit from Kaye £800
      18   Sold goods on credit to Nailor £360
      19   Sent cheque to Abel in settlement of his account
      20   Paid rent by cheque £200
      21   Paid delivery expenses by cheque £50
      24   Received from Hill £200 on account
      30   Drew cheques for personal expenses £200 and assistant's wages £320
      31   Settled the account of Green.

Required

(a) Record the foregoing in appropriate books of original entry.   **3 Marks**
(b) Post the entries to the ledger accounts.   **4 Marks**
(c) Balance the ledger accounts where necessary.   **4 Marks**

(d) Extract a trial balance at 31 May 19X4.

4 Marks

Total Marks = 15

Note. You are not required to complete any entries in personal accounts, nor are folio references required.

10 OMEGA

At 1 May 19X3 amounts owing to Omega by his customers in respect of their April purchases were:

	£
Alpha	210
Beta	1,040
Gamma	1,286
Delta	279
Epsilon	823

The amounts owing by Omega to his suppliers at 1 May were:

	£
Zeta	2,173
Eta	187
Theta	318

Sales made by Omega during May were as follows.

	£
Gamma	432
Epsilon	129
Beta	314
Epsilon	269
Alpha	88
Delta	417
Epsilon	228

Purchases during May:

	£
Eta	423
Zeta	268
Eta	741

Returns inwards: (ie sales returns)

	£
Epsilon	88

Cash payments:

	£
Eta	187
Theta	318
Zeta	1,000

Cash receipts:

	£
Beta	1,040
Delta	279
Gamma	826
Epsilon	823

Required

(a) Open accounts for Omega's customers and suppliers and record therein the 1 May balances.

(b) Record the transactions in the appropriate personal and impersonal accounts.

(c) Balance the personal accounts where necessary.

(d) Extract a list of debtors at 31 May showing in separate columns:

(i) the total amounts owing;
(ii) amounts owing in respect of May;
(iii) amounts owing in respect of April.

Note. You need not enter dates or narrative in the accounts.

11 HUBBLE

On 28.2.19X8, which is one month before the end of his financial year, the ledger accounts of A Hubble were as follows.

CASH

	£		£
Capital	9,500	Rent	2,750
Bank loan	3,000	Creditors	700
Sales	11,200	Interest	350
Debtors	400	Electricity	400
		Telephone	180
		Drawings	1,300

CAPITAL

	£		£
		Cash	9,500

BANK LOAN

	£		£
		Cash	3,000

SALES

	£		£
		Cash	11,200
		Debtors	4,600

DEBTORS

	£		£
Sales	4,600	Cash	400

RENT

	£		£
Cash	2,750		

PURCHASES

	£		£
Creditors	2,100		

CREDITORS

	£		£
Cash	700	Purchases	2,100

INTEREST

	£		£
Cash	350		

ELECTRICITY

	£		£
Cash	400		

TELEPHONE

	£		£
Cash	180		

DRAWINGS

	£		£
Cash	1,300		

During the last month of his financial year, A Hubble recorded the following transactions.

(a) He bought goods for £2,000, half for credit and half for cash.

(b) He paid the following:

    (i)   interest £20;
    (ii)   electricity £25;
    (iii)   telephone £12.

(c) He made sales of £3,500 of which £500 were for cash.

(d) He received £220 from debtors

Required

(a) Post the transactions for March 19X8 into the ledger accounts.

(b) Balance off the ledger accounts and draw up a trial balance.

(c) Prepare a balance sheet as at 31.3.19X8 and a trading, profit and loss account for the year ended 31.3.19X8.

12   RENT, RATES AND INSURANCE

From the information given below you are required:

(a) to calculate the charge to the profit and loss account for the year ended 30 June 19X6 in respect of rent, rates and insurance;

(b) to state the amount of accrual or prepayment for rent, rates and insurance as at 30 June 19X6.

The accruals and prepayments as at 30 June 19X5 were as follows.

	£
Rent accrued	2,000
Rates prepaid	1,500
Insurance prepaid	1,800

Payments made during the year ended 30 June 19X6 were as follows.

19X5		£
10 August	Rent, three months to 31 July 19X5	3,000
26 October	Insurance, one year to 31 October 19X6	6,000
2 November	Rates, six months to 31 March 19X6	3,500
12 December	Rent, four months to 30 November 19X5	4,000
19X6		
17 April	Rent, four months to 31 March 19X6	4,000
9 May	Rates, six months to 30 September 19X6	3,500

13   HACKER   *45 mins*

Hacker commenced business as a retail butcher on 1 January 19X0. The following is a summary of the transactions which took place during the first three months of trading.

(a) Cash sales amounted to £3,000, including £500 of sales on credit cards.

(b) Credit sales totalled £1,600 and of this £300 was outstanding at the end of the period.

(c) On the commencement of business Hacker had paid £4,000 into the business, and a full year's rent of £600 had been paid immediately.

(d) A delivery van was purchased on 1 January at a cost of £900. It was agreed that this should be depreciated at the rate of 20% per annum.

(e) During the period suppliers had been paid £1,600 for meat and invoices totalling £400 remained unpaid at 31 March.

(f) The stock of meat at the close of business on 31 March was valued at cost at £360.

(g) Sundry expenses (all paid during the period and relating to it) amounted to £400, and during March Hacker drew £200 from the business.

Required

(a) Write up the ledger accounts and cash book of Hacker.   **8 Marks**

(b) Extract a trial balance.   **7 Marks**

(c) Prepare a trading and profit and loss account for the three months ending 31 March 19X0, and balance sheet at that date.   **10 Marks**

Total Marks = 25

Tutorial note. Keep firmly in your mind the fact that you are preparing quarterly accounts, whereas some expenses are given as an annual amount.

You might also be interested in the new idea given in (a), that sales on credit cards can be treated in the same way as sales paid by cheque - ie as cash sales.

14   JAMES   *27 mins*

James opened a shop on 1 July 19X2 and during his first month in business, the following transactions occurred.

19X2

1 July	James contributes £20,000 in cash to the business out of his private bank account.
2 July	He opens a business bank account by transferring £18,000 of his cash in hand.
5 July	Some premises are rented, the rent being £500 per quarter payable in advance in cash.
6 July	James buys some second-hand shop equipment for £300 paying by cheque.
9 July	He purchases some goods for resale for £1,000 paying for them in cash.
10 July	Seddon supplies him with £2,000 of goods on credit.
20 July	James returns £200 of the goods to Seddon.
23 July	Cash sales for the week amount to £1,500.
26 July	James sells goods on credit for £1,000 to Frodsham.
28 July	Frodsham returns £500 of the goods to James.
31 July	James settles his account with Seddon by cheque, and is able to claim a cash discount of 10%.
31 July	Frodsham sends James a cheque for £450 in settlement of his account, any balance remaining on his account being treated as a cash discount.
31 July	During his initial trading, James has discovered that some of his shop equipment is not suitable, but he is fortunate in being able to dispose of it for £50 in cash. There was no profit or loss on disposal.
31 July	He withdraws £150 in cash as part payment towards a holiday for his wife.

Required

(a) Enter the above transactions in James' ledger accounts, balance off the accounts and bring down the balances as at 1 August 19X2.   **8 Marks**

(b)   Extract a trial balance as at 31 July 19X2.   **7 Marks**

Total Marks = 15

15   GEORGE   *27 mins*

George is a wholesaler and the following information relates to his accounting year ending 30 September 19X2.

(a)   Goods are sold on credit terms, but some cash sales are also transacted.

(b)   At 1 October 19X1 George's trade debtors amounted to £30,000 against which he had set aside a provision for doubtful debts of 5%.

(c)   On 15 January 19X2 George was informed the Fall Ltd had gone into liquidation, owing him £2,000. This debt was outstanding from the previous year.

(d)   Cash sales during the year totalled £46,800, whilst credit sales amounted to £187,800.

(e)   £182,500 was received from trade debtors.

(f)   Settlement discounts allowed to credit customers were £5,300.

(g)   Apart from Fall Ltd's bad debt, other certain bad debts amounted to £3,500.

(h)   George intends to retain the provision for doubtful debts account at 5% of outstanding trade debtors as at the end of the year, and the necessary entry is to be made.

You are required to enter the above transactions in George's ledger accounts and (apart from the cash and bank and profit and loss accounts) balance off the accounts and bring down the balances as at 1 October 19X2.

15 Marks

16   AFTER THE STOCK COUNT   *36 mins*

After its end of year physical stock count and valuation, the accounts staff of Caveat Emptor Ltd have reached a valuation of £153,699 at cost for total stocks held as at the year end.

However, on checking the figures, the chief bookkeeper has come across the following additional facts.

(a)   On one of the stock sheets, a sub-total value of £6,275 had been carried forward on to the next sheet as £6,725.

(b)   260 units of stock number 73113X which cost £0.60 each have been extended into the total value column at £6 each.

(c)   The purchasing department has informed the accounts department that it is in possession of a number of free samples given to them by potential suppliers Their estimated value, at purchase cost, would be £1,750. They were not included in the stock referred to above.

(d)   The stock count includes £4,658 of goods bought on credit and still not paid for as at the year end.

(e)   The stock count includes damaged goods which originally cost £2,885. These could be repaired at a cost of £921 and sold for £3,600.

(f)   The stock count excludes 300 units of stock item 730052 which were sold to a customer Seesaft Ltd on a sale or return basis, at a price of £8 each. The original cost of the units was £5 each. Seesaft Ltd has not yet indicated to Caveat Emptor Ltd whether these goods have been accepted, or whether they will eventually be returned.

(g)   The stock count includes 648 units of stock item 702422. These cost £7.30 each originally but because of dumping on the market by overseas suppliers, a price war has flared up and the unit price of the item has fallen to £6.50. The price reduction is expected to be temporary, lasting less than a year or so, although some observers of the market predicted that the change might be permanent. Caveat Emptor Ltd has already decided that if the price reduction last longer than six months, it will reduce its resale price of the item from £10.90 to about £10.

Required

Calculate the closing stock figure for inclusion in the annual accounts of Caveat Emptor Ltd, making whatever adjustments you consider necessary in view of items (a) to (g). Explain your treatment of each item.

20 Marks

17 A COMPANY'S PLANT AND MACHINERY   *45 mins*

A company's plant and machinery account at 31 December 19X8 and the corresponding depreciation provision account broken down into years of purchase, are as follows.

Year of purchase	Plant and machinery at cost	Depreciation provision
	£	£
19X0	20,000	20,000
19X2	30,000	30,000
19X4	100,000	90,000
19X6	70,000	35,000
19X7	50,000	15,000
19X8	30,000	3,000
	300,000	193,000

Depreciation is at the rate of 20% per annum on cost. It is the company's policy to assume that all purchases, sales or disposals of plant occurred on 30 June in the relevant year for the purposes of calculating depreciation, irrespective of the precise date on which these events occurred.

During 19X9 the following transactions took place.

(a) Purchase of plant and machinery amounted to £150,000.
(b) Plant that had been bought in 19X2 for £17,000 was scrapped.
(c) Plant that had been bought in 19X4 for £9,000 was sold for £500.
(d) Plant that had been bought in 19X6 for £24,000 was sold for £8,500.

Required

(a) Calculate the provision for depreciation of plant and machinery for the year ended 31 December 19X9. In calculating this provision you should bear in mind that it is the company's policy to show any profit or loss on the sale or disposal of plant as a completely separate item in the profit and loss account.   **12 Marks**

(b) Show the following as at 31 December 19X8 and 31 December 19X9:

   (i)   plant and machinery, at cost;
   (ii)   depreciation provision (ie accumulated deprecation);
   (iii) the net book value of plant and machinery;
   (iv)   the profit or loss on sales or disposals of plant and machinery.   **13 Marks**

Tutorial note. It would help you to reconcile the figures as at 31 December 19X8 with the figures as at 31 December 19X9 for items (i) and (ii) by calculating the 1 January figures, and then making adjustments for disposals and additional purchases during 19X9 in order to arrive at the figures for 31 December 19X9.

Total Marks = 25

18 SPARK   *54 mins*

Spark has been trading for a number of years as an electrical appliance retailer and repairer in premises which he rents at an annual rate of £1,500 payable in arrears. Balances appearing in his books at 1 January 19X1 were as follows.

	£	£
Capital account		1,808
Motorvan		1,200
Fixtures and fittings		806
Provision for depreciation on motor van		720
Provisions for depreciation on fixtures and fittings		250
Stock at cost		366
Debtors for credit sales		
Brown	160	
Blue	40	
Stripe	20	
		220
Cash at bank		672
Cash in hand		5
Loan from Flex		250
Creditors for supplies		
Live	143	
Negative	80	
Earth	73	
		296
Amount owing for electricity		45
Rates paid in advance		100

Although Sparks has three credit customers the majority of his sales and services are for cash, out of which he pays various expenses before banking the balance.

The following transactions took place during the first four months of 19X1.

	January £	February £	March £	April £
Suppliers' invoices				
Live	468	570	390	602
Negative	-	87	103	64
Earth	692	-	187	-
Capital introduced		500		
Bankings of cash (from cash sales)	908	940	766	1,031
Expenditure out of cash sales before banking				
Drawings	130	120	160	150
Stationery	12	14	26	21
Travelling	6	10	11	13
Petrol and van repairs	19	22	37	26
Sundry expenses	5	4	7	3
Postage	12	10	15	19
Cleaner's wages	60	60	65	75
Goods invoiced to credit customers				
Brown	66	22	10	12
Blue	120	140	130	180
Stripe	44	38	20	48
Cheque payments (other than those to suppliers)				
Telephone	40	49	59	66
Electricity	62	47	20	106
Rates	-	-	220	-
Motor van (1 February 19X1)	-	800	-	-
Unbanked at the end of April	-	-	-	12

Spark pays for goods by cheque one month after receipt of invoice, and receives a settlement discount of 15% from each supplier.

Credit customers also pay be cheque one month after receipt of invoice, and are given a settlement discount of 10% of the invoice price.

Required

(a) Write up the ledger accounts of Spark for the four months to 30 April 19X1, and extract a trial balance after balancing off the accounts.   **15 Marks**

(b) Prepare:

   (i)   trading and profit and loss accounts for the four months;

   (ii)   a balance sheet on 30 April 19X1;

   after dealing with the following matters.

   (i)   The payment of £800 for a new motor van represents the balance paid to the garage after being granted a part-exchange value of £500 on the old van.

   (ii)   Depreciation is provided at the rate of 20% per annum on the cost of motor vans and at the rate of 10% on the cost of fixtures and fittings. No depreciation is to be provided in the period of disposal.

   (iii) Interest on the loan from Flex is to be accrued at 10% per annum and credited to his account.

   (iv)   Amounts owing at 30 April 19X1 were electricity £22, and telephone £15. The payment for rates was for six months in advance from 1 March.

   (v)   Included in the payments for telephone was one of Spark's private bills of £37 which is to be charged to him.

   (iv)   Stock at cost on 30 April 19X1 amounted to £390.   **15 Marks**

Total Marks = 30

19   INTANGIBLE   *27 mins*

The accounts of Intangible Ltd at 1 January 19X6 include deferred development costs of £26,500. During the year ended 31 December 19X6 Intangible Ltd purchased a new business. The consideration paid to the proprietor included £4,800 in respect of goodwill. The company also spent £7,900 on research and £3,500 on development activities.

The directors of Intangible Ltd intend to write off goodwill evenly over its estimated economic life of four years. They believe that £22,600 of development costs should be carried forward at 31 December 19X6.

Show the ledger accounts for goodwill and research and development in the books of Intangible Ltd.

15 Marks

20   FRANK MERCER   *36 mins*

On 10 January 19X9, Frank Mercer received his monthly bank statement for December 19X8. The statement showed the following.

MIDWEST BANK PLC

F Mercer: Statement of Account

Date	Particulars	Debits	Credits	Balance
19X8		£	£	£
Dec 1	Balance			1,862
Dec 5	417864	243		1,619
Dec 5	Dividend		26	1,645
Dec 5	Bank Giro Credit		212	1,857
Dec 8	417866	174		1,683
Dec 10	417867	17		1,666
Dec 11	Sundry Credit		185	1,851
Dec 14	Standing Order	32		1,819
Dec 20	417865	307		1,512
Dec 20	Bank Giro Credit		118	1,630
Dec 21	417868	95		1,535
Dec 21	416870	161		1,374
Dec 24	Bank charges	18		1,356
Dec 27	Bank Giro Credit		47	1,403
Dec 28	Direct Debit	88		1,315
Dec 29	417873	12		1,303
Dec 29	Bank Giro Credit		279	1,582
Dec 31	417871	25		1,557

His cash book for the corresponding period showed:

CASH BOOK

19X8		£	19X8		Cheque no	£
Dec 1	Balance b/d	1,862	Dec 1	Electricity	864	243
Dec 4	J Shannon	212	Dec 2	P Simpson	865	307
Dec 9	M Lipton	185	Dec 5	D Underhill	866	174
Dec 19	G Hurst	118	Dec 6	A Young	867	17
Dec 26	M Evans	47	Dec 10	T Unwin	868	95
Dec 27	J Smith	279	Dec 14	B Oliver	869	71
Dec 29	V Owen	98	Dec 16	Rent	870	161
Dec 30	K Walters	134	Dec 20	M Peters	871	25
			Dec 21	L Philips	872	37
			Dec 22	W Hamilton	873	12
			Dec 31	Balance c/d		1,793
		2,935				2,935

Required

(a) Bring the cash book balance of £1,793 up to date as at 31 December 19X8.

10 Marks

(b) Draw up a bank reconciliation statement as at 31 December 19X8.   **10 Marks**

Total Marks = 20

21   **CAMFORD**   *27 mins*

The Treasurer of the Camford School Fund is attempting to reconcile the balance shown in the cash book with that appearing on the bank pass sheets. According to the cash book, the balance at the bank as at 31 May 19X2 was £1,900, whilst the bank pass sheets disclosed an overdrawn amount £470. Upon investigation, the treasurer identified the following discrepancies.

(a) A cheque paid to Summer Ltd for £340 had been entered in the cash book at £430.

(b) Cash paid into the bank for £100 had been entered in the cash book as £90.

(c) A transfer of £1,500 to the Midlands Savings Bank had not been entered in the cash book.

(d) A receipt of £10 shown on the bank statement had not been entered in the cash book.

(e) Cheques drawn amounting to £40 had not been paid into the bank.

(f) The cash book balance had been incorrectly brought down at 1 June 19X1 as a debit balance of £1,200 instead of a debit balance of £1,100.

(g) Bank charges of £20 do not appear in the cash book.

(h) Receipts of £900 paid into the bank on 31 May 19X2 do not appear on the bank pass sheets until 1 June 19X2.

(i) A standing order payment of £30 had not been entered in the cash book.

(j) A cheque for £50 previously received and paid into the bank had been returned by the subscriber's bank marked 'account closed'.

(k) The bank received a direct debit of £100 from an anonymous subscriber.

(l) Cheques paid into the bank had been incorrectly totalled. The total amount should have been £170 instead of £150.

You are required to draw up a bank reconciliation statement as at 31 May 19X2.

15 Marks

22   APRIL SHOWERS   *27 mins*

April Showers sells goods on credit to most of its customers. In order to control its debtor collection system, the company maintains a sales ledger control account. In preparing the accounts for the year to 31 October 19X3 the accountant discovers that the total of all the personal accounts in the sales ledger amounts to £12,802, whereas the balance on the sales ledger control account is £12,550.

Upon investigating the matter, the following errors were discovered.

(a) Sales for the week ending 27 march 19X3 amounting to £850 had been omitted from the control account.

(b) A debtor's account balance of £300 had not been included in the list of balances.

(c) Cash received of £750 had been entered in a personal account as £570.

(d) Discounts allowed totalling £100 had not been entered in the control account.

(e) A personal account balance had been undercast by £200

(f) A contra item of £400 with the purchase ledger had not been entered in the control account.

(g) A bad debt of £500 had not been entered in the control account.

(h) Cash received of £250 had been debited to a personal account.

(i) Discounts received of £50 had been debited to Bell's sales ledger account.

(j) Returns inwards valued at £200 had not been included in the control account.

(k) Cash received of £80 had been credited to a personal account as £8.

(l) A cheque for £300 received from a customer had been dishonoured by the bank, but no adjustment had been made in the control account.

Required

(a) Prepare a corrected sales ledger control account, bringing down the amended balance as at 1 November 19X3.   **8 Marks**

(b) Prepare a statement showing the adjustments that are necessary to the list of personal account balances so that it reconciles with the amended sales ledger control account balance.   **7 Marks**

Total Marks = 15

23 **FRONTLOADER**   *36 mins*

Frontloader Ltd is a business which acts as a distributor of washing machines entirely on credit terms to a wide range of customers. The following balances were extracted from its ledgers at 30 June 19X5:

	£	£
Sales		723,869
Creditors: balance at 30 June 19X4		49,781
Debtors: balance at 30 June 19X4	84,611	
Purchases of washing machines	342,916	
Discounts allowed	8,214	
Discounts received		6,978
Cash received from debtors	699,267	
Cash paid to creditors		321,853
Returns inwards	36,925	
Carriage outwards	5,264	
Overdraft interest	12,748	
Provision for doubtful debts as at 30 June 19X4		4,813

Subsequent enquiries reveal the following.

A cheque for £1,246 from A Brown, a customer, has been returned by the bank marked 'refer to drawer'. Bad debts totalling £6,854 are to be written off, and the provision for doubtful debts is to be raised to 8% of the debtor balances at 30 June 19X5.

On the last day of the year a cheque is received for £1,000 from the liquidator of J Smith Limited. This customer had owed Frontloader £7,500 when it ceased to trade in March 19X2, and the debt had been written off as a bad debt in the year ended 30 June 19X2. No entry in respect of this cheque has yet been made in the books.

You are required to prepare for the year ended 30 June 19X5:

(a) the debtors ledger control account;   **8 Marks**
(b) the bad and doubtful debts account; and   **6 Marks**
(c) the balance sheet entry for debtors.   **6 Marks**

Total Marks = 20

24 **HYPER**

The following extracts are taken from Hyper Ltd's accounts for the quarter ended 30 June 19X1.

	£
Debtors balance, 1 April 19X1	40,000
Creditors balance, 1 April 19X1	22,000
VAT creditor, 1 April 19X1	4,100

Transactions during the quarter were as follows.

	£
Invoiced sales, including VAT	141,000
Purchases on credit, including VAT	84,600
Payments made for credit purchases	92,700
Receipts from debtors	128,300
Payment to VAT creditor	4,100

The rate of VAT during the quarter was 17.5% and this rate applied to all purchases and sales.

Required

Prepare the ledger account entries necessary to give effect to these transactions.

25   PAYROLL   *36 mins*

As at 1 November 19X3, the following balances existed in the ledger of Payroll Ltd.

	£
Creditors	800
Bad debts provision	450
Wages control	38
PAYE income tax deductions	35
National Insurance contributions liability	44

During the year ended 31 October 19X4 the following transactions occurred.

	£
Gross wages earned	2,000
Cash paid to suppliers	5,400
Discounts received	100
Debtors and creditors accounts set off against each other and settled by contra	700
Sales on credit	12,000
Purchases on credit	6,000
Cash received from customers	11,800
Discounts allowed	300
Bad debts written off against the provision	200
Bad debts previously written off now recovered in cash	50
Increase in the bad debts provision charged to profit and loss account	100
Net wages paid in cash	1,330
PAYE income tax deducted from employees' wages	407
National Insurance contributions deducted from employees' wages	260
National Insurance contributions, employer's contribution	290
Cash paid to Inland Revenue for:	
PAYE income tax deductions	400
Employer's and employees' National Insurance contributions	546
Debtors at 31 October 19X4 amounted to £1,000	

There were no cash sales or cash purchases during the year.

You are required to write up the following accounts in the company's ledger for the year ended 31 October 19X4.

(a) Creditors
(b) Debtors
(c) Provision for doubtful debts
(d) Wages control
(e) PAYE income tax deductions
(f) National Insurance contributions liability

                                                          20 Marks

26   CHI KNITWEAR   *36 mins*

Chi Knitwear Ltd is an old fashioned firm with a hand-written set of books. A trial balance is extracted at the end of each month, and a profit and loss account and balance sheet are computed. This month however the trial balance will not balance, the credits exceeding debits by £1,536.

You are asked to help and after inspection of the ledgers discover the following errors.

(a) A balance of £87 on a debtors account has been omitted from the schedule of debtors, the total of which was entered as debtors in the trial balance.

(b) A small piece of machinery purchased for £1,200 had been written off to repairs.

(c) The receipts side of the cash book had been undercast by £720.

(d) The total of one page of the sales day book had been carried forward as £8,154, whereas the correct amount was £8,514.

(e) A credit note for £179 received from a supplier had been posted to the wrong side of his account.

(f) An electricity bill in the sum of £152, not yet accrued for, is discovered in a filing tray.

(g) Mr Smith whose past debts to the company had been the subject of a provision, at last paid £731 to clear his account. His personal account has been credited but the cheques has not yet been entered in the cash book.

Required

(a)	Write up the suspense account to clear the trial balance difference.	**10 Marks**
(b)	State the effect on the accounts of correcting each error.	**10 Marks**

Total Marks = 20

27   DONALD BROWN
36 mins

Donald Brown, a sole trader, extracted the following trial balance on 31 December 19X0.

TRIAL BALANCE AS AT 31 DECEMBER 19X0

	Debit £	Credit £
Capital at 1 January 19X0		26,094
Debtors	42,737	
Cash in hand	1,411	
Creditors		35,404
Fixtures and fittings at cost	42,200	
Discounts allowed	1,304	
Discounts received		1,175
Stock at 1 January 19X0	18,460	
Sales		491,620
Purchases	387,936	
Motor vehicles at cost	45,730	
Lighting and heating	6,184	
Motor expenses	2,862	
Rent	8,841	
General expenses	7,413	
Balance at bank		19,861
Provision for deprecation		
Fixtures and fittings		2,200
Motor vehicles		15,292
Drawings	26,568	
	591,646	591,646

The following information as at 31 December is also available.

(a) £218 is owing for motor expenses.

(b) £680 has been prepaid for rent.

(c) Depreciation is to be provided of the year as follows.

> Motor vehicles: 20% on cost
> Fixtures and fittings: 10% reducing balance method

(d) Stock at the close of business was valued at £19,926.

Required

Prepare Donald Brown's trading and profit and loss account for the year ended 31 December 19X0 and his balance sheet at that date.

20 Marks

28   HERBERT HOWELL   *36 mins*

The following trial balance has been extracted from the ledger of Herbert Howell, a sole trader, as at 31 May 19X9, the end of his most recent financial year.

HERBERT HOWELL
TRIAL BALANCE AS AT 31 MAY 19X9

	Dr £	Cr £
Property, at cost	90,000	
Equipment, at cost	57,500	
Provisions for depreciation (as at 1 June 19X8)		
- property		12,500
- equipment		32,500
Stock, as at 1 June 19X8	27,400	
Purchases	259,600	
Sales		405,000
Discounts allowed	3,370	
Discounts received		4,420
Wages and salaries	52,360	
Bad debts	1,720	
Loan interest	1,560	
Carriage out	5,310	
Other operating expenses	38,800	
Trade debtors	46,200	
Trade creditors		33,600
Provision for bad debts		280
Cash on hand	151	
Bank overdraft		14,500
Drawings	28,930	
13% Loan		12,000
Capital, as at 1 June 19X8		98,101
	612,901	612,901

The following additional information as at 31 May 19X9 is available.

(a) Stock as at the close of business was valued at £25,900.

(b) Depreciation for the year ended 31 May 19X9 has yet to be provided as follows:

property   - 1% using the straight line method;
equipment - 15% using the straight line method;

(c) Wages and salaries are accrued by £140.

(d) 'Other operating expenses' includes certain expenses prepaid by £500. Other expenses included under this heading are accrued by £200.

(e) The provision for bad debts is to be adjusted so that it is 0.5% of trade debtors as at 31 May 19X9.

(f) 'Purchases' includes goods valued at £1,040 which were withdrawn by Mr Howell for his own personal use.

Required

Prepare Mr Howell's trading and profit and loss account for the year ended 31 May 19X9 and his balance sheet as at 31 May 19X9.

20 Marks

29   BRENDA BAILEY   *45 mins*

The following trial balance has been extracted from the accounts of Brenda Bailey, a sole trader.

BRENDA BAILEY
TRIAL BALANCE AS AT 30 JUNE 19X9

	Dr £	Cr £
Sales		427,726
Purchases	302,419	
Carriage inwards	476	
Carriage outwards	829	
Wages and salaries	64,210	
Rent and rates	12,466	
Heat and light	4,757	
Stock at 1 July 19X8	15,310	
Drawings	21,600	
Equipment at cost	102,000	
Motor vehicles at cost	43,270	
Provision for depreciation		
Equipment		22,250
Motor vehicles		8,920
Debtors	50,633	
Creditors		41,792
Bank		3,295
Sundry expenses	8,426	
Cash	477	
Capital		122,890
	626,873	626,873

The following information as at 30 June 19X9 is also available.

(a) £350 is owing for heat and light.

(b) £620 has been prepaid for rent and rates.

(c) Depreciation is to be provided for the year as follows:

Equipment   - 10% on cost
Motor vehicles - 20% on cost.

(d) Stock at the close of business was valued at £16,480.

Required

Prepare Brenda Bailey's trading and profit and loss account for the year ended 30 June 19X9 and her balance sheet at that date.

25 Marks

30   HELPFUL COMPUTERS   *36 mins*

Computers are increasingly being used for accounts work in all types of business.

(a) What makes accounting systems relatively easy to computerise?   **10 Marks**
(b) Why are computers so helpful in processing accounting data?   **10 Marks**

Total Marks = 20

31   GILTAN GOLF CLUB

The treasurer of the Giltan Golf Club has prepared the following receipts and payments account for the year ended 31 March 19X8.

	£		£
Balance at 1 April 19X7	682	Functions	305
Subscriptions	2,930	Repairs	146
Functions	367	Telephone	67
Sale of land	1,600	Extensions to clubhouse	600
Bank interest	60	Furniture	135
Bequest	255	Heat and light	115
Sundry income	46	Salary and wages	2,066
		Sundry expenses	104
		Balance c/d:	
		Bank	2,300
		Cash	102
			2,402
	5,940		5,940

You are required to prepare an income and expenditure account for the year ended 31 March 19X8 and a balance sheet at that date. The treasurer has supplied the following additional information.

(a) Subscriptions received included £65 which had been in arrears at 31 March 19X7 and £35 which had been paid for the year commencing 1 April 19X8.

(b) Land sold had been valued in the club's books at cost £500.

(c) Accrued expenses:

	31 March 19X7	31 March 19X8
	£	£
Heat and light	32	40
Wages	12	14
Telephone	14	10
	58	64

(d) Depreciation is to be charged on the original cost of assets appearing in the books at 31 March 19X8 as follows.

Buildings	5 per cent
Fixtures and fittings	10 per cent
Furniture	20 per cent

(e) The following balances are from the club's books at 31 March 19X7.

	£
Land at cost	4,000
Buildings at cost	3,200
Buildings provision for depreciation	860
Fixtures and fittings at cost	470
Fixtures and fittings provision for depreciation	82
Furniture at cost	380
Furniture provision for depreciation	164
Subscriptions in arrears (including £15 from a lapsed member who had emigrated)	80
Subscriptions in advance	30
Accrued expenses	58
Bank	600
Cash	82
Accumulated fund	7,618

32   IMPROVIDENT ACTUARIES   *54 mins*

The following balances were taken from the books of the Improvident Actuaries Society Golf Club as at 1 January 19X5.

	£	£
Course at cost		70,000
Clubhouse at cost		15,000
Building fund - represented by investments:		
£20,000 4% consolidated stock	7,400	
Deposit with building society	10,000	
		17,400
Subscriptions in advance (19X5)		400
Creditors for bar supplies		350
Life membership fund		4,000
Subscriptions in arrear		600
Bar stock		4,800
Clubhouse equipment at cost		3,200
Cash in hand	100	
Cash at bank	850	
		950

An analysis of the bank account operated by the club showed the following summary of receipts and payments during the year ended 31 December 19X5.

Receipts	£
Subscriptions	25,000
Life members	2,000
Sale of instruction manuals	700
Green fees	300
Sale of old carpet from clubhouse	22
Bar takings	28,500
Consolidated stock interest	800

Payments	£
Upkeep of course	16,150
General clubhouse expenses (including bar wages of £4,200)	12,150
Petty cash (expenses paid to treasurer)	1,550
Bar supplies	23,150
Purchase of instruction manuals	250
Piano	500
Deposited with building society	800
Replacement carpet for clubhouse	1,260

The following information is significant for the preparation of the club's accounts.

(a)   The club maintains a building fund separate from the capital fund and life membership fund. The building fund is invested in consolidated stock and a building society, whilst the capital fund and life membership fund are represented by the general assets of the club.

(b)   The building society has been instructed to credit the interest on the club's account direct to the account at each half year. The society computes interest half yearly on 30 June and 31 December. This year the interest amounted to £740. Interest paid on the consolidated stock is also added to the building fund by paying it into the building society account.

(c)   There were four life members at the beginning of the year, one of whom has since died. Two other life members have, however, joined the club.

(d)   Renewals of clubhouse furnishings are to be treated as revenue expenditure.

(e)   Outstanding at 31 December 19X5 were:

	£
Creditors for bar supplies	1,600
Subscriptions in advance (19X6)	900
Subscriptions in arrear (19X5)	300
Bar chits not yet settled	35

(f)   Bar stocks at 31 December 19X5 were valued at £4,300.

(g)   It is a rule of the club that a cash float of £100 shall be maintained in the treasurer's hands. To this end an imprest petty cash account is operated.

(h)   An insurance premium of £480 has been paid by cheque during 19X5 for the year to 31 March 19X6.

Required

(a)   Prepare an income and expenditure account for the year ended 31 December 19X5.   **15 Marks**

(b)   Prepare a balance sheet as at that date.   **15 Marks**

Total Marks = 30

33   ROBERT FULLER   *54 mins*

Robert Fuller started his own business selling antiques on 1 May 19X3. Immediately prior to this date he had bought premises at a cost of £93,200 and shelving and fittings for £7,800. He had also taken possession of stock costing £14,000 although £4,600 of this total still remained unpaid at 1 May 19X3. A bank loan of £50,000 had been received on 29 April 19X3 which carried an interest rate of 10% pa. Interest was to be paid quarterly in arrears. On 1 May 19X3 Mr Fuller had £11,740 debit balance in his bank account and £280 cash in hand.

Mr Fuller enjoyed his first year in business. He found the majority of customers to be friendly people who were knowledgeable about antiques. He enjoyed lengthy conversations with a few of his customers and soon built up a good reputation. A few people purchased goods at regular intervals.

On 30 April 19X4 Mr Fuller summarised his cash book entries for the financial year as follows.

CASH BOOK

	Discount £	Cash £	Bank £		Discount £	Cash £	Bank £
1 May 19X3							
Balance b/f		280	11,740	Cash register			3,600
Customer				Purchases	170	420	88,420
payments	180	1,990	171,900	Delivery van			10,800
Rent		600	6,600	Casual wages		340	1,880
Contra			1,970	Heat and light			620
				New fittings			4,800
				Cleaning material			140
				Postage /stationery		80	
				Contra		1,970	
				Vehicle expense			3,240
				Drawings			18,000
				Misc expenses			11,910
				Bank interest			3,750
				Balance c/f		60	45,050
		2,870	192,210			2,870	192,210

The delivery van was purchased on 1 August 19X3 and was expected to have an effective life of three years. The residual value is expected to be negligible. The anticipated loss in value is expected to be: 50% in the first year of use, 30% in the second year of use, 20% in the third year of use.

Mr Fuller has decided to depreciate other fixed assets by 20% per annum based on assets held at the year end with the exception of premises which he anticipates will retain its original value.

The flat above the antique shop was let to a tenant from 1 August 19X3 at a rent of £600 per month, payable quarterly in advance.

Other information available at 30 April 19X4 is as follows.

An electricity bill for £180 in respect of the quarter ending 31 May 19X4 was unpaid. Postage stamps worth £20 purchased during Mr Fuller's financial year had not yet been used. Customers owed £2,140 and suppliers were owed £7,740. Stock-in-trade was valued at £15,500.

Required

(a) Prepare Mr Fuller's trading and profit and loss account for the year ended 30 April 19X4 and a balance sheet at that date. **18 Marks**

(b) Clearly show the calculation of Mr Fuller's capital account balance at 30 April 19X4. **4 Marks**

(c) Note four fundamental accounting concepts/conventions you have applied in constructing Mr Fuller's final accounts. Give an example from your answer for each concept/convention you have referred to. **8 Marks**

Total Marks = 30

34   HIGHTON   *45 mins*

A Highton is in business as a general retailer. He does not keep a full set of accounting records; however it has been possible to extract the following details from the few records that are available.

	1 April 19X1 £	31 March 19X2 £
Freehold land and buildings at cost	10,000	10,000
Motor vehicle (cost £3,000)	2,250	
Stock, at cost	3,500	4,000
Trade debtors	500	1,000
Prepayments: motor vehicle expenses	200	300
property insurance	50	100
Cash at bank	550	950
Cash in hand	100	450
Loan from Highton's father	10,000	
Trade creditors: accruals	1,500	1,800
electricity	200	400
motor vehicle expenses	200	100

Extract from a rough cash book for the year to 31 March 19X2

	£
Receipts	
Cash sales	80,400

	£
Payments	
Cash purchases	17,000
Drawings	7,000
General shop expenses	100
Telephone	100
Wages	3,000

Extract from the bank pass sheets for the year to 31 March 19X2

	£
Receipts	
Cash banked	52,850
Cheques from trade debtors	8,750

	£
Payments	
Cheques to suppliers	47,200
Loan repayment (including interest)	10,100
Electricity	400
Motor vehicle expenses	1,000
Property insurance	150
Rates	300
Telephone	300
Drawings	1,750

Note. Depreciation is to be provided on the motor vehicle at a rate of 25% per annum on cost.

You are required to prepare a trading and profit and loss account for the year to 31 March 19X2, and a balance sheet as at that date.

25 Marks

35 CHURCH   *45 mins*

The summarised balance sheet of Richard Church, photographic retailer, as at 31 March 19X2, is as follows.

	Cost	*Depn*	*NBV*
	£	£	£
Shop equipment and fittings	15,000	3,000	12,000
Motor vehicles	6,000	1,500	4,500
	21,000	4,500	16,500
Stock at or below cost		10,420	
Trade debtors		6,260	
Rent paid in advance		650	
Bank		6,690	
		24,020	
Trade creditors		4,740	
Accrued expenses: heating and lighting		380	
		5,120	
Net current assets			18,900
Loan: S Chappell			(3,000)
			32,400
Capital account: R Church			32,400

Despite professional advice, Richard Church has not maintained an accounting system, but produces the following information regarding the financial year ended 31 March 19X3.

(a) Total sales and sales returns were £152,600 and £3,500 respectively. An average gross profit to sales ratio of 30 per cent is maintained during the year.

(b) The trade debtors figure at 31 March 19X3 was £5,620, on which figure it has been decided to make a provision for doubtful debts of 5 per cent at the year end. During the course of the financial year trade debts amounting to £470 had been written off.

(c) The trade creditors figure at 31 March 19X3 was £6,390. Discounts received from suppliers amounted to £760 in the financial year.

(d) Stock, at or below cost at 31 March 19X3, indicates an increased investment of £4,000 in stock over that one year earlier. Drawings from stock by Richard

Church during the year amounted to £600 and were included in payments made to suppliers; otherwise no records of these drawings were made.

(e) Payments for shop salaries for the year were £15,840, and for heating, lighting, rent and rates and other administration expenses amounted to £3,460. At 31 March 19X3 rent paid in advance amounted to £480, and heating bills outstanding were £310.

(f) Shop fittings acquired during the year, and paid for, amounted to £2,000. Depreciation on shop equipment and fittings is provided annually at the rate of 10 per cent on the original cost of assets held at the financial year end. Similarly, depreciation on the motor vehicle is to be provided at the rate of 25% on original cost.

(g) On 31 March 19X3 the loan from S Chappell was repaid.

(h) Cash drawings during the financial period by Richard Church amounted to £9,000.

Required

(a) Prepare a trading and profit and loss account for the year ended 31 March 19X3.

(b) Prepare the balance sheet as at 31 March 19X3.

25 Marks

36   **EXCEL**   *45 mins*

The following balances were extracted from the accounting records of Excel Ltd, a car hire and taxi service company in respect of the year ended 30th November 19X5.

	£
Motor cars	111,200
Depreciation - motor cars to 30th November 19X4	46,320
Revenue from business operations	510,500
Ordinary shares - 200,000 of £1 each, allotted and fully paid	200,000
Retained profits at 30th November 19X4	127,200
Drivers' wages and expenses	245,200
Motor vehicle expenses	
Licence and insurance	7,500
Repairs etc.	35,460
Petrol and oil	45,310
Trade debtors	62,530
Administration expenses	30,460
Advertising expenses	12,540
Directors' remuneration	40,000
12% Debentures issued 1st September 19X5	
(interest payable January and July)	120,000
Interim dividend on ordinary shares	12,000
Freehold premises at cost	420,000
Stock at 30th November 19X4	
Petrol and oil	1,200
Vehicle spares	700
Share premium	40,000
Cash at bank	19,920

Additional information relevant to the year ended 30th November 19X5 is as follows.

(a) Trade debtors include bad debts of £890; in addition, it is considered necessary to make a provision for doubtful debts of 3% of debtors.

(b) The following expenses were outstanding at 30th November 19X5:

	£
Advertising	800
Auditor's fee	2,000
Repairs	1,450

(c) Prepayments in respect of licences and insurance amounted to £1,500.

(d) Stocks at 30th November 19X5 were:

	£
Petrol and oil	1,640
Vehicle spares	3,170

(e) All the motor vehicles were bought after 1st December 19X1. The depreciation of the vehicles is provided from the date of purchase to the date of sale at the rate of 25% per annum on the straight line method. The motor vehicles figure is made up as follows.

	£
Cost to 30th November 19X4	85,200
Additions - 1 September 19X5	32,000
Sale proceeds 1 September 19X5 (cost £24,000 on 1 December 19X2)	6,000

(f) A final ordinary share dividend of 12p per share is proposed for the year ended 30th November 19X5.

Required

(a) Prepare the profit and loss appropriation accounts for the year ended 30 November 19X5.   **13 Marks**

(b) Prepare the balance sheet as on the above date.   **12 Marks**

Total Marks = 25

37   PEAKEWAR   *43 mins*

Peakewar Ltd, a manufacturing and trading company, has extracted the following trial balance from its ledgers on 31 October 19X9.

	Debit £'000	Credit £'000
Premises at cost	200	
Plant and equipment at cost	180	
Vehicles at cost	64	
Accumulated depreciation at 1 November 19X8		
Premises		32
Plant and equipment		102
Vehicles		24
Ordinary shares (£1 each)		150
Share premium		50
Profit and loss reserve		283
Stocks: direct materials (1 November 19X8)	12	
work in progress (1 November 19X8)	8	
finished goods	16	
Purchases of direct materials	164	
Sales		671
Production overhead incurred	104	
Selling overhead	26	
Administration overhead	49	
Trade debtors and creditors	46	28
PAYE creditor		13
VAT creditor		28
Cash in hand	3	
Balance at bank	329	
Direct manufacturing wages	180	
	1,381	1,381

The following information is also relevant.

(a) On 1 November 19X8 the company sold a piece of plant for £6,000. It had originally cost the company £20,000 on 1 November 19X5. The proceeds from the sale were recorded as a credit to the sales account and a debit to the bank account.

(b) The company provides for depreciation using the following rates.

Premises	4% per annum on cost
Plant and equipment	20% per annum on cost
Vehicles	25% per annum reducing balance

The depreciation of premises and plant and equipment is treated as a manufacturing overhead, the depreciation of vehicles is apportioned 50% to manufacturing overhead, 25% to selling overhead and 25% to administration overhead.

No entries have yet been made for depreciation in respect of the year ended 31 October 19X9.

(c) Closing stocks of raw materials on 31 October 19X9 were valued at cost as £14,000 but some of these items had been in stock for ten years and had never been used. These items had an original cost of £3,000 but it was believed that their only value was as scrap for which £1,000 would be realised.

(d) Closing work in progress on 31 October 19X9 was valued at £17000.

	£
Direct labour	8,000
Direct materials	5,000
Production overhead	4,000

(e) Unfortunately, the closing finished goods stock could not be counted until 3 November 19X9 when it had a total production cost of £13,000. The following transactions took place during the three days after the company's year end but before the stock-take.

Sales to customers	£5,000 at selling price
Returns by customers	£1,250 at selling price
Work in progress completed	£2,000 at total production cost

The company priced the goods sold to/returned by customers during this period using a mark-up of 25% on total production cost.

Required

(a) Record the disposal of plant in the plant disposal account in the ledger of the company, showing clearly any profit/loss on disposal.   **4 Marks**

(b) Prepare the manufacturing, trading and profit and loss account of the company for the year ended 31 October 19X9.   **8 Marks**

(c) Prepare the balance sheet of the company at 31 October 19X9.   **6 Marks**

(d) Explain the basis of your valuation of raw material, work in progress and finished goods stock on 31 October 19X9, relating your answer to stock valuation theory as appropriate.   **6 Marks**

Total Marks = 24

38   MATTHEWS

The financial details which follow are in respect of Matthews Ltd.

PROFIT AND LOSS ACCOUNT EXTRACT FOR THE YEAR ENDED 31 MAY 19X4

	£'000
Sales	1,284
Cost of goods sold	708
Operating profit	88
Interest payable	(23)
Net profit	65
Corporation tax	(20)
Dividends	(17)
Retained profit	28

BALANCE SHEETS AS AT 31 MAY

	19X3	*19X4*
	£'000	£'000
Fixed assets at cost	780	812
Cumulative depreciation	(485)	(546)
	295	266
Stock	118	154
Debtors	96	167
Cash in hand	12	-
Trade creditors	179	210
Bank overdraft	-	23
Proposed dividends	17	17
Corporation tax	14	18
12% debenture	200	180
	111	139
Ordinary shares @ £1	40	40
Retained profits	71	99
	111	139

Note. No fixed assets were sold between 31 May 19X3 and 31 May 19X4.

Required

Prepare a cash flow statement in respect of Matthews Ltd for the year ended 31 May 19X4.

39   WEAKNESSES   *27 mins*

The managing director of H plc read a newspaper report of a fraud with had recently come to the attention of the police. The perpetrators had sent invoices to several thousand companies. These requested payment for an entry in a trade directory.

The directory did not, however, exist. The newspaper report claimed that approximately 700 companies had paid £2,000 each for an entry in this alleged directory. H plc's managing director asked whether the company had received one of these invoices. It was discovered that H plc was one of the companies which had paid the £2,000 charge. The reason for this payment was investigated.

H plc's accounting system was recently computerised. All invoices are keyed straight into a standard accounting package. The company's accounting department is short staffed and so the default settings on the package have been set to minimise the amount of clerical effort required to process transactions. If, for example, an invoice is received from a new supplier, the program will automatically allocate an account number and open an account in the purchase ledger. At the end of every month, the program calculates the amount which is due to each creditor; a cheque for each creditor is automatically printed out for the total of all of the invoices from that creditor input during the month. When the system was first installed, the accountant used to review creditors' accounts prior to the cheque run as a check that the system was not being abused. This review was, however, discontinued because of pressure of work and because there were too many invoices to review properly.

The managing director was most disturbed by this description of the purchases system and decided that it was in urgent need of improvement. The company's accountant was ordered to redesign the system. The accountant was authorised to employ additional staff if the extra expense could be justified.

Required

(a) Describe three weaknesses in H plc's existing purchases system. **6 Marks**

(b) How should the purchases and creditors system should be reorganised?

9 Marks

Total Marks = 15

40 **A AND B** *36 mins*

Business A and Business B are both engaged in retailing, but seem to take a different approach to this trade according to the information available. This information consists of a table of ratios, shown below.

Ratio	Business A	Business B
Current ratio	2:1	1.5:1
Quick assets (acid test) ratio	1.7:1	0.7:1
Return on capital employed (ROCE)	20%	17%
Return on owner's equity (ROOE)	30%	18%
Debtors turnover	63 days	21 days
Creditors turnover	50 days	45 days
Gross profit percentage	40%	15%
Net profit percentage	10%	10%
Stock turnover	52 days	25 days

Required

(a) Explain briefly how each ratio is calculated. **10 Marks**

(b) Describe what this information indicates about the differences in approach between the two businesses. If one of them prides itself on personal service and one of them on competitive prices, which do you think is which and why?

10 Marks

Total Marks = 20

1   USERS OF ACCOUNTING INFORMATION

The people who might be interested in financial information about a large public company may be classified as follows.

(a) *Managers of the company*. These are people appointed by the company's owners to supervise the day-to-day activities of the company. They need information about the company's financial situation as it is currently and as it is expected to be in the future. This is to enable them to manage the business efficiently and to take effective control and planning decisions.

(b) *Shareholders of the company*, ie the company's owners. These will want to assess how effectively management is performing its stewardship function. They will want to know how profitably management is running the company's operations and how much profit they can afford to withdraw from the business for their own use.

(c) *Trade contacts*, including suppliers who provide goods to the company on credit and customers who purchase the goods or services provided by the company. *Suppliers* will want to know about the company's ability to pay its debts; *customers* need to know that the company is a secure source of supply and is In no danger of having to close down.

(d) *Providers of finance to the company*. These might include a bank which permits the company to operate an overdraft, or provides longer-term finance by granting a loan. The bank will want to ensure that the company is able to keep up with interest payments, and eventually to repay the amounts advanced.

(e) *The Inland Revenue*, who will want to know about business profits in order to assess the tax payable by the company, and also the *Customs and Excise*.

2   DEFINITIONS

(a) The *going concern* concept is the assumption that, when preparing accounts, the business will continue trading for the foreseeable future, without closing down or even running down its activities to a significant extent.

If a business is to be closed down, for example, then any stock on hand will have to be valued at the amount they will realise in a forced sale. But if the business is regarded as a going concern, then the value of any unsold stock at the end of an accounting period will be carried forward to the next period and will eventually be matched against income earned in that subsequent period.

(b) The *accruals concept* is that, when profit is being calculated, revenue earned must be matched against the expenditure incurred in earning it. For example, suppose you were calculating profit for the year ended 31 December 19X8 and had got as far as working out that gross profit was £12,000. To calculate net profit, expenses must be deducted - suppose rent paid in 19X8 was £700. Then only that part of the £700 relating to 19X8 should be deducted from the gross profit. If £200 was actually a prepayment for rent in 19X9, then that £200 must be matched against next year's income, not against the £12,000 for 19X8.

(c) The *consistency concept* states that in preparing accounts consistency should be observed in two respects.

   (i)   Similar items within a single set of accounts should be given similar accounting treatments.

   (ii) The same treatment should be applied from one period to another in accounting for similar items. This enables valid comparisons to be made from one period to the next.

For example, suppose a business owns a fleet of cars. Then the consistency concept rules that each car should be depreciated in the same way (by whatever method the business deems most appropriate) and once that depreciation policy has been set, it should be applied consistently from one year to the next.

A business can change its accounting methods, but it should explain clearly why it is doing so, and it should show the effects of the change on the profits for the relevant year in its financial statements.

(d) The *prudence concept* is that where alternative procedures, or alternative valuations, are possible, the one selected should be the one which gives the most cautious presentation of the business's financial position or results. For example, stocks should be stated in the balance sheet at the lower of cost or net realisable value rather than their selling price: to value the stock at selling price would be to anticipate making a profit before the profit had been earned, and would not be 'prudent'.

The other aspect of the prudence concept is that where a loss is foreseen, it should be anticipated and taken into account immediately. If a business purchases stock for £1,200 but because of a sudden slump in the market only £900 is likely to be realised when the stock is sold, the prudence concept dictates that the stock should be valued at £900. It is not enough to wait until the stock is sold, and then recognise the £300 loss. It must be recognised as soon as it is foreseen.

3   FINANCIAL REPORTING

(a)   Shareholders require information on a company and its performance to make investment decisions, and to assist in voting at general meetings. This information should be provided in sufficient detail to allow informed decision-making but without obscuring the important issues.

The shareholders' primary interest lies in the earnings and dividend trends revealed by the profit and loss account, as these are traditionally the main factors in share valuation. Further information on future projects and dividend policy will make it easier to establish trends. Comparison with other companies is facilitated by presentation of information in a similar format by all companies.

Additionally, shareholders in large public companies will wish to check the stewardship of the directors to whom they have delegated the company's management. Where shareholders are in close touch with management (or comprise the management), this is not as important.

Finally, many investors nowadays wish to avoid investment in companies whose ecological, social and political activities are at odds with their own attitudes. The corporate report should therefore give full details of all investments, products, overseas locations, charitable and political donations and initiatives etc.

(b)   In times of high inflation, growth in dividends and earnings can be insufficient to keep ahead of rising prices. Under the historical cost basis of accounting, this is not obvious from the accounts because they are not stated in 'real' terms, ie adjusted to show what the results would have been if there had no been no inflation in the period.

The two most common alternatives to historical cost accounting are current cost accounting (CCA) and current purchasing power accounting (CPP).

Under CCA, assets are valued at replacement cost. Various adjustments to profit are made so that the current cost profit 'represents the surplus arising from the ordinary activities of the company in the period after allowing for the impact of price changes on the net assets needed to maintain its operating capital' (ASC Handbook Accounting for the effects of changing prices).

CCA's aim is to make it easier to assess how well the company is maintaining its operating capacity. By contrast, under CPP the aim is to measure how well the equity investors' capital has been maintained in the period. All non-monetary assets are restated after adjustment for changes in the retail price index since acquisition. An adjustment to profit is made to reflect the reduction in value in real terms of long-term debt when inflation rises and the loss of value when non-monetary items (eg stock) are turned into monetary items (eg debtors).

The application of general price indices means that for businesses affected by non-standard levels of inflation, the adjusted accounts have little relevance to the company's operating capacity. However, the investor needs to know how the investment has performed in terms of increasing his purchasing power.

A disadvantage of both CCA and CPP is that neither has gained general acceptance in the UK and neither is straightforward to interpret, even for the more financially sophisticated investor, especially as no consistent application has been made mandatory. Accounts prepared to allow for inflation are therefore not directly comparable with most similar enterprises' accounts.

A more important point for most investors is to examine the company's liquidity, which is stretched in times of inflation because of the constant increases in the replacement costs of materials and in labour costs. This can be gauged from the balance sheet, flow of funds statement and notes. The investor needs to know whether sufficient funds are being generated to cover dividend payments as well as other liabilities and new investment plans and to maintain current levels of operation. More fundamentally, the company must remain solvent if the investment of shareholders is to remain secure.

To this end, companies need to disclose future commitments under leases and other financing agreements, together with contingent liabilities and guarantees.

4 THE ACCOUNTING EQUATION

Transaction	Assets		=	Capital		+	Liabilities	
		£			£			£
Start of business	Cash	5,000	=		5,000	+		0
(a)	Cash	3,200	=		5,000	+		0
	Shelves	1,800						
		5,000						
(b)	Cash	1,200	=		5,000	+		0
	Shelves	1,800						
	Books	2,000						
		5,000						
(c)	Cash	2,700	=		5,000	+		0
	Shelves	1,800		Profit	500			
	Books	1,000						
		5,500			5,500			
(d)	Cash	2,500	=		5,000	+		0
	Shelves	1,800		Profit	500			
	Books	1,000		Drawings	(200)			
		5,300			5,300			
(e)	Cash	3,000	=		5,000	+	Loan	500
	Shelves	1,800		Profit	500			
	Books	1,000		Drawings	(200)			
		5,800			5,300			500
(f)	Cash	3,000	=		5,000	+	Loan	500
	Shelves	1,800		Profit	500		Creditor	1,000
	Books	1,000		Drawings	(200)			
	Carpets	1,000			5,300			1,500
		6,800						
(g)	Cash	3,000	=		5,000	+	Loan	500
	Shelves	1,800		Profit	700		Creditor	1,000
	Books	600		Drawings	(200)			
	Carpets	1,000			5,500			1,500
	Debtor	600						
		7,000						

5 FINANCIAL STATEMENTS

A balance sheet is a 'snapshot' of the financial position of a business. It is a statement of the liabilities, assets and capital of the business at a given moment in time. It is basically the same as the accounting equation, but written out in more detail.

The trading profit and loss account is not a static picture like the balance sheet, but is a record of income generated and expenditure incurred over the relevant accounting period.

Capital expenditure is expenditure which results in the acquisition of fixed assets (or an improvement in their earning capacity). It is not charged as an expense in the trading, profit and loss account.

Revenue expenditure is any other expenditure such as purchase of goods and expenses incurred to keep the business running (for example repairs, wages, electricity and so on). It is accounted for in the trading, profit and loss account.

Capital expenditure: (a), (d)
Revenue expenditure: (b), (c), (e), (f)

(Note that the value of the transactions is irrelevant.)

6 BUSINESS TRANSACTIONS

(a) *Purchase of goods on credit*

   (i) The supplier's invoice would be the original document.

   (ii) The original entry would be made in the purchase day book.

(b) *Allowances to credit customers on the return of faulty goods*

   (i) The usual documentation is a credit note. Occasionally, however, a customer may himself issue a debit note.

   (ii) The book of original entry would be the sales returns day book.

(c) *Petty cash reimbursement*

   (i) The original documents for the data would be receipts and a petty cash voucher.

   (ii) The transaction would be entered in the petty cash book.

(d) *Credit card sale*

   (i) The original document would be the credit card sales voucher or, strictly speaking, a copy of it.

   (ii) The original entry would be made in the cash book. This is because a credit card sale is like a cash sale as far as the retailer is concerned. The credit card company pays immediately, or very soon after the transaction has taken place. There is no need to set up a debtor.

7 BEECHFIELD

(a)

PETTY CASH BOOK

Receipts	Date	Narrative	Total	Stationery	Cleaning	Enter-tainment	Travel	Postages
£	19X9		£	£	£	£	£	£
	Nov							
350	1	Cash						
	2	Materials	5		5			
	3	Stamps	10					10
	6	Envelopes	12	12				
	8	Taxi fare	32				32	
	10	Petrol	17				17	
	14	Typing paper	25	25				
	15	Materials	4		4			
	16	Bus fare	2				2	
	20	Visitors' lunch	56			56		
	21	Mops and brushes	41		41			
	23	Stamps	35					35
	27	Envelopes	12	12				
	29	Visitors' lunches	30			30		
	30	Photocopying paper	40	40				
			321	89	50	86	51	45
321	30	Cash						
	30	Balance c/d	350					
671			671					
	Dec							
350	1	Balance b/d						

(b)

STATIONERY

19X9			£	19X9		£
1.11		Balance b/d	X			
30.11		Petty cash book	89			X
etc						

POSTAGES

19X9		£	19X9		£
1.11	Balance b/d	X			
30.11	Petty cash book	45			
etc					

8 JOCKFIELD

(a),(b),(c)

PETTY CASH BOOK

Receipts £	Date	Narrative	Total £	Postage £	Travelling £	Cleaning £	Stationery £	Motor £
300	May 1	Cash						
	May 2	Postage	18	18				
	May 3	Travelling	12		12			
	May 5	Cleaning	15			15		
	May 7	Petrol	22					22
	May 8	Travelling	25		25			
	May 9	Stationery	17				17	
	May 11	Cleaning	18			18		
	May 14	Postage	5	5				
	May 15	Travelling	8		8			
	May 18	Stationery	9				9	
	May 18	Cleaning	23			23		
	May 20	Postage	13	13				
	May 24	Van service	43					43
	May 26	Petrol	18					18
	May 27	Cleaning	21			21		
	May 29	Postage	5	5				
	May 30	Petrol	14					14
			286	41	45	77	26	97
286	May 31	Cash						
		Balance c/d	300					
586			586					
300	June 1	Balance b/d						

(d) The totals in the analysis column are posted to the relevant ledger accounts (the cash account will be CR £286, the relevant accounts will be debited the analysed amounts).

9 J OCKEY

(a) The relevant books of prime entry are the cash book, the sales day book, the purchase day book.

CASH BOOK (RECEIPTS)

Date	Narrative	Total £	Capital £	Sales £	Debtors £
May 1	Capital	5,000	5,000		
May 13	Sales	200		200	
May 16	Bruce	700			700
May 24	Hill	200			200
		6,100	5,000	200	900

CASH BOOK (PAYMENTS)

Date May	Narrative	Total £	Fixtures and fittings £	Creditors £	Rent £	Delivery expenses £	Drawings £	Wages £
1	Store Fitments Ltd	2,000	2,000					
19	Abel	650		650				
20	Rent	200			200			
21	Delivery expenses	50				50		
30	Drawings	200					200	
30	Wages	320						320
31	Green	300		300				
		3,720	2,000	950	200	50	200	320

SALES DAY BOOK

Date	Customer	Amount £
May 4	Bruce	700
May 11	Hill	580
Mat 18	Nailor	360
		1,640

PURCHASE DAY BOOK

Date	Customer	Amount £
May 2	Abel	650
May 9	Green	300
May 17	Kaye	800
		1,750

(b) and (c)

The relevant ledger accounts are for cash, sales, purchases, creditors, debtors, capital, fixtures and fittings, rent, delivery expenses, drawings and wages. Because this is not the end of the accounting period, balances on sales and expense accounts are not transferred to P & L but are simply carried down to be continued in the next month.

CASH ACCOUNT

	£		£
May receipts	6,100	May payments	3,720
		Balance c/d	2,380
	6,100		6,100

SALES ACCOUNT

	£		£
Balance c/d	1,840	Cash	200
		Debtors	1,640
	1,840		1,840

PURCHASES ACCOUNT

	£		£
Creditors	1,750	Balance c/d	1,750

DEBTORS ACCOUNT

	£		£
Sales	1,640	Cash	900
		Balance c/d	740
	1,640		1,640

CREDITORS ACCOUNT

	£		£
Cash	950	Purchases	1,750
Balance c/d	800		
	1,750		1,750

CAPITAL ACCOUNT

	£		£
Balance c/d	5,000	Cash	5,000

FIXTURES AND FITTINGS ACCOUNT

	£		£
Cash	2,000	Balance c/d	2,000

RENT ACCOUNT

	£		£
Cash	200	Balance c/d	200

DELIVERY EXPENSES ACCOUNT

	£		£
Cash	50	Balance c/d	50

DRAWINGS ACCOUNT

	£		£
Cash	200	Balance c/d	200

WAGES ACCOUNT

	£		£
Cash	320	Balance c/d	320

(d) Trial balance as at 31 May 19X4:

Account	Dr	Cr
	£	£
Cash	2,380	
Sales		1,840
Purchases	1,750	
Debtors	740	
Creditors		800
Capital		5,000
Fixtures and fittings	2,000	
Rent	200	
Delivery expenses	50	
Drawings	200	
Wages	320	
	7,640	7,640

10   OMEGA

(a),(b),(c)

ALPHA

	£		£
Opening balance	210		
May sales	88	Balance c/d	298
	298		298

BETA

	£		£
Opening balance	1,040	Cash	1,040
May sales	314	Balance c/d	314
	1,354		1,354

GAMMA

	£		£
Opening balance	1,286	Cash	826
May sales	432	Balance c/d	892
	1,718		1,718

DELTA

	£		£
Opening balance	279	Cash	279
May sales	417	Balance c/d	417
	696		696

EPSILON

	£		£
Opening balance	823	Cash	823
May sales	129	Returns	88
May sales	269	Balance c/d	538
May sales	228		
	1,449		1,449

ZETA

	£		£
Cash	1,000	Opening balance	2,173
Balance c/d	1,441	May purchases	268
	2,441		2,441

ETA

	£		£
Cash	187	Opening balance	187
Balance c/d	1,164	May purchases	423
		May purchases	741
	1,351		1,351

THETA

	£		£
Cash	318	Opening balance	318

SALES ACCOUNT

	£		£
		May sales	1,877

PURCHASES ACCOUNT

	£		£
May purchases	1,432		

RETURNS ACCOUNT

	£		£
May returns	88		

CASH ACCOUNT

	£		£
May receipts	2,968	May payments	1,505

(d)   DEBTORS AS AT 31 MAY

	April £	May £	Total £
Alpha	210	88	298
Beta	-	314	314
Gamma	460	432	892
Delta	-	417	417
Epsilon	-	538	538
	670	1,789	2,459

11   **HUBBLE**

Rather than write out the ledger accounts all over again, the question may be answered as follows.

(a)   The postings necessary for each transaction are:

		£	£
DEBIT	Purchases	2,000	
CREDIT	Cash		1,000
CREDIT	Creditors		1,000
DEBIT	Interest	20	
CREDIT	Cash		20
DEBIT	Electricity	25	
CREDIT	Cash		25
DEBIT	Telephone	12	
CREDIT	Cash		12
DEBIT	Cash	500	
DEBIT	Debtors	3,000	
CREDIT	Sales		3,500
DEBIT	Cash	220	
CREDIT	Debtors		220

(b)   Once these have been posted and the accounts balanced off, the trial balance is:

Account	Dr	Cr
	£	£
Cash	18,083	
Capital		9,500
Bank loan		3,000
Sales		19,300
Debtors	6,980	
Rent	2,750	
Purchases	4,100	
Creditors		2,400
Interest	370	
Electricity	425	
Telephone	192	
Drawings	1,300	
	34,200	34,200

(*Note.* If you are not confident of your arithmetic, you may find it safer to write out and balance off all the ledger accounts individually.)

PROFIT AND LOSS (LEDGER) ACCOUNT

	£		£
Rent	2,750	Sales	19,300
Purchases	4,100		
Interest	370		
Electricity	425		
Telephone	192		
Balance (net profit taken to			
balance sheet)	11,463		
	19,300		19,300

(c)   A HUBBLE BALANCE SHEET AS AT 31 MARCH 19X8

	£	£
Assets		
Cash	18,083	
Debtors	6,980	
	25,063	
Current liabilities		
Creditors	(2,400)	
		22,663
Long-term liabilities		
Loan		(3,000)
		19,663
Capital		
Capital as at 1.4.19X7		9,500
Add profit for year		11,463
Less drawings		(1,300)
Capital as at 31.3.19X8		19,663

A HUBBLE
TRADING, PROFIT AND LOSS ACCOUNT
FOR THE YEAR ENDED 31 MARCH 19X8

	£	£
Sales		19,300
Less cost of sales		4,100
Gross profit		15,200
Less other expenses		
Rent	2,750	
Interest	370	
Electricity	425	
Telephone	192	
		3,737
Net profit		11,463

12   RENT, RATES AND INSURANCE

(a)   *Rent for the year ending 30 June 19X6*

	£
1 July 19X5 to 31 July 19X5 = £3,000/3	1,000
1 August 19X5 to 30 November 19X5	4,000
1 December 19X5 to 31 March 19X6	4,000
Accrued, 1 April 19X6 to 30 June 19X6 = 3/4 × £4,000	3,000
Charge to profit and loss for year ending 30 June 19X6	12,000

Rates for the year ending 30 June 19X6

	£	£
Rates prepaid last year, relating to this year		1,500
1 October 19X5 to 31 March 19X6		3,500
1 April 19X6 to 30 September 19X6	3,500	
Less prepaid July to September (3/6)	1,750	
April to June 19X6		1,750
Charge to profit and loss for year ending 30 June 19X6		6,750

Insurance for the year ending 30 June 19X6

	£	£
Insurance prepaid last year, relating to this year		1,800
1 November 19X5 to 31 October 19X6	6,000	
Less prepaid July to October (4/12)	2,000	
		4,000
Charge to profit and loss for year ending 30 June 19X6		5,800

(b)   The accrual or prepayment for each expense can be summarised from the workings in part (a).

As at 30 June 19X6

	£
Rent accrued	3,000
Rates prepaid	1,750
Insurance prepaid	2,000

13   HACKER

(a)

CASH BOOK

	£		£
Capital	4,000	Rent	600
Debtors - cash received	1,300	Delivery van	900
Cash sales	3,000	Creditors	1,600
		Sundry expenses	400
		Drawings	200
		Balance c/d	4,600
	8,300		8,300
Balance b/d	4,600		

SALES

	£		£
Trading a/c *	4,600	Cash book	3,000
		Debtors - credit sales	1,600
	4,600		4,600

DEBTORS

	£		£
Sales - on credit	1,600	Cash book	1,300
		Balance c/d	300
	1,600		1,600
Balance b/d	300		

CAPITAL

	£		£
Drawings *	200	Cash book	4,000
Balance c/d *	6,165	Profit and loss a/c *	2,365
	6,365		6,365
		Balance b/d	6,165

RENT

	£		£
Cash book	600	Profit and loss a/c *	150
		Prepayment c/d *	450
	600		600
Balance b/d	450		

DELIVERY VAN

	£		£
Cash book	900		

CREDITORS

	£		£
Cash book	1,600	∴ Purchases *	2,000
Balance c/d	400		
	2,000		2,000
		Balance b/d	400

PURCHASES

	£		£
Creditors	2,000	Trading a/c*	2,000

SUNDRY EXPENSES

	£		£
Cash book	400	Profit and loss a/c *	400

DRAWINGS

	£		£
Cash book	200	Capital a/c*	200

(b)

TRIAL BALANCE

	Dr	Cr
	£	£
Cash book	4,600	
Sales		4,600
Debtors	300	
Capital		4,000
Rent	600	
Delivery van	900	
Creditors		400
Purchases	2,000	
Sundry expenses	400	
Drawings	200	
	9,000	9,000

Note. The asterisked entries will be made after the trial balance has been extracted.

(c) TRADING AND PROFIT AND LOSS ACCOUNT
FOR THE THREE MONTHS ENDING 31 MARCH

	£	£
Sales		4,600
Purchases	2,000	
Less closing stock	360	
Cost of sales		1,640
Gross profit		2,960
Rent	150	
Sundry expenses	400	
Depreciation on van ($^3/_{12} \times 20\% \times £900$)	45	
		595
Net profit (to capital account)		2,365

STOCK ON HAND AT END OF THREE MONTHS

	£		£
Trading a/c	360		

PROVISION FOR DEPRECIATION

	£		£
		Profit and loss a/c	45

BALANCE SHEET AT 31 MARCH

	£	£
Fixed assets		
Van: cost	900	
less depreciation	45	
		855
Current assets		
Stock at cost	360	
Debtors	300	
Prepayments	450	
Cash	4,600	
	5,710	
Creditors	400	
		5,310
		6,165
Hacker's capital		
Original capital		4,000
Profit	2,365	
Less drawings	200	
Retained profit		2,165
		6,165

14   JAMES

> *Tutorial note.* This question introduces a distinction between the cash account (representing cash in hand) and the bank account (representing cash at bank). When cash in hand is paid into the bank the transaction is accounted for as a payment from the cash account and a receipt of cash by the bank account.

(a)

CASH ACCOUNT

		£			£
1.7.X2	Capital	20,000	2.7.X2	Bank	18,000
23.7.X2	Sales	1,500	5.7.X2	Rent	500
31.7.X2	Equipment	50	9.7.X2	Purchases	1,000
			31.7.X2	Drawings	150
				Balance c/d	1,900
		21,550			21,550
1.8.X2	Balance b/d	1,900			

CAPITAL ACCOUNT

		£			£
31.7.X2	Balance c/d	20,000	1.7.X2	Cash	20,000
			1.8.X2	Balance b/d	20,000

BANK ACCOUNT

		£			£
2.7.X2	Cash	18,000	6.7.X2	Equipment	300
31.7.X2	Debtors	450	31.7.X2	Creditors	1,620
				Balance c/d	16,530
		18,450			18,450
1.8.X2	Balance b/d	16,530			

RENT ACCOUNT

		£			£
5.7.X2	Cash	500	31.7.X2	Balance c/d	500
31.7.X2	Balance b/d	500			

EQUIPMENT ACCOUNT

		£			£
6.7.X2	Bank	300	31.7.X2	Cash	50
				Balance c/d	250
		300			300
1.8.X2	Balance b/d	250			

PURCHASES ACCOUNT

		£			£
9.7.X2	Cash	1,000	31.7.X2	Balance c/d	3,000
10.7.X2	Creditors (Seddon)	2,000			
		3,000			3,000
1.8.X2	Balance b/d	3,000			

CREDITORS ACCOUNT

		£			£
20.7.X2	Purchase returns	200	10.7.X2	Purchases	2,000
31.7.X2	Bank	1,620			
	Discounts received	180			
		2,000			2,000

PURCHASES RETURNS ACCOUNT

		£			£
31.7.X2	Balance c/d	200	20.7.X2	Creditors	200
			1.8.X2	Balance b/d	200

SALES ACCOUNT

		£			£
31.7.X2	Balance c/d	2,500	23.7.X2	Cash	1,500
			26.7.X2	Debtors (Frodsham)	1,000
		2,500			2,500
			1.8.X2	Balance b/d	2,500

DEBTORS ACCOUNT

		£			£
26.7.X2	Sales	1,000	28.7.X2	Sales returns	500
			31.7.X2	Bank	450
				Discounts allowed	50
		1,000			1,000

SALES RETURNS ACCOUNT

		£			£
28.7.X2	Debtors	500	31.7.X2	Balance c/d	500
1.8.X2	Balance b/d	500			

DISCOUNTS RECEIVED ACCOUNT

		£			£
31.7.X2	Balance c/d	180	31.7.X2	Creditors	180
			1.8.X2	Balance b/d	180

DISCOUNTS ALLOWED ACCOUNT

		£			£
31.7.X2	Debtors	50	31.7.X2	Balance c/d	50
1.8.X2	Balance b/d	50			

DRAWINGS ACCOUNT

		£				£
31.7.X2	Cash	150	31.7.X2	Balance c/d		150
1.8.X2	Balance b/d	150				

(b)   TRIAL BALANCE AS AT 31 JULY 19X2

	Debit	Credit
	£	£
Cash	1,900	
Capital		20,000
Bank	16,530	
Rent	500	
Equipment	250	
Purchases	3,000	
Purchase returns		200
Sales		2,500
Sales returns	500	
Discounts received		180
Discounts allowed	50	
Drawings	150	
	22,880	22,880

15   GEORGE

DEBTORS ACCOUNT

		£			£
1.10.X1	Balance b/f (b)	30,000	15.1.X2	Bad debts-Fall Ltd (c)	2,000
30.9.X2	Sales (d)	187,800	30.9.X2	Cash (e)	182,500
				Discounts allowed (f)	5,300
				Bad debts (g)	3,500
				Balance c/d	24,500
		217,800			217,800
1.10.X2	Balance b/d	24,500			

SALES ACCOUNT

		£			£
30.9.X2	Trading P & L a/c	234,600	30.9.X2	Cash (d)	46,800
				Debtors (d)	187,800
		234,600			234,600

BAD DEBTS ACCOUNT

		£			£
15.1.X2	Debtors-Fall Ltd (c)	2,000	30.9.X2	Trading P & L a/c	5,500
30.9.X2	Debtors (g)	3,500			
		5,500			5,500

PROVISION FOR DOUBTFUL DEBTS ACCOUNT

		£			£
30.9.X2	Balance c/d (h)		1.10.X1	Balance b/f (b)	
	5% × £24,500	1,225		5% × £30,000	1,500
	Trading P & L a/c - reduction in provision	275			
		1,500			1,500
			1.10.X2	Balance b/d	1,225

DISCOUNTS ALLOWED ACCOUNT

		£			£
30.9.X2	Debtors	5,300	30.9.X2	Trading P & L a/c	5,300

CASH ACCOUNT (EXTRACT)

		£
30.9.X2	Debtors	182,500
	Sales	46,800

TRADING PROFIT AND LOSS ACCOUNT (EXTRACT)

		£			£
30.9.X2	Bad debts	5,500	30.9.X2	Sales	234,600
	Discounts allowed	5,300		Provision for doubtful debts	275

16   AFTER THE STOCK COUNT

		Adjustment	
		Add to stock value	Subtract from stock value
Item	*Explanation*	£	£
(a)	The sub-total error has over-valued stocks by £(6,725 – 6,275)		450
(b)	This arithmetical error has over-valued the stock item by £(6 – 0.6) per unit for 260 units		1,404
(c)	Free samples received are not trading items and should be excluded from the valuation		
(d)	Goods in stock should be included in the valuation regardless of whether or not they have been paid for yet.		
(e)	Cost £2,885. Net realisable value £(3,600 – 921) = £2,679. The stock should be valued at the lower of cost and NRV. Since NRV is lower, the original valuation of stocks (at cost) will be reduced by £(2,885 – 2,679)		206
(f)	Stocks issued on sale or return and not yet accepted by the customer should be included in the stock valuation and valued at the lower of cost and NRV, here at £5 each (cost)	1,500	
(g)	The cost (£7.30) is below the current and fore-seeable selling price (£10 or more) which is assumed to be the NRV of the item. Since, the current valuation is at the lower of cost and NRV no change in valuation is necessary		
		1,500	2,060

	£	£
Original valuation of stocks, at cost		153,699
Adjustments and corrections:		
to increase valuation	1,500	
to decrease valuation	(2,060)	
		(560)
Valuation of stocks for the annual accounts		153,139

17   A COMPANY'S PLANT AND MACHINERY

(a) (i)   Fixed assets purchased in 19X0 and 19X2 cannot be depreciated further, because they are already fully depreciated.

(ii)   Fixed assets purchased in mid-19X4 had been depreciated by 90% (4½ years) by 31 December 19X8. All these assets will be fully depreciated by mid-19X9, when some of them are sold for £500.

(iii)   Fixed assets purchased in 19X6 and sold in 19X9 would be 60% depreciated at the time of sale. Fixed assets purchased in 19X6 and not sold would be 70% depreciated by the end of the year.

Year of purchase		Plant and machinery at cost £	Depreciation charge as a % of cost	Depreciation charge P & L account £
19X0		20,000 (fully depreciated)-	0%	0
19X2		30,000 (fully depreciated)-	0%	0
19X4		100,000 (note (ii) above)	10%	10,000
19X6	Assets sold in 19X9	24,000 (sold in mid-year)	10%	2,400
	Assets not sold in 19X9	46,000	20%	9,200
19X7		50,000	20%	10,000
19X8		30,000	20%	6,000
19X9		150,000 (bought in mid-year)	10%	15,000
Total provision for depreciation for the year				52,600

(b) (i) *Plant and machinery*

Year of purchase	At cost, as at 31 Dec 19X8 £	Disposals during 19X9 £	Additions during 19X9 £	At cost, as at 31 Dec 19X9 £
19X0	20,000			20,000
19X2	30,000	(17,000)		13,000
19X4	100,000	(9,000)		91,000
19X6	70,000	(24,000)		46,000
19X7	50,000			50,000
19X8	30,000			30,000
19X9	-		150,000	150,000
Total	300,000	(50,000)	150,000	400,000

(ii) *Provision for depreciation*

Year of purchase	Accumulated depreciation as at 31 Dec 19X8 £	Accumulated depreciation on items disposed of in 19X9 £	Provision for depreciation £	Accumulated depreciation as at 31 Dec 19X9 £
19X0	20,000	-	-	20,000
19X2	30,000	(17,000)	-	13,000
19X4	90,000	(9,000)	10,000	91,000
19X6	35,000	(14,400) *	11,600	32,200 **
19X7	15,000	-	10,000	25,000
19X8	3,000	-	6,000	9,000
19X9	-	-	15,000	15,000
Total	193,000	(40,400)	52,600	205,200

* 60% depreciated at time of sale, 60% × £24,000 = £14,400.
** 70% depreciated 70% × £46,000 = £32,200.

(iii)

	31 Dec 19X8 £	31 Dec 19X9 £
Fixed assets		
Plant and machinery at cost	300,000	400,000
Provision for depreciation	193,000	205,200
Net book value	107,000	194,800

(iv)

	Disposal of item of plant purchased in		
	19X2 £	19X4 £	19X6 £
Cost of plant disposed of	17,000	9,000	24,000
Accumulated depreciation on plant disposed of (see (ii))	17,000	9,000	14,400
Net book value of plant at date of disposal	0	0	9,600
Net sale price	0	500	8,500
Profit/(loss) on disposal	0	500	(1,100)

There is a total loss of £600 on sale/disposal of the three items.

18   **SPARK**

(a)   Check the balances on your ledger accounts with the trial balance shown below.

	Debit £	Credit £
Cash book		
Bank (note below) (W1)	1,703	
Cash (unbanked at end of period) (W2)	12	
Nominal ledger		
Drawings	560	
Postage and stationery	129	
Travelling expenses	40	
Motor expenses	104	
Cleaning expenses	260	
Sundry expenses	19	
Telephone	214	
Electricity	190	
Motor vans	2,000	
Rates	320	
Fixtures and fittings	806	
Capital		2,308
Purchases	3,163	
Discounts received		419
Credit sales		830
Cash sales		4,764
Discount allowed	81	
Provision for depreciation:		
motor van		720
fixtures and fittings		250
Stock at 1 January 19X1	366	
Loan - Flex		250
Sales ledger		
Brown	12	
Blue	180	
Stripe	48	
Purchase ledger		
Live		602
Negative		64
Earth		
	10,207	10,207

Workings

1   *Cash at bank*

	£
Opening balance	672
Bankings of cash (908+940+766+1,031)	3,645
Capital introduced	500
Received from customers	
90% × (160+66+22+10+40+120+140+130+20+44+38+20) = 90% of 810	729
	5,546
Less cheque payments (telephone, electricity, rates, van)	(1,469)
Payments to suppliers	
85% × (143+468+570+390+80+87+103+73+692+187) = 85% × 2,793	(2,374)
Closing balance	1,703

2   *Cash in hand*

	£		£
Balance b/d	5	Bank	3,645
∴ Sales	4,764	Drawings	560
		Stationery	73`
		Travel	40
		Petrol and van	104
		Sundry	19
		Postage	56
		Cleaner	260
		Balance c/d	12
	4,769		4,769

(b) (i)   SPARK- TRADING AND PROFIT AND LOSS ACCOUNT FOR THE FOUR MONTHS ENDED 30 APRIL 19X1

	£	£	£
Sales			5,594
Opening stock		366	
Purchases		3,163	
		3,529	
Closing stock		390	
			3,139
Gross profit			2,455
Discount received			419
Profit on sale of motor van			20
			2,894
Rent (W1)		500	
Rates (W2)		174	
Electricity		212	
Telephone (W3)		192	
Motor expenses		104	
Travelling		40	
Postage and stationery		129	
Cleaning		260	
Sundry expenses		19	
Depreciation (W4)			
Motor van	65		
Fixtures and fittings	27		
		92	
Discount allowed		81	
Loan interest (W5)		8	
			1,811
Net profit			1,083

Workings

1	Rent:	4/12 × £1,500 = £500; Accrual of £500 at 30 April
2	Rates:	£100 + 2/6 × £220 = £174; Prepayment of £146 at 30 April
3	Telephone:	£214 + £15 - £37 = £192
4	Depreciation:	Motor van: 20% × £1,300 × 3/12 = £65
	Fixtures:	10% × £806 × 4/12 = £27
5	Loan interest:	10% × £250 × 4/12 = £8

(ii)   SPARK - BALANCE SHEET AS AT 30 APRIL 19X2

	Cost	Dep'n	
	£	£	£
Fixed assets			
Motor van	1,300	65	1,235
Fixtures and fittings	806	277	529
	2,106	342	1,764
Current assets			
Stock at cost		390	
Debtors		240	
Payments in advance		146	
Cash at bank		1,703	
Cash in hand		12	
		2,491	
Current liabilities			
Trade creditors	666		
Accrued expenses	537		
		1,203	
			1,288
			3,052
Loan account: Flex			258
			2,794

Capital account	£
Balance at 1 January	1,808
Capital introduced	500
Profit for the four months	1,083
	3,391
Less drawings	597
	2,794

19 INTANGIBLE

> *Tutorial note.* The important point is to distinguish between the amounts actually spent during the year and the amounts charged to profit and loss account.

PURCHASED GOODWILL

	£		£
Cash	4,800	P & L a/c - amortisation	1,200
		Balance c/d	3,600
	4,800		4,800
Balance b/d	3,600		

RESEARCH AND DEVELOPMENT EXPENDITURE

	£		£
Balance b/f	26,500	P & L a/c *	15,300
Cash: research and	7,900	Development expenditure c/d	22,600
development	3,500		
	37,900		37,900
Balance b/d	22,600		

* The P & L charge includes the £7,900 spent on research. The balance (£15,300 - £7,900) = £7,400 consists of amortisation of development expenditure.

20 FRANK MERCER

(a)

CASH BOOK

19X8		£	*19X8*		£
Dec 31	Balance b/f	1,793	Dec 31	Bank charges	18
Dec 31	Dividend	26	Dec 31	Standing order	32
			Dec 31	Direct debit	88
				Balance c/d	1,681
		1,819			1,819

(b) BANK RECONCILIATION AS AT 31 DECEMBER 19X8

	£	£
Balance per bank statement		1,557
Add unrecorded lodgements:		
V Owen	98	
K Walters	134	
		232
Less unpresented cheques:		
B Oliver (869)	71	
L Philips (872)	37	
		(108)
Balance per cash book (corrected)		1,681

21   CAMFORD

The first step is to correct the errors in the cash book.

CASH BOOK

	£		£
Uncorrected balance b/f	1,900	Transfer to Midlands Savings	
Transposition error (a)	90	Bank - previously omitted (c)	1,500
Cash lodgement understated (b)	10	Error in bringing down balance at	
		1.6.X1 (f)	100
Sundry receipt omitted (d)	10	Bank charges (g)	20
Subscription credited directly (k)	100	Standing order (i)	30
		Subscriptions - cheque returned (j)	50
		Corrected balance c/d	410
	2,110		2,110
Corrected balance b/d	410		

BANK RECONCILIATION STATEMENT AS AT 31 MAY 19X2

	£	£	
Balance shown by bank statement		470	o/d
Unpresented cheques (e)		40	
		510	o/d
Outstanding lodgements (h)	900		
Error on bank statement (l)	20		
		920	
Balance shown in cash account		410	

22   APRIL SHOWERS

> *Tutorial note*. The question specifically requires the correction of the control account before the correction of the list of balances.

(a)   SALES LEDGER CONTROL ACCOUNT

	£		£
Uncorrected balance b/f	12,550	Discounts omitted (d)	100
Sales omitted (a)	850	Contra entry omitted (f)	400
Bank - cheque dishonoured (l)	300	Bad debt omitted (g)	500
		Returns inwards omitted (j)	200
		Amended balance c/d	12,500
	13,700		13,700
Balance b/d	12,500		

Note. Items (b), (c), (e), (h), (i) and (k) are matters affecting the personal accounts of customers. They have no effect on the control account.

(b)   STATEMENT OF ADJUSTMENTS TO LIST OF PERSONAL ACCOUNT BALANCES

	£	£
Original total of list of balances		12,802
Add: debit balance omitted (b)	300	
debit balance understated (e)	200	
		500
		13,302
Less: transposition error (c): understatement of cash received	180	
cash debited instead of credited (2 × £250) (h)	500	
discounts received wrongly debited to Bell (i)	50	
understatement of cash received (l)	72	
		802
		12,500

23   FRONTLOADER

> *Tutorial note.* One problem you must deal with in answering this question is identifying which items in the ledgers are relevant to the debtors ledger control account. Irrelevant items are creditors and purchases of washing machines (purchase ledger), discounts received, cash paid to creditors, carriage outwards (it is assumed that Frontloader Ltd must bear these costs itself, and does not charge them to customers) and overdraft interest. The provision for doubtful debts, also, does not appear in the debtors ledger control account, although it is relevant to a solution to part (b) of the question.

Workings

	£
Sales	723,869
Less discounts allowed	8,214
	715,655
Less returns inwards	36,925
Net sales	678,730
Opening debtors	84,611
Opening debtors plus net sales	763,341
Cash received from debtors (excluding J Smith)	699,267
Closing debtors before adjustments for the subsequent entries	64,074
Subsequent entries:	
Bad debts written off	6,854
	57,220
A Brown's cheque dishonoured. A Brown becomes a debtor again	1,246
Closing debtors	58,466

A small problem arises in deciding how to record the payment of £1,000 by J Smith. J Smith's debt was written off in 19X2, and some money is finally received in 19X5. The revenue will be recorded in the debtors ledger by:

(a)   adding £1,000 to debtors;
(b)   recording the cash paid of £1,000.

These items are shown in the debtors ledger control account below.

(a)   DEBTORS LEDGER CONTROL ACCOUNT

	£		£
Opening balance	84,611	Cash received (debit bank a/c)	699,267
Sales on credit (credit sales a/c)	723,869	Discounts allowed	8,214
A Brown's dishonoured cheque		Returns inwards (debit sales a/c)	36,925
(credit bank a/c)	1,246	Bad debts written off (debit bad	
J Smith: bad debt written back		debts a/c)	6,854
(credit bad debts a/c)	1,000	Cash received from J Smith	
		(debit back a/c)	1,000
		Closing balance c/d	58,466
	810,726		810,726
Opening balance b/d	58,466		

(b)   The provision for doubtful debts as at 30 June 19X5 should be 8% of £58,466 = £4,677. The reduction in the provision for doubtful debts in the year is £(4,813 − 4,677) = £136.

BAD AND DOUBTFUL DEBTS

	£		£
Debtors a/c: bad debts written off	6,854	Provision for doubtful debts b/d	4,813
Provision for doubtful debts:		Debtors a/c: bad debt of J Smith	
closing balance c/d	4,677	written back	1,000
		P&L account (balance)	5,718
	11,531		11,531
		Balance b/d	4,677

The amount written off to the P&L account consists of the net amount of bad debts written off (£5,854) less the reduction in the provision for doubtful debts (£136). These separate amounts could be itemised separately in the account.

(c)

	£
Debtors	58,466
Less provision for doubtful debts	4,677
	53,789

24   HYPER

Initial workings

1   Invoiced sales excluding VAT $= \dfrac{£141,000}{117.5} \times 100 = £120,000 \therefore VAT = £21,000$

2   Purchases excluding VAT $= \dfrac{£84,600}{117.5} \times 100 = £72,000 \therefore VAT = £12,600ÿ$

DEBTORS

	£		£
Balance b/f	40,000	Bank	128,300
Sales and VAT creditor	141,000	Balance c/f	52,700
	181,000		181,000

CREDITORS

	£		£
Bank	92,700	Balance b/f	22,000
Balance c/f	13,900	Purchases and VAT creditor	84,600
	106,600		106,600

VAT CREDITOR

	£		£
Creditors (W2)	12,600	Balance b/f	4,100
Bank	4,100	Debtors (W1)	21,000
Balance c/f	8,400		
	25,100		25,100

SALES

	£		£
		Debtors (W1)	120,000

PURCHASES

	£		£
Creditors (W2)	72,000		

BANK ACCOUNT (EXTRACT)

	£		£
Debtors	128,300	Creditors	92,700
		VAT creditor	4,100

25   PAYROLL

(a)

CREDITORS

	£		£
Cash	5,400	Balance b/f	800
Discounts received	100	Purchases	6,000
Debtors - contra	700		
Balance c/d	600		
	6,800		6,800
Balance b/d	600		

(b)

DEBTORS

	£		£
Balance b/d (bal. fig.)	2,000	Creditors - contra	700
Sales	12,000	Cash	11,800
		Discounts allowed	300
		Bad debts	200
		Balance c/d	1,000
	14,000		14,000
Balance b/d	1,000		

(c)

PROVISION FOR DOUBTFUL DEBTS

	£		£
Debtors	200	Balance b/f	450
Balance c/d	400	Cash - bad debt recovered	50
		P&L a/c: increase in provision	100
	600		600
		Balance b/d	400

(d)

WAGES CONTROL

	£		£
Bank	1,330	Balance b/f	38
PAYE control	407	Wages expense a/c - gross	
NIC control	260	wages	2,000
Balance c/d	41		
	2,038		2,038
		Balance b/d	41

(e)

PAYE CONTROL

	£		£
Cash	400	Balance b/f	35
Balance c/d	42	Wages control	407
	442		442
		Balance b/d	42

(f)

NIC CONTROL

	£		£
Cash	546	Balance b/f	44
Balance c/d	48	Wages control - employees	260
		Wages expense a/c - employer	290
	594		594
		Balance b/d	48

26   CHI KNITWEAR

(a)

SUSPENSE ACCOUNT

	£		£
Opening balance	1,536	Debtors - balance omitted	87
Sales - under-recorded	360	Cash book - receipts undercast	720
		Creditors: credit note posted to wrong side	358
		Cash book: Mr Smith's debt paid but cash receipt not recorded	731
	1,896		1,896

Notes

(i)   Error (b) is an error of principle, whereby a fixed asset item (capital expenditure) has been accounted for as revenue expenditure. The correction will be logged in the journal, but since the error did not result in an inequality between debits and credits, the suspense account would not have been used.

(ii)   The electricity bill has been omitted from the accounts entirely. The error of omission means that both debits and credits will be logged in the journal, but the suspense account will not be involved, since there is equality between debits and credits in the error.

(b)   (i)   The error means that debtors are understated. The correction of the error will increase the total amount for debtors to be shown in the balance sheet.

(ii)   The correction of this error will add £1,200 to fixed assets at cost (balance sheet item) and reduce repair costs by £1,200. The P & L account will therefore show an increased profit of £1,200, less any depreciation now charged on the fixed asset.

(iii)   The undercasting (ie under-adding) of £720 on the receipts side of the cash book means that debits of cash will be £720 less than they should have been. The correction of the error will add £720 to the cash balance in the balance sheet.

(iv)   This transposition error means that total sales would be under-recorded by £8,514 - £8,154 = £360 in the sales account. The correction of the error will add £360 to total sales, and thus add £360 to the profits in the P & L account.

(v)   The credit note must have been issued for a purchase return to the supplier by the business. It should have been debited to the creditor's account, but instead has been credited. Assuming that the purchase returns account was credited correctly, the effect of the error has been to overstate total creditors by 2 × £179 = £358, and this amount should be credited from the suspense account and debited to the creditors account. The effect will be to reduce the total for creditors in the balance sheet by £358.

(vi)   The electricity bill, when entered in the accounts, will increase creditors by £152, and reduce profits (by adding to electricity expenses) by £152, assuming that none of this cost is a prepayment of electricity charges.

(vii)   Since the cheque has not yet been recorded in the cash book, the correction of the error will add £731 to the cash balance in the balance sheet. At the same time, the provision for doubtful debts can be reduced, which will increase the net amount for debtors in the balance sheet by £731 (ie debtors less provision for doubtful debts, although the reduction in gross debtors by £731 has already been accounted for, due to the cash received) and increase profits by £731.

27   DONALD BROWN

Tutorial note. You should note these points.

(a)   Discounts allowed are an expense of the business and should be shown as a deduction from gross profit. Similarly, discounts received is a revenue item and should be added to gross profit.

(b)   The figure for depreciation in the trial balance represents accumulated depreciation up to and including 19W9. You have to calculate the charge for the year 19X0 for the profit and loss account and add this to the trial balance figure to arrive at the accumulated depreciation figure to be included in the balance sheet.

DONALD BROWN
TRADING AND PROFIT AND LOSS ACCOUNT
FOR THE YEAR ENDED 31 DECEMBER 19X0

	£	£
Sales		491,620
Less cost of sales		
Opening stock	18,460	
Purchases	387,936	
	406,396	
Closing stock	19,926	
		386,470
Gross profit		105,150
Discounts received		1,175
		106,325
Less expenses:		
discounts allowed	1,304	
lighting and heating	6,184	
motor expenses	3,080	
rent	8,161	
general expenses	7,413	
depreciation (W)	13,146	
		39,288
Net profit		67,037

Working: depreciation charge

Motor vehicles: £45,730 × 20% = £9,146
Fixtures and fittings: 10% × £(42,200 − 2,200) = £4,000
Total: £4,000 + £9,146 = £13,146.

DONALD BROWN
BALANCE SHEET AS AT 31 DECEMBER 19X0

	Cost £	*Depreciation* £	*Net* £
Fixed assets			
Fixtures and fittings	42,200	6,200	36,000
Motor vehicles	45,730	24,438	21,292
	87,930	30,638	57,292
Current assets			
Stock		19,926	
Debtors		42,737	
Prepayments		680	
Cash in hand		1,411	
		64,754	
Current liabilities			
Creditors	35,404		
Accruals	218		
Bank overdraft	19,861		
		55,483	
Net current assets			9,271
Net assets			66,563
Represented by:			
Capital			26,094
Net profit for year			67,037
			93,131
Less drawings			26,568
			66,563

28   **HERBERT HOWELL**

HERBERT HOWELL
TRADING AND PROFIT AND LOSS ACCOUNT
FOR THE YEAR ENDED 31 MAY 19X9

	£	£
Sales		405,000
Cost of sales:		
Opening stock	27,400	
Purchases (£259,600 – £1,040)	258,560	
	285,960	
Closing stock	25,900	
		260,060
Gross profit		144,940
Discounts received		4,420
		149,360
Discounts allowed	3,370	
Loan interest	1,560	
Bad and doubtful debts (W1)	1,671	
Carriage out	5,310	
Wages and salaries	52,500	
Depreciation (W2)	9,525	
Other operating expenses (W3)	38,500	
		112,436
Net profit		36,924

HERBERT HOWELL
BALANCE SHEET AS AT 31 MAY 19X9

	Cost £	Dep'n £	Net book value £
Fixed assets			
Property (W4)	90,000	13,400	76,600
Equipment (W4)	57,500	41,125	16,375
	147,500	54,525	92,975
Current assets			
Stock		25,900	
Trade debtors	46,200		
Less provision for doubtful debts (W1)	231		
		45,969	
Prepayment		500	
Cash on hand		151	
		72,520	
Current liabilities			
Bank overdraft		14,500	
Trade creditors		33,600	
Accruals (140 + 200)		340	
		48,440	
Net current assets			24,080
Total assets less current liabilities			117,055
Long-term liabilities			
13% loan			12,000
			105,055
Capital			
Balance at 1 June 19X8			98,101
Net profit for the year			36,924
Drawings (£28,930 + £1,040)			(29,970)
Balance at 31 May 19X9			105,055

Workings

		£
1	*Bad debts*	
	Provision required: 0.5% × £46,200	231
	Provision b/f	280
	Decrease required	(49)
	Add bad debts	1,720
	Bad and doubtful debts expense for the year	1,671

		£
2	*Depreciation*	
	Property: 1% × £90,000	900
	Equipment: 15% × £57,500	8,625
		9,525

		£
3	*Other operating expenses*	
	As trial balance	38,800
	Less prepayment	(500)
	Add accrual	200
		38,500

4	*Provision for depreciation*	*Property* £	*Equipment* £
	Balance b/f	12,500	32,500
	Charge for the year (W2)	900	8,625
	Balance c/f	13,400	41,125

29 BRENDA BAILEY

TRADING AND PROFIT AND LOSS ACCOUNT
FOR THE YEAR ENDED 30 JUNE 19X9

	£	£
Sales		427,726
Opening stock	15,310	
Purchases	302,419	
Carriage inwards	476	
	318,205	
Less closing stock	16,480	
Cost of sales		301,725
Gross profit		126,001
Carriage outwards	829	
Wages and salaries	64,210	
Rent and rates (12,466 – 620)	11,846	
Heat and light (4,757 + 350)	5,107	
Depreciation - equipment	10,200	
- motor vehicles	8,654	
Sundry expenses	8,426	
		109,272
Net profit for the year		16,729

BRENDA BAILEY
BALANCE SHEET AS AT 30 JUNE 19X9

	Cost £	Dep'n £	Net book value £
Fixed assets			
Equipment	102,000	32,450	69,550
Motor vehicles	43,270	17,574	25,696
	145,270	50,024	95,246
Current assets			
Stock		16,480	
Debtors		50,633	
Prepayments		620	
Cash		477	
		68,210	
Current liabilities			
Bank overdraft		3,295	
Creditors		41,792	
Accruals		350	
		45,437	
Net current assets			22,773
			118,019
Capital			
Balance at 1 July 19X8			122,890
Add profit for the year			16,729
			139,619
Less drawings			21,600
Balance at 30 June 19X9			118,019

30   HELPFUL COMPUTERS

(a)   A computer always has to be told what to do. It will not think for itself. The instructions which tell it what to do (and when to do it) are given in programs - or in a collection of programs (depending on the complexity of the application being used on the computer). The easiest way to think of a program is that it is made up of a set of rules. So a computer operates within a framework of rules which tell it exactly what to do.

Accounting systems also exist within a framework of clearly defined, standard rules. The rules govern the regular, routine movement of transaction data through the accounting system. Although the actual accounting system might differ from business to business, the rules on which they are based do not. If a credit sale is made, for instance, then the relevant entries are made in the sales ledger and the debtors ledger. All businesses would make the same entries, although how they go about doing so might differ.

It is because both computer and accounting systems are based on clearly defined rules that accounting systems are relatively easy to computerise. The logical steps already existing within the accounting system can be transcribed into logical steps within the computer system. It would be much harder to computerise a system which was not based on standard rules, because first such rules would have to be created (in order to be able to set the program rules for the computer).

(b)   Computers are widely used today because of their ability to process large volumes of data quickly, accurately and economically. Faced with an enormous load of paperwork, a company no longer has to employ an equally enormous army of clerks. It buys a computer instead.

Unlike clerks, computers never suffer from fatigue, or boredom, or even hangovers. They are capable of processing large volumes of data accurately for long periods of time without ill-effects - apart from the occasional failure of an electronic component, or hiccup in the software.

So computers are particularly good at repetitive, time-consuming tasks on large amounts of data. Accounting data tends to occur in such a way that large volumes of data require similar processing (eg invoice details, or payroll details). Standard programs can be developed fairly easily to deal with these volumes of data (eg invoice application, payroll package). In other words, accounting data happens to be the sort of data for which a standard computer program can be produced fairly easily.

Computers are also able to store and summarise large quantities of data. Once the accounting data has been captured (ie put into a form suitable for the computer) it can be stored on (for example) disk or tape, from which:

(i)   it can be quickly retrieved for amendment or inspection;

(ii)   records can be summarised and printed on request; and

(iii)   exceptions can be reported whenever they occur.

All of the above would be repetitive and time-consuming in a manual accounting system, but are the very activities at which a computer excels.

31   GILTAN GOLF CLUB

> *Tutorial note.* In this problem, there is no bar trading account to deal with. The expenses of the functions should be netted off against the income from the functions. Subscriptions for the year consist of total cash received from subscriptions (£2,930) minus the cash received which relates to arrears from the previous year (£65) and payments in advance for the next year (£35), plus arrears for the current year (£30).
>
> The income of the previous year (to 31 March 19X7) included £15 owed as subscriptions in arrears by the member who has now emigrated. This £15, added to income last year, must now be deducted as an expense in the current year to even things out.
>
> Where there are accrued expenses, brief workings are shown to indicate how the expenditure for the year is calculated.
>
> The bequest of £255 to the club should be added directly to the accumulated fund. It is not a part of the regular income and expenditure of the club, and so should be excluded from the income and expenditure account.
>
> The surplus on the sale of the land (£1,600 − £500) should be added directly to the accumulated fund, since the fixed asset has not been subject to depreciation charges in the past.

INCOME AND EXPENDITURE ACCOUNT
FOR THE YEAR ENDED 31 MARCH 19X8

	£	£
Income		
Subscriptions £(2,930 − 65 − 35 + 30 − 15)		2,845
Functions: income	367	
less expenses	305	
		62
Bank interest received		60
Sundry income		46
		3,013
Expenditure		
Repairs	146	
Telephone £(67 − 14 + 10)	63	
Heat and light £(115 − 32 + 40)	123	
Salary and wages £(2,066 + 14 − 12)	2,068	
Sundry expenses	104	
Depreciation		
Buildings (5% × £3,800)	190	
Fixtures and fittings (10% × £470)	47	
Furniture (20% × £515)	103	
		2,844
Surplus transferred to accumulated fund		169

BALANCE SHEET AS AT 31 MARCH 19X8

	Cost	Dep'n	Net
	£	£	£
Fixed assets			
Land	3,500	-	3,500
Buildings	3,800	1,050	2,750
Fixtures and fittings	470	129	341
Furniture	515	267	248
	8,285	1,446	6,839
Current assets			
Bank		2,300	
Cash		102	
		2,402	
Current liabilities			
Accrued expenses		64	
Subscriptions in advance		35	
		99	
			2,303
			9,142
Accumulated fund			
Balance at 1 April 19X7			7,618
Surplus for year			169
Surplus on sale of land			1,100
Bequest			255
			9,142

32 IMPROVIDENT ACTUARIES

Tutorial notes and workings

This question involves a bar trading account, membership subscriptions, life membership, death of a life member and a building fund. Deal with one item at a time.

(a) *Bar trading account.* We must first of all calculate bar sales and bar purchases.

	£
Bar takings	28,500
Bar chits not yet settled at 31 December	35
	28,535
Bar chits unsettled as at start of year	0
Bar sales	28,535
Creditors for bar supplies as at 31 December	1,600
Cash payments for bar supplies	23,150
	24,750
Less creditors for bar supplies as at start of year	350
Purchases of bar supplies	24,400

BAR TRADING ACCOUNT FOR THE YEAR TO
31 DECEMBER 19X5

	£		£
Opening stocks	4,800	Sales	28,535
Purchases	24,400		
	29,200		
Less closing stocks	4,300		
	24,900	Loss on bar trading	
Wages	4,200	(to I & E account)	565
	29,100		29,100

(b)

ANNUAL SUBSCRIPTIONS

	£		£
Subscriptions in arrears b/d 1 Jan	600	Subscriptions in advance b/d 1 Jan	400
∴ Subscriptions income		Cash (subscriptions received)	25,000
(I & E account)	24,200		
Subscriptions in advance c/d 31 Dec	900	Subscriptions in arrears c/d 31 Dec	300
	25,700		25,700
Subscriptions in arrears b/d	300	Subscriptions in advance b/d	900

(If you do this calculation by the T account method, as shown above, you need to remember that subscriptions in arrears are debtors, and so a debit balance b/d, just as subscriptions in advance are liabilities of the club and so a credit balance b/d.)

(c) *Life membership.* Presumably, the method of accounting for life membership here is to keep all payments in a life membership fund until a life member dies, when his or her contributions should be transferred direct to the accumulated fund. Since there were four life members at the start of the year, and the life membership fund stood at £4,000, £1,000 will be transferred from this fund to the accumulated fund.

LIFE MEMBERSHIP FUND

	£		£
Accumulated fund (death of member)	1,000	Balance b/d	4,000
Balance c/d	5,000	Cash (new members)	2,000
	6,000		6,000
		Balance b/d	5,000

(d) *The building fund.* The building fund is a capital fund of the club, and it is represented directly by investments in consolidated stock and a building society account, which are assets (investments) of the club. The accounts for these assets, shown below in T account form, are a mirror image of the building fund (capital) and we should always expect the balance on the building fund account to be equal to the combined balance on the accounts of the two investments.

BUILDING SOCIETY ACCOUNT
(INVESTMENT = ASSET OF CLUB)

	£		£
Balance b/f	10,000		
Cash (new deposits with building society during year)	800		
Interest (added to account)	740	Balance c/f	11,540
	11,540		11,540

Presumably the £800 paid into the building society during the year is the interest on the consolidated stock, amounting to 4% of £20,000 = £800 (see note (b) of question).

4% CONSOLIDATED STOCK
(INVESTMENT = ASSET)

	£		£
Balance b/f	7,400	Balance c/f	7,400

This account is unchanged, because no new stock is bought during the year, and no stock has been sold. (*Note.* The consolidated stock will be a government security, on which a fixed rate of interest (here 4%) is paid on the nominal or face value of the stock, here £20,000.)

The building fund is a mirror image of these investment accounts.

BUILDING FUND

	£		£
		Balance b/f £(10,000+7,400)	17,400
		Cash paid into building society	800
Balance c/f	18,940	Building society interest	740
	18,940		18,940

(e) *General expenses*. A few further figures have still to be calculated in order to prepare a full solution.

	£
Club house expenses (£12,150 − £4,200)	7,950
Petty cash	1,550
	9,500
Less insurance prepayment (one quarter of £480)	120
	9,380

(f) *Accumulated fund*. The balance b/f at the start of the year will be the difference between club assets and liabilities, minus the sum of the life membership fund and the building fund.

	£	£
Assets as at 1 January 19X5		
£(70,000+15,000+17,400+600+4,800+3,200+950)		111,950
Less current liabilities (400 + 350)	750	
Life membership fund	4,000	
Building fund	17,400	
		22,150
		89,800

(g) *Cash at bank*

	£
Cash at bank, 1 January	850
Total receipts in year	57,322
	58,172
Total payments in year	55,810
Cash at bank, 31 December	2,362

(h) We now have the basic information to prepare an income and expenditure account and balance sheet. It is assumed that the piano bought during the year is a fixed asset. Unusually, we are given no information about depreciation of the club equipment or club house itself, and so depreciation should be ignored.

Suggested solution

(a) INCOME AND EXPENDITURE ACCOUNT
YEAR ENDED 31 DECEMBER 19X5

	£	£	£
Income			
Subscriptions			24,200
Green fees			300
Profit on manuals £(700 - 250)			450
			24,950
Expenditure			
Course upkeep		16,150	
General expenses		9,380	
Renewals of club furniture *		1,238	
Bar loss:			
Cost of sales	24,900		
Wages	4,200		
	29,100		
Takings	28,535		
		565	
			27,333
Deficit for year taken to accumulated fund			2,383

* *Note*. Net cost of renewals is a revenue expenditure = £1,260 - £22 (from sale of old carpet).

(b) IMPROVIDENT ACTUARIES
BALANCE SHEET AS AT 31 DECEMBER 19X5

	£	£
Fixed assets		
Course at cost		70,000
Clubhouse at cost		15,000
Clubhouse equipment at cost	3,200	
Additions - piano	500	
		3,700
Building fund		
£20,000 4% consolidated stock at cost	7,400	
Deposit with building society	11,540	
		18,940
Current assets		
Bar stocks	4,300	
Subscriptions in arrears	300	
Prepayment of insurance premium	120	
Debtors (bar chits unsettled)	35	
Bank	2,362	
Cash in hand (petty cash)	100	
	7,217	
Current liabilities		
Subscriptions in advance	900	
Creditors	1,600	
	2,500	
		4,717
		112,357

	£	£
Funds employed		
Accumulated fund as at 1 January		89,800
Transfer from life membership fund		1,000
		90,800
Less deficit for the year		2,383
Accumulated fund as at 31 December		88,417
Life membership fund as at 1 January	4,000	
Less transfer to capital fund	(1,000)	
Add new life members	2,000	
Life membership fund as at 31 December		5,000
Building fund as at 1 January	17,400	
Add interest:		
consolidated stock	800	
building society	740	
Building fund as at 31 December		18,940
Funds employed		112,357

33 ROBERT FULLER

> *Tutorial note.* This question required you to apply accounting concepts, conventions and practices by the construction of accounts from incomplete information.
>
> Possible traps for the unwary include incorrect calculation of sales and purchases, inclusion of drawings as an expense in the P&L and a poor appreciation of depreciation.

(a) ROBERT FULLER
     TRADING AND PROFIT AND LOSS ACCOUNT
     FOR THE YEAR ENDED 30 APRIL 19X4

	£	£
Sales (171,900 + 1,990 + 180 + 2,140)		176,210
Cost of sales		
Opening stock	14,000	
Purchases (W1)	9,150	
Closing stock	(15,500)	
		(90,650)
Gross profit		85,560
Other income		
Rent (9 × £600)		5,400
Discounts received		170
Expenses		
Discounts allowed	180	
Casual wages	2,220	
Heat and light (620 + 120) (W5)	740	
Cleaning	140	
Postage (80 – 20)	60	
Vehicle expenses	3,240	
Miscellaneous	11,910	
Bank interest (£50,000 × 10%)	5,000	
Depreciation (W2)	7,290	
		(30,780)
Net profit		60,350

ROBERT FULLER
BALANCE SHEET AS AT 30 APRIL 19X4

	£	£
Fixed assets		
Tangible fixed assets (W3)		112,910
Current assets		
Stock	15,500	
Debtors (W4)	2,160	
Cash at bank and in hand	45,110	
	62,600	
Creditors: amounts falling due in less than one year (W5)	(10910)	
Net current assets		51,860
Creditors: amounts falling due after more than one year		
Bank loan		(50,000)
		114,770
Capital account (see (b))		72,420
Current account (W6)		42,350
		114,770

Workings

1   *Purchases*

CREDITORS

	£		£
Cash purchases	420	B/F	4,600
Bank purchases	88,420	Purchases	92,150
Discount	170	(bal.Fig)	
C/F	7,740		
	96,750		96,750

			£
2	*Depreciation charge*		
	Delivery van £(10,800 × 50% × 9/12)		4,050
	Fittings £(7,800 + 3,600 + 4,800) × 20%		3,240
			7,290

3   *Fixed assets*

	£
Cost	
Premises	93,200
Fittings	7,800
Cash register	3,600
Delivery van	10,800
New fittings	4,800
	120,200
Less depreciation (W2)	(7,290)
	112,910

4   *Debtors*

	£
Trade debtors	2,140
Prepayments - stamps	20
	2,160

5   *Creditors*

		£
Trade creditors		7,740
Discounts received		
Rents received in advance (£600 × 3)		1,800
Electricity to 30 April (180 × 2/3)		120
Bank interest(£50,000 × 10%)	5,000	
Amount paid	(3,750)	
		1,250
		10,910

6   *Current account*

	£
Profit for year	60,350
Drawings	(18,000)
	42,350

(b)

CAPITAL ACCOUNT

	£		£
Bank loan	50,000	Premises	93,200
		Fittings	7,800
		Stock (14,000 – 4,600)	9,400
		Bank balance	11,740
Capital introduced	72,420	Cash in hand	280
	122,420		122,420
		1.5.X3	
		Capital introduced	72,420

	£
Capital at 1.5.X3	72,450
Profit for year	60,350
Drawings	(18,000)
Capital at 30.4.X4	114,770

(c)   *Going concern*. Accounts have been prepared on the basis that the business will continue for the foreseeable future, for example, fixed assets have not been valued on a 'break-up' basis.

Accruals. Revenue and costs are accrued, ie recognised, as they are earned or incurred, for example electricity costs relating to the period but not paid for have been accrued for.

Consistency. Consistency of accounting treatment of like items, for example all fixtures and fittings have been depreciated.

Prudence. Revenue and profits are not anticipated, for example only rents relating to the year to 30 April 19X4 are included even though cash has been received.

34   HIGHTON

TRADING PROFIT AND LOSS ACCOUNT
FOR THE YEAR ENDED 31 MARCH 19X2

	£	£
Sales: cash	80,400	
credit (W1)	9,250	
		89,650
Cost of sales		
Opening stock	3,500	
Purchases: cash	17,000	
credit (W2)	47,500	
	68,000	
Less closing stock	4,000	
		64,000
Gross profit		25,650
Expenses		
Depreciation of motor vehicle (25% × £3,000)	750	
Motor vehicle expenses (W3)	800	
Property insurance £(50 + 150 – 100)	100	
Loan interest	100	
Electricity £(400 + 400 – 200)	600	
General shop expenses	100	
Telephone £(100 + 300)	400	
Wages	3,000	
Rates	300	
		6,150
Net profit		19,500

BALANCE SHEET AS AT 31 MARCH 19X2

	£	£
Fixed assets		
Freehold land and buildings at cost		10,000
Motor vehicle: cost	3,000	
accumulated depreciation	1,500	
		1,500
		11,500
Current assets		
Stock	4,000	
Trade debtors	1,000	
Prepayments	400	
Cash at bank	950	
Cash in hand	450	
	6,800	
Current liabilities		
Trade creditors	1,800	
Accruals	500	
	2,300	
Net current assets		4,500
		16,000

	£	£
Proprietor's capital		
At 1 April 19X4 (W4)*		5,250
Net profit for the year	19,500	
Less drawings £(7,000 + 1,750)	8,750	
Profit retained in business		10,750
		16,000

*The opening capital could be inserted as a balancing figure; W4 is included merely to prove the figure.

Workings

1   DEBTORS CONTROL ACCOUNT

	£		£
Opening balance	500	Bank	8,750
∴ Credit sales	9,250	Closing balance	1,000
	9,750		9,750

2   CREDITORS CONTROL ACCOUNT

	£		£
Bank	47,200	Opening balance	1,500
Closing balance	1,800	∴ Credit purchases	47,500
	49,000		49,000

3   MOTOR VEHICLE EXPENSES

	£		£
Prepayment b/f	200	Accrual b/f	200
Bank	1,000	∴ P & L account	800
Accrual b/f	100	Prepayment c/f	300
	1,300		1,300

4   PROPRIETOR'S CAPITAL AT 1 APRIL 19X1

	£	£
Assets		
Freehold land and buildings	10,000	
Motor vehicle	2,250	
Stock	3,500	
Debtors and prepayments	750	
Cash at bank and in hand	650	
		17,150
Liabilities		
Loan	10,000	
Creditors and accruals	1,900	
		11,900
		5,250

35   CHURCH

(a)   TRADING PROFIT AND LOSS ACCOUNT
         FOR THE YEAR ENDED 31 MARCH 19X3

	£	£
Sales (less returns)		149,100
Opening stock	10,420	
Purchases (balancing figure)	108,370	
	118,790	
Closing stock £(10,420 + 4,000)	14,420	
Cost of goods sold		104,370
Gross profit (30% × £149,100)		44,730
Add discounts received		760
		45,490
Expenses		
Bad debts	470	
Provision for doubtful debts (5% × £5,620)	281	
Salaries	15,840	
Heat, light etc (W5)	3,560	
Depreciation:		
shop fittings 10% × £(15,000 + 2,000)	1,700	
motor vehicle 25% × £6,000	1,500	
		23,351
Net profit		22,139

(b)   BALANCE SHEET AS AT 31 MARCH 19X3

	Cost	*Depreciation*	*Net*
	£	£	£
Fixed assets			
Shop equipment and fittings	17,000	4,700	12,300
Motor vehicle	6,000	3,000	3,000
	23,000	7,700	15,300
Current assets			
Stock		14,420	
Trade debtors less provision		5,339	
Rent paid in advance		480	
Bank		16,100	
		36,339	
Current liabilities			
Trade creditors		6,390	
Accrued expenses		310	
		6,700	
Net current assets			29,639
			44,939
Proprietor's capital			
Balance at 31 March 19X2			32,400
Profit for year		22,139	
Less drawings £(9,000 + 600)		9,600	
			12,539
			44,939

Workings

Note. No distinction is made in the question between cash transactions and bank transactions. A 'total cash account' must therefore be constructed instead of the more usual columnar bank and cash account.

1   TOTAL CASH ACCOUNT

	£		£
Balance b/f	6,690	Creditors (Working 3)	106,560
Debtors (W2)	149,270	Salaries	15,840
		Heat, light etc	3,460
		Shop fittings	2,000
		Loan - repayment	3,000
		Drawings	9,000
		Balance c/d	16,100
	155,960		155,960
Balance b/d	16,100		

2   TOTAL DEBTORS ACCOUNT

	£		£
Balance b/f	6,260	Bad debts	470
Sales	152,600	Returns inwards	3,500
		Cash (balancing figure)	149,270
		Balance c/d	5,620
	158,860		158,860
Balance b/d	5,620		

3   TOTAL CREDITORS ACCOUNT

	£		£
Discounts received	760	Balance b/f	4,740
Cash (balancing figure)	106,560	Purchases (W4)	108,970
Balance c/d	6,390		
	113,710		113,710
		Balance b/d	6,390

4   PURCHASES ACCOUNT

	£		£
Creditors	108,970	Trading account	108,370
		Drawings	600
	108,970		108,970

5   *Heat, light etc*

	£	£
Amounts paid in year		3,460
Add: rent prepayment at 31 March 19X2	650	
heating accrual at 31 March 19X3	310	
		960
		4,420
Less: rent prepayment at 31 March 19X3	480	
heating accrual at 31 March 19X2	380	
		860
P & L charge for year		3,560

36   EXCEL

(a)   EXCEL LIMITED
PROFIT AND LOSS ACCOUNT
FOR THE YEAR ENDED 30 NOVEMBER 19X5

	£	£
Revenue		510,500
Less loss on vehicle disposal		1,500
		509,000
Less expenses		
Wages and expenses	245,200	
Licences and insurance	6,000	
Repairs	34,440	
Petrol and oil	44,870	
Administration expenses	30,460	
Advertising expenses	13,340	
Directors' remuneration	40,000	
Bad debts	890	
Provision for doubtful debts	1,849	
Auditor's fees	2,000	
Debenture interest	3,600	
Depreciation	21,800	
		444,449
		64,551
Appropriations		
Interim share dividend	12,000	
Final proposal dividend	24,000	
		36,000
Retained profit		28,551
Retained profit 30/11/X4		127,200
Retained profit 30/11/X5		155,751

(b)   EXCEL LIMITED
BALANCE SHEET AS AT 30 NOVEMBER 19X5

	Cost	Depreciation	NBV
Fixed assets	£	£	£
Premises	420,000	-	420,000
Vehicles	93,200	51,620	41,580
	513,200	51,620	461,580
Current assets			
Stocks: petrol and oil	1,640		
spares	3,170		
		4,810	
Debtors	61,640		
Provision for doubtful debts	(1,849)		
		59,791	
Prepayments		1,500	
Cash		19,920	
		86,021	

	£	£
Creditors: amounts falling due within one year:		
Debenture interest	3,600	
Final share dividend	24,000	
Advertising accrual	800	
Auditors fee	2,000	
Repairs	1,450	
	31,850	
Net current assets		54,171
Total assets less current liabilities		515,751
Creditors: amounts falling due after more than one year		
12% debentures		(120,000)
		395,751
Capital and reserves		
Shares (200,000 at £1, fully paid)		200,000
Share premium		40,000
Profit and loss account		155,751
		395,751

Workings

1   *Provision for doubtful debts*

Provision = 3% × £(62,530 − 890) = £1,849

2   *Accounting treatment for stocks*

Because of the nature of the business, it is difficult to come to a 'cost of sales' figure for Excel Ltd. Consequently no attempt has been made to arrive at a gross profit figure. Stocks figures have therefore been incorporated into the relevant expense figures as follows.

	Petrol and oil	*Vehicle spares (repairs)*
	£	£
Charge shown in list of balances	45,310	35,460
Add opening stock	1,200	700
	46,510	36,160
Less closing stock	1,640	3,170
Charge to P & L account	44,870	32,990 *

* There is also a repairs accrual of £1,450, so the P & L charge for repairs is £32,990 + £1,450 = £34,440

3   *Motor vehicles and depreciation*

The motor vehicles figure of £111,200 is incorrect, as it has been made up incorrectly. The sales proceeds should not be shown in the motor vehicles account, but the £24,000 original cost disposed of should be. Journal entries to correct these errors are:

		£	£
DEBIT	Motor vehicles	6,000	
CREDIT	Motor vehicles disposals		6,000
DEBIT	Motor vehicle disposals	24,000	
CREDIT	Motor vehicles		24,000

In addition, depreciation in respect of the vehicle disposed of should be debited to depreciation account, and credited to disposals account (25% × £24,000 × 2 5 years = £16,500). Also, depreciation for the year should be calculated on the motor vehicles account balance.

The effect of all these adjustments is:

MOTOR VEHICLES

	£		£
Balance b/f	85,200	Sale proceeds	6,000
Additions	32,000	Disposals	24,000
Sales proceeds correction	6,000	Balance c/f	93,200
	123,200		123,200

DISPOSALS

Motor vehicles	£ 24,000	Sale proceeds	£ 6,000
		Depreciation	16,500
		P & L account	1,500
	24,000		24,000

DEPRECIATION

Disposals	£ 16,500	Balance b/f	£ 46,320
Balance c/f	51,620	P & L account	21,800 *
	68,120		68,120

		£
* £85,200 × 25% × 9/12	=	15,975
£93,200 × 25% × 3/12	=	5,825
		21,800

4   *Debenture interest*

| Accrued debenture interest | = | 12% × £120,000 × 3 months |
| | = | £3,600 |

37   PEAKEWAR

(a)

PLANT DISPOSAL ACCOUNT

	£'000		£'000
Plant at cost	20	Sales proceeds	6
		Depreciation *	12
		Loss on disposal to	
		manufacturing account	2
	20		20

* Annual depreciation on plant = £20,000 × 20% = £4,000

∴ Cumulative depreciation since 19X5 = 3 years × £4,000 = £12,000

(b)   PEAKEWAR LIMITED
MANUFACTURING TRADING AND PROFIT AND LOSS ACCOUNT
FOR THE YEAR ENDED 31 OCTOBER 19X9

	£'000	£'000
Direct materials		
Opening stock	12.0	
Purchases	164.0	
	176.0	
Closing stock (note (I))	(12.0)	
		164.0
Direct manufacturing wages		180.0
		344.0
Production overhead		
Overhead incurred	104.0	
Depreciation: premises (£200,000 × 4%)	8.0	
plant and equipment (note (ii))	32.0	
vehicles (note (iii))	5.0	
Loss on disposal of plant (from part (a))	2.0	
		151.0
		495.0
Work in progress		
Opening stock	8.0	
Closing stock	17.0	
		(9.0)
Production cost of goods completed c/d		486.0

	£'000	£'000
Sales (note (iv))		665.0
Cost of sales		
Opening stock of finished goods	16.0	
Production cost of goods completed b/d	486.0	
	502.0	
Closing stock of finished goods (note (v))	(14.0)	
		488.0
Gross profit		177.0
Selling overhead: incurred	26.0	
Depreciation of vehicles (note (iii))	2.5	
		28.5
Administration overhead: incurred	49.0	
Depreciation of vehicles (note (iii))	2.5	
		51.5
Net profit		97.0

(c) PEAKEWAR LIMITED
BALANCE SHEET AS AT 31 OCTOBER 19X9

	Cost	*Depreciation*	*Net*
	£'000	£'000	£'000
Fixed assets			
Premises	200	40	160
Plant and equipment (note (vi))	160	122	38
Vehicles	64	34	30
	424	196	228
Current assets			
Stocks: direct materials (note (i))	12		
	17		
finished goods (note (v))	14		
		43	
Trade debtors		46	
Balance at bank		329	
Cash in hand		3	
		421	
Current liabilities			
Trade creditors		28	
PAYE creditor		13	
VAT creditor		28	
		69	
Net current assets			352
			580
Financed by			
Ordinary £1 shares			150
Share premium			50
Profit and loss reserve (283 + 97)			380
			580

Notes

(i)   See part (d) of this solution.

(ii) Depreciation of plant and equipment

	£'000
Plant and equipment at cost as per trial balance	180
Less cost of plant sold	20
	160
Depreciation at 20%	32

(iii) Depreciation of vehicles

	£'000
Vehicles at cost	64
Less accumulated depreciation at 1 November 19X8	24
Net book value at 1 November 19X8	40
25% reducing balance depreciation	10

	£'000
Apportioned:	
manufacturing overhead 50%	5.0
selling overhead 25%	2.5
administration overhead 25%	2.5

(iv) *Sales value for the year*

	£'000
Sales as per trial balance	671
Less proceeds of plant sale incorrectly credited to sales account	6
	665

(v) Finished goods closing stock valuation

	£'000	£'000
Value as at 3 November 19X9		13
Add back net sales to customers since year end		
Sales at selling price	5.00	
Less returns at selling price	(1.25)	
Net sales at selling price	3.75	
Deduct profit mark-up (25/125)	(0.75)	
Net sales at cost		3
		16
Less production completed since year end		(2)
		14

(vi) *Plant and equipment*

	Cost £'000	Depreciation £'000	Net £'000
Balances at 1 November 19X8	180	102	78
Sale of plant	(20)	(12)	(8)
	160	90	70
Depreciation for year	-	32	32
	160	122	38

(d) *Raw materials stocks*

Stocks should be valued at the lower of cost and net realisable value. The items which have been in stock for ten years now have a net realisable value of £1,000 which is lower than the cost of £3,000. These items should therefore be valued at £1,000 and the total value of stock must be reduced accordingly.

	£'000
Raw material stock at cost	14
Less stock written down to net realisable value (3 – 1)	2
	12

Finished goods

The workings in note (v) were carried out to determine the cost of finished goods stock held at the balance sheet date. Since the sales values include a profit margin this must be removed to deduce the cost price of the stock.

38   MATTHEWS

MATTHEWS LIMITED
CASH FLOW STATEMENT FOR THE YEAR ENDED 31 MAY 19X4

	£'000
Net cash inflow from operating activities (W)	73
Returns on investments and servicing of finance	
Interest paid	(23)
Taxation	
Corporation tax (14 + 20 − 18)	(16)
Tax paid	
Capital expenditure	
Purchase of tangible fixed assets (812 − 780)	(32)
	2
Equity dividends paid	(17)
	(15)
Financing	
Repayment of debentures	(20)
Decrease in cash	(35)

Working

	£'000
Operating profit	88
Depreciation charge (546 − 485)	61
Increase in stocks	(36)
Increase in debtors	(71)
Increase in creditors	31
Net cash inflow for operating activities	73

39   WEAKNESSES

> *Tutorial note.* This is a 'problem' question. You should have resisted the temptation to write all you know about purchases systems.

(a)   Weaknesses in H plc's existing purchase system are as follows.

    (i)   Invoices are not approved before they are input. This could lead to the creation of fictitious liabilities.

    (ii)   New supplier accounts are opened automatically as a result of keying in an invoice without approval from a responsible official. It would thus be possible to create fictitious accounts.

    (iii)   Cheque payments for creditors' balances are issued without scrutiny of the account and approval. The could lead to inaccuracy in the account or the name of the supplier.

(b)   The purchases and creditors system should be reorganised as follows.

    (i)   Purchase invoices should only be input after they have been approved by the relevant department/official who should check them to orders and goods received notes.

    (ii)   New suppliers' accounts should only be opened with written approval from a responsible official. An audit report of new accounts opened in a particular period (eg a month) should be produced and reviewed.

    (iii)   The batching of invoices and cash payments will allow batch totals to be agreed to output totals.

    (iv)   Creditor accounts should be reconciled to suppliers' statements on a regular basis.

    (v)   Cheque payments should not be made without approval linked to a review of the relevant invoices.

40   A AND B

> *Tutorial note.* You are not required to discuss the ratios; this will only waste precious time which could be devoted to part (b), the interpretation question.

(a) (i) *Current ratio*

$$\frac{\text{Current assets}}{\text{Current liabilities}}$$

(ii) *Quick assets (acid test) ratio*

$$\frac{\text{Current assets - stock}}{\text{Current liabilities}}$$

(iii) *Return on capital employed (ROCE)*

$$\frac{\text{Net profit before interest}}{\text{Total long - term capital}}$$

(iv) *Return on owner's equity (ROOE)*

$$\frac{\text{Profit after tax}}{\text{Share capital plus reserves}}$$

(v) *Debtors turnover*

$$\frac{\text{Debtors}}{\text{Sales per day}} \text{, ie } \frac{\text{Debtors} \times 365}{\text{Sales}}$$

(vi) *Creditors turnover*

$$\frac{\text{Creditors}}{\text{Cost of sales per day}} \text{ ie } \frac{\text{Creditors}}{\text{Cost of sales}} \times 365$$

(vii) *Gross profit percentage*

$$\frac{\text{Gross profit}}{\text{Sales}}$$

(viii) *Net profit percentage*

$$\frac{\text{Net profit}}{\text{Sales}}$$

(ix) *Stock turnover*

$$\frac{\text{Average (or year - end) stock}}{\text{Cost of sales per day}} \text{, ie } \frac{\text{Stock} \times 365}{\text{Cost of sales}}$$

(b) (i) *Profitability*

A has a much higher gross profit margin than B. It may be assumed that B concentrates on volume, while A has a higher mark-up, because it serves a smaller clientele which is prepared to pay higher prices.

Turning to the net profit margin, this is the same for both businesses, reflecting the fact that the more exclusive business will have relatively higher operating costs.

(ii) *Liquidity*

The current and quick assets ratios both show that A has a higher working capital requirement than B. Comparing the current and quick ratios, B has high stocks relative to liabilities (0.9:1), compared with A (0.4:1). It may be inferred from this that A has significantly higher debtors. This reflects the fact that a more 'upmarket' retailer is far more likely to give extended credit to its more exclusive, and richer customers. The latter is also reflected in the higher debtors collection period. Stock moves more slowly in A than in B, perhaps reflecting the less conventional nature of the products sold.

(iii) *Efficiency and gearing*

ROCE is slightly higher for A than for B indicating more efficient use of assets (perhaps less store space is needed to display the products on sale). ROOE is significantly higher for A, suggesting that A has high long-term borrowings at an interest rate below 20%. B on the other hand probably has low long term borrowings, since ROCE and ROOE are about the same. Alternatively B's long term borrowings may be at an interest rate close to 18%.

(iv)   *Summary*

Accounting ratios cannot tell us everything about an organisation. In particular, they give no definite information on the size of A relative to B. However, even without this background information, the lower margins and faster stock turnover of B would suggest a high sales volume at low prices, while A clearly sells more slowly at a higher mark-up, suggesting a niche rather than a mass market.

Class
questions

1 PRUDENCE

(a) Given that prudence is the main consideration, briefly discuss under what circumstances, if any, revenue might be recognised when:

    (i)   goods have been acquired by the business which it confidently expects to resell very quickly;

    (ii)   a customer places a firm order for goods;

    (iii)   goods are delivered to the customer;

    (iv)   the customer is invoiced for goods;

    (v)   the customer pays for the goods;

    (vi)   the customer's cheque in payment for the goods has been cleared by the bank.

(b) Explain briefly how the prudence concept might be applied:

    (i)   to the valuation of stocks;
    (ii)   to the valuation of debtors;
    (iii)   to the valuation of land and buildings.

2 BAD AND DOUBTFUL DEBTS

The Lax Company began trading in 19X7 and makes all its sales on credit. The company suffers from a high level of bad debts and a provision for doubtful debts of 3% of outstanding debtors is made at the end of each year.

Information for 19X7, 19X8 and 19X9 is as follows.

	Year to 31 December		
	19X7	*19X8*	*19X9*
	£	£	£
Outstanding debtors at 31 December	44,000	55,000	47,000
Bad debts written off during year	7,000	10,000	8,000

Required

(a) State the amount to be shown in the profit and loss account for bad debts and provision for doubtful debts for the years ended 31 December 19X7, 19X8 and 19X9.

(b) State the value of debtors which would be shown in the balance sheet as at 31 December each year.

3 AB THE SOLE TRADER

AB, a sole trader, commenced trading on 1 January 19X0. He has provided you with the following details of his telephone costs.

Quarterly rental payable in advance on 1 January, 1 April, 1 July and 1 October	£15

Telephone calls payable in arrears	£
January to March 19X0 paid 1 April 19X0	159
April to June 19X0 paid 1 July 19X0	211
July to September 19X0 paid 1 October 19X0	183

He is to prepare his first accounts to 31 October 19X0 and estimates that the total cost of his calls for October 19X0 will be £74.

AB also pays rent quarterly in advance for his premises and has made payments as follows.

	£
1 January 19X0	600
1 April 19X0	750
1 July 19X0	750
1 October 19X0	750

Required

(a) Prepare AB's ledger accounts for telephone and rent for the period from 1 January 19X0 to 31 October 19X0, showing clearly the amounts to be transferred to his profit and loss account for the period together with any balances carried forward on 31 October 19X0.

(b) Explain the accruals concept in relation to profit measurement theory.

4 S TRADER
45 mins

S Trader carries on a merchanting business. The following balances have been extracted from his books on 30 September 19X1.

	£
Capital - S Trader at 1 October 19X0	24,239
Office furniture and equipment	1,440
Cash drawings - S Trader	4,888
Stock on hand - 1 October 19X0	14,972
Purchases	167,760
Sales	203,845
Rent	1,350
Lighting and heating	475
Insurance	304
Salaries	6,352
Stationery and printing	737
Telephone and postage	517
General expenses	2,044
Travellers' commission and expenses	9,925
Discounts allowed	517
Discounts received	955
Bad debts written off	331
Debtors	19,100
Creditors	8,162
Balance at bank to S Trader's credit	6,603
Petty cash in hand	29
Provision for doubtful debts	143

The following further information is to be taken into account.

(a) Stock on hand on 30 September 19X1 was valued at £12,972.

(b) Provision is to be made for the following liabilities and accrued expenses as at 30 September 19X1: rent £450; lighting and heating £136; travellers' commission and expenses £806; accountancy charges £252.

(c) Provision for doubtful debts is to be raised to 3% of the closing debtor balances.

(d) Office furniture and equipment is to be depreciated by 10% on book value.

(e) Mr Trader had removed stock costing £112 for his own use during the year.

Required

(a) Prepare trading and profit and loss accounts for the year ended 30 September 19X1 grouping the various expenses under suitable headings.

(b) Prepare a balance sheet as at that date.

25 Marks

5   STATIONERY AND TELEPHONE   *36 mins*

You are required, using the information given below, to compile a company's stationery and telephone account for the year ended 31 January 19X4 showing clearly the charge to profit and loss account.

The value of the company's stock of stationery on 31 January 19X3 was £241. At that date the prepaid telephone rental amounted to £20, there was an accrued liability of £137 for telephone calls during December 19X2 and January 19X3 and an accrued liability of £25 for stationery.

During the year ended 31 January 19X4, the following transactions occurred.

19X3		£	£
February 20	Purchase of stationery for		103
March 19	Payment of telephone account of		262
	consisting of rent for quarter ended		
	31 May 19X3	60	
	calls for December 19X2	79	
	January 19X3	58	
	February 19X3	65	
June 28	Payment of telephone account of		281
	consisting of rent for quarter ended		
	31 August 19X3	60	
	calls for March, April and May 19X3	221	
August 12	Purchase of stationery for		156
September 15	Payment of telephone account of		305
	consisting of rent for quarter ended		
	30 November 19X3	75	
	calls for June, July and August 19X3	230	
November 13	Purchase of stationery for		74
December 20	Payment of telephone account consisting		282
	consisting of rent for quarter ended		
	29 February 19X4	75	
	calls for September, October and		
	November 19X3	207	

At 31 January 19X4 the stock of stationery was valued at £199 and there was an accrued liability for stationery of £13. On March 23 19X4 a telephone account of £298 was paid consisting of:

	£
rent for the quarter ended 31 May 19X4	75
calls for December 19X3	86
January 19X4	63
February 19X4	74

Tutorial note. Opening and closing stocks of stationery should be included in the account.

20 Marks

6   DEF   *36 mins*

DEF Ltd has a computerised sales ledger which is not integrated with the remainder of its accounting records which are kept manually.

A summary report (produced by totalling the individual customer accounts) from the computer system at 30 September 19X8 is as follows.

SALES LEDGER CONTROL REPORT 30 SEPTEMBER 19X8

	£
Balance brought forward	15,438
Add: sales	74,691
repayments made	1,249
adjustments	23
Less: sales returns	2,347
payments received	71,203
bad debts written off	646
purchase ledger contra	139
discounts allowed	4,128
adjustments	58
Balance carried forward	12,880

The computerised customer records were inspected and two customers were found to have credit balances. These were as follows.

B Green	£434
J Jones	£158

The balances on the manually prepared sales ledger control account in the nominal ledger at the same date were as follows.

Debit	£12,814
Credit	£592

The accounts were reviewed and the following errors were found.

(a) One of the pages in the sales day book had been over-added by £850.

(b) The total on one page of the sales returns day book had been carried forward as £1,239 instead of £1,329.

(c) XT Ltd had settled its account of £474 by purchase ledger contra. This had not been entered on a computer journal.

(d) A sales return valued at £354 was entered in J Smith's account as a sale.

(e) A repayment of £217 made to B Green was entered in his account as a payment received from him.

(f) The balance on AS Ltd's account of £793 had been written off as a bad debt but was not entered on a computer journal.

(g) A sale to CG Ltd for £919 was entered in EG Ltd's account.

(h) Discount allowed to XYZ Ltd of £57 had not been entered in its account.

(i) The total of the discount received column in the cash book was under-added by £100.

Required

(a) (i)   Re-state the manual control account commencing with the balances given.

    (ii) Show a corrected computerised control account using the format given.

    (iii) Explain the effect of each of the items (a) to (i) above.   **14 Marks**

(b) What is an open item sales ledger system? How does such a system assist a company to control the amount of credit its customers obtain?   **6 Marks**

Total Marks = 20

7   ALEX AUTOS

The following information has been extracted from the incomplete records of Alex Autos for the year to 31 October 19X4.

	£
Provision for doubtful debts (at 1 November 19X3)	6,300
Cash paid to trade creditors	274,000
Cash received from trade debtors	663,000
Credit purchases	310,000
Credit sales	690,000
Discounts allowed	14,000
Discounts received	15,000
Purchases returned (all credit)	10,000
Sales returned (all credit)	8,000
Trade creditors (at 1 November 19X3)	43,000
Trade debtors (at 1 November 19X3)	63,000

The following additional information for the year to 31 October 19X4 is to be taken into account.

(a) The provision for doubtful debts should be made equal to 10% of the outstanding trade debtors as at 31 October 19X4.

(b) One of Alex Autos customers went into liquidation on 1 August 19X4 owing the company £7,000. It is most unlikely that this debt will ever be recovered.

(c) A cheque for £3,000 received from a trade debtor was returned by the bank marked 'account unknown'.

(d) Alex Autos owed a customer £4,000 and it was agreed that this amount should be offset against an amount owing to Alex Autos by the same customer.

You are required to write up the following accounts for the year to 31 October 19X4.

(a) Provision for doubtful debts
(b) Trade creditors' control account
(c) Trade debtors' control account

8   JC   *27 mins*

JC Ltd uses a computerised accounting system to record its transactions and produce a trial balance. The trial balance which was produced by the system at 31 March 19X0 showed that the bank balance was £12,879 overdrawn, but the bank statement which is reproduced below showed a balance on the same date of £5,467 credit. A bank account control report was printed by the accountant of JC Ltd so that the transactions could be compared.

JC LIMITED
COMPUTERISED ACCOUNTING SYSTEM
CONTROL REPORT
BANK ACCOUNT CODE 99 TRANSACTIONS FROM 1.3.X0 TO 31.3.X0

Date		Dr £	Cr £	Balance £
1.3.X0	Balance			4,201
2.3.X0	J Smith & Sons	1,405		
	White Brothers	697		6,303
4.3.X0	Brown & Co	234		6,537
7.3.X0	543987		279	
	543988		1,895	
	543989		11,987	(7,624)
10.3.X0	J Lake	1,386		(6,238)
12.3.X0	543990		1,497	
	543991		547	
	543992		296	(8,578)
17.3.X0	Grey Enterprises	2,569		
	Hunt Lodges	34		
	B Black	643		(5,332)
24.3.X0	543993		2,305	(7,637)
31.3.X0	543994		5,242	(12,879)

The bank statement for the same month was as follows.

STATEMENT OF ACCOUNT
NATTOWN BANK 31 March 19X0

March		Dr £	Cr £	Balance £
1	Balance			3,529
3	Counter credit		2,489	6,018
4	543986	237		5,781
6	Counter credit		2,102	7,883
7	Bank charges	195		
	543988	1,895		5,793
9	Counter credit		234	6,027
11	543985	68		5,959

March		Dr £	Cr £	Bal £
13	Brown & Co cheque dishonoured	234		
	543989	1,197		4,528
14	Counter credit		1,486	6,014
17	543990	1,497		
	543992	296		4,221
23	Counter credit		5,332	9,553
25	Standing order: rates	4,029		5,524
27	543991	57		5,467
31	Balance			5,467

The balances on 1 March 19X0 were reconciled, the difference being partly due to the following cheques which were unpresented on that date.

Cheque	543984	£1,512
	543985	£68
	543986	£237

Required

(a) Prepare a bank reconciliation statement at 31 March 19X0.   **12 Marks**

(b) List three reasons why bank reconciliation statements should be prepared regularly.   **3 Marks**

Total Marks = 15

9 **RECTIFY** *36 mins*

A summary of the cash book of Rectify Ltd for the year to 31 May 19X5 is as follows:

CASH BOOK

	£		£
Opening balance b/f	805	Payments	146,203
Receipts	145,720	Closing balance c/f	322
	146,525		146,525

After some investigation of the cash book and vouchers you discover the following facts.

(a) Bank charges of £143 shown on the bank statement have not yet been entered in the cash book.

(b) A cheque drawn for £98 has been entered in the cash book as £89, and another drawn at £230 has been entered as a receipt.

(c) A cheque received from a customer for £180 has been returned by the bank marked 'refer to drawer', but it has not yet been written back in the cash book.

(d) An error of transposition has occurred in that the opening balance of the cash book should have been brought down as £850.

(e) Cheques paid to suppliers totalling £630 have not yet been presented at the bank, whilst payments in to the bank of £580 on 31 May 19X5 have not yet been credited to the company's account.

(f) A cheque for £82 has been debited to the company's account in error by the bank.

(g) The company owes £430 to the electricity board.

(h) Standing orders appearing on the bank statement have not yet been entered in the cash book:

    (i) interest for the half year to 31 March on a loan of £20,000 at 11% pa;

    (ii) hire purchase repayments on the managing director's car - 12 months at £55 per month;

    (iii) dividend received on a trade investment - £1,147.

(i) A page of the receipts side of the cash book has been undercast by £200.

(j) The bank statement shows a balance overdrawn of £870.

Required

(a) Adjust the cash book in the light of the above discoveries. **10 Marks**

(b) Produce a statement reconciling the bank statement balance to the cash book balance. **10 Marks**

Total Marks = 20

10 **IN SUSPENSE** *27 mins*

The trial balance of MLN plc was extracted on 30 September 19X9 and showed the following totals.

DEBIT £1,605,668
CREDIT £1,603,623

A suspense account was opened and used to record the difference until it could be investigated but the company continued to prepare its draft accounts by applying the prudence concept to the treatment of the suspense account balance.

After investigation the following facts emerged.

(a) Discounts allowed of £1,248 had not been entered in the sales ledger control account.

(b) A credit sale of £857 to SEC Limited had not been entered in the sales day book.

(c) A contra entry between the sales and purchases ledgers had been entered in the control accounts as follows.

DEBIT   Sales ledger control   £731
CREDIT   Purchase ledger control   £731

(d) An invoice of £54 for telephones had been entered in the telephone account as £45 but was correctly entered in the creditors account.

(e) Bank charges of £66 had been correctly entered in the expense account but had not been entered in the cash book.

(f) One of the pages of the purchase day book had been incorrectly totalled as £11,269 instead of £11,629.

(g) During the year a fixed asset was sold for £740. Its original cost was £3,600 and its net book value at the date of disposal was £800. The only entry made was to debit the proceeds of sale to the bank account.

Required

(a) Record in the suspense account the effects of correcting (a) to (g) above.
5 Marks

(b) Reconcile the difference between the balance on the sales ledger control account in the original trial balance and the sum of the individual customer balances in the sales ledger; the original control account balance was £327,762.   **5 Marks**

(c) Prepare a statement of adjusted net profit showing both the original net profit of £412,967 as given by the draft accounts and the net profit after correcting items (a) to (g) above.   **5 Marks**

Total Marks = 15

11   BYRD

Old Mr Byrd has run his corner shop in one of London's twilight areas for many years. On 30 September 19X0, vandals looted his shop, taking all his stock and the till float of £75. Fortunately the windows had been boarded up and only minor damage was done to the premises themselves.

Mr Byrd was fully insured against theft and he has asked you to help him formulate an insurance claim. Investigations on your part reveal the following matters.

(a) *Net assets* on 1 January 19X0 were:

	£
Fixtures and fittings:	
Cost	900
Accumulated depreciation	400
Net book value	500
Stock	2,700
Debtors	430
Prepayments (rates)	30
Cash in bank	2,140
Cash float in till	30
Trade creditors	1,650
Accrued electricity	40

(b) Bank statements for the nine months from 1 January show:

		£
Receipts		
Cash and cheques banked		20,060
Investment income		182
		20,242
Payments		
Trade creditors		17,850
Rent (1 Jan - 31 Dec)		1,200
Electricity		155
Insurance:	theft	45
	life	107
Telephone		83
		19,440

(c) The following were paid in cash from the till.

	£
Trade creditors	2,400
Drawings (per month)	295

(d) Mr Byrd's gross profit margin on sales has averaged 20% in recent years.

(e) The fixtures and fittings are now thought to be worth only £200.

(f) A cheque for £52 in respect of the telephone bill for the quarter ending 29 September 19X0 is not shown on the bank statements until 3 October.

(g) Rates for the period 1 April - 1 October amount to £75 and have not yet been paid.

(h) Trade debtors and creditors amounted to £270 and £1,900 respectively on 30 September 19X0.

Required

(a) Prepare Mr Byrd's trading and profit and loss account for the nine months to 30 September 19X0.

(b) Prepare his balance sheet as at that date.

12   GD SPORTS   *36 mins*

The GD Sports Club committee has recently asked if you would prepare the club accounts for the year ended 31 March 19X8. You have agreed and have found that they do not keep any accounting records other than notes concerning the subscriptions of members and the amounts paid for expenses. During discussions with the club committee you discover the following matters.

(a) The club does not have a bank account and conducts all its transactions in cash, any surplus being paid into a building society account. Interest credited to this account for the year to 31 March 19X8 was £350.

(b) A summary of the payments for the year is as follows.

	£
Deposit to building society account	250
Purchase of dartboards	100
Heat/light	262
Repairs to snooker tables	176
Bar creditors	7,455
Rental of premises	1,000
Club match referees' fees and expenses	675
Trophies, etc (treated as an expense)	424
Refreshments for visiting teams	235

(c) The club has 100 members who each pay an annual subscription of £5. However, on 31 March 19X7 ten members had already paid their subscriptions for 19X7/X8.

On 31 March 19X8 two members who had not been seen in the club since August 19X7 had not paid subscriptions for 19X7/X8 and it has been decided that the amount due be written off and that their names be removed from the list of members.

(d) The club has only two sources of income from club members: subscriptions and bar sales. A profit margin of 30% of selling price is normally applied to determine bar selling prices but during the year £397 of goods were sold at cost.

(e) The club has the following other assets and liabilities.

	1 April 19X7	31 March 19X8
	£	£
Equipment	4,000	?
Building society account	4,600	5,200
Bar stocks	840	920
Bar creditors	630	470
Cash in hand	nil	nil
Creditor for heat/light	34	41

(f) Equipment is depreciated at 10% of the value of equipment held on 31 March each year.

You are required to prepare the following.

(a) A bar trading account for the ended 31 March 19X8   **8 Marks**

(b) An income and expenditure account for the year ended 31 March 19X8.

7 Marks

(c) A balance sheet at 31 March 19X8.   **5 Marks**

Total Marks = 20

13   **COMPUTERISED DEBTORS SYSTEM**   *27 mins*

(a) What are the advantages of using a computerised package in accounting for debtors?   **7 Marks**

(b) How are the conventions of conservatism and matching applied to the accounting treatment of debtors?   **8 Marks**

Total Marks = 15

14   NOCTURNE

The following balances appeared in the books of Nocturne Ltd as at 30 September 19X4.

	£
Sales	120,000
Purchases	65,700
Creditors	9,450
Furniture and equipment at cost	33,000
Freehold premises at cost	84,000
Depreciation: furniture and equipment	15,000
freehold premises	9,000
Debtors	19,044
Provision for doubtful debts	1,224
Bad debts	1,014
Sales returns	1,450
Wages and salaries	12,108
Administration expenses	4,686
Selling and distribution expenses	2,844
Financial expenses	654
Discounts received	2,646
Debenture interest (six months to 31 March 19X4)	600
8% debentures	15,000
Interim dividend on preference shares	900
10% £1 preference shares	18,000
£1 ordinary shares called up and fully paid	50,000
General reserve	7,500
Share premium	10,000
Retained profits at 1 October 19X3	11,000
Stock at 1 October 19X3	18,872
Cash at bank	9,000
Cash in hand	948
Goodwill at cost	14,000

Additional information relevant to the year ended 30 September 19X4 is as follows.

(a)   The provision for doubtful debts is to be revised at 5% of debtors.

(b)   Bank charges of £120 are outstanding at 30 September 19X4, as is £1,100 for accrued wages and salaries, and £350 for computer services.

(c)   Stock at 30 September 19X4 was £22,654.

(d)   Depreciation is to be provided of £1,000 on freehold premises, and at 10% on the written down value of furniture and equipment. Goodwill is to be amortised evenly over four years.

(e)   A final preference share dividend is to be declared and an ordinary share dividend of 6p per share is proposed for the year ended 30 September 19X4.

(f)   Taxation on the 19X3/X4 profits is estimated at £15,000.

Required

(a)   Prepare the trading and profit and loss statements for the year ended 30 September 19X4.

(b)   Prepare the balance sheet as at 30 September 19X4, indicating the shareholders' funds employed and the working capital figure.

25 Marks

15   EIGHT RATIOS
36 mins

You are given summarised information about two firms in the same line of business, A and B, as follows.

Balance sheets at 30 June

	A				B	
	£'000	£'000	£'000	£'000	£'000	£'000
Land			80			260
Buildings		120			200	
Less depreciation		40			-	
			80			200
Plant		90			150	
Less depreciation		70			40	
			20			110
			180			570
Stocks		80			100	
Debtors		100			90	
Bank		-			10	
		180			200	
Creditors	110			120		
Bank	50			-		
	160			120		
			20			80
			200			650
Capital brought forward			100			300
Profit for year			30			100
			130			400
Less: drawings			30			40
			100			360
Land revaluation			-			160
Loan (10% pa)			100			130
			200			650
Sales			1,000			3,000
Cost of sales			400			2,000

Required

(a) Produce a table of eight ratios calculated for both businesses.   **10 Marks**

(b) Write a report briefly outlining the strengths and weaknesses of the two businesses. Include comment on any major areas where the simple use of the figures could be misleading.   **10 Marks**

Total Marks = 20

Glossary
and Index

Account A record in the bookkeeping ledger in which is kept details of all the financial transactions relating to one individual supplier, customer, asset, liability or type of expense or receipt.

Accounting The recording of financial transactions and the preparation of accounting reports and financial statements from bookkeeping records in accordance with acknowledged methods and conventions.

Accounting equation Assets = Capital + Liabilities

Accrual Expense (usually) or revenue outstanding at the end of a trading period which needs to be *accrued* for inclusion with the accounting records for the period.

Accruals concept Revenue and costs are accrued, that is, recognised as they are earned or incurred, not as money is received or paid, matched with one another so far as their relationship can be established or justifiably assumed and dealt with in the profit and loss account of the period to which they relate (SSAP 2).

Acid test ratio Also known as *quick ratio*. This is a measure of a company's ability to meet its short term debts. It is a more stringent test of liquidity than the *current ratio*, because it assumes that stocks cannot necessarily be readily converted into liquid funds.

$$\text{Acid test ratio} = \frac{\text{Current assets} - \text{stock}}{\text{Current liabilities}}$$

Amortisation This is similar to *depreciation*, but is generally applied either to leasehold buildings, or to intangible fixed assets such as *research and development* or *goodwill*, rather than to machinery and equipment.

Applied research Original or critical investigation undertaken primarily to acquire new scientific or technical knowledge and directed towards a specific practical aim or objective.

Appropriation account The record of how the profit or loss has been allocated to distributions or reserves.

Asset Resource *owned* by a business and of value to that business. Assets are classified as *fixed* or *current*.

Asset turnover The ratio of sales in a year to the amount of net assets (capital employed).

Audit A systematic examination of the activities and status of an entity based primarily on investigation and analysis of its systems, controls, and records (CIMA *Official Terminology*). It is important to distinguish between *internal audit* and *external audit*.

Average cost A method of stock valuation whereby an average price is calculated for all material in stock and this average price is used to charge issues to production.

Bad debt A debtor who fails to pay his outstanding debt to a company within a reasonable time, after which the balance is written off.

Balance The difference between the totals of the debit and credit entries in an account.

Balance sheet A statement of the *liabilities*, *capital* and *assets* of a business at a given moment in time. It is like a 'snapshot' photograph since it captures on paper a still image of something which is constantly changing.

Bank reconciliation A comparison of a bank statement with the cash book. Differences between the balance on the bank statement and the balance in the cashbook will be errors or timing differences, and they should be identified and explored.

Bookkeeping The recording of monetary transactions.

Business equation $P = I + D - Ci$

where   P represents profit
I represents the increase in net assets after drawings have been taken out by the proprietor
D represents drawings
Ci represents the amount of extra capital introduced into the business during the period

Capital employed The total funds invested in a business made up of shareholders' funds and loan capital. It is equivalent in value to a company's net assets.

Capital expenditure Expenditure on fixed assets, the net cost of which is to be 'capitalised' and depreciated over the anticipated useful working life of the assets.

Capital Money put into a business by its owner(s) with the intention of earning a profit.

Cash account A record of receipts and payments of cash or cheques.

Cash cycle See *operating cycle*.

Cash flow The amount of money flowing into and out of a business during a period of time. It does not necessarily equate to costs and revenues over the same period.

Cash flow statement A statement produced either for management or for external reporting purposes showing, by broad category cash receipts and payments in a period. The term may also refer to a forecast for future period.

Company A company is a business which is separate legal entity formed by registration under the Companies Act.

Consistency concept The principle that there is uniformity of accounting treatment of like items whether each accounting period and from one period to the next. (SSAP 2 *Disclosure of Accounting Policies*)

Credit An entry recorded on the right hand side of the account which represents a decrease in the value of a company's assets or expenses or an increase in the value of its liabilities or revenues.

Creditor A person to whom a business owes money. A trade creditor is a person to whom a business owes money for debts incurred in the course of trading operations.

Creditors' turnover period This is the period of credit taken from suppliers. It is the length of time between the purchase of materials and the payment to suppliers. It may be calculated as:

$$\frac{\text{Average (or y/e) trade creditors}}{\text{Purchases}} \times 365$$

Current asset Current assets are either:

(a) items owned by the business with the intention of turning them into cash within one year; or

(b) cash, including money in the bank, owned by the business.

These assets are current in the sense that they are continually flowing through the business.

Current liabilities Debts of the business which must be paid within a fairly short period of time, by convention one year.

Current ratio A ratio which measures a company's liquidity by comparing its short term liabilities with the current assets out of which these liabilities will be met.

$$\text{Current ratio} = \frac{\text{current assets}}{\text{current liabilities}}$$

Debit An entry made on the left hand side of the account which represents an increase in the value of a business' assets or expenses or a decrease in the value of its liabilities or revenue.

Debt collection period This is the length of the credit period taken by the customer - it is the time between the sale of an item and the receipt of cash from the customer. It may be calculated as:

$$\frac{\text{Average debtors (or y/e debtors)}}{\text{Credit sales}} \times 365$$

Debtor A person who owes the business money. A trade debtor is a customer who buys goods without paying cash for them straight away.

Debtors' turnover See *debt collection period*.

Depreciation The measure of the wearing out, consumption or other loss of value of a fixed asset whether arising from use, effluxion of time, or obsolescence through technology and market changes (SSAP 12).

Development cost The cost of use of scientific or technical knowledge in order to produce new or substantially improved materials, devices, products or services; to install new processes or systems prior to the commencement of commercial production or commercial applications; or to improve substantially those already produced or installed. (SSAP 13)

Distribution cost The cost of warehousing saleable products and delivering them to customers. (CIMA *Official Terminology*)

Dividend A distribution to shareholders out of profits, usually in the form of cash, in proportion to the number of shares that they hold in the business.

Double entry (bookkeeping) The method by which a business records financial transactions. An account is maintained for every supplier, customer, asset, liability, and income and expense. Every transaction is recorded twice so that every *debit* is balanced by a *credit*.

Doubtful debts provision An amount charged against profit and deducted from debtors to allow for the non-recovery of a proportion of the debts. (CIMA *Official Terminology*)

External audit A periodic examination of the books of account and records of an entity carried out by an independent third party (the auditor), to ensure that they have been properly maintained, are accurate and comply with established concepts, principles, accounting standards, legal requirements and give a true and fair view of the financial state of the entity. (CIMA *Official Terminology*)

Financial accounting The classification and recording of monetary transactions of an entity in accordance with established concepts, principles, accounting standards and legal requirements and their presentation by means of profit and loss accounts, balance sheets and cash flow statements and at the end of an accounting period. (CIMA *Official Terminology*)

First in first out (FIFO) A method of stock valuation in which it is assumed that the first goods into stock will be the first to be issued for use or sale. Compare *LIFO* and *average cost*.

Fixed asset A fixed asset is an asset acquired for continuing use within the business with a view to earning income or making profits from its use either directly or indirectly. A fixed asset is not acquired for sale to a customer.

Fixed assets register A record showing details of individual fixed assets.

Fundamental accounting concepts The basic assumptions which underlie the periodic financial accounts of an entity.

Gearing The proportion of a company's capital employed that is tied up in loan capital. There are various ways of calculating the ratio, which may be found in Chapter 24.

Going concern concept The assumption that the entity will continue in operational existence for the foreseeable future. (SSAP 2)

Goodwill The excess of the price paid for a business over the fair market value of the individual assets and liabilities acquired.

Imprest system A method of controlling cash or stock. When the cash or stock has been reduced by disbursements or issues it is restored to its original level.

Income and expenditure account The *profit and loss account* of a non-trading organisation.

Intangible assets Assets which do not have a physical identity (such as *goodwill*, patents, trade marks unamortised research and development costs). They are classified as *fixed assets* because they cannot readily be converted into cash.

Internal audit An independent function established within an organisation to examine and evaluate its activities as a service to the organisation. The objective of internal auditing is to assist members of the organisation in the effective discharge of their responsibilities. To this end, internal auditing furnishes them with analyses, appraisals, recommendations, counsel and information concerning the activities reviewed.

Internal control system The system of controls, financial and otherwise, established to carry out the functions of an entity in an orderly and efficient manner, ensure adherence to management policies, safeguard assets and secure completeness and accuracy of records.

Last in first out (LIFO) A method of stock valuation which is the opposite of *FIFO*. Materials are charged to production in the reverse order of their receipt.

Ledger A collection of accounts eg a collection of suppliers' accounts is the purchase ledger.

Liabilities An amount *owed* to a business.

Loan capital Money that has been loaned to the company on a long-term basis at a pre-agreed rate of interest. The lenders of loan capital do not (normally) share in the profits of a business.

Long term liabilities Debts which are not payable within the *short term* and so any liability which is not current must be long-term.

Management accounting A management information system which analyses data to provide information as a basis for management action. The concern of a management accountant is to present accounting information in the form most helpful to management.

Mark-up The addition to the cost of goods or services which results in a selling price. The mark-up may be expressed as a percentage or as an absolute financial amount. (CIMA *Official Terminology*)

Materiality concept Information is material if its omission or misstatement could influence the economic decisions of users taken on the basis of the financial statements. Materiality depends on the size of the item or error judged in the particular circumstances of its omission or misstatement. Thus, materiality provides a threshold or cut-off point rather than being a primary qualitative characteristic that information must have if it is to be useful (ASB *Statement of Principles*).

Net assets The value of a company's total assets less its current liabilities, equivalent in value to its *capital employed*.

Net book value The historical cost of an asset less accumulated depreciation or other write down.

Net realisable value The price at which goods in stock could be currently sold less any costs which would be incurred to complete the sale. (SSAP 9)

Operating cycle This is a term used to describe the connection between working capital and cash movements in and out. The cycle is usually measured in days or months. It is also called the *cash cycle*.

Partnership The relationship which exists between persons carrying on businesses in common with a view to profit. (Partnership Act 1890)

Prepayments Amounts of money already paid by the business for benefits which have not yet been enjoyed but will be enjoyed within the next accounting period.

Profit and loss account A record of income earned and expenditure incurred over a given period.

Profit margin This is ratio of profit to sales and may also be called profit percentage. For example, if a company makes a profit of £20,000 on sales of £100,000 its profit margin is 20%.

Prudence concept The principle that revenue and profits are not anticipated, but are included in the profit and loss account only when realised in the form either of cash or of other assets, the ultimate cash realisation of which can be assessed with reasonable certainty; provision is made for all known liabilities (expense and losses) whether the amount of these is known with certainty or is a best estimate in the light of the information available (SSAP 2).

Pure research Experimental or theoretical work undertaken primarily to acquire new scientific or technical knowledge for its own

sake rather than directed towards any specific aim or application (SSAP 13).

Receipts and payments account A record of cash paid and received used by some (usually small) non-trading organisations.

Reserves Profit which has been re-invested in the business.

Return on capital employed (ROCE) The amount of profit as a percentage of capital employed. In your CIMA examination it should be calculated as:

$$\frac{\text{Net profit before tax and interest}}{\text{Average capital employed}}$$

Revenue expenditure Expenditure incurred for the purpose of the trade of the business or to maintain the existing earning capacity of fixed assets.

Share capital The amount of money invested in a company by its risk-taking shareholders.

Share premium The excess of the share price over the nominal value of the share.

Shareholders funds The amount of part of a company's capital owned by its shareholders. It is made up of share capital plus profits not distributed by the business.

Short term investments Stocks and shares of other businesses currently owned but with the intention of selling them in the near future.

Sole trader A person who carries on a business with sole legal responsibility. A sole trader's business is *not* a separate *legal* entity from the owner, but it is a separate accounting entity.

Stock turnover This is the length of time an item is held in stores before it is used. It may be calculated as:

$$\frac{\text{Average stocks held (or y/e stocks held)}}{\text{Cost of sales}}$$

Suspense account A temporary account opened for a number of reasons of which the most common are:

(a) the trial balance does not balance
(b) the bookkeeper of a business does not know where to post one side of a transaction.

Tangible asset An asset having a physical identity, eg plant and machinery.

Trial balance A list of all the balances in a company's ledger accounts. Such a listing is generally used as the first step in the preparation of the final accounts and is used to prove that the total of all the debit balances is equal to the total of all the credit balances.

Work-in-progress Any material component, product or contract at an intermediate stage of completion.

Working capital The difference between current assets and current liabilities.

ORDER FORM

For further question practice on Stage 1 *Financial Accounting Fundamentals*, BPP publish a companion Practice & Revision Kit (January 1997). This contains a bank of questions, mostly drawn from past examinations, plus a full test paper. Fully worked suggested solutions are provided for all questions, including the test paper. The new edition will be published in January 1998.

You may also wish to make use of our innovative revision product, CIMA Passcards. Published in February 1997 they are designed to act as last-minute revision notes and memory prompters. A new edition will be available in February 1998.

To order your Practice & Revision Kit and Passcards ring our credit card hotline on 0181-740 2211. Alternatively, send this page to our Freepost address or fax it to us on 0181-740 1184.

To: BPP Publishing Ltd, FREEPOST, London W12 8BR   **Tel: 0181-740 2211**
                                                            Fax: 0181-740 1184

Forenames (Mr / Ms): _____

Surname: _____

Address: _____

_____

Post code: _____   Date of exam (month/year):_____

Please send me the following books: Price   Quantity   Total
                                                            £   £

CIMA Stage 1 *Financial Accounting Fundamentals* Kit   8.95   ....

CIMA Stage 1 *Financial Accounting Fundamentals* Passcards 4.95   ....

Postage and packaging:

UK: £2.00 for first plus £1.00 for each extra   ....

Europe (inc ROI): £2.50 for first plus £1.00 for each extra   ....

Rest of the World: £5.00 for first plus £3.00 for each extra   ....

We guarantee delivery to all UK addresses inside 3 working days. Orders to all EU addresses should be received within 4 working days. All other orders to overseas addresses should be received within 12 working days.

I enclose a cheque for £ _____ **or charge to Access/Visa/Switch**

Card number | | | | | | | | | | | | | | | | | | | |

Start date (Switch only) _____ **Expiry date** _____ **Issue no. (Switch only)**_____

Signature _____

Data correct at time of publication

To order any further titles in the CIMA range, please use the form overleaf.

ORDER FORM

To order your CIMA books, ring our credit card hotline on 0181-740 2211. Alternatively, send this page to our Freepost address or fax it to us on 0181-740 1184.

To: BPP Publishing Ltd, FREEPOST, London W12 8BR   **Tel: 0181-740 2211**
Fax: 0181-740 1184

Forenames (Mr / Ms): _____

Surname: _____

Address: _____

_____

Post code: _____   Date of exam (month/year):_____

Please send me the following books:

	Price 6/97 Text £	Price 1/97 Kit £	Price 2/97 Passcards £	Quantity Text	Kit	Passcards	Total £
Stage 1							
Financial Accounting Fundamentals	17.95	8.95	4.95	....	....	....	....
Cost Accounting and Quantitative Methods	17.95	8.95	4.95	....	....	....	....
Economic Environment	17.95	8.95	4.95	....	....	....	....
Business Environment and Information Technology	17.95	8.95	4.95	....	....	....	....
Stage 2							
Financial Accounting	17.95	8.95	4.95	....	....	....	....
Operational Cost Accounting	17.95	8.95	4.95	....	....	....	....
Management Science Applications	17.95	8.95	4.95	....	....	....	....
Business and Company Law	17.95	8.95	4.95	....	....	....	....
Stage 3							
Financial Reporting	18.95	9.95	5.95	....	....	....	....
Management Accounting Applications	18.95	9.95	5.95	....	....	....	....
Organisational Management and Development	18.95	9.95	5.95	....	....	....	....
Business Taxation (FA 97 Con) (6/97 Text, 6/97 P/c, 9/97 Kit)	18.95	9.95	5.95	....	....	....	....
Business Taxation (FA 97 Lab)	18.95	9.95	5.95	....	....	....	....
Stage 4							
Strategic Financial Management	18.95	9.95	5.95	....	....	....	....
Strategic Management Accountancy and Marketing	18.95	9.95	5.95	....	....	....	....
Information Management	18.95	9.95	5.95	....	....	....	....
Management Accounting Control Systems	18.95	9.95	5.95	....	....	....	....

Postage and packaging:

UK: Texts £3.00 for first plus £2.00 for each extra   ....

      Kits and Passcards £2.00 for first plus £1.00 for each extra   ....

Europe (inc ROI): Texts £5.00 for first plus £4.00 for each extra   ....

      Kits and Passcards £2.50 for first plus £1.00 for each extra   ....

Rest of the World: Texts £8.00 for first plus £6.00 for each extra   ....

      Kits and Passcards £5.00 for first plus £3.00 for each extra   ....

We guarantee delivery to all UK addresses inside 3 working days. Orders to all EU addresses should be received within 4 working days. All other orders to overseas addresses should be received within 12 working days.

I enclose a cheque for £ _____ **or charge to Access/Visa/Switch**

Card number | | | | | | | | | | | | | | | | | | | |

Start date (Switch only) _____   **Expiry date** _____   **Issue no. (Switch only)**___

Signature _____

REVIEW FORM & FREE PRIZE DRAW

All original review forms from the entire BPP range, completed with genuine comments, will be entered into one of two draws on 31 January 1998 and 31 July 1998. The names on the first four forms picked out on each occasion will be sent a cheque for £50.

Name: _____   Address: _____

_____

_____

How have you used this Text?
(Tick one box only)

☐ Home study (book only)

☐ On a course: college _____

☐ With 'correspondence' package

☐ Other _____

Why did you decide to purchase this Text?
(Tick one box only)

☐ Have used complementary Kit

☐ Have used BPP Texts in the past

☐ Recommendation by friend/colleague

☐ Recommendation by a lecturer at college

☐ Saw advertising

☐ Other _____

During the past six months do you recall seeing/receiving any of the following?
(Tick as many boxes as are relevant)

☐ Our advertisement in *CIMA Student*

☐ Our advertisement in *Management Accounting*

☐ Our advertisement in *Pass*

☐ Our brochure with a letter through the post

Which (if any) aspects of our advertising do you find useful?
(Tick as many boxes as are relevant)

☐ Prices and publication dates of new editions

☐ Information on Text content

☐ Facility to order books off-the-page

☐ None of the above

Have you used the companion Practice & Revision Kit for this subject?   ☐ Yes   ☐ No

Your ratings, comments and suggestions would be appreciated on the following areas

	Very useful	Useful	Not useful
Introductory section (How to use this text, study checklist, etc)	☐	☐	☐
Introduction to chapters	☐	☐	☐
Syllabus coverage	☐	☐	☐
Exercises and examples	☐	☐	☐
Chapter roundups	☐	☐	☐
Test your knowledge quizzes	☐	☐	☐
Illustrative questions	☐	☐	☐
Content of suggested solutions	☐	☐	☐
Glossary and index	☐	☐	☐
Structure and presentation	☐	☐	☐

	Excellent	Good	Adequate	Poor
Overall opinion of this Text	☐	☐	☐	☐

Do you intend to continue using BPP Study Texts/Kits?   ☐ Yes   ☐ No

Please note any further comments and suggestions/errors on the reverse of this page.

Please return to: Neil Biddlecombe, BPP Publishing Ltd, FREEPOST, London, W12 8BR

REVIEW FORM & FREE PRIZE DRAW (continued)

Please note any further comments and suggestions/errors below

FREE PRIZE DRAW RULES

1   Closing date for 31 January 1998 draw is 31 December 1997. Closing date for 31 July 1998 draw is 30 June 1998.

2   Restricted to entries with UK and Eire addresses only. BPP employees, their families and business associates are excluded.

3   No purchase necessary. Entry forms are available upon request from BPP Publishing. No more than one entry per title, per person. Draw restricted to persons aged 16 and over.

4   Winners will be notified by post and receive their cheques not later than 6 weeks after the relevant draw date. Lists of winners will be published in BPP's *focus* newsletter following the relevant draw.

5   The decision of the promoter in all matters is final and binding. No correspondence will be entered into.